SpringBoard®
English
Language Arts

STUDENT EDITION   ENGLISH IV

About The College Board

The College Board is a mission-driven not-for-profit organization that connects students to college success and opportunity. Founded in 1900, the College Board was created to expand access to higher education. Today, the membership association is made up of over 6,000 of the world's leading educational institutions and is dedicated to promoting excellence and equity in education. Each year, the College Board helps more than seven million students prepare for a successful transition to college through programs and services in college readiness and college success—including the SAT® and the Advanced Placement Program®. The organization also serves the education community through research and advocacy on behalf of students, educators, and schools. For further information, visit collegeboard.org.

ISBN: 978-1-4573-1298-4

4 5 6 7 8   22 23 24 25 26

Printed in the United States of America

Acknowledgements

The College Board gratefully acknowledges the outstanding work of the classroom teachers who have been integral to the development of this program. The end product is testimony to their expertise, understanding of student learning needs, and dedication to rigorous and accessible English Language Arts instruction.

Lance Balla
Everett School District
Everett, Washington

Carisa Barnes
San Diego Unified School District
San Diego, California

Leia Bell
Hillsborough County Public Schools
Tampa, Florida

Alysa Broussard
Lafayette Parish School System
Lafayette, Louisiana

Robert J. Caughey
San Dieguito Union High School District
San Diego, California

Susie Challancin
Bellevue School District 405
Bellevue, Washington

Doug Cole
Cherry Creek School District
Greenwood Village, Colorado

Cari Davis
Rio Rancho Public School District
Rio Rancho, New Mexico

Paul De Maret
Poudre School District Fort Collins, Colorado

Sylvia Ellison
Hillsborough County Public Schools
Hillsborough, Florida

Karen Fullam
Hillsborough County Public Schools
Tampa, Florida

Michael Gragert
Plano Independent School District
Plano, Texas

Nancy Gray
Brevard County Schools
Viera, Florida

Charise Hallberg
Bellevue School District 405
Bellevue, Washington

T.J. Hanify
Bellevue School District 405
Bellevue, Washington

Jessi Hupper
Peninsula School District
Gig Harbor, Washington

Nimat Jones
ICEF Public Schools, Los Angeles, California

Karen Kampschmidt
Fort Thomas Independent School District
Fort Thomas, Kentucky

Karen Kennedy
Peninsula School District
Peninsula, Washington

LeAnn Klepzig
Bradley County Schools
Cleveland, Tennessee

Susie Lowry
Volusia County School District Deland, Florida

Michelle Lewis
Spokane Public School
Spokane, Washington

John Marshall
Mead School District Mead, Washington

Cassandra Mattison
Hillsborough County Public Schools Tampa, Florida

Glenn Morgan
San Diego Unified School District San Diego, California

John Murray
Garland Independent School District Sachse, Texas

Kristen J. Ohaver
Charlotte-Mecklenburg Schools Charlotte, North Carolina

Amanda Olinger
Harrisburg School District
Harrisburg, South Dakota

Julie Pennabaker
Quakertown Community School District Quakertown, Pennsylvania

Bryan Sandala
School District of Palm Beach County West Palm Beach, Florida

Angela Seiler
Rio Rancho Public School District Rio Rancho, New Mexico

Amanda Shackelford
Lafayette Parish School System Lafayette, Louisiana

Kimberlyn Slagle
Lafayette Parish School System Lafayette, Louisiana

Sarah Smith Arceneaux
Lafayette Parish School System Lafayette, Louisiana

Holly Talley
Hillsborough County Public Schools Ruskin, Florida

Derek Thomas
Hillsborough County Public Schools Tampa, Florida

Maria Torres-Crosby
Hillsborough County Public Schools Tampa, Florida

Susan Van Doren
South Lake Tahoe, California

JoEllen Victoreen
San José Unified School District
San José, California

Rebecca Wenrich
Peninsula School District Gig Harbor, Washington

Research and Planning Advisors

We also wish to thank the members of our SpringBoard Advisory Council and the many educators who gave generously of their time and their ideas as we conducted research for both the print and online programs. Your suggestions and reactions to ideas helped immeasurably as we created this edition. We gratefully acknowledge the teachers and administrators in the following districts.

ABC Unified School District
Cerritos, California

Allen Independent School
District
Allen, Texas

Bellevue, School District 405
Bellevue, Washington

Burnet Consolidated
Independent School District
Burnet, Texas

Community Unit School
District 308
Oswego, Illinois

Fresno Unified
School District
Fresno, California

Frisco Independent
School District
Frisco, Texas

Garland Independent
School District
Garland, Texas

Grapevine-Colleyville
Independent School District
Grapevine, Texas

Hamilton County Schools
Chattanooga, Tennessee

Hesperia Unified
School District
Hesperia, California

Hillsborough County Public
Schools
Tampa, Florida

ICEF Public Schools
Los Angeles, California

IDEA Public Schools
Weslaco, Texas

Irving Independent
School District
Irving, Texas

Keller Independent
School District
Keller, Texas

KIPP Houston
Houston, Texas

Lafayette Parish Schools
Lafayette Parish, Louisiana

Los Angeles Unified
School District
Los Angeles, California

Lubbock Independent
School District
Lubbock, Texas

Mansfield Independent
School District
Mansfield, Texas

Midland Independent
School District
Midland, Texas

Milwaukee Public Schools
Milwaukee, Wisconsin

New Haven School District
New Haven, Connecticut

Ogden School District
Ogden, Utah

Rio Rancho Public Schools
Rio Rancho, New Mexico

San José Unified
School District
San José, California

Scottsdale Unified
School District
Scottsdale, Arizona

Spokane Public Schools
Spokane, Washington

Tacoma Public Schools
Tacoma, Washington

SpringBoard English Language Arts

Lori O'Dea
Executive Director
Content Development

Natasha Vasavada
Executive Director
Pre-AP & SpringBoard

Doug Waugh
Vice President
SpringBoard & Pre-AP Programs

Sarah Balistreri
Senior Director
ELA Content Development

Florencia Duran Wald
Senior Director
ELA Content Development

Julie Manley
Senior Director
Professional Learning

Joely Negedly
Senior Director
Pre-AP Humanities

Jessica Brockman
Product Manager
English Language Arts

Suzie Doss
Director
SpringBoard Implementation

Jennifer Duva
Director
English Language Arts

Spencer Gonçalves
Director
Digital Content Development

Rebecca Grudzina
Senior Editor
English Language Arts

Georgia Scurletis
Senior Instructional Writer
Pre-AP English Language Arts

Abigail Johnson
Editor
English Language Arts

Casseia Lewis
Assistant Editor
English Language Arts

Natalie Hansford
Editorial Assistant
English Language Arts

Table of Contents

ACTIVITY	Unit 1: Perception Is Everything	

CONTENTS

Embedded Assessment 2:
Writing a Reflective Essay **140**

CONTENTS

CONTENTS

ACTIVITY | Unit 4: Creating Perspectives

CONTENTS

Resources

Texts not included in these materials.

Introduction to SpringBoard English Language Arts

About SpringBoard ELA

SpringBoard was built around a simple belief: if you give students and teachers the best materials, engaging methods, and ongoing support, then student success will surely follow. Developed by teachers, SpringBoard brings your classroom to life with materials that help you practice the skills and learn the knowledge you need to excel in high school and beyond. Read on to find out how SpringBoard will support your learning.

Instructional Materials

SpringBoard English Language Arts supplies a Student Edition and Teacher Edition, in print and digital form, for grades 6–12. In addition to using the English Language Arts curriculum, you can sharpen your reading, writing, and language skills with materials including Language Workshop, Close Reading Workshop, and Writing Workshop.

Design that Begins with the End in Mind

- Based on the Understanding by Design model, SpringBoard teaches the skills and knowledge that matter most to meet AP and college and career readiness standards.

- You will start each unit by unpacking the assessment, so you know where you're heading and why the skills you're developing matter.

- Each activity starts with clear, standards-aligned learning targets.

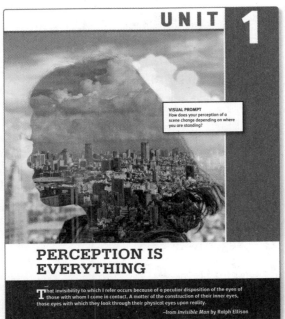

The Practice of Reading Closely

- SpringBoard puts a special focus on close reading, giving you strategies and structure for developing this key skill.

- You will encounter compelling texts—fiction, nonfiction, poetry, drama, visuals, and film.

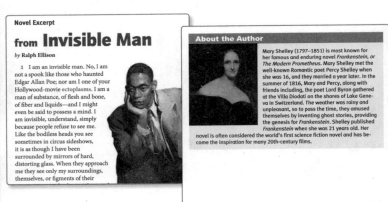

A Living System of Learning

- SpringBoard puts you and your classmates in charge of your learning to create a more dynamic classroom experience.

- With a flexible design and rich library of tools and resources, SpringBoard helps your teacher personalize instruction for your class.

Bringing the Classroom to Life

When you enter a SpringBoard classroom you don't hear a teacher talking in the front of the room. You hear a buzz of excitement, with students working together and taking charge of how they learn. That's what the teachers who designed SpringBoard wanted for their classrooms, so they created a curriculum and materials that are focused on real classroom needs, encouraging teacher and student involvement.

SpringBoard translates the expectations of state standards into engaging daily lessons. We believe that reading, writing, speaking, and listening should all be learned together. You'll see examples of our integrated approach throughout our materials. And we put a special focus on close reading, giving you strategies and structure for developing this key skill.

Our Approach to Reading

In SpringBoard ELA, we move right into compelling texts—fiction, nonfiction, poetry, drama, visuals, and film—and offer the tools, supports, and approaches that will help you get the most out of every reading.

The Practice of Reading Closely

Texts take center stage in the SpringBoard ELA classroom, where you will prepare for close, critical reading of a wide range of materials. With guidance from your teacher, you will develop the habits of close reading that will serve you for a lifetime.

- **As You Read:** You prepare to read and annotate the text for notable elements like genre characteristics, important use of words, and text structures.

- **First Reading:** You read on your own, with a partner, in a group, or with the class. You annotate the text as you begin to uncover its meaning.

- **Making Observations:** Your teacher guides you to pause during or right after the first reading to observe the small details within a text in order to arrive at a deeper understanding of the whole.

- **Returning to the Text:** You continue to deepen your understanding of the text by responding to a series of text-dependent questions. You will use text evidence, speak with new vocabulary words, reflect on your classmates' ideas, and make connections among texts, ideas, and experiences.

- **Working from the Text:** You use the text as a source as you move from reading and analysis to productive work, including academic discussion and writing.

Reading Independently

As a SpringBoard student, you'll practice good reading habits in class so that you can read challenging texts in other classes and on your own. Independent reading is an integral part of every SpringBoard English Language Arts unit. At the beginning of the year, you will learn how to make a plan for independent reading. **Independent Reading Lists** for each unit give you a jump-start on selecting texts by offering a list of suggested titles, including a number of Spanish-language titles, that connect to the themes, genres, and concepts of the SpringBoard unit.

While you work your way through each unit, you will respond to **Independent Reading Links** that lead you to make connections between the reading you're doing on your own and the skills and knowledge you're developing in class. Twice per unit, **Independent Reading Checkpoints** give you a chance to reflect on and synthesize your independent reading in an informal writing assignment or discussion.

Reading to Build Knowledge

SpringBoard units are designed so that you can delve deeply into an overarching topic, theme, or idea. Each unit will pose essential questions that relate to the ideas and texts within the unit, and you will return to these questions again and again, each time refining your responses with new understanding and new evidence to support your point of view. You will also deepen your knowledge of key topics by conducting both on-the-spot and extended research, asking and answering questions, evaluating multiple sources, and synthesizing your findings.

Twice a unit, you will go on a **Knowledge Quest**. Each Knowledge Quest begins with a Knowledge Question and supporting questions to focus your reading. After reading several texts that explore a topic, theme, or idea, you will get to return to the Knowledge Question and show your growing understanding of the topic by responding to a writing prompt or engaging in a discussion.

At the end of a Knowledge Quest, you will be encouraged to continue building your knowledge of the topic by going to **Zinc Reading Labs** and finding related texts to read. Zinc Reading Labs offers a variety of informational and literary texts that you can choose based on your interests. Vocabulary sets for each text let you learn new words and practice using them.

Your independent reading can also enhance your understanding of the topics you are studying in class if you want it to. SpringBoard's **Independent Reading Lists** include suggested books that relate to the topics and themes from each unit. By choosing those books you can see a different side of the topic, learn new words, and find other topics you want to learn more about.

Reading to Gain Perspectives

Gaining Perspectives features use a text as a jumping off point for examining an issue relevant to you. You will be asked to consider the perspectives of others and to empathize with others who have different points of view. You will also be asked to think about social and ethical norms and to recognize the family, school, and community resources available to you. Each Gaining Perspectives feature concludes with a writing task in which you will summarize the discussion you have with your classmates.

Our Approach to Writing

SpringBoard English Language Arts provides you with the support you need to write in all the major modes, emphasizing argumentative, informational, and narrative. You will write often, and you will learn to become a critical reviewer of your own and your peers' work through frequent opportunities for revision and editing. You will learn to plan with purpose, audience, topic, and context in mind; develop drafts with engaging ideas, examples, facts and commentary; revise for clarity, development, organization, style, and diction; and edit using the conventions of the English language.

The Craft of Writing

As you read texts by skilled authors, you will observe the many choices those authors make. You'll tune in to the ways authors purposefully use words, sentences, and structures to convey meaning. After analyzing and critiquing others' work, you will learn to apply your understanding of author's craft to your own writing. A few SpringBoard features help you do just that:

- **Writing prompts** lead up to the Embedded Assessments and give you practice with writing texts in multiple genres, including personal narratives, argumentative essays, letters, research papers, and more. Writing to Sources writing prompts drive you back to texts you have read or viewed to mine for evidence.

- **Focus on the Sentence** tasks help you process content while also practicing the craft of writing powerful sentences.

- **Grammar & Usage** features highlight interesting grammar or usage concepts that appear in a text, both to improve your reading comprehension and to help you attend to these concepts as you craft your own texts.

- **Language & Writer's Craft** features address topics in writing such as style, word choice, and sentence construction.

- **Language Checkpoints** offer in-depth practice with standard English conventions and guide you to develop an editor's checklist to use as a reference each time you check your own or a peer's written work.

Modes of Writing

SpringBoard helps you become a better academic writer by giving you authentic prompts that require you to use sources, and showing you how to work through the writing process. Over the course of the year you will have the chance to write narratives, arguments, and informational texts, and you will develop a wide range of writing skills:

- Consider task, audience, and purpose when structuring and organizing your writing.

- Incorporate details, reasons, and textual evidence to support your ideas.

- Generate research questions, evaluate sources, gather relevant evidence, and report and cite your findings accurately.

- Use research-based strategies that will guide you through the writing process.

Writing with a Focus on the Sentence

SpringBoard English Language Arts leverages sentence writing strategies that were developed by The Writing Revolution. These evidence-based strategies are part of the Hochman Method, the Writing Revolution's system for helping students learn to write across all content areas and grades. The Writing Revolution emphasizes the importance of embedding writing and grammar instruction into content. That's why SpringBoard's **Focus on the Sentence** tasks integrate sentence-level writing into the curriculum. These tasks not only help you learn and practice important grammar concepts and sentence forms, but they also provide a chance for you to process and demonstrate your understanding of texts, images, class discussions, and other content.

Our Approach to Vocabulary

Vocabulary is threaded throughout each unit and developed over the course of the SpringBoard English Language Arts year. You will have ample opportunities to read and hear new words, explore their meanings, origins, and connotations, and use them in written and oral responses.

- Important academic and literary terms that you will need to actively participate in classroom discussions are called out in your book.
- Challenging vocabulary terms found in reading passages are glossed at the point of use.
- Periodic Word Connections boxes guide you through the process of exploring a word with multiple meanings and nuances, an interesting etymology, a telling root or affix, a helpful Spanish cognate, a relationship to another word, or a connection to another content area.

Zinc Reading Labs

Zinc Reading Labs combines the best features of a typical vocabulary program with those of a typical reading program and makes reading and learning new words a game. Zinc offers a variety of nonfiction and fiction texts that you can choose from based on individual needs and interest. Each article has a corresponding vocabulary set that pre-teaches challenging words through spaced repetition, to help you genuinely learn and internalize the vocabulary. Additional vocabulary games focus on SAT/ACT power words and foundational words for English language learners.

Pre-AP Connections

SpringBoard shares Pre-AP's core principles and encourages you to build skills that you will use in high school and beyond. These principles are evident in every SpringBoard activity.

 Close Observation and Analysis
... to notice and consider

When reading, your teacher will guide you to pause to make observations and notice details in the text before analyzing or explaining. Only after you have noticed and enjoyed elements of the text do you then return to the text for deeper analysis and inferential thinking. This close reading sequence helps you interact and engage with the text in increasingly meaningful ways.

 Evidence-Based Writing
... with a focus on the sentence

SpringBoard offers varied and frequent writing opportunities, with specific attention to developing complex and precise sentences as the building block to sophisticated paragraph and essay length writing. Instead of being isolated from reading, sentence-level grammar and writing exercises are integrated into the curriculum to enhance your comprehension and your ability to compose a variety of texts.

 Higher-Order Questioning
... to spark productive lingering

Each unit opens with two essential questions that relate to the topics, themes, and texts within that unit. You return to these questions throughout the unit and refine your answers as new evidence is presented. SpringBoard also encourages you to craft your own questions, and to dig deeply into the texts you read. After each reading passage, you evaluate the meaning of the text and examine the choices that the author made when writing it.

 Academic Conversations
... to support peer-to-peer dialogue

SpringBoard classrooms are places where students like you engage in collaborative learning. You will participate in discussion groups, writing groups, debates, Socratic seminars, literature circles, and oral interpretations and performances. These activities create an environment where you can share, compare, critique, debate, and build on others' ideas to advance your learning.

PSAT/SAT Connections

We want you to be rewarded for the hard work you do in your English Language Arts courses, including when you sit down to take important assessments. Therefore, SpringBoard English Language Arts focuses on the same essential knowledge and skills that are the center of the Evidence-Based Reading and Writing sections of the SAT Suite of Assessments (SAT, PSAT/NMSQT, PSAT™ 10, and PSAT™ 8/9). To make our alignment transparent, we conducted a research study, the results of which showed strong to exemplary alignment between the SpringBoard ELA courses and the corresponding SAT Suite tests. This means that you are getting ready for the SAT, PSAT/NMSQT, PSAT™ 10, and PSAT™ 8/9 in the classroom every day.

Tools and Supports

SpringBoard Digital

SpringBoard puts you in charge of what you learn and gives students and teachers the flexibility and support they need. SpringBoard Digital is an interactive program that provides always-available online content that's accessible from any device—desktop computer, laptop, tablet, or interactive whiteboard. The student edition allows you to interact with the text, respond to prompts, take assessments, and engage with a suite of tools, all in the digital space. Teachers get access to a correlations viewer that embeds correlations at point of use, a lesson planner, progress reports, grading, messaging, and more.

Zinc Reading Labs

All SpringBoard users have access to Zinc Reading Labs, where you can find a huge library of reading material chosen specifically to align with the SpringBoard English Language Arts curriculum. Zinc offers:

- Fresh and engaging nonfiction and fiction content for independent reading.
- Interactive games, quizzes, and tasks that build skills and confidence.
- Freedom of choice: Zinc's massive and ever-growing library means that all students should find texts they want to read.

Turnitin Revision Assistant

When you develop drafts of an available Embedded Assessment through SpringBoard Digital, you can use a tool called Turnitin Revision Assistant. This online tool gives instant feedback to students as they write so they can polish their drafts and practice their revision skills. The feedback model Revision Assistant uses is based on scoring by SpringBoard teachers, and it's trained to assess the same rubric areas that they assess.

Revision Assistant offers:

- A template to help you create an outline.
- Actionable, instant feedback in specific areas such as structure, use of language, and ideas.
- Identification of strengths and weakness in your writing.

A Letter to the Student

Dear Student,

Welcome to the SpringBoard program! We created this program with you in mind: it puts you and your classmates at the center of your learning and equips you with the skills and knowledge you need to excel in high school and beyond.

The energy and excitement you bring to class helps you and your classmates learn. You will explore compelling themes through readings, classroom discussions, and projects. You will dive into fascinating texts—some of which you'll choose on your own—from different genres including myths, poems, biographies, plays, and films. You will engage in lively discussions, debates, and performances so that you become confident sharing and presenting your ideas. You will write frequently to sharpen your ability to craft effective sentences, paragraphs, and longer texts. And you'll start each unit with a clear understanding of where you're headed by unpacking the skills and knowledge you'll need to do well on the assessment at the end.

SpringBoard helps you make connections between the concepts you're reading and writing about in class and the real world. Instead of just memorizing how to do things, you'll draw on your own and your classmates' experiences and knowledge to come to new and deeper understandings. When questions arise from the materials you're studying in class, you'll learn how to do both quick and longer-term research to find answers. Plus, you'll have access to tools and resources that are built right into the program, including powerful learning strategies, independent reading lists to help you select texts to read outside of class, and digital tools that you can access any time from any device—desktop computer, laptop, or tablet.

We want students to be rewarded for the hard work they do in their English Language Arts course. That's why the SpringBoard program focuses on the essential knowledge and skills that will prepare you for the challenging work you'll do in your high school classes, in AP courses, and in college.

Students from around the country are talking about how much they like the SpringBoard approach to learning. We hope you enjoy learning with SpringBoard, too.

Sincerely,

The SpringBoard Team

VISUAL PROMPT
How does your perception of a scene change depending on where you are standing?

PERCEPTION IS EVERYTHING

That invisibility to which I refer occurs because of a peculiar disposition of the eyes of those with whom I come in contact. A matter of the construction of their inner eyes, those eyes with which they look through their physical eyes upon reality.

—from *Invisible Man* by Ralph Ellison

GOALS

- To apply Reader-Response and Cultural Criticism in determining an author's purpose, audience, and message
- To evaluate the effectiveness of an author's organizational and stylistic choices in texts across genres
- To strategically use text evidence to support commentary and critiques of an author's work
- To write texts that use a logical structure, precise language, and effective genre characteristics

VOCABULARY

ACADEMIC
imperialism
marginalize
paradox
perception
rhetorical devices

LITERARY
Cultural Criticism
diction
literary criticism
literary theories
prologue
Reader-Response Criticism

ACTIVITY	CONTENTS	

📦 My Independent Reading List

_____
_____
_____
_____
_____
_____
_____
_____
_____
_____
_____
_____
_____
_____
_____
_____
_____
_____
_____
_____
_____
_____
_____
_____

Learning Strategies

Graphic Organizer
Marking the Text
Paraphrasing
Think-Pair-Share

My Notes

Learning Targets

- Preview the big ideas of the unit.
- Create a plan for reading independently.
- Identify and analyze the knowledge and skills needed to complete Embedded Assessment 1.

Preview

In this activity, you will explore the big ideas and tasks of the unit and make plans for your independent reading.

About the Unit

In this unit, you will examine the choices authors make to inform and shape the perception of readers. You will begin by deeply evaluating and critiquing poetry and then apply these skills to more complex literary and argumentative texts. This unit also introduces literary theories, which you will use to interpret texts and the world. Studying literary theory is a means to make you aware that the world is full of ideologies, theories, and biases through which we construct an understanding of our individual experiences and the world around us. You will apply Reader-Response Criticism in the first half of this unit and Cultural Criticism in the latter half.

Essential Questions

Based on your current knowledge, how would you answer these questions?

1. Why do writers make particular choices when composing a text?

2. How does the interaction between a reader and a text create meaning?

3. What does it mean to be a stranger in a village?

Unpacking Embedded Assessment 1

Closely read the assignment for Embedded Assessment 1: Writing a Rhetorical Analysis Essay.

 Write an essay in which you critique and evaluate how the author of "Tipping System Exacerbates Unfair Pay at Restaurants" builds an argument to convince her audience that restaurant workers deserve fair wages from their employers instead of tips. In your essay, explain and evaluate how Kathleen Kingsbury uses one or more of the features in the directions that precede the passage (or features of your own choosing) to develop her argument. Be sure that your critique focuses on the most relevant features of the passage. Your essay should not explain whether you agree with Kingsbury's claims, but rather it should explain and evaluate how Kingsbury builds an argument to persuade the audience. Paraphrase the assignment in your own words. What do you need to know to be able to complete this assessment successfully? What skills must you have to complete the task successfully?

Planning Independent Reading

To enhance this unit's focus, look for literature or nonfiction that includes multiple perspectives. Each of the literary theories you will study in this course can help you analyze and understand your independent reading texts in new and enlightening ways. Consider how these readings connect to what you read in the unit and to your own perspectives. Choose exceptional readings to recommend to and discuss with your peers. To help you choose the right book, use the following questions as a guide.

- What have you enjoyed reading in the past? What is your favorite book or favorite type of book? Who is your favorite author?

- When you select a potential book, preview it. What do the front and back covers show you? What type of visual is shown? What types of fonts and colors are used? Are there awards or brags that tell you about the book?

- Read the first few pages. Are they interesting? How does the author try to hook you to keep reading? What can you tell about the characters and setting so far? Does this seem too hard, too easy, or just right?

- How do you think literary theory might change your perspective of the texts you are reading independently?

Reading Discussion Groups

Follow your teacher's oral guidance through a book pass. Practice previewing each book by looking at the covers and reading the first few pages.

4. In your Reader/Writer Notebook, record each book's title and author, something from your previewing that stands out to you, and your rating of the book.

5. After previewing each book and thinking about the goals of this unit, do you want to continue reading the book you brought to the group or choose something else?

   Create an Independent Reading Plan to help you set personal reading goals. Keep this plan in your Reader/Writer Notebook.

   I have chosen to read _____

   _____ .

   by (author) _____ .

   because (reason from previewing) _____

   _____ .

   I will set aside time to read at (time, place) _____

   _____ .

   I should finish this text by (date) _____

6. Record your daily reading pace in your Independent Reading Log. Write a brief daily report in your log responding to what you have read. Include in your report questions or predictions about what you have read.

7. Respond to the Independent Reading Links you encounter throughout the unit.

© 2021 College Board. All rights reserved.

Learning Strategies

Marking the Text
OPTIC

VOCABULARY

ACADEMIC
A **perception** is one person's interpretation of sensory or conceptual information.

LITERARY
Literary criticism is the formal practice of interpreting, evaluating, and explaining the meaning and significance of literary works. Scholars often use specific **literary theories**— systematic, conceptual methods of analyzing texts— when they engage in literary criticism.

My Notes

Learning Targets

- Understand the fundamentals of literary criticism and six literary theories.
- Apply literary theories to analyze, question, and interpret images.
- Summarize your observations and understanding of the impact of literary theories.

Preview

In this activity, you will be introduced to six literary theories and their definitions. You will use the key assumptions of a critical perspective to analyze and question illustrations.

Literary Criticism

Our experiences, relationships, and interactions shape how we perceive the world around us. How one person perceives an event unfolding in front of them can be dramatically different than how another perceives the same event. These varied **perceptions** are at the heart of **literary criticism**.

Literary criticism does not always involve being negative or critical about a piece of writing. Instead, it is a formal practice that scholars of literature use to interpret, evaluate, and explain the meaning and significance of literary works. Because we all bring different perceptions to the classroom, *how* we analyze, interpret, and evaluate literature varies greatly. But literary criticism doesn't require scholars to agree. In fact, it encourages scholars to engage in ongoing discourse about the meaning of literary works and their significance to the broader human experience.

Becoming skilled at literary criticism has benefits beyond the study of literature, too. Learning to read a text from various critical perspectives can help readers become agile and skillful thinkers who are capable of exploring the world outside the boundaries of one's own limited perceptions.

☑ Focus on the Sentence

Write two complete sentences in response to what you have learned so far about literary criticism. The first should be a statement that paraphrases the definition of literary criticism in your own words. The second should be a question you have about literary criticism.

Statement: _____

_____

Question: _____

_____

Literary Theory

Scholars use a number of different literary theories, sometimes called critical theories or lenses, to uncover meaning in literary works. Each theory is made up of a set of assumptions or concepts that a reader applies to the text in order to understand it in new ways.

Studying literary theories can help a reader to become aware of competing perceptions of truth and to learn that a text can be understood through a filter of ideologies, values, and perspectives. Being able to apply different theories to a text expands a reader's worldview and adds dimensions to understanding a text.

The following six literary theories will give you the tools to understand texts in novel and challenging ways over the course of this school year. These are not the only literary theories that exist, but they are among the most commonly used theories for exploring literature. Imagine each theory as a lens, like a pair of tinted glasses, that adds color to the interpretation of a text. No single lens or theory provides the clearest view of the world. Instead, each one allows a reader to make meaning from a piece of literature in a different way.

As you read each definition, underline words and phrases that strike you as most essential to understanding the theory.

Literary Theory	Key Assumptions
Reader-Response Criticism Reader Response Criticism focuses on a reader's active engagement with a text. The reader's response to any text is shaded by the reader's own experiences, ethics, moral values, and general views of the world. For example, the response to *To Kill a Mockingbird* may depend on the reader's sense of outrage on behalf of someone unjustly accused of a crime.	• When encountering a text, the reader creates meaning from a personal interaction with the text. • A discussion of a text should take into account the reader as well as the reading situation. • Different readers formulate different acceptable interpretations because a text allows for a range of acceptable interpretations for which textual support is available.
Cultural Criticism Cultural Criticism asserts that differing religious beliefs, ethnicities, class identifications, political beliefs, and individual viewpoints affect how texts are created and interpreted. What it means to be a part of—or excluded from—a specific cultural group contributes to an understanding of texts in relation to culture.	• Ethnicity, religious beliefs, social class, and other cultural features are crucial components in formulating plausible interpretations of a text. • It is essential to examine the relationship between dominant cultures and those with less power or authority.
Archetypal Criticism Archetypes are universal symbols—images, characters, motifs, or patterns that recur in the myths, dreams, oral traditions, songs, literature, and other texts of peoples widely separated by time and place. Archetypal Criticism deals with the similarities of these patterns in the literature of widely diverse cultures. For example, most cultures have stories that present a version of the Hero's Journey.	• Certain images recur in texts from diverse cultures that share a common interpretation—water, sun, colors, trees, and settings such as gardens and deserts. • Certain characters recur—the hero, the trickster, the great mother, the wise old man, the prodigal son. • Certain motifs and patterns recur—creation stories, the quest, voyage to the underworld, journey, and initiation.

Literary Theory	Key Assumptions
Marxist Criticism Marxist Criticism asserts that economics provides the foundation for all social, political, and ideological reality. Economic inequalities between classes create conflict and a power structure that influences all other aspects of life. For example, status in the community in *Their Eyes Were Watching God* can be examined from an economic point of view.	• All aspects of humanity are based on the struggle for economic power. • The basic struggle in human society is between the haves and the have-nots. • The struggle between social classes is inevitable but also drives social transformation.
Feminist Criticism Feminist interpretation focuses on relationships between genders. It examines the patterns of thought, behavior, values, enfranchisement, and power in relations between and within the sexes. A Feminist reading of *Their Eyes Were Watching God*, for example, may examine the novel as an example of a heroine's journey.	• Issues of gender and sexuality are central to artistic expression. • A patriarchal society conveys the notion of male dominance through the images of women in its texts. • Fictional portrayals of female characters often reflect and create stereotypical social and political attitudes about women. • Many classic literary texts lack complex female figures and treat the female reader as an outsider. • Texts authored by women may have different viewpoints than texts authored by men.
Historical Criticism While acknowledging the importance of the literary text, the Historical approach recognizes the significance of historical information in interpreting literature. This perspective assumes that texts both influence and are influenced by the times in which they are created. For example, an interpretation of *Things Fall Apart* by Chinua Achebe may be enhanced by an understanding of the effects of colonialism in present-day African life.	• A text cannot be separated from its historical context, which is a web of social, cultural, economic, personal, and political factors. • An understanding of a text is enhanced by the study of beliefs and artifacts (such as diaries, films, paintings, and letters) in existence when the text was created.

Introducing the Strategy: OPTIC

OPTIC is an acronym for **o**verview, **p**arts, **t**itle, **i**nterrelationships, and **c**onclusion. This strategy is useful for close analysis of visual texts, including paintings, photographs, advertisements, maps, charts, or graphs. By viewing the details of an image in this order, readers develop an interpretation of the image's meaning or theme.

Viewing through the Lenses

In small groups, use the **OPTIC** strategy to closely examine each of the following images. Then return to each image for a second look, this time through the lens of the literary theories.

1. Record your observations about the image you are viewing. Follow the steps of the OPTIC strategy outlined here.

   Overview: Write notes on what the image appears to be about.

   Parts: Zoom in on the different parts of the image. Describe any details that seem important.

   Title: Highlight the words of the title if there is one.

   Interrelationships: How are the elements of the image related?

   Conclusion: Draw a conclusion about the image as a whole. What does the visual mean?

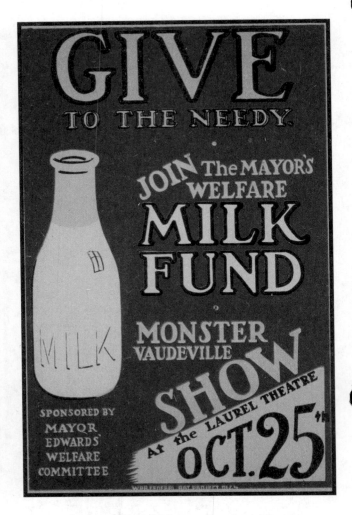

2. Briefly share your observations with your group in a clear and concise summary. Listen as your group members share their observations, and respond by offering additional ideas or asking questions.

3. Assign one of the literary theories to each member of your group. Revisit the images, this time imagining that you are viewing the image through the lens of your assigned theory. What questions do you have or observations can you make about the images when you are viewing from the perspective of a critical theory? Record your ideas in the graphic organizer.

Image	Questions and Observations Using Literary Theories
	Reader-Response: Cultural: Archetypal: Marxist: Feminist: Historical:
	Reader-Response: Cultural: Archetypal: Marxist: Feminist: Historical:
	Reader-Response: Cultural: Archetypal: Marxist: Feminist: Historical:
	Reader-Response: Cultural: Archetypal: Marxist: Feminist: Historical:

4. **Discussion:** Share your most relevant or interesting questions and observations in a class discussion. Listen as your classmates share their discoveries and follow up by asking questions and purposefully offering ideas and judgments.

☑ Check Your Understanding

Based on the information in your the graphic organizer, did your understanding of each image change after applying literary theories? How does a viewer's perspective create meaning in a given text?

Learning Strategies

Think-Pair-Share
TP-CASTT
Summarizing
Activating Prior Knowledge

My Notes

Learning Targets

- Analyze how two poems from different periods treat the same theme.
- Apply the Reader-Response Criticism to an analysis of a poem.

Preview

In this activity, you will read and analyze two poems. Then, you will learn about Reader-Response Criticism and revisit your analysis of the poems through this lens.

Introducing the Strategy: Metacognitive Markers

Metacognition refers to the thinking you do about your own learning. Using metacognitive markers involves marking the text with symbols to reflect the thinking you are doing as you read. After reading, you can scan the text and use your metacognitive markers to quickly find evidence when you are talking or writing about a text. Here are the markers:

- ? Use a question mark for questions you have about the text.
- ! Use an exclamation point for a reaction to what you are reading.
- * Use an asterisk for a comment about the text.

As You Read

- Use metacognitive markers to interact with the text.
- Circle unknown words and phrases. Try to determine the meaning of the words by using context clues, word parts, or a dictionary.

About the Author

Phillis Wheatley (c. 1753–1784) was age 13 when she wrote her first published poem. Born in West Africa, Wheatley was kidnapped at the age of eight and brought to Boston on a slave ship. Her life was unusual for a slave, as her owners encouraged Wheatley to read and provided her with lessons in multiple subjects. In 1773, she published *Poems on Various Subjects, Religious and Moral* and became the first African American and the third American woman to publish a book of poems. Wheatley wrote several poems to honor George Washington and visited him at his invitation in 1776. Though she was freed from slavery, Wheatley was never able to find support for her second volume of poetry.

Poetry

On Being Brought from Africa to America

by **Phillis Wheatley**

T'was mercy brought me from my Pagan land,
Taught my **benighted** soul to understand
That there's a God, that there's a Saviour too:
Once I redemption neither sought nor knew.
5 Some view our **sable** race with scornful eye,
"Their colour is a diabolic die."
Remember, Christians, Negros, black as Cain,
May be refin'd, and join th' angelic train.

Making Observations
- What's your first impression about the theme of the poem?
- What emotions do you feel after reading the poem?

benighted: unenlightened
sable: black

My Notes

About the Author

Emma Lazarus (1849–1887) was born in New York City, the daughter of Jewish immigrants who came to the United States from Portugal during the time of the American Revolution. Lazarus received an extensive education at home and demonstrated the ability to analyze and write poetry at a young age. She wrote "The New Colossus" as a contribution to a fundraiser to generate money for the construction of a pedestal for the Statue of Liberty. Lazarus initially refused, but another writer convinced her to use the opportunity to express the plight of refugee immigrants. After Lazarus's death, a friend helped renew public interest in the poem. In 1903, it was inscribed on a plaque that remains on display inside the pedestal.

Poetry

The New Colossus[1]

by **Emma Lazarus**

Not like the brazen giant of Greek fame,

With conquering limbs astride from land to land;

Here at our sea-washed, sunset gates shall stand

A mighty woman with a torch, whose flame

5 Is the imprisoned lightning, and her name

Mother of Exiles. From her beacon-hand

Glows world-wide welcome; her mild eyes command

The air-bridged harbor that twice cities frame.

"Keep, ancient lands, your storied pomp" cries she

10 With silent lips. "Give me your tired, your poor,

Your huddled masses yearning to breathe free,

The wretched refuse of your teeming shore.

Send these, the homeless, tempest-tossed to me:

I lift my lamp beside the golden door!"

---

[1] **Colossus:** refers to the Colossus of Rhodes, one of the seven wonders of the ancient world.

Making Observations

- What details or images stand out to you the most?
- What questions about the theme will you ask yourself as you reread the poem?

Returning to the Text

- Reread the poems to answer these text-dependent questions.
- Write any additional questions you have about the text in your Reader/Writer Notebook.

1. The first stanza of "On Being Brought from Africa," introduces a **paradox**. Using evidence from the poem, describe the paradox.

   _____

   _____

   _____

   _____

ACADEMIC

A **paradox** is a statement that appears to contain two contradictory or incompatible points, but upon closer examination it can reveal a hidden truth to the reader or viewer.

VOCABULARY

2. What can you infer about the meaning of the word *diabolic* from its use in the poem? Write a definition in your own words. Verify your definition by checking a dictionary.

   _____

   _____

   _____

   _____

3. How would you describe the tone of "On Being Brought from Africa," and does it shift? Cite specific words and phrases to support your answer.

   _____

   _____

   _____

   _____

   _____

4. Consider the title "The New Colossus." Consult a dictionary and other reference materials to explain the connection and importance of the title to the poem.

_____

_____

_____

_____

5. What type of verse is "The New Colossus," and how does its structure contribute to the overall effect of the poem?

_____

_____

_____

_____

Introducing the Strategy: TP-CASTT

This reading strategy is used to analyze a poetic text by identifying and discussing each topic in the acronym: **T**itle, **P**araphrase, **C**onnotation, **A**ttitude, **S**hift, **T**itle again, and **T**heme. The strategy is a guide designed to lead you in an analysis of a literary text. It is a good idea to begin at the top and work your way down the elements. However, you will find that as you study one element, you will naturally begin to explore others. For example, a study of connotation often leads to a discussion of tone and shifts. Revisiting the title often leads to a discussion of the theme, or author's message.

Working from the Text

6. Use the **TP-CASTT** strategy to analyze the poems. Record your responses in the graphic organizer that follows. Read each poem several times, each time discussing aspects of the TP-CASTT strategy and recording your responses.

Strategy	Response
Title: Look at the title without looking at the rest of the poem. What do you think the poem will be about?	
Paraphrase: After diffusing the text, translate the most challenging lines of the poem into your own words (you may need to reread the text several times). Then briefly summarize the poem in such a way that the meaning is maintained.	
Connotation: Mark the text by highlighting the diction (words and phrases) used for positive effect (color 1) and/or negative effect (color 2). Then study the diction to determine a pattern and record your analysis.	
Attitude (Tone): Consider the speaker's attitude in the poem. How does her attitude change from the start of the poem to its end?	

Strategy	Response
Shift: Look for shifts, or changes in the poem. These shifts are meant to draw your attention, and might take the form of punctuation, transition words, stanza length, or structural changes. Identify a shift in the poem.	
Title: Look at the title again. How is your interpretation of it different now that you've analyzed the poem more deeply? Can you confirm or correct your initial hypotheses?	
Theme: Determine the author's message conveyed in the poem. Identify a theme in the poem (such as family or the human condition). Then, write a statement about the underlying theme of the poem.	

☑ Check Your Understanding

Choose a line from each poem that illustrates a related theme found in both poems. In a few sentences, analyze the two poems' treatment of a related theme.

Reader-Response Criticism

Your personal attitudes, beliefs, and experiences influence how you derive meaning from text. Examining the way in which you understand a text involves using critical lenses. A critical lens is a way of judging or analyzing a work of literature.

Reader-Response Criticism suggests that readers' perspectives often determine their perceptions. The critical lens of Reader-Response Criticism asks you to be aware of your personal attitudes, beliefs, and experiences as you read. It focuses on the relationships among the reader, the reader's situation, and the text. The theory suggests that the process of making meaning relies not only on the text itself, but also on the qualities and motivations of the individual who is interacting with the text.

The diagram illustrates this idea:

LITERARY

Reader-Response Criticism focuses on a reader's active engagement with a piece of print or nonprint text. The reader's response to any text is shaped by the reader's own experiences, social ethics, moral values, and general views of the world.

My Notes

Reading Situation
The circumstances surrounding the reading, including purposes

↓

Meaning

↗   ↖

Reader
Person engaged in the reading process

Text
What is being read

My Notes

The Elements of Reader-Response Criticism

The Reader

Reader-Response critical theory examines the person doing the reading. In Reader-Response criticism, the reader is seen not as a passive recipient of the meaning in the text, but as an active co-creator of meaning. Any text presents gaps which the reader, through imaginative engagement with the text, completes. Over time, the responses of readers form a range of meanings ascribed to a text. Because of the centrality of the reader in the construction of meaning, reader-response criticism does not view texts as having single, fixed meanings. Instead, reader-response theorists believe a range of defensible interpretations can be produced. To apply this theory, you must examine how your own opinions, attitudes, beliefs, and background knowledge factor into your perspective.

The Reading Situation

The reading situation includes *why* you are engaged in reading, *when* you are reading, and *where* you are reading. All of these factors affect your perception.

Why: What is your purpose for reading? You may be reading a text because the subject matter interests you, your teacher assigned it, or you need to learn something in order to complete a task.

When: Perhaps a story was written hundreds of years ago, but you are reading it in the 21st century. Your perspective will differ from that of the writer and of the text's original readers.

Where: If you are reading a text written by someone from a community like yours, you may understand the text more readily or relate to the author in certain ways that you don't if you are reading a text by someone from a very different locale.

The Text

The text is defined as whatever is being read, viewed, or heard, and may include videos, audio, and websites. Textual features vary, depending on the source. For example, a textbook presents text differently from the way a magazine or a pamphlet does. Numerous other factors, from level of difficulty to the font, influence the text.

☑ Check Your Understanding

Think about your initial analysis of "On Being Brought from Africa to America" and "The New Colossus." Describe the Reader, the Reading Situation, and the Text. How did the interaction of these three elements influence your understanding and analysis of the poem? In particular, examine the way your Metacognitive Markers demonstrate your responses as a reader and illuminate the ways you constructed meaning in the text.

📦 INDEPENDENT READING LINK

Read and Respond

Think about your independent reading text. In what ways does your personal response to the text depend on where and why you are reading the text? Consider how your own experiences and background affect your reading of the text and how someone with a different background might view it differently. Then, write a short reflection on your response in your Reader/Writer Notebook.

Applying Reader-Response Criticism

Learning Targets

- Identify poetic devices and evaluate how they contribute to the mood and meaning of a poem.
- Evaluate a poem, paying special attention to the interaction of form, sound, and wordplay.
- Evaluate how three poems from the same period treat similar themes.

Preview

In this activity, you will analyze how a poet uses sound, form, figurative language, and structure to convey meaning. After analyzing a poem in one small group, you will join another group who studied a different poem to share your analyses in a collaborative discussion.

Introducing the Strategy: QHT

QHT is a strategy for thinking about your own understanding of vocabulary words. The letters stand for **Q**uestions, **H**eard, and **T**each:

Q: words you may have seen but you are not sure about their meaning

H: words you have heard before but may not know them well

T: words you know so well you could teach them to someone else

To use QHT, think about how well you know each term and label each term with a letter.

Tools for Poets: Reviewing Poetic Devices

Poetic devices are literary techniques that authors use to strengthen and enhance their work. These devices are often used in poetry, but writers often employ these literary techniques in all types of writing. Before reading your assigned poem, review the different poetic devices listed in the following chart. Developing an understanding of these devices will help you to identify and discuss the strategic choices that a writer makes.

1. Expand your background knowledge about these poetic devices by marking each word with Q, H, or T.

Poetic Device	Q/H/T	Your Definition
alliteration		
assonance		
consonance		
hyperbole		

Learning Strategies

Discussion Groups
Marking the Text
QHT
Think-Pair-Share

My Notes

Poetic Device	Q/H/T	Your Definition
imagery		
meter		
extended metaphor		
personification		
rhyme scheme		

My Notes

2. Work with a partner to record definitions for each term. For terms you know well or have heard before, write your own definition. Then use the glossary to validate your understanding. Use a glossary to look up the terms that you have labled "Q." Record a paraphrased definition for each term in the chart.

As You Read

- Underline any poetic devices that you notice in the poem.
- Circle unknown words and phrases. Try to determine the meaning of the words by using context clues, word parts, or a dictionary.

About the Author

E. E. Cummings (1894–1962) was an experimental poet whose work continues to enjoy widespread popularity. During his career, Cummings examined traditional themes such as love and childhood, but he explored these themes with innovative methods, such as incorporating typography into the poem's meaning, or using words such as *if* and *because* as nouns. Cummings's work was not at first successful, but he began to receive greater recognition in 1945 when his work was discovered and championed by a new generation of rebellious young poets who saw him as a kindred spirit. In 1950, he was awarded a fellowship by the American Academy of Poets, and later (1958) the Bollingen Prize in Poetry. By the time of his death in 1962, Cummings had published almost one thousand poems.

Poetry

in Just –

by **E. E. Cummings**

in Just-
spring   when the world is mud-
luscious the little
lame balloonman

5 whistles   far   and wee
and eddieandbill come
running from marbles and
piracies and it's
spring

10 when the world is puddle-wonderful
the queer
old balloonman whistles
far   and   wee
and bettyandisabel come dancing=

15 from hop-scotch and jump-rope and
it's
spring
and
     the

20   goat-footed
balloonMan   whistles
far
and
wee

Making Observations
- What imagery catches your attention?
- Which of the poet's structural or stylistic choices stand out to you?

My Notes

About the Author

Sylvia Plath (1932–1963) captured the intensity of her turbulent life in an autobiographical novel and personal, revealing poetry. An accomplished scholar and writer, Plath won many awards as a young woman, including a scholarship to Smith College and a Fulbright fellowship to Newnham College in Cambridge University. She is most remembered for two collections of her poems, *The Colossus and Other Poems* (1960) and *Ariel* (1965), and a novel, *The Bell Jar* (1963). In 1981, almost two decades after her death, her works were published in *The Collected Poems* and awarded the Pulitzer Prize.

Poetry

Mushrooms

by **Sylvia Plath**

Overnight, very
Whitely, **discreetly**,
Very quietly
Our toes, our noses
5 Take hold on the **loam**,
Acquire the air.
Nobody sees us,
Stops us, betrays us;
The small grains make room.
10 Soft fists insist on
Heaving the needles,
The leafy bedding,
Even the paving.
Our hammers, our rams,
15 Earless and eyeless,
Perfectly voiceless,
Widen the **crannies**,
Shoulder through holes. We
Diet on water,

discreetly: without attracting attention
loam: soil that plants thrive in
crannies: cracks

20 On crumbs of shadow,

Bland-mannered, asking

Little or nothing.

So many of us!

So many of us!

25 We are shelves, we are

Tables, we are meek,

We are edible.

Nudgers and shovers

In spite of ourselves.

30 Our kind multiplies:

We shall by morning

Inherit the earth.

Our foot's in the door.

Making Observations

- What imagery catches your attention?
- Which of the poet's structural or stylistic choices stand out to you?

My Notes

My Notes

About the Author

Anne Sexton (1928–1974) pursued poetry in her adult life as a means of coping with depression. Sexton's work reflects the emotional turmoil that filled her life, and she often wrote about controversial and difficult subjects. Her writing was known for its brilliant imagery. A very popular poet in her lifetime, Sexton won numerous honors and awards, including the Pulitzer Prize for Poetry in 1967. In addition to her poetry, Sexton wrote several children's books and a play, and collaborated with a jazz-rock group known as Anne Sexton and Her Kind.

Poetry

Water

by **Anne Sexton**

We are fishermen in a flat scene.

All day long we are in love with water.

The fish are naked.

The fish are always awake.

5 They are the color of old spoons

and caramels.

The sun reaches down

but the floor is not in sight.

Only the rocks are white and green.

10 Who knows what goes on in the halls below?

Making Observations
- What imagery catches your attention?
- Which of the poet's structural or stylistic choices stand out to you?

Returning to the Text

- Reread your assigned poem to answer these text-dependent questions.
- Write any additional questions you have about the poem in your Reader/Writer Notebook.

"in Just—"

3. What happens when the "balloonman whistles far and wee"?

_____

_____

_____

_____

4. What can you infer about how the speaker feels about springtime? Use specific evidence from the poem to support your answer.

_____

_____

_____

5. What effect do the short line lengths (lines 16–19 and 22–24) have on the sound of the poem?

_____

_____

_____

6. How does Cummings's use of line breaks and spacing contribute to the mood of the poem? Can you identify conscious patterns?

_____

_____

_____

"Mushrooms"

7. What human characteristics does Plath attribute to the mushrooms? What effect does her use of personification have on the reader's understanding of the mushrooms?

_____

_____

_____

_____

8. How does the word "whitely" in line 2 add to the description of the mushrooms' growing?

_____

_____

_____

_____

9. Identify the central metaphor in the poem. What idea is the metaphor conveying? Use evidence to support your interpretation

_____

_____

_____

_____

10. Which poetic devices does Plath employ and how do they affect your understanding of the poem? Use text evidence to support your response.

_____

_____

_____

_____

11. What is Plath's key idea in this poem? What languge does she use to convey this to her audience?

_____

_____

_____

_____

"Water"

12. Based on details from the poem, what do you think the water represents?

_____

_____

_____

_____

_____

13. Analyze the use of personification in the poem, paying attention to line 7. What effect does the poet create through the use of this figurative language?

_____

_____

_____

_____

14. Consider the lines, "They are the color of old spoons/ and caramels." Why do you think Sexton used these words to describe the fish? What effect does it have on you as a reader?

_____

_____

_____

_____

15. What is the significance of the line "All day long we are in love with water" within the context of the rest of the poem? Use text evidence to support your interpretation.

_____

_____

_____

_____

My Notes

Working from the Text

16. Reflect on this statement by W. H. Auden, and then discuss it with a partner. How does it apply to Reader-Response Criticism?

    "What a poem means is the outcome of a dialogue between the words on the page and the person who happens to be reading it; that is to say, its meaning varies from person to person."

17. In preparation for a group discussion, revisit the poem you worked with closely and analyze it from the perspective of Reader-Response Criticism. Write a short, interpretive response.

    • How do your experiences, attitudes, and values as the reader contribute to your understanding of the text?
    • What elements of the text itself affect your perception of the poem's meaning?
    • How did the reading situation affect your interpretation?

18. Now that you have used Reader-Response Criticism, share your interpretation of the poem with your group. To what extent do you and your peers agree on an interpretation of the poem?

19. How does the poet use poetic devices and precise language to achieve a specific effect? Compare the poetic style of Cummings and Plath to Sexton. Discuss the choices that the poet made to convey a specific message to his or her audience. Refer to the list of poetic devices at the beginning of the activity as needed.

20. Compare and contrast how all three poets treat nature as a theme in the poems you have studied.

☑ Check Your Understanding

How did your interpretation of the poem change after considering the poet's deliberate word choice?

Creating Meaning

Learning Targets

- Analyze the way a poet uses imagery and diction to create particular effects.
- Evaluate and critique how an author uses language to convey a sensory experience to readers.

Preview

In this activity, you will read a poem before evaluating and critiquing the poet's use of imagery, sensory details, and diction. Then you will write a literary analysis explaining how the poet's language choices contribute to the poem's effect.

As You Read

- Underline any memories the author describes that prompt you to create mental images.
- Circle unknown words and phrases. Try to determine the meaning of words by using context clues, word parts, or a dictionary.

Poetry

I Remember

by **Edward Montez**

from **Calafia: The California Poetry Project**
Ishmael Reed, Project Director

I remember the scent of acorn soup cooking and deer meat frying in
quiet evenings of summer.

And shivering under thin blankets in winter and watching the wall
paper dance to the force of the winter winds outside.

5   I remember the cry of an owl in the night and I knew it was an
ominous warning, a cry of death.

I remember running in the dust behind the medicine truck when it
came to the reservation, lifesavers was a free treat.
And grandpa sitting in his favorite resting chair under his favorite
10 shade tree with his dog "Oly" by his side.

I remember running naked and screaming with my aunt in hot
pursuit, a stick in her hand, she always caught me.

And every summer we would swim in the river and let the sun bake
us until we were a shade less than purple, basking on the riverbank,
15 undisturbed, at peace.

Learning Strategies

Brainstorming
Discussion
Rereading
Think-Pair-Share

 INDEPENDENT READING LINK

Read and Connect

Select a passage from your independent reading that contains strong imagery or particularly effective diction. Which words or phrases stand out? Why do you think the author chose to use those specific words or phrases to convey his or her message? Write a paragraph in which you evaluate the author's language choices.

My Notes

My Notes

And I remember grandma toiling in the bean fields while I played with my army truck on the fender of a "49" Plymouth.

I remember going to the movies in town on Saturday nights with fifty cents in my pocket, thirty-five cents for the ticket and the rest
20 was mine.

Eating popcorn and drinking water from a discarded coke cup and rooting for the Indians to win, and they never did, but that was yesterday.

Making Observations

- What sights, smells, or sounds do you notice in this poem?
- How would you describe the speaker's childhood?

Returning to the Text

- Reread the poem to answer these text-dependent questions.
- Write any additional questions you have about the text in your Reader/Writer Notebook.

1. What phrase repeats at the beginning of most stanzas? Why do you think the poet chooses to repeat this phrase?

2. How does the poet include the reader in his memory?

3. How does the poet's **diction** affect your understanding of the memories described?

4. How does the poem end? What details from earlier in the poem help the reader make meaning from the final stanza?

LITERARY

Diction is the writer's choice of words. Writers make stylistic choices about which words to use to convey a particular voice and tone.

VOCABULARY

Working from the Text

5. Writers often use precise details and diction to appeal to the reader. Use your annotations to evaluate the details Montez includes in his poem. As you complete the graphic organizer, focus on how the poet uses specific imagery, details, and diction to retell a childhood memory.

	Example from the Text (Underline key words and phrases.)	What is the effect of word choice in this line?	Replace one or more of the key words/phrases. How does the line's meaning or effect change?
Visual Imagery (sight)			
Auditory Imagery (sound)			
Tactile Imagery (touch)			
Olfactory / Gustatory Imagery (smell/taste)			

Evaluating and Critiquing Author's Craft

6. Now that you have evaluated some of the key elements of the poem, evaluate the poet's use of language. Use the following questions to guide your discussion with a partner.

   • Which lines might evoke an emotional response in readers?

   • Which lines illuminate a theme found in the poem?

   • How effective is the poet's diction in helping the reader understand the speaker's memories?

7. **Quickwrite:** Do you think Montez's use of imagery, specific details and diction is effective? Use specific evidence from the text to support your commentary.

☑ Check Your Understanding

Think about Edward Montez's poem "I Remember" and write a new response to the unit Essential Question: Why do writers make particular choices when composing a text?

☑ Writing Prompt: Informational

Revisit any of the poems you have read so far in this unit. Write a paragraph explaining how the poet purposefully uses language in the poem to convey meaning or to create a specific effect on the reader. Be sure to:

• Describe key genre characteristics such as precise language, structural elements, and the use of poetic devices.

• Incorporate examples from a poem read in this unit.

• Use academic vocabulary and standard English capitalization, punctuation, and spelling.

Exploring Poetic Form

© 2021 College Board. All rights reserved.

Learning Strategies

Brainstorming
Discussion Groups

WORD CONNECTIONS

Etymology

The word **allegory** comes from the Greek *allegoria*, which literally means "a speaking about something else." In literature, allegory describes a type of extended metaphor in which authors represent complex or abstract ideas about the real world through characters, events, or other elements. George Orwell's 1945 novel *Animal Farm* is among the most well-known examples of allegory in literature. The story, which focuses on a group of animals who overthrow their human farm owners, serves as a sharp commentary on the rise of communism under Josef Stalin.

My Notes

Learning Targets

- Analyze and evaluate the effects of literary devices and form in an allegorical poem.
- Write an original poem that includes figurative language, literary devices, and a distinct poetic form to achieve a desired effect.

Preview

In this activity, you will move from analyzing how an author crafts a poem to writing your own poem. After reading a poem and analyzing the author's use of figurative language, structure, and punctuation, you will research and discuss poetic forms with a partner. Then you will strategically incorporate various literary elements to achieve a desired effect in your own writing.

As You Read

- Highlight descriptive languge the author uses.
- Circle unknown words and phrases. Try to determine the meaning of the words by using context clues, word parts, or a dictionary.

About the Author

William Blake (1757–1827) was among the earliest Romantic poets in mid 18th-century England. Blake and the other Romantics wrote with an emphasis on human feelings and emotions, as well as with a deeply felt concern about the effects of technology and industrialization on the human spirit and human interactions. Blake incorporates into his poems his own visions of God and the supernatural realm, but they often return to common Romantic themes: the plight of the innocent in danger and despair and the inherent alienation of the human condition. These themes are especially present in his *Songs of Experience* (1794), which includes the poem "A Poison Tree." That volume was later combined with its predecessor, *Songs of Innocence* (1789), and given the subtitle *Shewing the Two Contrary States of the Human Soul*.

Poetry

A Poison Tree

by **William Blake**

I was angry with my friend;
I told my wrath, my wrath did end.
I was angry with my foe:
I told it not, my wrath did grow.

5   And I waterd it in fears,
Night & morning with my tears:
And I sunned it with smiles,
And with soft deceitful **wiles**.

And it grew both day and night.
10 Till it bore an apple bright.
And my foe beheld it shine,
And he knew that it was mine.

And into my garden stole,
When the night had veild the pole;
15 In the morning glad I see;
My foe outstretched beneath the tree.

Making Observations
- What happens to the speaker's foe?
- What imagery stands out to you in this poem?

wiles: tricks or lies

Returning to the Text

- Reread the poem to answer these text-dependent questions.
- Write any additional questions you have about the text in your Reader/Writer Notebook.

1. What message is Blake trying to convey to the reader?

_____

_____

_____

_____

2. What causes the speaker's wrath to grow? Cite specific details from the text to support your response.

_____

_____

_____

_____

3. How does the rhyme scheme affect the meaning of the poem?

_____

_____

_____

_____

4. How does the author develop a moral lesson in this poem?

_____

_____

_____

_____

Working from the Text

5. Analyze the effect of various elements in the poem using the chart that follows:

Element	Quotation	Effect
rhyme		
word choice		
repetition		
punctuation		

On the Spot Research

6. With your group, use the following questions to conduct research on one of the following poetic forms: *villanelle*, *sonnet*, *ode*, *haiku*, *pantoum*, *concrete poem*, *prose poem*, *ballad*, *limerick*. Jot down notes about the form you have selected.

- What do you notice about the form?
- What is the rhyme scheme? For example: *aabb, abcabc, abad*.
- Which syllables are stressed and unstressed?
- What mood or feeling does the form typically create?
- What is a well-known example of a poem that uses this form?
- What poets are most associated with the form?

7. With a partner, discuss how you would use your respective poetic forms to write about a childhood memory. Spend a few minutes brainstorming ideas for an original poem using either of the forms. As you brainstorm ideas, consider the purpose of your poem:

- Will it tell a story, teach a lesson, or focus on a single image, such as a scene from nature?
- Will the tone be playful, melancholy, or reflective?

After brainstorming, write down any interesting words or images you may want to incorporate into your poem.

☑ Check Your Understanding

What choices does a writer consider when composing a poem? How can diction, punctuation, and rhythm have a specific effect on the reader?

📝 Writing Prompt: Literary

Select one of the poetic forms you researched and discussed. Write an original poem using elements from this form. Be sure to:

- Consider the effect you wish your poem to have on the reader and its overall message.
- Use inventive diction, original language.
- Make appropriate use of tone and voice.
- Use sound, structure, and rhythm to enhance meaning.

Learning Strategies

Graphic Organizer
Quickwrite
Sketching
Visualizing

My Notes

Learning Targets

- Evaluate the effectiveness of an author's diction and syntax.
- Analyze how an author's purpose and audience contribute to language and stylistic choices.
- Compare how two different authors use language, diction, and syntax to connect with their audience.

Preview

In this activity, you will read the prologue and analyze an author's use of diction and syntax. Then you will consider how an author's purpose and intended audience affect language and stylistic choices. Finally, you will compare the ways the two writers have made language choices to achieve particular effects on their reader.

As You Read

- Highlight statements where the narrator defines what he is and what he is not.
- Circle unknown words and phrases. Try to determine the meaning of the words by using context clues, word parts, or a dictionary.

About the Author

Although Ralph Ellison's novelistic output is small, its influence is huge. Ellison (1914–1994) is best known for his novel *Invisible Man* (1952). In his masterpiece, an unnamed narrator struggles against racism and urban alienation to find an identity. Ellison employs an all-embracing style—combining elements of African American folklore, Native American mythology, and classical allusions—which he likens to a jazz musician's improvisation on traditional themes. Ellison is also known for his short stories and for nonfiction writing on literature, music, and African American issues. Though Ellison detested being labeled a black writer, he accepted the label *minority writer*, because, as he put it, "the individual is a minority."

Novel Excerpt

from Invisible Man

by **Ralph Ellison**

1   I am an invisible man. No, I am not a spook like those who haunted Edgar Allan Poe; nor am I one of your Hollywood-movie **ectoplasms**. I am a man of substance, of flesh and bone, of fiber and liquids—and I might even be said to possess a mind. I am invisible, understand, simply because people refuse to see me. Like the bodiless heads you see sometimes in circus sideshows, it is as though I have been surrounded by mirrors of hard, distorting glass. When they approach me they see only my surroundings, themselves, or figments of their imagination—indeed, everything and anything except me.

2   Nor is my invisibility exactly a matter of a biochemical accident to my **epidermis**. That invisibility to which I refer occurs because of a peculiar disposition of the eyes of those with whom I come in contact. A matter of the construction of their inner eyes, those eyes with which they look through their physical eyes upon reality. I am not complaining, nor am I protesting either. It is sometimes advantageous to be unseen, although it is most often rather wearing on the nerves. Then too, you're constantly being bumped against by those of poor vision. Or again, you often doubt if you really exist. You wonder whether you aren't simply a phantom in other people's minds. Say, a figure in a nightmare which the sleeper tries with all his strength to destroy. It's when you feel like this that, out of resentment, you begin to bump people back.

3   And, let me confess, you feel that way most of the time. You ache with the need to convince yourself that you do exist in the real world, that you're a part of all the sound and the anguish, and you strike out with your fists, you curse and you swear to make them recognize you. And, alas, it's seldom successful.

GRAMMAR & USAGE

Sentence Variety
Effective writers vary sentence length for effect. Too many long, complex sentences can lose the reader, yet too many short sentences can sound choppy or unsophisticated. Short sentences can also sometimes lack clarity by not including transitions to show relationships between ideas. However, short sentences can be used for effect, making an important idea stand out.

Notice the difference in length between the last two sentences in the prologue. Consider the way Ellison conveys relationships among the ideas within the long, next-to-last sentence. How does this add to the impact of the final short sentence?

ectoplasms: ghosts
epidermis: skin

Making Observations
- How does the narrator define himself?
- What are your initial thoughts about the narrator's perspective?

VOCABULARY

LITERARY

A **prologue** occurs at the beginning of a literary work and takes place within the narrative action.

My Notes

Returning to the Text

- Reread the **prologue** to answer these text-dependent questions.
- Write any additional questions you have about the text in your Reader/Writer Notebook.

1. According to the text, what does the narrator view as the reason for his invisibility?

2. How would you describe the narrator's diction and syntax in the first two paragraphs of the prologue? What effect does this have on the tone of the passage? Use text evidence to support your answer.

3. What details explain what causes the narrator to begin to "bump people back"? How do these details contribute to texts overall message?

4. What is the effect of the author's use of semicolons and dashes in the first paragraph?

Working from the Text

5. In the prologue from *Invisible Man*, the narrator contrasts how he believes himself to be in reality with how others perceive him. Working with a partner, create two quick illustrations in in your Reader/Writer Notebook that demonstrate the narrator's contrasting perceptions of self. Use words or phrases from the text to write a short caption for each of your illustrations.

How the Narrator Sees Himself	How Others See the Narrator
Caption:	Caption:

6. If the prologue from *Invisible Man* had been written as an argument instead of a work of fiction, what would the central claim be? Use your own words to state the text's central message in the form of a claim.

7. When making an argument, authors often try to appeal to their audience's emotions, intellect, or sense of morality and justice. How does Ellison's use of language—including word choice and sentence structure—support the claim you wrote in the previous step? Which type of appeal appears most evident in this text?

8. How might the effect of this piece be different if the author had chosen to write a nonfiction argumentative text instead of a novel? Why do you think Ellison chose to communicate his message through fiction rather than nonfiction?

LANGUAGE & WRITER'S CRAFT: Syntax

Syntax is the way words are arranged to form phrases, clauses, and sentences. Authors choose different kinds of sentence structures depending on the sentence's function and the intended effect on the reader. Read the descriptions and the examples provided. Then revisit the prologue from *Invisible Man* to find additional examples, and explain how each is used to advance the tone or theme of the text. Record your ideas in the chart that follows.

Analyzing Elements of Syntax in *Invisible Man*	Additional Examples from the Text
A **fragment** is a word group that is not a complete sentence. It may be lacking a subject, a verb, or both. Although you should usually avoid using fragments, they are sometimes used for effect. **Example:** *Nor is my invisibility exactly a matter of a biochemical accident to my epidermis.*	**Additional Example:** *Say, a figure in a nightmare which the sleeper tries with all his strength to destroy.* **Function:**
A **complex sentence** contains one independent clause and one or more dependent, or subordinate, clauses. **Example:** *Like the bodiless heads you see sometimes in circus sideshows, it is as though I have been surrounded by mirrors of hard, distorting glass.*	**Additional Example:** *I am invisible, understand, simply because people refuse to see me.* **Function:**
Parallel structure is the use of the same pattern of words to show that two or more ideas are related and have the same level of importance. **Example:** *You ache with the need to convince yourself that you do exist in the real world, that you're a part of all the sound and the anguish, and you strike out with your fists, you curse and you swear to make them recognize you.*	**Additional Example:** *I am a man of substance, of flesh and bone, of fiber and of liquids—and I might even be said to possess a mind.* **Function:**

PRACTICE Choose two or three sentences from the passage and rewrite them using different syntax, diction, and vocabulary for effect (use a thesaurus for the vocabulary as needed). Then write new sentences that build off the sentences you've rewritten. Include a fragment, a complex sentence, and one using parallel structure.

☑ Check Your Understanding

With a partner discuss why writers make particular choices when composing a text. How might the intended purpose or audience contribute to an author's decisions?

INDEPENDENT READING LINK

Read and Discuss

Select a passage from your independent reading that showcases the author's writing style. Analyze the way the author's style helps communicate a perspective. Share your analysis with a partner and discuss how the styles of your authors compare.

✍ Writing Prompt: Literary Analysis

Write a short essay in which you analyze and compare the use of language, including diction and syntax, in the prologue to *Invisible Man* to the use of language in one of the poems you have read so far in the unit. Compare the ways the two writers have made language choices to achieve particular effects on their reader. Be sure to:

- Begin with a clear comparative thesis statement.
- Explain the effectiveness of each author's word choice.
- Incorporate text evidence to support your analysis.
- Organize information in a logical structure.

Exploring Rhetoric

Learning Strategies

Questioning the Text
SOAPSTone

VOCABULARY

ACADEMIC

Rhetorical devices are specific techniques that are used in writing to create a literary effect or enhance the effectiveness of an author's message. For example, in argumentative texts authors often try to appeal to the reader's emotions and sense of logic in order to persuade the reader.

My Notes

Learning Targets

- Evaluate an author's purpose and determine the target audience in an argumentative text.
- Identify and analyze how an author uses rhetorical devices to build an effective argument.

Preview

In earlier activities, you looked closely at the choices authors make in poetry and literary texts to connect with their audience. Now you will apply what you've learned about the effectiveness of diction, text structure, and figurative language to the study of arguments. In this activity, you will analyze an argumentative text and how the author uses rhetorical devices to persuade her audience.

Introducing the Strategy: SOAPSTone

SOAPSTone stands for **S**peaker, **O**ccasion, **A**udience, **P**urpose, **S**ubject, and **T**one. It is a reading and writing tool for analyzing the relationship among a writer, his or her purpose, and the target audience of the text. SOAPSTone guides you in asking questions to analyze a text or to plan for writing a composition.

- **Speaker:** The speaker could be the author or a character or narrator the author invents.
- **Occasion:** The occasion is the time and place of the text; it is the context that prompted the writing.
- **Audience:** The audience is the person or persons to whom the piece is directed.
- **Purpose:** The purpose is the reason behind the text or what the writer wants the audience to think as a result of reading or hearing the text.
- **Subject:** The subject is the focus of the text.
- **Tone:** Tone is the speaker's attitude toward the subject.

📝 Opening Writing Prompt

Read the About the Author for Aruna Kashyap and the title of the argument and answer the following question.

- Based on the title and the details in the author's biography, what do you think the author's purpose and subject will be?

As You Read

- Look for details about the speaker, occasion, audience, purpose, subject, and tone (SOAPSTone elements). Note these details in a two-column SOAPSTone chart in your Reader/Writer Notebook.
- Circle unknown words and phrases. Try to determine the meaning of the words by using context clues, word parts, or a dictionary.

About the Author

Aruna Kashyap is senior counsel for the women's rights division of Human Rights Watch, an international nonprofit organization that advocates for human rights worldwide. With a background in litigation, Kashyap spent the early years of her career working as a lawyer for the India Center for Human Rights and Law. Her work now focuses on women's labor and economic rights and violence against women.

Argumentative Text

Clothing Brands Need to Step Up and Keep Women Safe in Their Factories

by **Aruna Kashyap**

1   In a recent survey of experts, countries were ranked according to how safe they are for women. India came out as the most dangerous, followed by Afghanistan and Syria. Leaving aside the survey's obvious challenges – including its attempt to use six measures to compare 10 very different countries – it paints a dire picture for women's safety in the world. One area in which women everywhere face discrimination, inequality, harassment or violence in their everyday lives is in their workplace. Governments and corporations must contend with how to keep women safe when they are working.

2   Globally, [women's rights] movements have forced many companies to revisit their gender pay gap and anti-harassment policies. The momentum has spurred discussions for a new international labor standard that squarely addresses violence and harassment in the workplace.

3   As in the apparel industry, for example, where women make up much of the global workforce. Apparel companies should do more to create work spaces free of violence and harassment... This is not just for the benefit of their own employees, but also for the customers and clients walking into their stores; the models who are the face of their clothes; and the workers producing their clothes and shoes in factories around the world.

My Notes

Worker sews garments inside a factory in Gazipur, Bangladesh. Bangladesh is the world's second largest apparel exporter after China.

4   In May, when I was speaking to garment workers about the conditions in factories, I met Roja R., a married woman in her thirties who worked in a factory in the Indian city of Mysore making clothing for international brands. She told me the cutting section supervisor had been stalking her. She said he misused his access to her cell number, calling her after work hours to harass her. He promised that if she submitted to his demands, he would give her a more manageable workload and assured her that he would quickly approve requests for time off work.

5   Roja resisted. She complained to the factory administration. But the person she spoke with laughed and told her: "This is normal practice and you need to adjust." Nobody in the factory's management took the steps that Indian law requires to stop harassment. That includes setting up an internal complaints committee and **disseminating** and publicly displaying the names and contact information of committee members. Companies are also supposed to develop a policy against harassment and widely publicize it through harassment-prevention training programs.

6   The harassment went on for months, Roja said. She was losing sleep. Coming from a conservative family, she worried that her husband would find out, blame her and stop her from going to work. By the time I met her, the problems still hadn't been resolved. Another of her co-workers also told me she was harassed in a different part of the same factory.

7   Even in their desperation for some respite from the harassment, they had one plea: They wanted the clothing brands they work for to help fix the problem, but not by cutting ties with the factory. If the factory lost business,

disseminating: sharing publicly

these women could lose their jobs. They feared not just for their own livelihoods, but also for those of their colleagues.

8   The factory's management exploited this fear. The women say supervisors had threatened them, telling them that any mention of harassment or other complaints to the monitors who inspect factories for labor compliance would cause problems. The women were told: "You will take away food from many mouths. Do you want everyone to eat mud?"

9   Brands need to be held accountable for monitoring and remediating labor conditions in factories they source from, rather than being allowed to conveniently distance themselves from labor abuses.

10   No doubt a brand should be able to cut ties with a factory that is a repeat offender, one that shows zero willingness to put in place legal protections and to abide by international human rights standards. But before taking that step, companies need to find ways to help factories improve and ensure that workers can safely raise their issues.

11   Investing in the underlying **infrastructure** that translates paper codes of conduct into actual practice is key to any meaningful effort. Brands should take steps toward this goal.

12   First, they should publish information about the factories that supply their products, which makes it easier for workers to find out which brands buy from that factory and whom to contact when problems occur. Many apparel companies have been leaders on transparency, but many others have yet to follow good industry practices for making details about their business easily available.

13   Second, brands should recognize the limits of social and labor compliance checks (known as "social audits" in industry **parlance**), in which it may not be possible to address issues like harassment effectively. Monitors are expected to document "evidence" or sufficiently corroborate complaints they get from workers before they can report it. Studies by CARE and other organizations show how often workers themselves under-report and sometimes do not even recognize harassment.

14   Third, merely having monitors check periodically whether or not a workplace has a complaint system is not good enough. The absence of well-trained, independent and gender-sensitive committees to look into complaints, coupled with a lack of strong anti-retaliation procedures, risk stripping these systems of any credibility. In numerous cases from South Asia, I have found that women workers who dared to speak up … had experienced retaliation.

15   That included factory management not allowing the **complainant** to work, suddenly finding fault with her productivity and quality of work, or warning that she was a troublemaker.

 INDEPENDENT READING LINK

Read and Connect

Think about your independent reading text, and the issues the characters are concerned with. What is an argument one of the characters makes, or might make, in response to their concerns? Analyze how you think the character would present their argument. Would they use appeals to reason, to logic, or to ethics? Would they employ logical fallacies? Now choose another character from your text and consider how they would react to the argument. Would they agree or disagree? What counterargument might they make?

My Notes

infrastructure: system
parlance: language
complainant: person or group filing a legal complaint

My Notes

16 Another problem is that often brands do their own training and monitoring. In fact, it may be more effective for multiple brands buying garments from the same factory to pool their resources to create a single, comprehensive and effective system for that factory.

17 They could ensure that there are effective and accessible grievance-**redress** systems for workers if their problems are not resolved at the factory level. Instead of requiring workers to find and use a different complaints procedure for each brand, which is time-consuming and difficult for workers, there should be a simple and effective process for them to lodge complaints. And the process should result in clear outcomes when problems are found. Without effective grievance redress that leads to binding outcomes, brands should know that their talk of protecting workers' rights is pure rhetoric.

18 In late May and early June, governments, employers' and workers' organizations concluded the first round of negotiations for a binding International Labor Organization (ILO) standard to address violence and harassment in the workplace supplemented by a non-binding recommendation. Another round of discussions will follow next year.

19 Apparel and footwear companies should call on employers' organizations and governments to **unequivocally** support a binding standard in next year's negotiations. That would be a major step toward helping make the world a safer place for women.

Making Observations

- After reading the argument for the first time, what did you learn about the author's purpose?
- Which ideas from the argument stand out to you the most?

redress: resolution
unequivocally: clearly and strongly

Returning to the Text

- Reread the argument to answer these text-dependent questions.
- Write any additional questions you have about the argument in your Reader/Writer Notebook.

1. What are three actions that Kashyap argues brands should take to improve conditions for their workers?

_____

_____

_____

_____

2. What is the most likely reason that Kashyap included story of Roja R.? How does this example affect her argument?

_____

_____

_____

_____

3. How does Kashyap's language affect your perception of her argument? Is her use of language appropriate for her topic and audience?

_____

_____

_____

_____

4. In paragraph 10, what is the counterclaim that Kashyap addresses and how does she respond to it? Why do you think she advises against this solution?

_____

_____

_____

_____

5. How is the text structured? What purpose does this structure achieve?

_____

_____

_____

_____

Working from the Text

6. With a partner, use the SOAPSTone strategy to analyze how Aruna Kashyap builds her argument. Use your notes from the first reading of the text to help support your answers.

Element	Who/What?
Speaker	
Occasion	
Audience	
Purpose	
Subject	
Tone	

7. Continue working with a partner to trace the author's use of rhetorical appeals in the text. Name specific examples from the text.

- Appeals to readers' emotions
- Appeals to readers' sense of logic
- Appeals to ethics and other features that show the writer's credibility/trustworhiness

8. Use Reader-Response Criticism to think about how the reading situation, the text, and you as a reader interact to make meaning from this text. How do your own beliefs, experiences, and values influence your likeliness to be persuaded by the author's argument?

 Gaining Perspectives

You read about how working conditions in some countries are not safe and improvements need to be made. The author of the text gives some ideas on what could be done to improve conditions. Choose a manufacturer such the maker of your favorite clothing or backpack. Conduct On the Spot research to learn about where and how the product is manufactured. How can you ensure that the people who created this item for you are fairly treated? What options are available for you, as a consumer, to influence working conditions? Consider traditional methods as well as social media platforms. Present your ideas to the class and choose which option would be most beneficial to create social change.

LANGUAGE & WRITER'S CRAFT: Hyphenation

Hyphens have many uses and can change the meaning of a sentence. Hyphens are used to join two or more words that function as a single adjective before a noun.

Example: *Globally, [women's rights] movements have forced many companies to revisit their gender pay gap and <u>anti-harassment</u> policies.*

PRACTICE Look over "Clothing Brands Need to Step Up and Keep Women Safe in Their Factories" again. List the five other examples of hyphenation from the text. If the hyphenated word functions as an adjective, write the noun it modifies.

 Check Your Understanding

What one language selection or rhetorical choice did the author make that added to the persuasiveness of this argumentative text? If you were the author, what might you have done differently to make the piece more persuasive?

Critiquing and Evaluating an Argument

Learning Strategies

Activating Prior Knowledge
Marking the Text

My Notes

Learning Targets

- Explain and evaluate the reasoning in a significant U.S. text as well as its effectiveness in the area of public advocacy.
- Analyze how two or more texts address similar themes or topics, including the purpose and rhetorical approach of each.
- Critique and evaluate the effectiveness of a speech's structure, appeals, evidence, and treatment of counterarguments.
- Integrate ideas from multiple texts to build knowledge and vocabulary about advocacy on social issues.

Preview

In this activity, you will review the characteristics and structural elements of an argument before reading and critiquing a speech and a piece of legislation.

Reviewing the Structure of an Argument

Before reading the arguments in this part of the unit, review the following structural elements of an argument.

The Hook
- Grabs readers' attention and catches their interest
- May establish a connection between reader and writer and provide background information
- Might be an anecdote, image, definition, or quotation

The Claim
- Usually comes in the opening section of a text
- States the author's main point
- Can be straightforward and direct (for instance, "I believe that ...")

Concessions and Rebuttals
- Recognize arguments made by the other side
- Build credibility by showing ability to discuss each side with apparent objectivity
- Grant that the other side has some validity
- Argue against the opposing viewpoint by showing that the author's side has more validity

Support
- Sets out the reasoning behind an argument
- Provides evidence of the claim (data, quotations, anecdotes, and the like)
- May include appeals to logic, emotions, or ethics

Call to Action

- Draws the argument to a close and restates the claim
- May make a final, new appeal to values
- May voice a final plea
- Sums up the argument and asks the reader to do something or take action

Opening Writing Prompt

Read Florence Kelley's biography and the first two paragraphs of her speech and then respond to the following question.

- Consider this introduction through the lens of Reader-Response. How does the reader (you or Kelley's intended audience, the National American Woman Suffrage Association) and the situation (her delivery of the speech in 1905 or reading it in present day) affect the meaning and impact of the introduction? Are Kelley's words affected by the shift in audience?

As You Read

- Mark the text where you notice the elements of a good argument: hook, claim, concessions and refutations, support, and call to action. (You can even abbreviate them as H, C, C&R, S, and C2A.)
- Circle unknown words and phrases. Try to determine the meaning of the words by using context clues, word parts, or a dictionary.

About the Author

Florence Kelley (1859–1932) was an American social worker and reformer. Starting in 1892 in Chicago, Kelley did extensive investigative work delving into slum and sweatshop conditions. Her findings and articles sparked legislators to limit women's working hours, prohibit child labor, and regulate sweatshops. She was also instrumental in groundbreaking legislation for minimum wages. She delivered the following speech before the convention of the National American Woman Suffrage Association in Philadelphia on July 22, 1905. This association fought to allow women the right to vote in elections, which was achieved on a national level in 1920.

KNOWLEDGE QUEST

Knowledge Question:

How can you make a convincing case about a problem that inspires people to take action?

In Activity 1.9, you will read a speech and a text that examine the topic of advocacy. While you read and build knowledge about the topic, think about your answer to the Knowledge Question.

My Notes

textile: woven fabric
repealed: overturned
enfranchised: allowed to vote

Speech

to the National American Woman Suffrage Association

by **Florence Kelley**

1   We have, in this country, two million children under the age of sixteen years who are earning their bread. They vary in age from six and seven years (in the cotton mills of Georgia) and eight, nine and ten years (in the coal-breakers of Pennsylvania), to fourteen, fifteen and sixteen years in more enlightened states.

2   Tonight while we sleep, several thousand little girls will be working in textile mills, all the night through, in the deafening noise of the spindles and the looms spinning and weaving cotton and wool, silks and ribbons for us to buy.

3   In Alabama the law provides that a child under sixteen years of age shall not work in a cotton mill at night longer than eight hours, and Alabama does better in this respect than any other southern state. North and South Carolina and Georgia place no restriction upon the work of children at night; and while we sleep little white girls will be working tonight in the mills in those states, working eleven hours at night.

4   In Georgia there is no restriction whatever! A girl of six or seven years, just tall enough to reach the bobbins, may work eleven hours by day or by night. And they will do so tonight, while we sleep.

5   Nor is it only in the South that these things occur. Alabama does better than New Jersey. For Alabama limits the children's work at night to eight hours, while New Jersey permits it all night long. Last year New Jersey took a long backward step. A good law was repealed which had required women and [children] to stop work at six in the evening and at noon on Friday. Now, therefore, in New Jersey, boys and girls, after their 14th birthday, enjoy the pitiful privilege of working all night long.

6   In Pennsylvania, until last May it was lawful for children, 13 years of age, to work twelve hours at night. A little girl, on her thirteenth birthday, could start away from her home at half past five in the afternoon, carrying her pail of midnight luncheon as happier people carry their midday luncheon, and could work in the mill from six at night until six in the morning, without violating any law of the Commonwealth.

7   If the mothers and the teachers in Georgia could vote, would the Georgia Legislature have refused at every session for the last three years to stop the work in the mills of children under twelve years of age?

8   Would the New Jersey Legislature have passed that shameful repeal bill enabling girls of fourteen years to work all night, if the mothers in New Jersey were enfranchised? Until the mothers in the great industrial states

are enfranchised, we shall none of us be able to free our consciences from participation in this great evil. No one in this room tonight can feel free from such participation. The children make our shoes in the shoe factories; they knit our stockings, our knitted underwear in the knitting factories. They spin and weave our cotton underwear in the cotton mills. Children braid straw for our hats, they spin and weave the silk and velvet wherewith we trim our hats. They stamp buckles and metal ornaments of all kinds, as well as pins and hat-pins. Under the sweating system, tiny children make artificial flowers and neckwear for us to buy. They carry bundles of garments from the factories to the **tenements**, little beasts of burden, robbed of school life that they may work for us.

Textile workers were often so young that they had to stand on the spinning frames to replace empty bobbins.

9   We do not wish this. We prefer to have our work done by men and women. But we are almost powerless. Not **wholly** powerless, however, are citizens who enjoy the right of **petition**. For myself, I shall use this power in every possible way until the right to the ballot is granted, and then I shall continue to use both.

10   What can we do to free our consciences? There is one line of action by which we can do much.

11   We can enlist the workingmen on behalf of our enfranchisement just in proportion as we strive with them to free the children. No labor organization in this country ever fails to respond to an appeal for help in the freeing of the children.

12   For the sake of the children, for the Republic in which these children will vote after we are dead, and for the sake of our cause, we should enlist the workingmen voters, with us, in this task of freeing the children from toil!

🖉 Knowledge Quest
- What strikes you about Kelley's speech?
- Who and what is Kelley advocating for?
- What part of Kelley's speech inspires you to want to act?

My Notes

_____

_____

_____

_____

_____

_____

_____

_____

_____

_____

_____

_____

tenements: overcrowded apartment buildings
wholly: completely
petition: making a formal written request for change

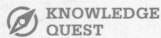
KNOWLEDGE QUEST

Knowledge Question:
How can you make a convincing case about a problem that inspires people to take action?

My Notes

bureau: a government agency
mortality: death rate

As You Read

- Mark the text where you notice what type of text it is, its purpose, and any evidence that the text is consistent with U.S. constitutional principles. (Abbreviate your markings as T, P, and E.)
- Circle unknown words and phrases. Try to determine the meaning of words by using context clues, word parts, or a dictionary.

About the Document

In addition to advocating for significant changes in child labor laws, Florence Kelley was also instrumental in the founding of the U.S. Children's Bureau. Kelley and her friend Lillian D. Wald conceived the idea in 1903. Their goal was to establish a federal agency to promote child health and welfare. A friend of Wald's informed President Theodore Roosevelt of the idea, and he immediately invited Kelley and Wald to the White House to discuss it. For years, individuals and groups campaigned to have the idea signed into law. After 11 bills, the act to create the Children's Bureau was finally passed by Congress in 1912. President William Howard Taft signed the bill on April 9, 1912.

Informational Text

Children's Bureau Act

An Act To establish in the Department of Commerce and Labor a **bureau** to be known as the Children's Bureau.

1   *Be it enacted by the Senate and House of Representatives of the United States of America in Congress assembled,* That there shall be established in the Department of Commerce and Labor a bureau to be known as the Children's Bureau.

2   That the said bureau shall be under the direction of a chief, to be appointed by the President, by and with the advice and consent of the Senate, and who shall receive an annual compensation of five thousand dollars. The said bureau shall investigate and report to said department upon all matters pertaining to the welfare of children and child life among all classes of our people, and shall especially investigate the questions of infant **mortality**, the birth-rate, orphanage, juvenile courts, desertion, dangerous occupations, accidents and diseases of children, employment, legislation affecting children in the several states and territories. But no official, or agent, or representative of said bureau shall, over the objection of the head of the family, enter any house used exclusively as a family residence. The chief of said bureau may from time to time publish the results of these investigations in such manner and to such extent as may be prescribed by the Secretary of Commerce and Labor.

3   That there shall be in said bureau, until otherwise provided for by law, an assistant chief, to be appointed by the Secretary of Commerce and Labor, who shall receive an annual compensation of two thousand four hundred dollars;

one private secretary to the chief of the bureau, who shall receive an annual compensation of one thousand five hundred dollars; one statistical expert, at two thousand dollars; two clerks of class four; two clerks of class three; one clerk of class two; one clerk of class one; one clerk, at one thousand dollars; one copyist, at nine hundred dollars; one special agent, at one thousand four hundred dollars, one special agent, at one thousand two hundred dollars, and one messenger at eight hundred and forty dollars

4   That the Secretary of Commerce and Labor is hereby directed to furnish sufficient quarters for the work of this bureau at an annual rental not to exceed two thousand dollars..

5   That this Act shall take effect and be in force from and after its passage.

Approved, April 9, 1912.

⌀ Knowledge Quest

- What questions about children's rights does this text raise for you?
- How is advocacy represented in the text?

Returning to the Text

- Reread the speech to answer these text-dependent questions.
- Write any additional questions you have about the speech in your Reader/ Writer Notebook.

"to the National American Woman Suffrage Association"

1. What factual information does Kelley present about child labor? How is she making appeals to her audience's logic, emotions, or sense of ethics with this information?

   _____

   _____

   _____

   _____

2. Where does Kelley state her claim? How is it effective in its placement and rhetorical style?

   _____

   _____

   _____

3. KQ How does the phrase "little beasts of burden" affect the tone and effectiveness of Kelley's speech to inspire people to take action?

   _____

   _____

   _____

4. KQ What is Kelley's call to action, and how does it relate to her claim about the need for women's suffrage?

   _____

   _____

   _____

5. What argument does Kelley make over the course of her speech? Who is her intended audience?

   _____

   _____

   _____

Children's Bureau Act

6. What do the first five lines of the Act establish? Why is this structure important to the effectiveness of the text?

_____

_____

_____

_____

7. According to Section 2, who directs the bureau and what rights does it have? How are these rights effective in their placement?

_____

_____

_____

_____

8. KQ A *premise* is an idea on which an action is based. Upon what premise do you think the Act is based? What evidence from the text supports your ideas?

_____

_____

_____

_____

9. Summarize the purpose of Sections 3, 4, and 5. Why do you think these sections were placed at the end of the text?

_____

_____

_____

_____

10. KQ How are the Children's Bureau Act and the speech to the National American Woman Suffrage Association similar in their approach to advocacy?

_____

_____

_____

_____

Working from the Text

"to the National American Woman Suffrage Association"

11. Use the graphic organizer that follows to analyze Kelley's use of the elements of argument.

Element of Argument	Analysis
The Hook: Does the speaker grab readers' attention from the opening sentence? If so, how is this accomplished?	
The Claim: Does Kelley state her claim in a direct, straightforward way?	
Concessions and Rebuttals: Does Kelley discuss the merits of the counterargument to establish her credibility and objectivity? Does she rebut the opposing argument?	
Support: Does Kelley offer compelling evidence to support her claim? If so, how is this evidence presented?	
Call to Action: Does Kelley present a clear call to action? If so, what actions does the author want the readers to take?	

12. In a small group compare the effectiveness and the various elements of Kelley's speech and the Children's Bureau Act. Use the following questions to guide your discussion:

- What is the purpose of each text? How is structure used to convey the purpose of each?
- What types of evidence does Kelley use in her speech? Is evidence used in the Act? Why or why not?
- What topic is presented in each of the documents? How are rhetoric and structure used to emphasize the topic in each?
- What is the historical significance of each document? Do both texts shape the future? How?

☑ Focus on the Sentence

Use the following subordinating conjunctions to write three sentences evaluating or critiquing the rhetorical choices in both texts.

Because Kelley repeats the phrase "while we sleep," _____

_____

Although the details about child labor laws are compelling, _____

_____

In order to effectively establish credibility as a newly established government entity, _____

_____

Knowledge Quest

Think about how Kelley advocated for the rights of children. Write an informative text that tells people how they can make a convincing case about a problem that inspires people to take action. Be sure to:

- Clearly introduce the topic and logically organize your ideas.
- Cite evidence from the text that represents the most significant and relevant details.
- Use precise language and topic-specific vocabulary.

INDEPENDENT READING LINK

You can continue to build your knowledge about advocacy by reading other articles at ZINC Reading Labs. Search for keywords such as *social issues* or *advocacy*.

 ZINC

Explain How an Author Builds an Argument

Learning Strategies

Brainstorming
Drafting
Rereading

My Notes

Learning Targets

- Analyze the structure of an argument.
- Write a timed rhetorical analysis essay that includes an introduction and conclusion, uses relevant and accurate textual evidence, and adheres to standard English conventions.

Preview

In this activity, you will read and analyze an argumentative text and then write a rhetorical analysis of the text in a timed setting.

Introduction

This activity is designed to help you practice writing a rhetorical analysis essay similar to the one you will write for the Embedded Assessment. In this activity, however, you will practice writing in a timed setting. You will have 50 minutes to read, analyze, and write about the text, so be sure to use your time wisely. Read the prompt carefully, annotate the text, and leave yourself time to quickly review what you have written at the end. Your essay will be evaluated in the areas of reading, analysis, and writing.

Prompt

As you read the passage, consider how the authors, Riskin and Farrell, use

- evidence, such as facts or examples, to support claims,
- reasoning to develop ideas and to connect claims and evidence,
- stylistic or persuasive elements, such as word choice or appeals to emotion, to add power to the ideas expressed.

Write an essay in which you explain how Riskin and Farrell build an argument to persuade their audience that child labor in the U.S. agricultural sector is a disgrace and needs to be changed. In your essay, analyze how Riskin and Farrell use one or more of the features listed previously (or features of your own choice) to strengthen the logic and persuasiveness of their argument. Be sure that your analysis focuses on the most relevant features of the passage. Your essay should not explain whether you agree with Riskin and Farrell's claims but rather explain how the authors build an argument to persuade their audience. Conclude your essay by restating the main ideas in your analysis, including your evaluation of the authors' use of rhetorical elements.

Argumentative Text

Profiting on the Backs of Child Laborers

October 12, 2000

by **Victoria Riskin and Mike Farrell, co-chairs of the California committee (south) of Human Rights Watch**

1   Damaris was 13 years old when she began working in the broccoli and lettuce fields of Arizona. During peak season, she would often work 14 hours a day in 100-degree temperatures. For months on end she suffered frequent nosebleeds and nearly passed out on several occasions. Despite illness from exposure to dangerous pesticides, she kept on working. "It was very difficult," she told Human Rights Watch. "I just endured it."

2   Between 300,000 and 800,000 children like Damaris are working as hired laborers in commercial U.S. agriculture today. These farmworker children weed cotton fields, pick lettuce and cantaloupe, and climb rickety ladders in cherry and apple orchards. They often work 12 or more hours a day, sometimes beginning at 3 or 4 in the morning. They risk serious illness, including cancer and brain damage, from exposure to pesticides, and suffer high rates of injury from working with sharp tools and heavy machinery.

3   Despite long and grueling days, some child farmers are paid only $2 an hour. Many of them drop out of school, too exhausted to study. Nearly half of them never graduate from high school. Lacking other options, many are relegated to a lifetime of low-wage field labor that perpetuates the cycle of farmworker poverty through generations.

4   Agriculture is the most dangerous occupation open to minors in the United States. Work-related fatalities among child farm workers are five times higher than for children working in nonagricultural jobs, and an estimated 100,000 children suffer agriculture-related injuries annually in the United States.

5   The long-term effects of pesticide exposure are not yet completely known, but have been linked to cancer, brain tumors, brain damage and birth defects. Child farm workers interviewed by Human Rights Watch for a recent study described working in fields still wet with poison and being exposed to pesticide drift from spraying in nearby fields. One 16-year-old boy told us that he mixed and sprayed pesticides several times a week, but wore no mask or protective clothing because his employer told him he had nothing to worry about.

6   Despite the hazards of agricultural work, current U.S. labor law allows children working in agriculture to work at younger ages and for longer

My Notes

_____

_____

_____

_____

_____

_____

_____

_____

_____

_____

_____

_____

_____

_____

_____

_____

hours than minors in other jobs. Surprisingly, the 14-hour days worked by a 13-year-old are not prohibited by law. Children as young as 12 can legally work unlimited hours in agriculture. In contrast, kids cannot work in the fast-food industry before age 14 and are limited to no more than three hours of work on a school day until age 16. This legal double standard amounts to de facto race-based discrimination, since the vast majority of farmworker children are Latino and other racial minorities.

7   This shameful tolerance for abusive child labor in American fields stands in stark contrast to U.S. leadership in combating child labor overseas. The U.S. devotes $30 million a year to international programs to end abusive child labor—a tenfold increase from just two years ago. Last year, the U.S. became one of the first countries to ratify a new international convention to eliminate the worst forms of child labor, including such practices as child slavery, debt bondage, sexual exploitation, and forced labor. Congress recently acted to deny trade preferences to countries that fail to meet their legal obligations to end such abusive child labor.

8   This commitment to abolish inappropriate child labor abroad must be matched by a commitment to protect children from abusive labor here in the United States. Labor laws that exempt agriculture from basic child labor restrictions date back to 1938, a time when nearly a quarter of Americans still lived on farms, and Congress was understandably reluctant to regulate the ability of children to work their parents' land. The reality today is vastly different. The overwhelming number of child farm workers are not working their families' farms, but are hired laborers in large-scale commercial agriculture…

9   Child labor in U.S. agriculture is America's shameful secret. Our laudable efforts to protect children from exploitative labor overseas appear deeply hypocritical unless matched by efforts … to protect children here at home.

Evaluating a Peer's Essay

Learning Targets

- Collaborate with a peer in giving and receiving constructive feedback.
- Formulate critical responses that are clearly articulated and explained.

Preview

In this activity, you will work collaboratively with classmates to read and evaluate each other's essays using the Embedded Assessment 1 Scoring Guide. You will then revise and edit your essay based on feedback you receive.

Learning Strategies

Close Reading
Marking the Text
Peer Editing
Sharing and Responding

My Notes

The Writing Process

The previous activity gave you practice writing in a timed setting, which you have likely experienced when taking exams. More often, writers engage in an ongoing process where they plan, draft, revise, and edit a piece of writing before eventually publishing it. Engaging in this process will strengthen your ability as a writer.

1. **Quickwrite:** Take a couple of minutes to jot down your thoughts about how the steps of the writing process can help you strengthen your skills as a writer. Then share your thoughts with a partner.

Reviewing the Scoring Guide

Use the following steps to help you as you review the Embedded Assessment Scoring Guide.

2. Review the Scoring Guide and read the descriptions for each element, left to right, before moving on to the next one. Make sure you understand how each is scored—if not, ask a partner or your teacher for clarification.

3. As you read, think about which elements you will need the most help with. Make notes to revisit these areas of your paper first.

4. Now read through your paper again, and look at each category of the Scoring Guide—Ideas/Comprehension, Structure, and Language.

5. Identify which of the three categories you made the most notes in.

6. Now write down ideas for concrete steps you can take to improve these areas in your paper—for instance, you might write "review sentence structure."

Giving and Receiving Feedback

7. Exchange drafts with a partner. Skim through your partner's paper and look for obvious errors. Are there typos, misspellings, confusing grammar, or sentences that are poorly written? Consult print or digital resources such as *Merriam-Webster's Dictionary*, *Merriam-Webster's Dictionary of Usage*, or *Garner's Modern American Usage* to help you resolve spelling and more complex usage questions.

My Notes

8. Read the paper again carefully. Use a pencil or pen to mark corrections. Circle or underline words or phrases that could use editing, and write an explanation in the margin. You might write "spelling," "lowercase," "insert comma," or notes like "This sentence feels off to me" or "not sure about this word choice."

9. Consult the Scoring Guide descriptions. Consider each element of the essay and make a check or other indication in the appropriate column. Note: sometimes you'll find an element that falls between two categories. Use your best judgment.

10. Write a brief summary for the author. Be sure and point out the things the essay does well, and be as detailed as possible about the areas that need improvement.

11. When you receive your own draft back, carefully look through each note and correction your partner made. Do you agree? Make note of any patterns that you see. For instance, you may realize that you have one grammatical issue that occurs repeatedly.

12. Have a conversation with your partner. This will give both of you the opportunity to ask detailed questions and discuss the issues in a deeper way.

☑ Check Your Understanding

List three concrete actions you will take in response to your classmate's feedback that will help you produce a strong essay for the Embedded Assessment. Put a star next to the action you will take first.

📖 Independent Reading Checkpoint

Think about the ideas and perspectives from your independent reading from this half of the unit, and look back over previous Independent Reading Links in this unit. Then create a short presentation about your reading to give to the class. The organization, content, and style of your speech should be appropriate for a formal classroom presentation.

As you prepare your presentation, use text evidence to support your ideas. Communicate your perspective clearly and distinctly. Organize your ideas so each topic in the presentation is clearly defined and listeners can follow your presentation easily. You should give a brief overview of the story and characters, discuss the central conflict of the story, and talk about the author's purpose, use of language, and poetic (if fiction) or rhetorical (if nonfiction) devices. Finally, discuss how you feel the reading was relevant to or enhanced your understanding of other readings in this unit.

Writing a Rhetorical Analysis Essay

 ASSIGNMENT

Write an essay in which you critique and evaluate how the author of "Tipping System Exacerbates Unfair Pay at Restaurants" builds an argument to convince her audience that restaurant workers deserve fair wages from their employers instead of tips. In your essay, explain and evaluate how Kathleen Kingsbury uses one or more of the features in the directions that precede the passage (or features of your own choosing) to develop her argument. Be sure that your critique focuses on the most relevant features of the passage. Your essay should not explain whether you agree with Kingsbury's claims. Instead it should explain and evaluate how Kingsbury builds an argument to persuade the audience.

Planning and Prewriting: Take time to plan for writing your essay.	■ What prewriting strategies will you use, such as reading and annotating the source text, to prepare for writing? ■ What features of argumentative texts will you keep in mind as you read the source text? ■ How will you consider audience and purpose when planning your writing? ■ How can you use your knowledge of the genre characteristics of rhetorical analysis as you plan your writing?
Drafting: Determine how you will include the elements of a rhetorical analysis that will assure a successful draft.	■ How will you use genre characteristics and craft to produce a focused, structured, and coherent essay? ■ How will you use an organizational structure appropriate to your purpose, audience, topic, and context? ■ How can you develop your draft with details, examples, and commentary that support your analysis? ■ How will you review your draft to ensure that your essay follows your plan?
Evaluating and Revising: Review and revise to make your work the best it can be.	■ How can you revise your draft to improve clarity, development, organization, style, diction, and sentence fluency, both within and between sentences? ■ How can you use feedback from your peers and criteria from the Scoring Guide to inform your revision?
Checking and Editing: Confirm that your final draft is ready for publication.	■ What resources, such as a style guide, will you use to make sure your final draft demonstrates a command of standard English conventions? ■ How will you make sure to publish the final draft in a way that is appropriate for your audience?

Reflection

After completing this Embedded Assessment, think about how you went about accomplishing this assignment and respond to the following question:

• Consider this assignment from the perspective of Reader-Response Criticism. How was your critique influenced by the reader (you) and the reading situation (an assessment)? How might your essay be different if you read the text at a different time and for a different purpose?

SCORING GUIDE

Scoring Criteria	Exemplary	Proficient	Emerging	Incomplete
Ideas	The essay demonstrates: • an in-depth understanding of the text's central idea(s) and key details • skillful use of textual evidence and support for claims • freedom from factual errors or interpretations of the text • a well-considered evaluation of the structure, features, and/or stylistic techniques used by the author.	The essay demonstrates: • an effective understanding of the text's central idea(s) and key details • appropriate use of textual evidence and support for claims • freedom from significant factual errors or interpretations of the text • an adequate evaluation of the structure, features, and/or stylistic techniques used by the author.	The essay demonstrates: • a very basic understanding of the text's central idea(s) and key details • limited use of textual evidence and/or weak support for claims • possible errors of fact or interpretation of the text • a limited evaluation of the structure, features, and/or stylistic techniques used by the author.	The essay demonstrates: • little to no understanding of the text's central idea(s) and key details • little to no use of textual evidence and/or relevant support for claims • numerous errors of fact and/or interpretation of the text • little to no evaluation of the structure, features, and/or stylistic techniques used by the author.
Structure	The essay includes: • a logical structure with an insightful claim and effective order • cohesive, well-developed paragraphs that develop specific ideas and support the essay • clear transitions that connect ideas smoothly within and between paragraphs.	The essay includes: • a logical structure with a plausible claim and effective order • cohesive paragraphs that develop ideas and support the essay • transitions that connect ideas within and between paragraphs.	The essay includes: • an inadequate structure with an unclear claim • paragraphs with little to no cohesion, under-developed ideas, and/or limited support for the essay • minimal transitions within and/or between paragraphs.	The essay includes: • a missing or inadequate structure with no identifiable claim • paragraphs with a complete lack of cohesion, unclear ideas, and/or no support for the essay • few if any transitions within and/or between paragraphs.
Use of Language	The essay demonstrates: • an effective command of language, with advanced vocabulary and precise word choice • a wide variety of sentence structures that strategically emphasize key points • few or no errors in a standard English conventions.	The essay demonstrates: • an adequate command of language, with appropriate vocabulary and precise word choice • a variety of sentence structures that support key points • slight errors in standard English conventions.	The essay demonstrates: • little command of language, with simplistic vocabulary and/or vague word choice • repetitive or incomplete sentence structures • several errors in standard English conventions.	The essay demonstrates: • no command of language, with incorrect vocabulary and/or confusing word choice • a number of incomplete sentences • many errors in standard English conventions.

About the Author

Kathleen Kingsbury joined the *New York Times* as deputy editorial page editor in 2017. Prior to that, Kingsbury served on the editorial board of the *Boston Globe* where, in 2015, she won a Pulitzer Prize for a series of editorials called "Service Not Included." The series, including the editorial "Tipping System Exacerbates Unfair Pay at Restaurants," gave readers insight into the high rates of poverty experienced by workers in the restaurant and food services industry.

Prompt

As you read the passage, consider how Kathleen Kingsbury uses

- evidence, such as facts or examples, to support claims,
- reasoning to develop ideas and to connect claims and evidence,
- stylistic or persuasive elements, such as word choice or appeals to emotion, to add power to the ideas expressed.

Editorial

Tipping System Exacerbates Unfair Pay at Restaurants

by **Kathleen Kingsbury**

1   Tipping is said to have started in the Roman Empire as a means to reward servants and slaves. Americans adopted the custom only after the Civil War, but it stuck: Diners doled out some $40 billion in gratuities in 2012, according to industry experts. Yet the entrenchment of tipping has given restaurant owners a pretext to avoid paying their workers a proper wage. The tip system should be uprooted—or at least returned to its roots as a purely voluntary reward for excellent service.

2   Other than restaurants, few other industries let bosses rely mainly on customers' generosity to set employee wages. Owners are happy to save on labor costs. Back when tips still came mainly in cash (and therefore could conveniently be left off income tax forms), this arrangement probably made sense to workers, too.

3   That's changed in the era of credit card payments. Only the wait staff at the priciest establishments can count on big tips leading to livable incomes. Wage theft—the nonpayment of owed wages or tips—is now commonplace at restaurants. Overall, the vast majority of servers and other front-of-the-house employees have been left with little control over how much income they make each week.

My Notes

4   A busy Friday evening shift can mean good money, only to be followed by a slow Sunday afternoon where tips total $20 for a whole shift. If a diner doesn't like his meal, his dissatisfaction with the kitchen could reduce the take-home pay of his server, the busser who cleared his table, and even the host who seated him. Work performed outside regular shifts typically goes unpaid, and bad weather or illness may lead to no pay at all.

5   Rakel Papke earned good tips as a waitress at Braza Bar and Grill, a popular Everett restaurant. Yet in nine months of working there, she received only six paychecks—and, she says, those checks arrived only after she asked. "They basically only paid me to keep me quiet," Papke adds. So she recently filed a formal complaint with Attorney General Martha Coakley's office, asking her former employer for the more than $4,000 she is owed in back pay.

6   Some of the volatility that Papke and others like her experience would be eased if restaurant-goers routinely left higher tips. But while most people are accustomed to adding a 15 to 20 percent gratuity regardless of the quality of service, others set their own tipping standards, which may include a host of factors beyond a server's control. Still others—angry customers, foreigners who don't understand the custom—leave nothing at all. American restaurants could emulate most of the rest of the developed world, where service charges are automatically tacked on to dinner tabs. Some eateries in New York and California have made headlines for simply including the cost of labor in their menu prices and banning tips altogether.

7   More realistic, however, would be systemic change through stronger wage laws and better enforcement of those regulations. The Massachusetts Legislature is currently debating whether to raise the minimum wage, and the state Senate last November voted to raise the minimum for tipped workers, pegging it to 50 percent of the minimum for other workers.

...

8   Even better, however, would be to pass a law that would prohibit a separate tipped minimum wage, as seven other states have done. Workers would be guaranteed $8, or whatever the current full minimum wage is. Then, any tips they received would be what most customers already see them as—bonuses.

9   The nation's largest state, California, for decades has not allowed tipped workers' base pay to fall below the regular minimum wage. From fusion bistros in Los Angeles to sushi bars in San Francisco where the fish is flown in daily, the industry is booming and expected to expand by 9.1 percent over the next decade. In fact, in California and the six other states without a separate tipped wage—Alaska, Nevada, Montana, Minnesota, Oregon, and Washington state—job growth in the industry is expected to exceed Massachusetts' over the next 10 years, in some cases by more than double. The poverty rate for tipped workers in these states was 12.1 percent, compared with 16.1 percent in states with the lowest tipped minimum, according to a 2011 analysis by the Economic Policy Institute.

...

10 Women, who make up about 73 percent of tipped workers, are disproportionately harmed. Waitresses in some gritty bars and grills say they feel compelled to flirt with customers and laugh at offensive jokes just to preserve their income. Even then, they earn an average of $0.50 less per hour than male tipped workers, government statistics show. Doing away with the tipped minimum and giving these women a steadier paycheck would be the quickest way to restore their dignity.

11 Under the current system, restaurants must pay wait staff $2.63 an hour. A server's wages plus her tips for every two-week pay period must also average out to at least $8 an hour, the regular state minimum wage. If not, then her employer is legally required to make up the difference.

12 Reality is messier. The government agencies that enforce wage laws largely depend on violations being reported, and some restaurant owners have found they can underpay workers without consequence. Nationwide, an Aspen Institute study suggests that nearly 40 percent of restaurant workers earn at or below the federal minimum wage of $7.25, even with tips factored in.

13 A 2009 study of 4,400 workers in New York, Los Angeles, and Chicago found that more than one-quarter of tipped workers were not even paid the lower tipped minimum wage, and 12 percent had seen their tips stolen by an employer or supervisor, which is illegal…

14 Ending the tipped minimum wage would be the first step to preventing this kind of abuse. Frequenting and encouraging eateries that include a service charge in the price of a meal is another.

15 Until then, tip well.

© 2021 College Board. All rights reserved.

Learning Strategies

Graphic Organizer
Marking the Text
Close Reading

My Notes

Learning Targets

- Reflect on big ideas for the second half of the unit.
- Create a plan for reading independently.
- Identify and analyze the knowledge and skills needed to complete Embedded Assessment 2 successfully.

Preview

In this activity, you will explore the big ideas and tasks of the second half of the unit and make a plan for your independent reading.

Making Connections

In the first part of this unit, you looked closely at the choices authors make to shape the perception of readers. You used Reader-Response Criticism to examine a variety of texts to understand how your own perspective and experiences can affect how you interpret a text. In this part of the unit, you will continue to build reading, writing, and collaborative skills as you apply another literary theory—Cultural Criticism—to your reading. Using the lens of Cultural Criticism, you will interpret texts by analyzing elements of culture, such as religious beliefs, class identification, or political beliefs. By the end of the unit, you will have gained a deeper understanding of the texts you are reading and be prepared to write and present a reflective essay for Embedded Assessment 2.

Essential Questions

Reflect on your responses to the Essential Questions at the beginning of the unit. Would you change your responses now, and, if so, how?

1. Why do writers make particular choices when composing a text?

2. How does the interaction between a reader and a text create meaning?

3. What does it mean to be a stranger in a village?

Unpacking Embedded Assessment 2

Closely read the assignment for Embedded Assessment 2: Writing a Reflective Essay.

 Write and present a reflective essay that illustrates an event in which you or someone you know felt like a "stranger in the village" or was perceived as a stranger by some group.

With your class, create a graphic organizer as you "unpack" the requirements of Embedded Assessment 2. What knowledge must you have (what do you need to know) and what skills must you have (what must you be able to do) to be successful on this assignment?

My Notes

🎲 Planning Independent Reading

In the second half of the unit, continue your study of different perspectives by selecting an independent reading text that explores an aspect of culture. You might look at a reading in which the author examines his or her place in one's own or another's culture. Write a brief reflection in your Reader/Writer Notebook considering the text you have chosen from the perspective of Reader-Response Criticism.

What Is Cultural Criticism?

© 2021 College Board. All rights reserved.

Learning Strategies

Discussion Groups
Levels of Questions
Marking the Text
Rereading

VOCABULARY

LITERARY

Cultural Criticism focuses on the elements of culture and how they affect one's perceptions and understanding of texts.

ACADEMIC

To **marginalize** someone is to limit their participation in mainstream social, cultural, or economic activities.

My Notes

Learning Targets

- Use cultural context to understand a poem's language and meaning.
- Make connections between the ideas in a poem and society.
- Identify specific literary devices in a poem that serve the author's connection to the reader.

Preview

In this activity, you will read, analyze, and discuss a poem through the Cultural Criticism lens. You will then use this understanding to write an analytical paragraph about a stanza of the poem.

Cultural Criticism

Earlier in this unit you learned about literary theories and how to use Reader-Response criticism to analyze a text. In this half of the unit, you will apply **Cultural Criticism** to a series of texts.

Cultural Criticism is another critical lens through which a text can be viewed. This literary theory often explores works that are traditionally **marginalized** by mainstream society. This approach examines the effects of race, class, and gender perspectives in the analysis of texts. Cultural criticism evaluates whether these perspectives are dominant, mainstream, or marginalized. The following statements reflect four common ideas about the use of Cultural Criticism as a lens for understanding literature:

- Ethnicity, religious beliefs, sexual identity, and so on are crucial components in formulating interpretations of texts.
- While the emphasis is on diversity of approach and subject matter, Cultural Criticism is not the only means of exploring meaning in texts.
- An examination of the relationship between dominant cultures and marginalized cultures is essential.
- When looking at a text through the perspective of marginalized people, new understandings emerge.

Cultural Criticism often examines texts from the position of those individuals who are in some way marginalized or not part of the dominant culture.

As You Read

- Underline words and phrases that convey the writer's culture and the relationships between the people in the poem.
- Circle unknown words and phrases. Try to determine the meaning of the words by using context clues, word parts, or a dictionary.

About the Author

Luis J. Rodriguez (b. 1954) is recognized as a major figure in contemporary Chicano literature and has received numerous awards for his work as a poet and journalist. Rodriguez was born in El Paso, Texas but grew up in the Watts neighborhood of Los Angeles. As a teenager, he joined a gang, but he later found belonging in the Chicano movement. Works like *Always Running: La Vida Loca, Gang Days in L.A.*, and poetry collections like *The Concrete River* deal with the struggle to survive in a chaotic urban setting.

Poetry

Speaking with Hands

by **Luis J. Rodriguez**

There were no markets in Watts.
There were these small corner stores
we called *marketas*
who charged more money
5 for cheaper goods than what existed
in other parts of town.

The owners were often thieves in white coats
who talked to you like animals,
who knew you had no options;
10 who knew Watts was the preferred landfill
of the city.

One time, Mama started an argument
at the cash register.
In her broken English,

My Notes

15 speaking with her hands,

she had us children stand around her

as she fought with her grocer

on prices & quality & dignity.

Mama became a woman swept

20 by a sobering madness;

she must have been what Moses saw

in the burning bush,

a pillar of fire

consuming the still air

25 that reeked of overripe fruit

and bad meat from the frozen food

section.

She refused to leave

until the owner called the police.

30 The police came and argued too,

but Mama wouldn't stop.

They pulled her into the parking lot,

called her crazy …

and then Mama showed them crazy!

35 They didn't know what to do

but let her go, and Mama took us children

back toward home, tired of being tired.

Making Observations
- What is Mama's experience in the corner store?
- What details from the poem can you visualize?

Returning to the Text

- Reread the poem to answer these text-dependent questions.
- Write any additional questions you have about the poem in your Reader/Writer Notebook.

1. What idea does the author convey to the reader by using the phrase "preferred landfill of the city" to describe his neighborhood?

_____

_____

_____

_____

2. In stanza 3, why does the speaker's mother start "an argument at the cash register"? Use details from the text to make inferences about what she wants.

_____

_____

_____

_____

3. How does the author use imagery to tell us more about his mother in lines 19–24? How does this imagery help us understand what he feels about her?

_____

_____

_____

_____

4. Why do you think the author inserted an ellipsis (...) in line 33? What effect does it create for the reader?

_____

_____

_____

_____

My Notes

Working from the Text

5. Using the lens of Cultural Criticism, write Levels of Questions (three for each level)—literal, interpretative, and universal—to explore the preceding text. Discuss with your group the meaning of this poem when read through that lens.

- **Literal:** Why weren't there markets in Watts?
- **Interpretive:** Why is the speaker's mother frustrated by the corner store owner?
- **Universal:** In what ways are people in impoverished areas impacted by a lack of access to quality goods and services?

Literal: _____

Interpretative: _____

Universal: _____

☑ Check Your Understanding

How do you think different cultural backgrounds can influence how a reader understands Rodriguez's poem?

☑ Writing Prompt: Literary Analysis

Write a paragraph analyzing one stanza of the poem "Speaking with Hands" through the lens of Cultural Criticism. Does the author's work speak to larger cultural and societal issues? Be sure to:

- Include a clear topic sentence that responds to the prompt.
- Choose words that keep the author's meaning when you paraphrase or summarize lines in the stanza .
- Use evidence from the text, including direct quotations if appropriate, to support your ideas.
- Organize your ideas clearly and provide a concluding statement.
- Place modifiers correctly.

Applying Cultural Criticism

Learning Strategies

Activating Prior Knowledge
KWHL Chart
Socratic Seminar
Questioning the Text

Learning Targets

- Compare and contrast two different poets' perspectives in a Socratic Seminar.
- Use Cultural Criticism to analyze the concept of imperialism in written and visual texts.

Preview

In this activity, you will use Cultural Criticism to examine two poems that have contrasting views of imperialism. You will then participate in a Socratic Seminar to discuss and analyze the poems further. Finally, you will apply your knowledge of imperialism and of Cultural Criticism to a written analysis of a visual text.

ACADEMIC

Imperialism is the policy of extending the rule or influence of one country over other countries or colonies. The word also refers to the political, military, or economic domination of one country by another.

VOCABULARY

Applying Cultural Criticism to the Concept of Imperialism

In the last activity, you learned that Cultural Criticism suggests that being a part of—or excluded from—a specific group or culture contributes to and affects our understanding of texts. In the next series of activities, you will apply the concept of Cultural Criticism to the concept of imperialism.

Use the KWHL chart that follows to begin exploring the concept of imperialism. Fill in what you already know about imperialism, what you want to know, and how you will learn what you want to know. After reading and discussing the texts in this activity, return to the chart to fill in the last column with reflections on what you have learned.

Imperialism			
Know	Want to Know	How Will I Learn It?	What Have I Learned?

My Notes

> ### 📝 Opening Writing Prompt
>
> Read the titles of the two poems that you will encounter in this activity and respond to the following question.
>
> - Based on the titles what inference can you make about the subject of the poem? What connection might there be between the two poems?

As You Read

- Underline words and phrases that reveal the speaker's perspective on imperialism.
- Circle unknown words and phrases. Try to determine the meaning of the words by using context clues, word parts, or a dictionary.

About the Author

Rudyard Kipling (1865 –1936) was a British author known for his support of British colonialism and imperialism. Born to British parents in Bombay (now Mumbai), India, in 1865, Kipling was educated in England. He returned to India, where he worked for seven years as a journalist. Kipling was awarded the Nobel Prize for Literature in 1907. His children's books, including *Just So Stories* (1902), *Kim* (1901), and *The Jungle Books* (1894, 1895), are considered classics. "The White Man's Burden" was published in 1899.

Poetry

The White Man's Burden

by **Rudyard Kipling**

Take up the White Man's burden—

Send forth the best ye breed—

Go bind your sons to exile

To serve your captives' need;

5 To wait, in heavy harness,

On fluttered folk and wild—

Your new-caught **sullen** peoples,

Half devil and half child.

Take up the White Man's burden—

sullen: resentful

10   In patience to **abide**,

     To veil the threat of terror

     And check the show of pride;

     By open speech and simple,

     An hundred times made plain,

15   To seek another's profit,

     And work another's gain.

     Take up the White Man's burden—

     The savage wars of peace—

     Fill full the mouth of Famine,

20   And bid the sickness cease;

     And when your goal is nearest

     (The end for others sought)

     Watch **sloth** and **heathen** folly

     Bring all your hope to naught.

25   Take up the White Man's burden—

     No **tawdry** rule of kings,

     But toil of serf and sweeper—

     The tale of common things.

     The ports ye shall not enter,

30   The roads ye shall not tread,

     Go mark them with your living

     And mark them with your dead.

     Take up the White Man's burden—

     And reap his old reward:

35   The blame of those ye better

     The hate of those ye guard—

     The cry of hosts ye humour

     (Ah, slowly!) toward the light:—

     "Why brought ye us from bondage,

40   Our loved Egyptian night?"

My Notes

abide: continue to tolerate
sloth: laziness
heathen: uncivilized
tawdry: showy yet insubstantial

Take up the White Man's burden—

Ye dare not stoop to less—

Nor call too loud on Freedom

To cloak your weariness;

45 By all ye will or whisper,

By all ye leave or do,

The silent sullen peoples

Shall weigh your God and you.

Take up the White Man's burden!

50 Have done with childish days—

The lightly **proffered** laurel,

The easy ungrudged praise:

Comes now, to search your manhood

Through all the thankless years,

55 Cold, edged with dear-bought wisdom,

The judgment of your peers.

proffered: offered

My Notes

About the Author

Born in Massachusetts, George McNeill (1836–1906) grew up in an era when workers put in long hours and had few protections from poor or even dangerous working conditions. McNeill became a labor leader and activist who worked for improved working conditions (such as the eight-hour work day) and social reform. McNeill, a critic of imperialism, responded to Kipling with this satirical offering in 1899, a few months after Kipling's poem was published.

Poetry

The Poor Man's Burden

by **George McNeill**

Pile on the Poor Man's Burden—
Drive out the beastly breed;
Go bind his sons in exile
To serve your pride and greed;
5   To wait in heavy harness,
Upon your rich and grand;
The common working peoples,
The **serfs** of every land.
Pile on the Poor Man's Burden—
10   His patience will abide;
He'll veil the threat of terror
And check the show of pride.
By pious **cant** and humbug
You'll show his pathway plain,
15   To work for another's profit
And suffer on in pain.
Pile on the Poor Man's Burden—
Your savage wars increase,
Give him his full of Famine,
20   Nor bid his sickness cease.
And when your goal is nearest
Your glory's dearly bought,
For the Poor Man in his fury,
May bring your pride to naught.

WORD CONNECTIONS

Etymology
The word **serf** refers to the lowest class in medieval feudal society: the peasants who worked the land under a lord. *Serf* is an Old French word derived from the Latin word *servus*, meaning "servant" or "slave." Serfs were completely bound to the land owned by their lords, so they were, in a sense, slaves.

serfs: servant or slave
cant: insincere or hypocritical words

25 Pile on the Poor Man's Burden—
Your Monopolistic rings
Shall crush the serf and sweeper
Like iron rule of kings.
Your joys he shall not enter,

30 Nor pleasant roads shall tread;
He'll make them with his living,
And mar them with his dead.
Pile on the Poor Man's Burden—
The day of reckoning's near—

35 He will call aloud on Freedom,
And Freedom's God shall hear.
He will try you in the balance;
He will deal out justice true:
For the Poor Man with his burden

40 Weighs more with God than you.
Lift off the Poor Man's Burden—
My Country, grand and great—
The Orient has no treasures
To buy a Christian state,

45 Our souls brook not oppression;
Our needs—if read aright—
Call not for wide possession.
But Freedom's sacred light.

Making Observations
- How would you describe your intial reaction to each poem?
- What did you think each poem was about when you read the title? Did the poem confirm your hypothesis?

Returning to the Text

- Reread your assigned poem to answer these text-dependent questions.
- Write any additional questions you have about the poem in your Reader/Writer Notebook.

"The White Man's Burden"

1. How does the author use repetition to convey his message? What phrase is repeated in each stanza? What is different about this phrase in the final stanza?

_____

_____

_____

_____

2. The author used the image of a white man taking up a burden. Based on the context of the poem, who is the "White Man" and what is his "burden"?

_____

_____

_____

_____

3. What kind of figurative language does the speaker use to describe colonized people in stanza 3? Why does he express this attitude towards them?

_____

_____

_____

_____

4. How do the "silent sullen peoples" feel about the White Man who calls them "captives" but also serves their "need"? What do the words "silent" and "sullen" suggest about the speaker's attitude toward them?

_____

_____

_____

_____

5. What is the speaker's attitude toward imperialism and colonialism in the poem? Which lines from the poem indicate this attitude?

_____

_____

_____

_____

"The Poor Man's Burden"

6. Scan the first three stanzas of Kipling's poem. What language has McNeill borrowed from Kipling? How does he use irony as a literary device in this poem?

_____

_____

_____

_____

7. Who is the intended audience for McNeill's poem? What words or details tell you?

_____

_____

_____

_____

8. Who does "He" refer to lines 37–38? According to the speaker, what will he do? How does this compare to Kipling's presentation of a similar issue?

_____

_____

_____

_____

9. How does McNeill's tone shift at the end of the poem? How does he address the reader and how can this affect readers' response to the poem?

_____

_____

_____

_____

Working from the Text

Introducing the Strategy: Socratic Seminar

A **Socratic Seminar** is a focused discussion that is tied to an essential question, topic, or selected text. You participate by asking questions to initiate a conversation that continues with a series of responses and additional questions. In a Socratic Seminar, you must support your opinions and responses using specific textual evidence.

10. Reread the poems to compare their perspectives and to prepare for a Socratic Seminar. Respond to the pre-seminar questions and two to three of the questions generated from your reading. For each question, use details from each text to support your response. Pre-seminar questions:

   • What is each poet's attitude toward imperialism?
   • What is the difference between the "white man's burden" and the "poor man's burden"?
   • To what extent do these poems reflect different cultural perspectives?
   • How does the language and imagery used by these poets reflect the culture of their historical time period?

Participating in the Socratic Seminar

11. A successful seminar depends on the participants and their willingness to engage in the conversation. Be mindful of the following:

   • Focus on being part of a collaborative effort by making sure everybody has a chance to ask questions and offer insights. Acknowledge that not all participants will agree on every point.
   • Use evidence from the text to support your own ideas. Cite evidence from the text when you are responding to the ideas of others.
   • Make sure you speak respectfully to other participants. Summarize points of agreement or disagreement before justifying your own perspective.
   • Begin the seminar by asking one of the pre-seminar questions. From there, ask additional questions to explore one another's interpretation of the poems.

Post-Seminar Reflection

12. Review your responses to the pre-seminar questions and reflect on what you learned in the seminar. Add key learnings to the KWHL Chart at the beginning of this activity.

   • How has your understanding of imperialism improved?
   • How has your understanding of the lens of Cultural Criticism improved?
   • How would you rate your participation in the seminar?
   • What will you do differently in your next seminar?

My Notes

Analyzing an Advertisement

13. Choose an effective strategy, such as OPTIC, to analyze this advertisement from 1899.

14. Who is the target audience of this advertisement? What details support your answer?

15. What literary reference do you find in this advertisement? How does the advertisement use this reference to send a message? What effect does this create? Use details to support your answer.

☑ Check Your Understanding

In what ways is the perspective of imperialism portrayed in the advertisement similar to or different from the perspective of imperialism conveyed by the two poems you read in this activity?

📝 Writing Prompt: Literary Analysis

Think about the text, illustration, and layout of the Pears' Soap advertisement from an 1890s magazine. Write an interpretation of this advertisement using the lens of Cultural Criticism. Be sure to:

- Summarize the message of this advertisement.
- Include evidence from the advertisement to support your ideas.
- Use ideas and specific vocabulary terms from the Cultural Criticism lens in your interpretation of this advertisement.

Digging Deeper for Meaning

Learning Strategies

Discussion Groups
Graphic Organizer
Marking the Text
Sketching

My Notes

Learning Targets

- Analyze a reflective essay by closely reading the text.
- Analyze British literature from different time periods paying close attention to how each author develops a perspective on the effects of imperalism.
- Analyze how an author uses rhetorical devices to convey point of view and tone.

Preview

In this activity, you will read an essay and analyze the author's attitude toward her subject. Then you will compare the author's views of imperialism to the views reflected in Rudyard Kipling and George McNeill's poems.

As You Read

- Highlight any rhetorical strategies you observe in the text.
- Circle unknown words and phrases. Try to determine the meaning of the words by using context clues, word parts, or a dictionary.

About the Author

Jamaica Kincaid (b. 1949) was born Elaine Potter Richardson on the Caribbean island of Antigua, an island that would not gain full independence from British colonial rule until 1981. She was a precocious child and a voracious reader. At 17 years old, she was disillusioned by her family's lack of support for her talents, and moved to New York. Kincaid later became a staff writer for the *New Yorker*. By 1985, writing under her chosen name, she had earned acclaim for two books: *At the Bottom of the River*, a book of short stories, and *Annie John*, a semiautobiographical novel. Using life to inspire fiction, Kincaid cultivated a voice distinct from male Caribbean writers to explore the complexity of relationships, the effects and aftereffects of colonialism, and general alienation.

Essay

from "On Seeing England for the First Time"

by **Jamaica Kincaid**

Chunk 1

1 When I saw England for the first time, I was a child in school sitting at a desk. The England I was looking at was laid out on a map gently, beautifully, delicately, a very special jewel: it lay on a bed of sky blue—the background of the map—its yellow form mysterious, because though it looked like a leg of **mutton**, it could not really look like anything so familiar as a leg of mutton because it was England—with shadings of pink and green, unlike any shadings of pink and green I had seen before, squiggly veins of red running in every direction. England was a special jewel all right, and only special people got to wear it. The people who got to wear England were English people. They wore it well and they wore it everywhere: in jungles, in deserts, on plains, on top of the highest mountains, on all the oceans, on all the seas, in places where they were not welcome, in places they should not have been. When my teacher had pinned this map up on the blackboard, she said, "This is England"—and she said it with authority, seriousness, and adoration, and we all sat up. It was as if she had said, "This is Jerusalem, the place you will go to when you die but only if you have been good." We understood then—we were meant to understand then—that England was to be our source of myth and the source from which we got our sense of reality, our sense of what was meaningful, our sense of what was meaningless—and much about our own lives and much about the very idea of us headed that last list.

Chunk 2

2 At the time I was a child sitting at my desk seeing England for the first time, I was already very familiar with the greatness of it. Each morning before I left for school, I ate breakfast of half a grapefruit, an egg, bread and butter and a slice of cheese, and a cup of cocoa; or half a grapefruit, a bowl of oat porridge, bread and butter and a slice of cheese, and a cup of cocoa. The can of cocoa was often left on the table in front of me. It had written on it the name of the company, the year the company was established, and the words "Made in England." Those words, "Made in England," were written on the box the oats came in too. They would also have been written on the box the shoes I was wearing came in: a bolt of gray linen cloth lying on the shelf of a store from which my mother had bought three yards to make the uniform that I was wearing had written along its edge those three words. The shoes I wore were made in England; so were my socks and cotton undergarments and the satin ribbons I wore tied at the end of two **plaits** of my hair. My father, who might have sat next to me at breakfast, was a carpenter and cabinet maker. The shoes he wore to work would have been made in England, as were his khaki shirt and brown felt hat. Felt was not the proper material from which a hat that was expected to provide shade from the hot sun should be made, but my father must have seen and admired a

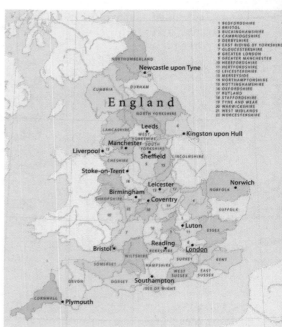

mutton: lamb
plaits: braids

My Notes

GRAMMAR & USAGE

Clauses

A clause is a group of words that has a subject and a verb. An **independent clause** expresses a complete thought and can stand alone as a sentence. A **dependent clause** does not express a complete thought and cannot stand alone. A sentence with an independent clause and one or more dependent clauses is **a complex sentence.** Complex sentences add variety to writing and establish relationships between ideas. Reread this complex sentence from Kincaid's essay:

"My father, who might have sat next to me at breakfast, was a carpenter and cabinet maker."

The dependent clause—*who might have sat next to me at breakfast*—cannot stand alone as a sentence. It is set off by commas because it is not essential to our understanding of who the father is. The rest of this complex sentence—*My father was a carpenter and cabinet maker*—forms the independent clause.

Find other examples of complex sentences in Jamaica Kincaid's essay. Determine which clauses are independent and which are dependent.

picture of an Englishman wearing such a hat in England, and this picture that he saw must have been so compelling that it caused him to wear the wrong hat for a hot climate most of his long life. And this hat—a brown felt hat—became so central to his character that it was the first thing he put on in the morning as he stepped out of bed and the last thing he took off before he stepped back into bed at night. As we sat at breakfast a car might go by. The car, a Hillman or a Zephyr, was made in England. The very idea of the meal itself, breakfast, and its substantial quality and quantity was an idea from England; we somehow knew that in England they began the day with this meal called breakfast and a proper breakfast was a big breakfast. No one I knew liked eating so much food so early in the day: it made us feel sleepy, tired. But this breakfast business was Made in England like almost everything else that surrounded us, the exceptions being the sea, the sky, and the air we breathed.

Chunk 3

3   At the time I saw this map—seeing England for the first time—I did not say to myself. "Ah, so that's what it looks like." Because there was no longing in me to put a shape to those three words that ran through every part of my life, no matter how small; for me to have had such a longing would have meant that I lived in a certain atmosphere, an atmosphere in which those three words were felt as a burden. But I did not live in such an atmosphere. My father's brown felt hat would develop a hole in its crown, the lining would separate from the hat itself, and six weeks before he thought that he could not be seen wearing it—he was a very vain man—he would order another hat from England. And my mother taught me to eat my food in the English way: the knife in the right hand, the fork in the left, my elbows held still close to my side, the food carefully balanced on my fork and then brought up to my mouth. When I had finally mastered it, I overheard her saying to a friend, "Did you see how nicely she can eat?" But I knew then that I enjoyed my food more when I ate it with my bare hands, and I continued to do so when she wasn't looking. And when my teacher showed us the map, she asked us to study it carefully, because no test we would ever take would be complete without this statement: "Draw a map of England." I did not know then that the statement "Draw a map of England" was something far worse than a declaration of war, for in fact a flat-out declaration of war would have put me on alert, and again in fact, there was no need for war—I had long ago been conquered. I did not know then that this statement was part of a process that would result in my erasure, not my physical erasure, but my erasure all the same. I did not know then that this statement was meant to make me feel in awe and small whenever I heard the word "England": awe at its existence, small because I was not from it. I did not know very much of anything then—certainly not what a blessing it was that I was unable to draw a map of England correctly.

Making Observations
- What visual images came to mind as you were reading this essay?
- What stands out to you the most about this narrator's childhood?

Returning to the Text

- Reread the essay to answer these text-dependent questions.
- Write any additional questions you have about the text in your Reader/Writer Notebook.

1. What does the repetition of the word "England" in paragraph 1 tell you about the author's point of view?

2. What can you infer from the speaker's tone in the opening paragraphs?

3. In Chunk 2, how does the speaker evoke England's presence in her daily life?

4. In Chunk 3, what rhetorical devices are used and how do they convey Kincaid's attitude toward "seeing England for the first time"?

5. How does the author's notion of England develop and change over the course of the essay?

Working from the Text

6. With a partner, consider the quotation, "England was a special jewel all right, and only special people got to wear it. The people who got to wear England were English people."

   • Why might the author have included this statement in the first paragraph of her essay?
   • What does this quotation reveal about the narrator's perception of England?
   • How might England's presence in the narrator's every day life cause her to feel like an outsider?

7. Answer each question in the chart that follows. As you fill in the chart think about how each text affects your understanding of the others. Note any ways your ideas or opinions change as you compare and contrast the texts.

Question:	The White Man's Burden	The Poor Man's Burden	On Seeing England for the First Time
What tone does each author use when addressing the reader? Who is the author's intended audience?			
What does each author believe about imperialism?			
What connotations does Western culture have for each author?			
How does each text reflect the author's cultural and historical context?			

☑ Check Your Understanding

How did analyzing texts from different time periods provide you with a new understanding or perspective of imperialism? Summarize how the texts from Kipling, McNeill, and Kincaid informed your perspective.

Learning Targets
- Place phrases and clauses correctly in sentences.
- Recognize and correct misplaced and dangling modifiers.

Preview

In this activity, you will develop an understanding of modifiers and how to use them to enhance your writing. Then, you will practice identifying and correctly placing modifiers, before incorporating them into your own writing.

Placing Modifiers Correctly

Part of being an effective writer is placing modifiers so that your meaning is clear. It is also important to know how to revise misplaced and dangling modifiers. A **modifier** is a word, phrase, or clause that makes the meaning of another word or word group more specific. In these examples, the words and word groups in boldface are modifiers:

a beautiful map

the map of England

an elegant map that makes England look like a jewel

Modifiers should be placed near the word or word group they modify. A **misplaced modifier** can create confusion or accidental humor. The following excerpt is a single sentence that includes many modifiers. If the modifiers were misplaced the reader could easily get confused.

> The England I was looking at was laid out on a map gently, beautifully, delicately, a very special jewel: it lay on a bed of sky blue—the background of the map—its yellow form mysterious, because though it looked like a leg of mutton, it could not really look like anything so familiar as a leg of mutton because it was England—with shadings of pink and green, unlike any shadings of pink and green I had seen before, squiggly veins of red running in every direction.

1. Read the following sentences, and identify the misplaced modifiers. Then rewrite each sentence, placing the modifier correctly. The first one has been done for you.

   a. Jamaica Kincaid was born in 1949 on the colonial island Antigua, <u>who eventually moved to New York and became a famous writer</u>.

   b. We discussed her reflections on being instructed to draw a map of England <u>during our English class</u>.

c. She discusses being a child and seeing a map of England <u>sitting at a desk in school</u>.

Correcting Dangling Modifiers

A modifier that does not clearly modify any word or word group in a sentence is a dangling modifier. While you can usually correct a misplaced modifier by rearranging the sentence, in the case of a dangling modifier, you may need to add or replace words to clarify your meaning.

Dangling: After reading the essay, a discussion took place. (Did the discussion read the essay?)

Revised: After reading the essay, we discussed it.

Now the phrase modifies *we*.

Dangling: Moving to New York, a career as a writer came next.

In this example, the phrase seems to modify *career*, but that doesn't make sense.

Revised: After Jamaica Kincaid moved to New York, she undertook a career as a writer.

- Read the following sentences, and underline each dangling modifier. Then, rewrite each sentence to make it clear.

d. <u>Coming from a family in an English colony</u>, the author's essay delivers a clear message about identity.

e. <u>Struck by the author's memories</u>, the experience seems to have changed her forever.

f. <u>Considering her young self conquered</u>, even so, the desire to eat with bare hands never went away.

Revising

Read the paragraph that follows from a student's essay analyzing "On Seeing England for the First Time." Work with a partner to check whether modifiers are placed correctly and whether each clearly modifies a word or word group. Underline any mistakes you notice, and rewrite the paragraph, correcting the mistakes. (Not all sentences include errors.)

[1] Drawn so that it resembled a jewel, the schoolgirl gazed at the map of England. [2] Surprised, it also looked a little like mutton, a popular English meat. [3] At the time, she didn't understand how colonial rule had colored her world and distorted her perception. [4] She would eventually explore what it means to grow up in a colonized Caribbean nation, reflecting on her experiences. [5] No longer a little girl, the essay demonstrates a canny understanding of history and identity.

☑ Check Your Understanding

Imagine you are editing a classmate's writing, and you notice these sentences:

Called Waladii by the native people for hundreds of years, Jamaica Kincaid was born on an island that the Spanish named Antigua. Reading about Antigua, slavery and colonization took a serious toll on the island.

Write an explanation so that your classmate understands the mistakes and how to correct them. Then add a question to your Editor's Checklist to remind yourself to check for correct use of modifiers.

Practice

Return to the essay you wrote in Activity 1.13, and check it for correct use and placement of modifiers. Work with a partner, and follow the steps listed.

- Underline any modifying words, phrases, and clauses.
- Check for correct placement and use.
- Rewrite to correct any misplaced or dangling modifiers.

Learning Strategies

Diffusing
Marking the Text
Levels of Questions
Quickwrite
Skimming/Scanning
Think-Pair-Share

My Notes

Learning Targets

- Analyze a reflective essay to explore an author's perspective on imperialism.
- Evaluate how the organizational structure of reflective essay can help you achieve your purpose.
- Draft a reflective essay applying the organizational structure studied.

Preview

In this activity, you will study George Orwell's reflective essay and apply the lens of Cultural Criticism to Orwell's commentary on imperialism. After working with the text, you will turn to your own writing and apply what you have learned about the structure of a reflective essay.

Organizational Structure of a Reflective Essay

A reflective essay is a kind of personal narrative in which the writer reflects on the significance of an incident.

Response
The author describes his or her feelings and thoughts concerning the encounter. This is the initial response, without the benefit of reflection.

Reflective Essay

Event
The author describes an incident or set of circumstances.

Reflection
The author reflects on the incident. This reflection usually occurs sometime after the event or incident. In the reflection, the author often transitions from describing a situation unique to him or her to a discussion more universal in nature.

1. Look back at the essay "On Seeing England for the First Time" in the previous activity. Work with a partner to try to identify the event, response, and reflection in that essay.

2. **Quickwrite:** Think about an event that taught you something valuable. Use the triangle graphic organizer to brainstorm details about the event, your response, and your reflection on the lessons learned. Then complete a quickwrite that includes these details. You will return to this draft later in the activity.

As You Read

- Use a question mark to note anything you do not understand or any place where you would like more information.
- Circle unknown words and phrases. Try to determine the meaning of the words by using context clues, word parts, or a dictionary.

About the Author

George Orwell (1903–1950) was born Eric Blair in what was then British India, where his father was a government official. After an education in England, Orwell worked in the Indian Imperial Police, though he left his position at the age of 24 to turn his hand to writing. Throughout his career, Orwell wrote under his pen name about the poor and working classes in Asia, England, and France. Working for the BBC during and after WWII, he wrote his two most famous works: *Animal Farm*, a satire of collectivism, and *1984*, a stinging critique of totalitarianism. Orwell, who famously said, "Good prose is like a window pane," is considered one of the most influential stylists of the 20th century. He wrote extensively on the art of prose, which he considered a powerful political tool.

Essay

Shooting an Elephant

by **George Orwell**

Chunk 1

1   In Moulmein, in lower Burma, I was hated by large numbers of people—the only time in my life that I have been important enough for this to happen to me. I was subdivisional police officer of the town, and in an aimless, petty kind of way an anti-European feeling was very bitter. No one had the guts to raise a riot, but if a European woman went through the **bazaars** alone somebody would probably spit betel juice over her dress. As a police officer I was an obvious target and was baited whenever it seemed safe to do so. When a nimble Burman tripped me up on the football field and the referee (another Burman) looked the other way, the crowd yelled with hideous laughter. This happened more than once. In the end the sneering yellow faces of young men that met me everywhere, the insults hooted after me when I was at a safe distance, got badly on my nerves. The young Buddhist priests were the worst of all. There were several thousands of them in the town and none of them seemed to have anything to do except stand on street corners and jeer at Europeans.

bazaars: open-air markets

2 All this was perplexing and upsetting. For at that time I had already made up my mind that imperialism was an evil thing and the sooner I chucked up my job and got out of it the better. Theoretically—and secretly, of course—I was all for the Burmese and all against their oppressors, the British. As for the job I was doing, I hated it more bitterly than I can perhaps make clear. In a job like that you see the dirty work of Empire at close quarters. The wretched prisoners huddling in the stinking cages of the lockups, the gray, cowed faces of the long-term convicts, the scarred buttocks of men who had been flogged with bamboos—all these oppressed me with an intolerable sense of guilt. But I could get nothing into perspective. I was young and ill-educated and I had to think out my problems in the utter silence that is imposed on every Englishman in the East. I did not know that the British Empire is dying, still less did I know that it is a great deal better than the younger empires that are going to **supplant** it. All I knew was that I was stuck between my hatred of the empire I served and my rage against the evil-spirited little beasts who tried to make my job impossible. With one part of my mind I thought of the British Raj as an unbreakable tyranny, as something clamped down, in *saecula saeculorum*[1], upon the will of **prostrate** peoples; with another part I thought that the greatest joy in the world would be to drive a bayonet into a Buddhist priest's guts. Feelings like these are the normal by-product of imperialism; ask any Anglo-Indian official, if you can catch him off duty.

Chunk 2

3 One day something happened which in a roundabout way was enlightening. It was a tiny incident in itself, but it gave me a better glimpse than I had had before of the real nature of imperialism—the real motives for which despotic governments act. Early one morning the subinspector at a police station the other end of the town rang me up on the phone and said that an elephant was ravaging the bazaar. Would I please come and do something about it? I did not know what I could do, but I wanted to see what was happening and I got onto a pony and started out. I took my rifle, an old. 44 Winchester and much too small to kill an elephant, but I thought the noise might be useful *in terrorem*[2]. Various Burmans stopped me on the way and told me about the elephant's doings. It was not, of course, a wild elephant, but a tame one which had gone "must." It had been chained up, as tame elephants always are when their attack of "must"[3] is due, but on the previous night it had broken its chain and escaped. Its mahout,[4] the only person who could manage it when it was in that state, had set out in pursuit, but had taken the wrong direction and was now twelve hours' journey away, and in the morning the elephant had suddenly reappeared in the town. The Burmese population had no weapons and were quite helpless against it. It had already destroyed somebody's bamboo hut, killed a cow and raided some fruit stalls and

supplant: replace
prostrate: overpowered

---

[1] *saecula saeculorum*: forever and ever
[2] *in terrorem*: in fright or terror
[3] *must*: a condition of dangerous frenzy
[4] *mahout*: the keeper and driver of an elephant

My Notes

devoured the stock; also it had met the municipal rubbish van and, when the driver jumped out and took to his heels, had turned the van over and inflicted violences upon it.

4   The Burmese subinspector and some Indian **constables** were waiting for me in the quarter where the elephant had been seen. It was a very poor quarter, a labyrinth of squalid huts, thatched with palm leaf, winding all over a steep hillside. I remember it was a cloudy, stuffy morning at the beginning of the rains. We began questioning the people where the elephant had gone and, as usual, failed to get any definite information. That is invariably the case in the East; a story always sounds clear enough at a distance, but the nearer you get to the scene of events the vaguer it becomes. Some of the people said that the elephant had gone in one direction, some said that it had gone in another, some professed not even to have heard of any elephant. I had made up my mind that the whole story was a pack of lies, when I heard yells a little distance away. There was a loud, scandalized cry of "Go away, child! Go away this instant!" and an old woman with a switch in her hand came round the corner of a hut, violently shooing away a crowd of naked children. Some more women followed, clicking their tongues and exclaiming; evidently there was something the children ought not to have seen. I rounded the hut and saw a man's dead body sprawling in the mud. He was an Indian, a black Dravidian5 coolie,6 almost naked, and he could not have been dead many minutes. The people said that the elephant had come suddenly upon him round the corner of the hut, caught him with its trunk, put its foot on his back, and ground him into the earth. This was the rainy season and the ground was soft, and his face had scored a trench a foot deep and a couple of yards long. He was lying on his belly with arms crucified and head sharply twisted to one side. His face was coated with mud, the eyes wide open, the teeth bared and grinning with an unendurable agony. (Never tell me, by the way, that the dead look peaceful. Most of the corpses I have seen looked devilish.) The friction of the great beast's foot had stripped the skin from his back as neatly as one skins a rabbit. As soon as I saw the dead man I sent an orderly to a friend's house nearby to borrow an elephant rifle. I had already sent back the pony, not wanting it to go mad with fright and throw me if it smelt the elephant.

Chunk 3

5   The orderly came back in a few minutes with a rifle and five cartridges, and meanwhile some Burmans had arrived and told us that the elephant was in the paddy fields below, only a few hundred yards away. As I started forward practically the whole white population of the quarter flocked out of the houses and followed me. They had seen the rifle and were all shouting excitedly that I was going to shoot the elephant. They had not shown much interest in the elephant when he was merely ravaging their homes, but it was different now that he was going to be shot. It was a bit of fun to them, as it would be to an English crowd; besides they wanted the meat. It made me vaguely uneasy.

---

5 *Dravidian*: belonging to an ancient race in India
6 *coolie*: servant

constables: police officers

My Notes

I had no intention of shooting the elephant—I had merely sent for the rifle to defend myself if necessary—and it is always unnerving to have a crowd following you. I marched down the hill, looking and feeling a fool, with the rifle over my shoulder and an ever growing army of people jostling at my heels. At the bottom, when you got away from the huts, there was a metaled road and beyond that a miry waste of paddy fields a thousand yards across, not yet plowed but soggy from the first rains and dotted with coarse grass. The elephant was standing eight yards from the road, his left side toward us. He took not the slightest notice of the crowd's approach. He was tearing up bunches of grass, beating them against his knees to clean them, and stuffing them into his mouth.

6   I had halted on the road. As soon as I saw the elephant I knew with perfect certainty that I ought not to shoot him. It is a serious matter to shoot a working elephant—it is comparable to destroying a huge and costly piece of machinery—and obviously one ought not to do it if it can possibly be avoided. And at that distance, peacefully eating, the elephant looked no more dangerous than a cow. I thought then and I think now that his attack of "must" was already passing off; in which case he would merely wander harmlessly about until the mahout came back and caught him. Moreover, I did not want in the least to shoot him. I decided that I would watch him a little while to make sure that he did not turn savage again, and then go home.

Chunk 4

7   But at that moment I glanced round at the crowd that had followed me. It was an immense crowd, two thousand at the least and growing every minute. It blocked the road for a long distance on either side. I looked at the sea of yellow faces above the garish clothes—faces all happy and excited over this bit of fun, all certain that the elephant was going to be shot. They were watching me as they would watch a conjurer about to perform a trick. They did not like me, but with the magical rifle in my hand I was momentarily worth watching. And suddenly I realized that I would have to shoot the elephant after all. The people expected it of me and I had got to do it; I could feel their two thousand wills pressing me forward irresistibly. And it was at this moment, as I stood there with the rifle in my hands, that I first grasped the hollowness, the **futility** of the white man's dominion in the East. Here was I, the white man with his gun, standing in front of the unarmed crowd—seemingly the leading actor of the piece; but in reality I was only an absurd puppet pushed to and fro by the will of those yellow faces behind. I perceived in this moment that when the white man turns tyrant it is his own freedom that he destroys. He becomes a sort of hollow, posing dummy, the conventionalized figure of a sahib[7]. For it is the condition of his rule that he shall spend his life in trying to "impress the natives," and so in every crisis he has got to do what the "natives" expect of him. He wears a mask, and his face grows to fit it. I had got to shoot the elephant. I had committed myself to doing it when I sent for the rifle. A sahib has got to act like a sahib; he has got to appear resolute, to know his own

futility: ineffectiveness

---

[7] *sahib*: native term for a European gentleman

mind and do definite things. To come all that way, rifle in hand, with two thousand people marching at my heels, and then to trail feebly away, having done nothing—no, that was impossible. The crowd would laugh at me. And my whole life, every white man's in the East, was one long struggle not to be laughed at.

Chunk 5

8   But I did not want to shoot the elephant. I watched him beating his bunch of grass against his knees, with that preoccupied grandmotherly air that elephants have. It seemed to me that it would be murder to shoot him. At that age I was not squeamish about killing animals, but I had never shot an elephant and never wanted to. (Somehow it always seems worse to kill a large animal.) Besides, there was the beast's owner to be considered. Alive, the elephant was worth at least a hundred pounds; dead, he would only be worth the value of his tusks, five pounds, possibly. But I had got to act quickly. I turned to the experienced-looking Burmans who had been there when we arrived, and asked them how the elephant had been behaving. They all said the same thing; he took no notice of you if you left him alone, but he might charge if you went too close to him.

9   It was perfectly clear to me what I ought to do. I ought to walk up to within, say, twenty-five yards of the elephant and test his behavior. If he charged I could shoot; if he took no notice of me, it would be safe to leave him until the mahout came back. But I also knew that I was going to do no such thing. I was a poor shot with a rifle and the ground was soft mud into which one would sink at every step. If the elephant charged and I missed him, I should have about as much chance as a toad under a steam roller. But even then I was not thinking particularly of my own skin, only of the watchful yellow faces behind. For at that moment, with the crowd watching me, I was not afraid in the ordinary sense, as I would have been if I had been alone. A white man mustn't be frightened in front of "natives"; and so, in general, he isn't frightened. The thought in my mind was that if anything went wrong those two thousand Burmans would see me pursued, caught, trampled on, and reduced to a grinning corpse like that Indian up the hill. And if that happened it was quite probable that some of them would laugh. That would never do.

My Notes

10   There was only one alternative. I shoved the cartridges into the magazine and lay down on the road to get a better aim. The crowd grew very still, and a deep, low, happy sigh, as of people who see the theater curtain go up at last, breathed from innumerable throats. They were going to have their bit of fun after all. The rifle was a beautiful German thing with cross-hair sights. I did not know then that in shooting an elephant one would shoot to cut an imaginary bar running from earhole to earhole. I ought, therefore, as the elephant was sideways on, to have aimed straight at his earhole; actually I aimed several inches in front of this, thinking the brain would be further forward.

My Notes

Chunk 6

11 When I pulled the trigger I did not hear the bang or feel the kick—one never does when a shot goes home—but I heard the devilish roar of glee that went up from the crowd. In that instant, in too short a time, one would have thought, even for the bullet to get there, a mysterious, terrible change had come over the elephant. He neither stirred nor fell, but every line of his body had altered. He looked suddenly stricken, shrunken, immensely old, as though the frightful impact of the bullet had paralyzed him without knocking him down. At last, after what seemed a long time—it might have been five seconds, I dare say—he sagged flabbily to his knees. His mouth slobbered. An enormous senility seemed to have settled upon him. One could have imagined him thousands of years old. I fired again into the same spot. At the second shot he did not collapse but climbed with desperate slowness to his feet and stood weakly erect, with legs sagging and head drooping. I fired a third time. That was the shot that did for him. You could see the agony of it jolt his whole body and knock the last remnant of strength from his legs. But in falling he seemed for a moment to rise, for as his hind legs collapsed beneath him he seemed to tower upward like a huge rock toppling, his trunk reaching skywards like a tree. He trumpeted for the first and only time. And then down he came, his belly toward me, with a crash that seemed to shake the ground even where I lay.

12 I got up. The Burmans were already racing past me across the mud. It was obvious that the elephant would never rise again, but he was not dead. He was breathing very rhythmically with long rattling gasps, his great mound of a side painfully rising and falling. His mouth was wide open—I could see far down into caverns of pink throat. I waited a long time for him to die, but his breathing did not weaken. Finally I fired my two remaining shots into the spot where I thought his heart must be. The thick blood welled out of him like red velvet, but still he did not die. His body did not even jerk when the shots hit him, the tortured breathing continued without a pause. He was dying, very slowly and in great agony, but in some world remote from me where not even a bullet could damage him further. I felt that I had got to put an end to that dreadful noise. It seemed dreadful to see the great beast lying there, powerless to move and yet powerless to die, and not even to be able to finish him. I sent back for my small rifle and poured shot after shot into his heart and down his throat. They seemed to make no impression. The tortured gasps continued as steadily as the ticking of a clock.

Chunk 7

13 In the end I could not stand it any longer and went away. I heard later that it took him half an hour to die. Burmans were bringing dahs[8] and baskets even before I left, and I was told they had stripped his body almost to the bones by afternoon.

14 Afterwards, of course, there were endless discussions about the shooting of the elephant. The owner was furious, but he was only an Indian and could do nothing. Besides, legally I had done the right thing, for a mad elephant has to

---

8 *dahs*: bowls

be killed, like a mad dog, if its owner fails to control it. Among the Europeans, opinion was divided. The older men said I was right, the younger men said it was a shame to shoot an elephant for killing a coolie, because an elephant was worth more than any Coringhee coolie. And afterwards I was very glad that the coolie had been killed; it put me legally in the right and gave me a sufficient pretext for shooting the elephant. I often wondered whether any of the others grasped that I had done it solely to avoid looking a fool.

Making Observations

- What are your first thoughts about the narrator?
- Which details help you visualize the scenes the narrator describes?
- What do you find most shocking in the story?

Returning to the Text

- Reread the essay to answer these text-dependent questions.
- Write any additional questions you have about the essay in your Reader/Writer Notebook.

3. Based on details in paragraphs 1 and 2, what can readers infer about what the narrator is like as a person? How does he respond to the hatred of the Burmese?

_____

_____

_____

_____

4. In the first two pragrapgraphs, how does Orwell use imagery to create a contrast between the people of Burma and the narrator? What is the effect on the reader?

_____

_____

_____

_____

5. In paragraph 3, what does the narrator mean when he uses the word "enlightening"?

_____

_____

_____

_____

6. Explain the sequence of events that leads to the narrator being called to "do something about" a rampaging elephant.

_____

_____

_____

7. Paragraph 4 ends very differently than it starts. Describe how the narrator reveals the important details in the paragraph.

_____

_____

_____

_____

8. What is the narrator's attitude toward shooting the elephant in paragraphs 5 and 6? What language does he use to convey this attitude? Provide evidence from the text to support your answer.

_____

_____

_____

_____

9. What makes the narrator change his mind about shooting the elephant? What does he understand about himself—as an Englishman and a white man—at the moment of this decision?

_____

_____

_____

_____

10. In paragraph 9, the narrator formulates a logical plan of action that will allow him to avoid shooting the elephant, but he does not follow it. Why not? What persistent thought or worry causes him to prepare to shoot the animal?

_____

_____

_____

_____

11. What miscalculation does the narrator make as he prepares to shoot the elephant? How does his error affect what happens next?

_____

_____

_____

_____

12. Reread Chunk 6 and mark the text for details describing the elephant's collapse. What do these details reveal about the writer's attitude?

_____

_____

_____

_____

13. What central idea about the value of life in imperial Burma is revealed by the "endless discussions about the shooting of the elephant" in the final paragraph?

_____

_____

_____

_____

Working from the Text

14. Revisit Orwell's essay and write Levels of Questions—literal, interpretative, and universal—to prepare for a Socratic Seminar. Apply a Cultural Criticism lens and your knowledge of imperialism as you develop your questions.

- **Literal:** Why was the elephant considered a problem?
- **Interpretive:** What does shooting the elephant mean to Orwell?
- **Universal:** What kind of forces might cause someone to do something against their conscience or better judgment?

Literal: _____

Interpretative: _____

Universal: _____

15. Discuss your questions with your assigned Socratic Seminar group. During the discussion, be sure to:

- Explicitly draw on your knowledge of imperialism as well as evidence from the text to support your ideas.
- Evaluate how cultural context influences the behavior of individuals and how they respond to moral conflicts.
- Ask thoughtful questions and offer insights that can deepen the group's understanding of the text and help the group move towards its goals.
- Respond thoughtfully to diverse perspectives and interpretations.
- Use appropriate eye contact, adequate volume, and clear pronunciation.

☑ Check Your Understanding

Orwell's "Shooting an Elephant" is a reflective essay. Look at your summary of the text for the event, response, and reflection, and compare with a partner. In what order do these three elements occur?

LANGUAGE & WRITER'S CRAFT:
Formal and Informal Style

You have learned that a reflective essay is a type of personal narrative in which the writer reflects on the significance of an incident or set of circumstances. Because such an essay reveals a writer's unique feelings and perceptions, yet also addresses universal issues and insights, the narrator may use a writing style that combines personal and formal elements.

Note how Orwell strikes a balance between the two styles in this example:

> Orwell's language and style demonstrate his political intelligence and awareness of the cruelty of imperialism: "hatred of the empire," "unbreakable tyranny," and "upon the will of the prostrate peoples." He conveys a more personal and emotional style when he uses less formal language, such as "evil spirited little beasts" and "into a Buddhist priests' guts."

> "All I knew was that I was stuck between my hatred of the empire I served and my rage against the evil spirited little beasts who tried to make my job impossible. With one part of my mind I thought of the British Raj as an unbreakable tyranny, as something clamped down, in saecula saeculorum, upon the will of prostrate peoples; with another part I thought that the greatest joy in the world would be to drive a bayonet into a Buddhist priest's guts."

PRACTICE Return to the Literary writing prompt in Activity 1.13. Analyze your writing and identify whether you used personal elements, formal elements, or a combination of both. In your Reader/Writer notebook, explain the style you used and why. If you would change your style based on what you have learned, explain your reasoning.

✏️ Writing Prompt: Literary

Using your quickwrite from the beginning of the activity, write a reflective essay about a significant event in your life that taught you a meaningful lesson. Be sure to:

- Engage the reader by establishing a clear incident, response, progression of events, and reflection.
- Use narrative techniques to develop experiences, events, and/or characters.
- Use precise words and phrases, telling details, and sensory language to convey a vivid picture of the experiences, events, setting, or characters.
- Sequence events to create a coherent narrative that builds toward the outcome.

📖 INDEPENDENT READING LINK
Read and Discuss

Select a point in your independent reading in which a character or the narrator experiences feeling like an outsider. Discuss with a partner or a group how the character reflects on this incident.

My Notes

Learning Strategies

Brainstorming
Graphic Organizer
Think-Pair-Share

KNOWLEDGE QUEST

Knowledge Question:

What challenges or difficulties might someone new to a place face?

Across Activities 1.17 and 1.18, you will read two texts and examine the theme of what it means to be a stranger in a new place. While you read and build knowledge about the theme, think about your answer to the Knowledge Question.

Learning Targets

- Analyze the thematic concept of "being a stranger in the village."
- Plan and outline a reflective essay that explores a personal experience.
- Draft an informative introduction to a reflective essay based on a personal incident.
- Integrate ideas from multiple texts to build knowledge and vocabulary about thematic concerns regarding being a stranger in a new place.

Preview

In this activity, you will explore the thematic concept of "being a stranger in the village" by analyzing an excerpt from an autobiography. Then you will reflect on a significant personal event and outline a reflective essay. A peer will review your outline and provide you with clear feedback. After receiving feedback, you will write a draft.

As You Read

- Underline words, phrases, or sentences that reveal the narrator's ideas about Chinese and British culture.
- Circle unknown words and phrases. Try to determine the meaning of the words by using context clues, word parts, or a dictionary.

My Notes

About the Author

Xiaolu Guo (b. 1973) is a Chinese-born filmmaker and writer who lives and works in London. She is bilingual in Chinese and English. She was born and raised in a poor rural village in China. At the age of 18 she won a scholarship to the Beijing Film Academy. Unhappy with the repressive atmosphere in China, she moved to London in 2002. Her works have received many awards, including Britain's National Book Circle of Critics Award for her autobiography in 2017. Although not strictly a science-fiction writer, she often employs many elements of that genre in her stories, films, and novels.

Autobiography

from Once Upon a Time in the East

by **Xiaolu Guo**

Leaving China

1   From 2001 onwards, Beijing was consumed with preparations for the 2008 Olympics. Everywhere you went, there was construction going on. Every bus route had to be redirected. Every building was covered in scaffolding. Highways were springing up around Beijing like thick noodles oozing from the ground, with complicated U-turns and roundabouts. Suddenly, many old residential houses were marooned in the middle of six-lane highways or under snaking flyovers. The city was perpetually surrounded by a moonscape of construction sites. Living in Beijing had become a visual and logistical torture. It was also becoming artistically impossible. There were increasing restraints put on my books and film scripts. I was desperately looking for a way out…

2   The opportunity came sooner than I could have hoped. I heard that the Chevening scholarship and the British Council were looking for talent in China. I had never heard of "Chevening." Someone told me it was a large historical mansion in Kent, England. This was as good as anything abroad, so why not? To apply for residency in a large mansion in England would be interesting. My mind was instantly filled with images from *The Forsyte Saga*— one of the most watched English television programs on the Chinese internet. The wealthy housewives of Beijing in particular loved the fancy houses and rich people dressed in elegant costumes riding about on white horses. So I applied as a film-maker. Eight months later, after many stressful exams, the British Council in Beijing called me in. "Congratulations! You are one of three people in China this year who've won the scholarship! You beat five hundred other candidates!" The English lady brought me a cup of tea with a big smile. She also handed me back my passport with a UK **visa** in it.

3   "Oh, thank you so much," I said, flipping through the pages to check. I couldn't really believe that I had received a year-long UK visa, the first visa ever in my Chinese passport. …

4   … I realized that I had to tell my parents the news at once. …

5   They were rather surprised but both thought it sounded like a great opportunity. …

6   "Your father says he is very proud of you!" my mother said. "All your years of studying now make sense." Then she added: "You said the scholarship is from England. Do you mean Great Britain?"

7   "Yes. Great Britain," I confirmed.

GRAMMAR & USAGE

Punctuating Dialogue

Writers use dialogue—the exact words of the characters—to reveal and develop character, advance the plot, and add life to writing. Direct dialogue is enclosed in quotation marks and set off from the rest of a sentence with a comma, a question mark, or an exclamation point. Commas and periods are always placed inside the quotation marks:

"Your father says he is very proud of you!" my mother said. "All your years of studying now make sense."

Question marks and exclamation points from the dialogue are placed inside the quotation marks:

"Do you have a Chinese passport?" She stared at me with a cold, calm intensity, clutching my British passport.

As you read, notice the way punctuation is used to set off dialogue from the surrounding text. Notice when dialogue is used purposefully to develop the conflict between characters and illuminate the theme.

visa: visitor's permit

My Notes

8 "That's great. Greater than United States, right?" my mother said, drawing her conclusions from her Maoist education of the 1960s. But I knew that she had no idea about either Britain or America. The only thing she knew about those countries was that they were in the West. "You should take a rice cooker with you. I heard that Westerners don't use rice cookers." …

9 I remember very well the day I left China. It was 1 April, and the notorious Beijing sandstorm season had begun. … I dragged my luggage towards the subway, choking in the sandy soup. This was my chance to escape the world I had grown up in. But that world was trying one last time to keep me. I will be walking under a gentle and moist English sky soon, I said to myself. It nurtures rather than hinders its inhabitants. I will breathe in the purest Atlantic sea air and live on an island called Britain. All this was destined to be nothing more than a memory.

Arrival

10 I spent a sleepless eleven hours sitting on the Air China Boeing 747 to London. . . Unable to read or sleep, I entered a kind of purgatorial state, until eventually, exhausted and zombie-like, we landed at Heathrow Airport. …

11 …There was no one to pick me up, and all I had was a reservation letter for a student hostel near Marylebone Station in central London. Dragging my luggage, I jumped into a taxi. Great Britain or—what was this country called exactly? The United Kingdom and Northern Ireland? As I looked out at the streets through the rain-drenched window of the taxi, it smelled damp and soggy. The air clung to my cheeks. The sky was dim and the city drew a low and squat outline against the horizon: not very impressive. We traveled slowly, through unfamiliar, traffic-jammed streets. Everything felt threatening: the policemen moving about the street corner with their hands resting on their truncheons, long queues of grey-faced people at bus stops but no one talking, fire engines shooting through the traffic with howling sirens. … I realized that I knew nothing about this country at all. I had planted myself in alien soil. And, most of all, my only tool of communication was a jumble of half-grammatically-correct sentences in this tongue they called English. In China I had learned that the population of Britain was equal to that of my little province, Zhejiang. Perhaps it was true, since the streets didn't look that grand, especially the motorways, which were even uglier than the ones in China. Everything was one size smaller, or even two. Still, here I was. As the Chinese say, *ruxiang suisu*—once in the village, you must follow their customs. …

12 Before I left China, I was desperately looking for something. Freedom, the chance to live as an individual with dignity. This was impossible in my home country. But I was also blindly looking for something connected to the West, something non-ideological, something imaginative and romantic. But as I walked along the London streets, trying to save every penny for buses or food, I lost sight of my previous vision. London seemed no more spiritually fulfilling than home. Instead, I was faced with a world of practical problems and difficulties. Perhaps I was looking for great writers to meet or great books to read, but I could barely decipher a paragraph of English. … Now I realized

there had been some truth to my own country's Communist education: the West was not milk and honey. …

Adopting a New Language

13 The year I came to England, I was nearing thirty. I spent several months in panicked activity as the thought of my age came bearing down on me—to be a thirty-year-old woman in China was to be unbearably old! I still remember that celebration in London with some of my classmates from the film school. It was actually the first birthday party I had organized in my entire life. Like most Chinese families at the time, mine never celebrated birthdays. But there I was, cooking Chinese dumplings for my Western friends. Everyone declared that thirty was a good age, the age at which you started to know yourself a little, when you were no longer confused and started achieving goals. But I spent that year very confused. I had lost my main tool: language. Here, I was nothing but a witless, dumb, low-class foreigner.

14 At the end of the Chevening scholarship I was supposed to go back to China. But I didn't want to. So I struggled to get all the required paperwork together and managed to extend my visa. Now the crucial question was: how do I make a living in the West? I had to survive somehow. But survival wasn't enough. I wanted dignity. I could only see myself making a living through writing, as I had done in China.

15 I didn't want to risk feeling even lonelier than I had in China. It was not just the physical loneliness, but cultural and intellectual isolation. By the time my thirtieth-birthday party drew to a close, I was clear about my direction: I would have to start writing in another tongue. I would use my broken English, even though it would be extremely difficult. …

16 When the birthday party was over, I mopped the floor and did the washing-up. An idea for a novel was already forming in my mind: I would make an advantage out of my disadvantage. I would write a book about a Chinese woman in England struggling with the culture and language. She would compose her own personal English dictionary. The novel would be a sort of phrasebook, recording the things she did and the people she met.

17 I had to overcome the huge obstacle of my poor English. I decided I didn't want to go to language classes because I knew my impatience would kill my will, my threshold for boredom being just too low. Instead, I decided to teach myself. Perhaps this was a huge mistake? As I studied day and night I grew more and more frustrated with English as a language, but also as a culture. The fundamental problem with English for me was that there is no direct connection between words and meanings; in Chinese, most characters are drawn and composed from images. **Calligraphy** is one of the foundations of the written language. When you write the Chinese for *sun*, it is 太阳 or 日, which means "an extreme manifestation of Yang energy." *Yang* signifies things with strong, bright and hot energy. So "extreme yang" can only mean the sun. But in English, *sun* is written with three letters, *s*, *u* and *n*, and none of them suggests any greater or deeper meaning. Nor does the word look anything like the sun! Visual imagination and philosophical understandings were useless

My Notes

calligraphy: artistic handwriting

when it came to European languages. Technically, the foremost difficulty for an Asian writer who wants to write in English is tense. Verb conjugations in English are, quite simply, a real drag. We Chinese never modify verbs for time or person, nor do we have anything like a subjunctive mood. All tenses are in the present. Because once you say something, you mean it in your current time and space. There is no past or future when making a statement. We only add specific time indicators to our verbs if we need them. Take the verb *to go*. In Chinese *to go* is 走, *zou*, and you can use *zou* in any context without needing to change it. But *zou* in English has all these forms: *goes, went, gone, going*. Mastering conjugations was a serious struggle for me, almost a dialectical critique of the **metaphysics** of grammar.

18 I particularly detested the *past-perfect progressive tense*, which I called the Annoying PPP: a continuous action completed at some point in the past. I felt giddy every time I heard the Annoying PPP; I just couldn't understand how anyone was able to grasp something so complex. For example, my grammar book said: *Peter had been painting his house for weeks, but he finally gave up.* My immediate reaction, even before I got to the grammatical explanation, was: my God, how could someone paint his house for weeks and still give up? I just couldn't see how time itself could regulate people's actions as if they were little clocks! As for the grammar, the word order *had been* and the added flourishes like *ing* made my stomach churn. They were bizarre decorations that did nothing but obscure a simple, strong building. My instinct was to say something like: *Peter tries to paint his house, but sadness overwhelms him, causing him to lay down his brushes and give up his dream. …*

19 Another curious realization came when I discovered that I used the first-person plural too much in my everyday speech. More than necessary, for sure. In the West, if I said "*We* like to eat rice," it would confuse people. They couldn't understand who this "we" was referring to. Instead, I should have said "*We Chinese* like to eat rice." After a few weeks, I swapped to the first-person singular, as in "I like to eat rice." But it made me uncomfortable. After all, how could someone who had grown up in a collective society get used to using the first-person singular all the time? The habitual use of "I" requires thinking of yourself as a separate entity in a society of separate entities. But in China no one is a separate entity: either you were born to a non-political peasant household or to a Communist party household. But here, in this foreign country, I had to build a world as a first-person singular—urgently.

20 Still, the desire and will to work on a first book in English propelled me through the difficulties. Every day, I wrote a detailed diary, filled with the new vocabulary I had learned. The diary became the raw material for my novel, the one I had imagined while mopping the floor after my thirtieth-birthday party: *A Concise Chinese–English Dictionary for Lovers. …*

To be Published and to be Known

21 After I finished the novel, I didn't know what to do with it. I knew it would have little chance at ever being published, since I had written it using such broken English in a country awash with BBC voices and the perfect

metaphysics: fundamental nature

My Notes

sentences of the Queen. And Britain was not like China, where writers could post their manuscripts directly to publishing houses. … While pacing up and down in Waterstones one day and wondering how the hell all these books had been published, I happened upon the book *Wild Swans*. I leafed through it. In the acknowledgements, the author Jung Chang thanked her agent. … In China, writers don't have agents because, in the world of Chinese socialism, agents have traditionally been viewed as parasites, members of the exploiting class. Although I had grown up with the same socialist propaganda … I sent my book to Jung Chang's agent that very day. A man called Toby Eady, at an address I had gleaned from an internet search. Who was this man? I wondered. What were the chances that he would pay any attention to a manuscript by an unknown Chinese author? …

22   Three months later, I received an unexpected phone call. . . informing that Random House wanted to meet me to discuss the book. . . Leaving my flat at east four hours ahead of the appointed time, I made my way to Pimlico. Sitting on a grey slab outside a rain-stained brown mansion building, called 'Random House,' I ate a prawn sandwich. I had no idea what the meeting would be about since no one had told me anything in advance. In those days I nodded my head, even before people began to speak. Eventually, I walked into the reception area. Disorientated by the number of floors and having to weave my way around mazes of paper-piled desks, I met some editors. They were very friendly and seemed to know a lot about me. One of them made me a cup of Earl Grey. But I still didn't understand what the meeting was about. … By the time I left the office, I didn't even understand that they had already made a good offer for my novel. At that time, even this word "offer" was alien to me. I didn't associate "an offer" with money or buying book rights, I thought it meant "Can I *offer* you a cup of tea, or a piece of cake?" It took me a whole week to understand that the offer was much bigger than a cup of tea. …

23   From the publication of my first English novel, I wrote intensely and all the time. I wrote three more books in English over the following three years.

Cutting up Nationality

24   … I managed to finish a new novel that I had been laboring on for years. Publication was due in a few months' time, but I began to worry that it would bring me trouble when I next tried to go back home, since the novel concerned the student massacre on Tiananmen Square in 1989 and the nature of **totalitarianism**. What if I was denied entry because of this book? I decided to make preparations before the novel came out. So I applied for a British passport since I had been living in the UK for nearly ten years by then.

25   I spent some months gathering the necessary documents for my **naturalization**. After a drawn-out struggle with immigration forms and lawyers, I managed to obtain a British passport. Now, I thought to myself, if there was any trouble with my books and films, I would feel a certain security in being a national of a Western country. Now I could go back to visit my sick father and see my family.

26   A week later, I applied for a Chinese visa with my British passport. After

totalitarianism: complete dictatorship by a centralized government

naturalization: process of becoming a citizen

My Notes

_____

_____

_____

_____

_____

_____

_____

_____

_____

_____

_____

_____

_____

_____

_____

_____

_____

_____

_____

_____

waiting at the Chinese Embassy in London for about half an hour, I found myself looking at the visa officer through a glass barrier. The woman wore horn-rimmed glasses and had her hair cut short, military-style. She looked like a resurrected Madame Mao. She took my British passport and scanned me up and down. Her face was stern, the muscles around her mouth stiff, just like all the other Communist officials, seemingly trained to keep their faces this way.

27 "Do you have a Chinese passport?" She stared at me with a cold, calm intensity, clutching my British passport. …

28 I had my Chinese passport in my bag, just in case. So I took it out and handed it to her through the narrow window.

29 She flipped through its pages. The way she handled it gave me a sudden stomach ache. I sensed something bad was coming.

30 "You know it's illegal to possess two passports as a Chinese citizen?" she remarked in her even-toned, slightly jarring voice.

31 "Illegal?" I repeated. My surprise was totally genuine. It had never occurred to me that having two passports was against Chinese law…

32 The woman glanced at me from the corner of her eye. . . I couldn't help but feel the judgment she had formed of me: a criminal! No, worse than that, I was a Chinese criminal who had muddied her own Chinese citizenship with that of a small, foreign state. And to top it all, I was ignorant of the laws of my own country.

33 She then flipped through my visa application, which was attached to my British passport, and announced: "Since this is the first time you are using your western passport, we will only issue you a two-week visa for China."

34 "What?" I was speechless. I had applied for a six-month family visit visa. Before I could even argue, I saw her take out a large pair of scissors and decisively cut the corner off my Chinese passport. She then threw it back out at me. It landed before me on the counter, disfigured and invalid.

35 I stared, without comprehension, at this once-trusted passport. The enormity of what had just happened slowly began registering itself in me. Although I was totally ignorant of most Chinese laws, I knew this for certain: when an embassy official cuts your passport, you are *no longer* a Chinese citizen. I stared back at Madame Mao with growing anger.

36 "How could you do that?" I stammered, like an idiot who knew nothing of how the world worked.

37 "This is the law. You have chosen the British passport. You can't keep the Chinese one." Case closed. She folded my visa application into my British passport and handed them to another officer, who took it, and all the other waiting passports, to a back room for further processing. She returned her tense face toward me, but she was no longer looking at me. I was already invisible.

My Notes

38 There I was, standing in front of the Chinese Embassy on Old Jewry, near Bank station. I was still struggling to believe what had just happened. Was that it? I had just lost my Chinese nationality? But I am Chinese, not British, I don't *feel* in any way British, despite my new passport. Little Madame Mao hadn't even asked me which passport I wanted to keep, the British or the Chinese. I suppose from her point of view I had already chosen by applying for another nationality, and in doing so, I had forfeited my birthright. For a few minutes I truly hated her, she became an emblem for everything I detested about my homeland, now no longer my country.

39 My tourist visa was ready a few days later. But for some reason, I never used it. Perhaps because I wasn't sure what I was supposed to do with a two-week stay. From the day I lost my Chinese passport, I came to the simple revelation that nationality did not declare who I was. I was a woman raised in China and in exile in Britain. I was a woman who wrote books and made films. I could have applied for a German passport if I had lived in Germany. But a passport and the nationality written on its cover would never define me.

40 As the old Chinese saying goes, uproot a tree and it will die; uproot a man and he will survive. I have always agreed with this proverb, especially in the years before I left China. But after the incident at the Chinese Embassy, I thought to myself: mere survival is a life without imagination, but a drifter's life with imagination is also a life without substance. As a new immigrant, everything felt intangible: I couldn't integrate fully with the locals, nor penetrate the heart of the Western culture that surrounded me. But the only way to overcome these problems was to root myself here, to transplant myself into this land and to grow steadily. So I began to plan a life exactly like every other first-generation immigrant, starting with making myself a proper home.

The view from the Thames of the Houses of Parliament in London.

Knowledge Quest

- What challenges does the author face that surprise you?
- How does the author's ability to deal with cultural pressures change throughout the essay?

Returning to the Text

- Reread the essay to answer these text-dependent questions.
- Write any additional questions you have about the text in your Reader/Writer Notebook.

1. What words and details in paragraphs 1–9 reveal the author's perception of China and England? What do these details reveal about her perspective of each country?

2. How does the author's impression of England change over time?

3. **KQ** What does the author's discussion of language in paragraph 19 imply about her perceptions of Chinese and Western culture? How does she respond to this difference?

4. What does the author's effort to learn English reveal about her character?

5. How does the author's diction help the reader connect with her reflective essay?

_____

_____

_____

_____

6. **KQ** How does the author explore the theme of identity in the text?

_____

_____

_____

_____

7. How does the author's use of a chronological narrative structure contribute to the text's purpose?

_____

_____

_____

_____

8. How does the the metaphor in the last paragraph, "uproot a tree and it will die; uproot a man and he will survive," contribute to the author's message?

_____

_____

_____

_____

Working from the Text

9. With a partner, answer the questions that follow to identify the event, response, and reflection in the passage.

   - What is the major incident in Xiaolu Guo's essay?
   - How does she respond to this event?
   - How does she reflect upon this event?
   - Think about how Xiaolu Guo and the narrator of "Shooting an Elephant" are both strangers in their environments. Respond to the first four items in the graphic organizer.

Stranger in the Village	
10. Brainstorm words related to village.	**11.** What does it mean to be part of the village, the group encountering the unfamiliar?
12. Brainstorm words related to stranger.	**13.** What does it mean to be the unfamiliar one, the stranger?
14. Listen to the song. How does the artist indicate the "stranger" and the "village"?	**15.** Brainstorm a list of films which you are familiar with, and for each one discuss this question: Who is the "stranger," and who or what is the "village"?

☑ Check Your Understanding

Based on the texts you have read so far, what does it mean to be a stranger in the village?

16. Review Embedded Assessment 2 and create an outline for your reflective essay. If necessary, come up with ideas by brainstorming, journaling, drawing, or discussion with others. When writing your outline be sure to:

    - Think about what kind of structure you want to use to achieve your purpose. Is there a clear event, response, reflection?
    - Connect the event in your narrative to the concept of being a stranger in a village.

Peer Review

17. Review a peer's outline. When providing feedback address the following questions:

    - Does the outline clearly and effectively address the prompt?
    - Is there a clear and coherent structure?
    - Does the event reflect the theme?

> ### ✍️ Writing Prompt: Informational
>
> Write a draft of an event in which you or someone you know felt like a "stranger in a village" or were perceived as a stranger. Be sure to:
>
> - Include a effective introduction with a clear event.
> - Use precise diction, sensory details, and stylistic devices to describe the event.
> - Use transitional phrases and dialogue to connect ideas smoothly.

Understanding the Stranger's Perception of the Village

Learning Strategies

Diffusing
Marking the Text
Previewing
Socratic Seminar
Think-Pair-Share

My Notes

Learning Targets

- Analyze the relationships between structure, thematic development, point of view, plot, and character in a reflective essay.
- Participate in a collaborative discussion by asking questions and using textual evidence to evaluate answers and responses.
- Integrate ideas from multiple texts to build knowledge and vocabulary about thematic concerns regarding being a stranger in a new place.

Preview

In this activity, you will read and discuss the essay "Stranger in the Village," analyzing its structure, style, and thematic concepts.

Making Adjustments While Reading

When faced with a complex text, readers sometimes need to pause and make adjustments when their understanding breaks down. When you don't understand something you are reading, try the following adjustments:

- Reread the word, phrase, or sentence that you do not understand. Reread out loud to see if hearing the sentence helps you understand it.
- Use your background knowledge to make sense of what you are reading.
- Ask questions about the text. Jot down questions in the My Notes section and return to them later to see if you know the answer after reading more of the text.
- Use annotations, like metacognitive markers, to note the parts of the text where you have questions or comments.

As You Read

- Make notes using metacognitive symbols (? ! *) to indicate the type of comment you wish to return to.
- Circle unknown words and phrases. Try to determine the meaning of the words by using context clues, word parts, or a dictionary.

About the Author

James Baldwin (1924–1987) was born in Harlem, into a poor household. By his early twenties he was earning a living as a freelance book reviewer and had become friends with many other writers, including the novelist Richard Wright, who encouraged him to write longer works. A grant enabled him to move to Paris in 1948. This move helped provide the critical distance he needed to write *Notes of a Native Son* and his first novel, *Go Tell It on the Mountain*—powerful works about the African American experience. After returning to the United States, he became a leading literary voice for civil rights. While his unsparing view of race issues in the United States drew criticism from his African American and white peers alike, he is now viewed as one of the most significant U.S. writers of the 20th century.

Essay

Stranger in the Village

by **James Baldwin**

KNOWLEDGE QUEST

Knowledge Question:
What challenges or difficulties might someone new to a place face?

My Notes

Chunk 1

1   From all available evidence no black man had ever set foot in this tiny Swiss village before I came. I was told before arriving that I would probably be a "sight" for the village; I took this to mean that people of my complexion were rarely seen in Switzerland, and also that city people are always something of a "sight" outside of the city. It did not occur to me—possibly because I am an American—that there could be people anywhere who had never seen a Negro.

Chunk 2

2   It is a fact that cannot be explained on the basis of the inaccessibility of the village. The village is very high, but it is only four hours from Milan and three hours from Lausanne. It is true that it is virtually unknown. Few people making plans for a holiday would elect to come here. On the other hand, the villagers are able, presumably, to come and go as they please—which they do: to another town at the foot of the mountain, with a population of approximately five thousand, the nearest place to see a movie or go to the bank. In the village there is no movie house, no bank, no library, no theater; very few radios, one jeep, one station wagon; and, at the moment, one typewriter, mine, an invention which the woman next door to me here had never seen. There are about six hundred people living here, all Catholic—I conclude this from the fact that the Catholic church is open all year round, whereas the Protestant chapel, set off on a hill a little removed from the village, is open only in the summertime when the tourists arrive. There are four or five hotels, all closed now, and four or five *bistros*,[1] of which, however, only two do any business during the winter. These two do not do a great deal, for life in the village seems to end around nine or ten o'clock. There are a few stores, butcher, baker, *epicerie*,[2] a hardware store, and a money-changer—who cannot change travelers' checks, but must send them down to the bank, an operation which takes two or three days. There is something called the *Ballet Haus*, closed in the winter and used for God knows what, certainly not ballet, during the summer. There seems to be only one schoolhouse in the village, and this for the quite young children; I suppose this to mean that their older brothers and sisters at some point descend from these mountains in order to complete their

---

[1] *bistros*: small informal restaurants
[2] *epicerie*: French for "grocery store"

James Baldwin visted Leukerbad, Switzerland in 1951.

disquietingly: disturbingly
jocularly: jokingly

education—possibly, again, to the town just below. The landscape is absolutely forbidding, mountains towering on all four sides, ice and snow as far as the eye can reach. In this white wilderness, men and women and children move all day, carrying washing, wood, buckets of milk or water, sometimes skiing on Sunday afternoons. All week long boys and young men are to be seen shoveling snow off the rooftops, or dragging wood down from the forest in sleds.

3   The village's only real attraction, which explains the tourist season, is the hot spring water. A **disquietingly** high proportion of these tourists are cripples, or semi-cripples, who come year after year—from other parts of Switzerland, usually—to take the waters. This lends the village, at the height of the season, a rather terrifying air of sanctity, as though it were a lesser Lourdes.[3] There is often something beautiful, there is always something awful, in the spectacle of a person who has lost one of his faculties, a faculty he never questioned until it was gone, and who struggles to recover it. Yet people remain people, on crutches or indeed on deathbeds; and wherever I passed, the first summer I was here, among the native villagers or among the lame, a wind passed with me—of astonishment, curiosity, amusement and outrage. That first summer I stayed two weeks and never intended to return. But I did return in the winter, to work; the village offers, obviously, no distractions whatever and has the further advantage of being extremely cheap. Now it is winter again, a year later, and I am here again. Everyone in the village knows my name, though they scarcely ever use it, knows that I come from America—though this, apparently, they will never really believe: black men come from Africa—and everyone knows that I am the friend of the son of a woman who was born here, and that I am staying in their chalet. But I remain as much a stranger today as I was the first day I arrived, and the children shout *Neger! Neger!* as I walk along the streets.

Chunk 3

4   It must be admitted that in the beginning I was far too shocked to have any real reaction. In so far as I reacted at all, I reacted by trying to be pleasant—it being a great part of the American Negro's education (long before he goes to school) that he must make people "like" him. This smile-and-the-world-smiles-with-you routine worked about as well in this situation as it had in the situation for which it was designed, which is to say that it did not work at all. No one, after all, can be liked whose human weight and complexity cannot be, or has not been, admitted. My smile was simply another unheard-of phenomenon which allowed them to see my teeth—they did not, really, see my smile and I began to think that, should I take to snarling, no one would notice any difference. All of the physical characteristics of the Negro which had caused me, in America, a very different and almost forgotten pain were nothing less than miraculous—or infernal—in the eyes of the village people. Some thought my hair was the color of tar, that it had the texture of wire, or the texture of cotton. It was **jocularly** suggested that I might let it all grow long and make myself a winter coat. If I sat in the sun for more than five minutes

---

[3] *Lourdes* is a town in southern France where the Blessed Virgin Mary appeared to St. Bernadette Soubirous in 1858. Today it is a place of pilgrimage and miracles.

some daring creature was certain to come along and gingerly put his fingers on my hair, as though he were afraid of an electric shock, or put his hand on my hand, astonished that the color did not rub off. In all of this, in which it must be conceded there was the charm of genuine wonder and in which there was certainly no element of intentional unkindness, there was yet no suggestion that I was human: I was simply a living wonder.

5   I knew that they did not mean to be unkind, and I know it now; it is necessary, nevertheless, for me to repeat this to myself each time that I walk out of the chalet. The children who shout *Neger!* have no way of knowing the echoes this sound raises in me. They are brimming with good humor and the more daring swell with pride when I stop to speak with them. Just the same, there are days when I cannot pause and smile, when I have no heart to play with them; when, indeed, I mutter sourly to myself, exactly as I muttered on the streets of a city these children have never seen, when I was no bigger than these children are now: *Your* mother *was a nigger.* Joyce[4] is right about history being a nightmare—but it may be the nightmare from which no one *can* awaken. People are trapped in history and history is trapped in them.

Chunk 4

6   There is a custom in the village—I am told it is repeated in many villages—of "buying" African natives for the purpose of converting them to Christianity. There stands in the church all year round a small box with a slot for money, decorated with a black figurine, and into this box the villagers drop their francs. During the carnaval which precedes Lent, two village children have their faces blackened—out of which bloodless darkness their blue eyes shine like ice—and fantastic horsehair wigs are placed on their blond heads; thus disguised, they solicit among the villagers for money for missionaries in Africa. Between the box in the church and blackened children, the village "bought" last year six or eight African natives. This was reported to me with pride by the wife of one of the *bistro* owners and I was careful to express astonishment and pleasure at the **solicitude** shown by the village for the souls of black folks. The *bistro* owner's wife beamed with a pleasure far more genuine than my own and seemed to feel that I might now breathe more easily concerning the souls of at least six of my kinsmen.

7   I tried not to think of these so lately baptized kinsmen, of the price paid for them, or the peculiar price they themselves would pay, and said nothing about my father, who having taken his own conversion too literally never, at bottom, forgave the white world (which he described as heathen) for having saddled him with a Christ in whom, to judge at least from their treatment of him, they themselves no longer believed. I thought of white men arriving for the first time in an African village, strangers there, as I am a stranger here, and tried to imagine the astounded populace touching their hair and marveling at the color of their skin. But there is a great difference between being the first white man to be seen by Africans and being the first black man to be seen

solicitude: concern

---

[4] *Joyce:* James Joyce is an important 20th-century Irish author.

My Notes

by whites. The white man takes the astonishment as tribute, for he arrives to conquer and to convert the natives, whose inferiority in relation to himself is not even to be questioned; whereas I, without a thought of conquest, find myself among a people whose culture controls me, has even, in a sense, created me, people who have cost me more in anguish and rage than they will ever know, who yet do not even know of my existence. The astonishment with which I might have greeted them, should they have stumbled into my African village a few hundred years ago, might have rejoiced their hearts. But the astonishment with which they greet me today can only poison mine.

8 And this is so despite everything I may do to feel differently, despite my friendly conversations with the *bistro* owner's wife, despite their three-year-old son who has at last become my friend, despite the *saluts* and *bonsoirs* which I exchange with people as I walk, despite the fact that I know that no individual can be taken to task for what history is doing, or has done. I say that the culture of these people controls me—but they can scarcely be held responsible for European culture. America comes out of Europe, but these people have never seen America, nor have most of them seen more of Europe than the hamlet at the foot of their mountain. Yet they move with an authority which I shall never have; and they regard me, quite rightly, not only as a stranger in their village but as a suspect latecomer, bearing no credentials, to everything they have—however unconsciously—inherited.

9 For this village, even were it incomparably more remote and incredibly more primitive, is the West, the West onto which I have been so strangely grafted. These people cannot be, from the point of view of power, strangers anywhere in the world; they have made the modern world, in effect, even if they do not know it. The most illiterate among them is related, in a way that I am not, to Dante, Shakespeare, Michelangelo, Aeschylus, Da Vinci, Rembrandt, and Racine; the cathedral at Chartres says something to them which it cannot say to me, as indeed would New York's Empire State Building, should anyone here ever see it. Out of their hymns and dances come Beethoven and Bach. Go back a few centuries and they are in their full glory—but I am in Africa, watching the conquerors arrive.

Chunk 5

10 The rage of the **disesteemed** is personally fruitless, but it is also absolutely inevitable: this rage, so generally discounted, so little understood even among the people whose daily bread it is, is one of the things that makes history. Rage can only with difficulty, and never entirely, be brought under the domination of the intelligence and is therefore not susceptible to any arguments whatever. This is a fact which ordinary representatives of the *Herrenvolk*,[5] having never felt this rage and being unable to imagine it, quite fail to understand. Also, rage cannot be hidden it can only be **dissembled**. This dissembling deludes the thoughtless, and strengthens rage and adds, to rage, contempt. There are,

[5] *Herrenvolk*: German for "master race"

WORD CONNECTIONS

Roots and Affixes
In paragraph 10, the prefix *dis-*, meaning "not or apart, in different directions," appears in **disesteemed**, **discounted**, and **dissembled**. The prefix *un-* also means not, but *dis-* adds a layer of meaning. For example, how does the word *discounted* differ in meaning from *uncounted*?

disesteemed: disrespected
dissembled: disguised

no doubt, as many ways of coping with the resulting complex of tensions as there are black men in the world, but no black man can hope ever to be entirely liberated from this internal warfare—rage, dissembling, and contempt having inevitably accompanied his first realization of the power of white men. What is crucial here is that, since white men represent in the black man's world so heavy a weight, white men have for black men a reality which is far from being reciprocal; and hence all black men have toward all white men an attitude which is designed, really, either to rob the white man of the jewel of his **naïveté** or else to make it cost him dear.

11 The black man insists, by whatever means he finds at his disposal, that the white man cease to regard him as an exotic rarity and recognize him as a human being. This is a very charged and difficult moment, for there is a great deal of will power involved in the white man's naïveté. Most people are not naturally reflective any more than they are naturally **malicious**, and the white man prefers to keep the black man at a certain human remove because it is easier for him thus to preserve his simplicity and avoid being called to account for crimes committed by his forefathers, or his neighbors. He is inescapably aware, nevertheless, that he is in a better position in the world than black men are, nor can he quite put to death the suspicion that he is hated by black men therefore. He does not wish to be hated, neither does he wish to change places, and at this point in his uneasiness he can scarcely avoid having recourse to those legends which white men have created about black men, the most usual effect of which is that the white man finds himself enmeshed, so to speak, in his own language which describes hell, as well as the attributes which lead one to hell, as being as black as night.

12 Every legend, moreover, contains its **residuum** of truth, and the root function of language is to control the universe by describing it. It is of quite considerable significance that black men remain, in the imagination, and in overwhelming numbers in fact, beyond the disciplines of salvation; and this despite the fact that the West has been "buying" African natives for centuries. There is, I should hazard, an instantaneous necessity to be divorced from this so visibly unsaved stranger, in whose heart, moreover, one cannot guess what dreams of vengeance are being nourished; and, at the same time, there are few things on earth more attractive than the idea of the unspeakable liberty which is allowed the unredeemed. When, beneath the black mask, a human being begins to make himself felt one cannot escape a certain awful wonder as to what kind of human being it is. What one's imagination makes of other people is dictated, of course, by the laws of one's own personality and it is one of the ironies of black-white relations that, by means of what the white man imagines the black man to be, the black man is enabled to know who the white man is.

13 I have said, for example, that I am as much a stranger in this village today as I was the first summer I arrived, but this is not quite true. The villagers wonder less about the texture of my hair than they did then, and wonder rather more about me. And the fact that their wonder now exists on another level is reflected in their attitudes and in their eyes. There are the children who make those delightful, hilarious, sometimes astonishingly grave overtures of

WORD CONNECTIONS

Roots and Affixes
Attribute comes from the Latin word *attribuere*, which means "to assign." It is related to the word *tribute*, which comes from the Latin word *tribuere*, meaning "to assign, allot, or pay."

naïveté: innocence
malicious: intending to cause harm
residuum: trace

My Notes

friendship in the unpredictable fashion of children; other children, having been taught that the devil is a black man, scream in genuine anguish as I approach. Some of the older women never pass without a friendly greeting, never pass, indeed, if it seems that they will be able to engage me in conversation; other women look down or look away or rather contemptuously smirk. Some of the men drink with me and suggest that I learn how to ski—partly, I gather, because they cannot imagine what I would look like on skis—and want to know if I am married, and ask questions about my *métier*.[6] But some of the men have accused *le sale nègre*—behind my back—of stealing wood and there is already in the eyes of some of them the peculiar, intent, paranoiac malevolence which one sometimes surprises in the eyes of American white men when, out walking with their Sunday girl, they see a Negro male approach.

Chunk 6

14 There is a dreadful abyss between the streets of this village and the streets of the city in which I was born, between the children who shout *Neger!* today and those who shouted *Nigger!* yesterday—the abyss is experience, the American experience. The syllable hurled behind me today expresses, above all, wonder: <u>I am a stranger here. But I am not a stranger in America and the same syllable riding on the American air expresses the war my presence has occasioned in the American soul.</u>

15 For this village brings home to me this fact: that there was a day, and not really a very distant day, when Americans were scarcely Americans at all but discontented Europeans, facing a great unconquered continent and strolling, say, into a marketplace and seeing black men for the first time. The shock this spectacle afforded is suggested, surely, by the promptness with which they decided that these black men were not really men but cattle. It is true that the necessity on the part of the settlers of the New World of reconciling their moral assumptions with the fact—and the necessity—of slavery enhanced immensely the charm of this idea, and it is also true that this idea expresses, with a truly American bluntness, the attitude which to varying extents all masters have had toward all slaves.

16 But between all former slaves and slave-owners and the drama which begins for Americans over three hundred years ago at Jamestown, there are at least two differences to be observed. The American Negro slave could not suppose, for one thing, as slaves in past epochs had supposed and often done, that he would ever be able to wrest the power from his master's hands. This was a **supposition** which the modern era, which was to bring about such vast changes in the aims and dimensions of power, put to death; it only begins, in unprecedented fashion, and with dreadful implications, to be resurrected today. But even had this supposition persisted with undiminished force, the American Negro slave could not have used it to lend his condition dignity, for the reason that this supposition rests on another: that the slave in exile yet remains related to his past, has some means—if only in memory—of revering and sustaining the forms of his former life, is able, in short, to maintain his identity.

[6] *métier*: profession

supposition: belief

Chunk 7

17 This was not the case with the American Negro slave. He is unique among the black men of the world in that his past was taken from him, almost literally, at one blow. One wonders what on earth the first slave found to say to the first dark child he bore. I am told that there are Haitians able to trace their ancestry back to African kings, but any American Negro wishing to go back so far will find his journey through time abruptly arrested by the signature on the bill of sale which served as the entrance paper for his ancestor. At the time—to say nothing of the circumstances—of the enslavement of the captive black man who was to become the American Negro, there was not the remotest possibility that he would ever take power from his master's hands. There was no reason to suppose that his situation would ever change, nor was there, shortly, anything to indicate that his situation had ever been different. It was his necessity, in the words of E. Franklin Frazier,[7] to find a "motive for living under American culture or die." The identity of the American Negro comes out of this extreme situation, and the evolution of this identity was a source of the most intolerable anxiety in the minds and the lives of his masters.

18 For the history of the American Negro is unique also in this: that the question of his humanity, and of his rights therefore as a human being, became a burning one for several generations of Americans, so burning a question that it ultimately became one of those used to divide the nation. It is out of this argument that the venom of the epithet *Nigger!* is derived. It is an argument which Europe has never had, and hence Europe quite sincerely fails to understand how or why the argument arose in the first place, why its effects are so frequently disastrous and always so unpredictable, why it refuses until today to be entirely settled. Europe's black possessions remained—and do remain—in Europe's colonies, at which remove they represented no threat whatever to European identity. If they posed any problem at all for the European conscience, it was a problem which remained comfortingly abstract: in effect, the black man, *as a man*, did not exist for Europe. But in America, even as a slave, he was an inescapable part of the general social fabric and no American could escape having an attitude toward him. Americans attempt until today to make an abstraction of the Negro, but the very nature of these abstractions reveals the tremendous effects the presence of the Negro has had on the American character.

19 When one considers the history of the Negro in America it is of the greatest importance to recognize that the moral beliefs of a person, or a people, are never really as **tenuous** as life—which is not moral—very often causes them to appear; these create for them a frame of reference and a necessary hope, the hope being that when life has done its worst they will be enabled to rise above themselves and to triumph over life. Life would scarcely be bearable if this hope did not exist. Again, even when the worst has been said, to betray a belief is not by any means to have put oneself beyond its power; the betrayal of a belief is not the same thing as ceasing to believe. If this were not so there would be no

tenuous: fragile or unstable

---

[7] *E. Franklin Frazier* was an American sociologist who studied race relations.

My Notes

moral standards in the world at all. Yet one must also recognize that morality is based on ideas and that all ideas are dangerous—dangerous because ideas can only lead to action and where the action leads no man can say. And dangerous in this respect: that confronted with the impossibility of remaining faithful to one's beliefs, and the equal impossibility of becoming free of them, one can be driven to the most inhuman excesses. The ideas on which American beliefs are based are not, though Americans often seem to think so, ideas which originated in America. They came out of Europe. And the establishment of democracy on the American continent was scarcely as radical a break with the past as was the necessity, which Americans faced, of broadening this concept to include black men.

20 This was, literally, a hard necessity. It was impossible, for one thing, for Americans to abandon their beliefs, not only because these beliefs alone seemed able to justify the sacrifices they had endured and the blood that they had spilled, but also because these beliefs afforded them their only bulwark[8] against a moral chaos as absolute as the physical chaos of the continent it was their destiny to conquer. But in the situation in which Americans found themselves, these beliefs threatened an idea which, whether or not one likes to think so, is the very warp and woof[9] of the heritage of the West, the idea of white supremacy.

21 Americans have made themselves notorious by the **shrillness** and the brutality with which they have insisted on this idea, but they did not invent it; and it has escaped the world's notice that those very excesses of which Americans have been guilty imply a certain, unprecedented uneasiness over the idea's life and power, if not, indeed, the idea's validity. The idea of white supremacy rests simply on the fact that white men are the creators of civilization (the present civilization, which is the only one that matters; all previous civilizations are simply "contributions" to our own) and are therefore civilization's guardians and defenders. Thus it was impossible for Americans to accept the black man as one of themselves, for to do so was to jeopardize their status as white men. But not so to accept him was to deny his human reality, his human weight and complexity, and the strain of denying the overwhelmingly undeniable forced Americans into rationalizations so fantastic that they approached the **pathological**.

22 At the root of the American Negro problem is the necessity of the American white man to find a way of living with the Negro in order to be able to live with himself. And the history of this problem can be reduced to the means used by Americans—lynch law and law, segregation and legal acceptance, terrorization and concession—either to come to terms with this necessity, or to find a way around it, or (most usually) to find a way of doing both these things at once. The resulting spectacle, at once foolish and dreadful, led someone to make the quite accurate observation that "the Negro-in-America is a form of insanity which overtakes white men."

shrillness: irritating intensity
pathological: insane

---

[8] *bulwark*: defense
[9] *warp and woof*: foundation

23 In this long battle, a battle by no means finished, the unforeseeable effects of which will be felt by many future generations, the white man's motive was the protection of his identity; the black man was motivated by the need to establish an identity. And despite the terrorization which the Negro in America endured and endures sporadically until today, despite the cruel and totally inescapable ambivalence of his status in his country, the battle for his identity has long ago been won. He is not a visitor to the West, but a citizen there, an American; as American as the Americans who despise him, the Americans who fear him, the Americans who love him—the Americans who became less than themselves, or rose to be greater than themselves by virtue of the fact that the challenge he represented was inescapable. He is perhaps the only black man in the world whose relationship to white men is more terrible, more subtle, and more meaningful than the relationship of bitter possessed to uncertain possessors. His survival depended, and his development depends, on his ability to turn his peculiar status in the Western world to his own advantage and, it may be, to the very great advantage of that world. It remains for him to fashion out of his experience that which will give him sustenance, and a voice. The cathedral at Chartres, I have said, says something to the people of this village which it cannot say to me; but it is important to understand that this cathedral says something to me which it cannot say to them. Perhaps they are struck by the power of the spires, the glory of the windows; but they have known God, after all, longer than I have known him, and in a different way, and I am terrified by the slippery bottomless well to be found in the crypt, down which heretics were hurled to death, and by the obscene, inescapable gargoyles jutting out of the stone and seeming to say that God and the devil can never be divorced. I doubt that the villagers think of the devil when they face a cathedral because they have never been identified with the devil. But I must accept the status which myth, if nothing else, gives me in the West before I can hope to change the myth.

24 Yet, if the American Negro has arrived at his identity by virtue of the absoluteness of his estrangement from his past, American white men still nourish the illusion that there is some means of recovering the European innocence, of returning to a state in which black men do not exist. This is one of the greatest errors Americans can make. The identity they fought so hard to protect has, by virtue of that battle, undergone a change: Americans are as unlike any other white people in the world as it is possible to be. I do not think, for example, that it is too much to suggest that the American vision of the world—which allows so little reality, generally speaking, for any of the darker forces in human life, which tends until today to paint moral issues in glaring black and white—owes a great deal to the battle waged by Americans to maintain between themselves and black men a human separation which could not be bridged. It is only now beginning to be borne in on us—very faintly, it must be admitted, very slowly, and very much against our will—that this vision of the world is dangerously inaccurate, and perfectly useless. For it protects our moral high-mindedness at the terrible expense of weakening our

sustenance: strength
heretics: nonbelievers

My Notes

grasp of reality. People who shut their eyes to reality simply invite their own destruction, and anyone who insists on remaining in a state of innocence long after that innocence is dead turns himself into a monster.

Chunk 8

25 The time has come to realize that the interracial drama acted out on the American continent has not only created a new black man, it has created a new white man, too. No road whatever will lead Americans back to the simplicity of this European village where white men still have the luxury of looking on me as a stranger. I am not, really, a stranger any longer for any American alive. One of the things that distinguishes Americans from other people is that no other people has ever been so deeply involved in the lives of black men, and vice versa. This fact faced, with all its implications, it can be seen that the history of the American Negro problem is not merely shameful, it is also something of an achievement. For even when the worst has been said, it must also be added that the perpetual challenge posed by this problem was always, somehow, perpetually met. It is precisely this black-white experience which may prove of indispensable value to us in the world we face today. This world is white no longer, and it will never be white again.

⊘ Knowledge Quest

- How do the villagers react to Baldwin when he first arrives in Switzerland?
- What strikes you about how the author defines a stranger throughout the passage?

☑ Focus on the Sentence

Use details from the text to complete the sentences that follow. James Baldwin

feels like a stranger in the village because _____

_____

_____

James Baldwin feels like a stranger in the village, but _____

_____

_____

James Baldwin feels like a stranger in the village, so _____

_____

_____

perpetual: never-ending

Returning to the Text

- Reread the essay to answer these text-dependent questions.
- Write any additional questions you have about the text in your Reader/Writer Notebook.

1. What is the event described in the first paragraph and why might it be significant?

_____

_____

_____

_____

2. How does Baldwin use setting in paragraphs 2–3 to develop the plot?

_____

_____

_____

_____

3. How does Baldwin feel about the village? Why does he keep returning to it? How does his behavior create an inner conflict? How does it contribute to the theme of being as stranger in the village?

_____

_____

_____

_____

4. **KQ** What is the significance of the last sentence in paragraph 4? Characterize Baldwin's tone or attitude as he writes about the village. Find diction that contributes to the tone.

_____

_____

_____

_____

5. How does Baldwin use dashes in Chunks 2 and 3? What impact does this syntax have on the reader?

_____

_____

_____

_____

6. What is the irony of the villagers' custom described in Chunk 4? How does Baldwin use irony to reveal cultural differences between him and the villagers?

_____

_____

_____

_____

7. **KQ** Which details in paragraphs 8–9 does the author use to develop a theme of "stranger in a village"? What idea is conveyed by this phrase?

_____

_____

_____

_____

8. What does Baldwin mean when he says in paragraph 10 that "the rage of the disesteemed is personally fruitless, but it is also absolutely inevitable"? What feeling does his choice of diction suggest?

_____

_____

_____

_____

9. How does Baldwin analyze the actions and attitudes of "the white man" in paragraph 11? Use details to support your answer.

_____

_____

_____

_____

10. According to the details in paragraph 13, how have the villagers' attitudes changed toward Baldwin over time?

_____

_____

_____

_____

11. In paragraph 15, what is the new description of the village in which Baldwin is a stranger? What does this say about the history and culture of that village?

_____

_____

_____

_____

12. How does Baldwin use the word "Neger" to examine the nature of racism?

_____

_____

_____

_____

13. How does Baldwin characterize the "American Negro slave" in paragraph 17? Use details to support your answer.

_____

_____

_____

_____

14. Paraphrase the essential conflict Baldwin presents in paragraph 19–21?

_____

_____

_____

_____

15. What, according to Baldwin, is the main foundation of the belief in white supremacy?

_____

_____

_____

_____

16. How does the author reflect on his experience? How does he use this reflection to achieve his purpose?

_____

_____

_____

_____

Working from the Text

- To prepare for a Socratic Seminar, review the pre-seminar questions that follow and use them as a model to create sophisticated questions stemming from your study of Baldwin's essay.
- **Literal:** How does Baldwin compare his interactions with Swiss villagers with his life in America?
- **Interpretive:** What connections does Baldwin make between the historical past, his present day, and the future?
- **Universal:** How can you connect Baldwin's essay to a personal experience or other texts that you have read?

Model Socratic Seminar Questions:

Write your own Socratic Seminar questions. Remember to pose these questions as Levels of Questions, emphasizing interpretive questions more than literal or universal questions.

Literal: _____

_____

Interpretive: _____

_____

Universal: _____

_____

Knowledge Quest

Think about the challenges that authors Guo and Baldwin describe as strangers in new places. In your small group, discuss the challenges or difficulties someone new to a place might face. Be sure to:

- Draw on your observations as well as evidence from the text to support your ideas.
- Respond thoughtfully to diverse perspectives and interpretations.
- Ask thoughtful questions and build on the ideas of the group to deepen understanding.

 INDEPENDENT READING LINK

You can continue to build your knowledge about the impact of cultural factors on newcomers by reading these and other articles at ZINC Reading Labs. Search for keywords such as *immigration* or *American Dream*.

 ZINC

 Independent Reading Checkpoint

Review your independent reading and reflect on the characters, events, and ideas in the text using the lens of Cultural Criticism. Write a brief summary of your analysis, taking into consideration cultural factors such as religion, political affiliation, ethnicity, and/or class identification.

Writing a Reflective Essay

© 2021 College Board. All rights reserved.

 ASSIGNMENT

Write and present a reflective essay that illustrates an event in which you or someone you know felt like a "stranger in the village" or were perceived as a stranger by some group.

Planning and Prewriting: Make a plan for writing your essay.	■ What prewriting strategies will you use to explore your memories and capture ideas needed for a reflective essay organized around the concept of "stranger in the village"? ■ How can you best use the general structure of event/response/reflection to plan and organize your reflective essay? ■ What have you learned from literary examples that you've read in this unit that can help you develop your theme? ■ What sorts of tools will you use to record your ideas and structure the essay (for example an outline, or a graphic organizer)? ■ How can you use point of view, setting, plot, and characterization to develop your essay?
Drafting: Determine how you will include the elements of a reflective essay that will assure a successful draft.	■ What stylistic devices (voice, diction, figurative language, detail, and the like) will you include to bring the reader into your reflective essay? ■ What literary devices will you use (imagery, irony, allegory, metaphor/ simile, etc.) to develop your theme? ■ How will you identify and use the appropriate tone, voice and vocabulary? ■ How will you review your draft to ensure that your reflective essay's structure includes a clear topic, supporting details, and a strong conclusion?
Evaluating and Revising Your Draft: Review and revise to make your work the best it can be.	■ How can you solicit feedback from others, such as peers, that will help you to know what needs to be improved or revised for clarity, organization, syntax, diction, and rhetorical devices? ■ How will you evaluate transitions within and between sentences? ■ How can you use the Scoring Guide to help guide your revision?
Checking and Editing: Confirm that your final draft is ready for publication and presentation.	■ How will you use print or digital resources to clarify the meaning of words? ■ What style manual will you consult for grammatical correctness, technical accuracy, format, and correct structure? ■ How will you present your work to an audience? (Will you read it out loud? Or will you have a peer read it to you?)

Reflection

After completing this Embedded Assessment, think about how you went about accomplishing this assignment, and respond to the following question:

• How did the structure of the reflective essay help you develop the theme?

SCORING GUIDE

Scoring Criteria	Exemplary	Proficient	Emerging	Incomplete
Ideas	The essay • thoroughly demonstrates a perceptive understanding of the relationship between the event and the thematic concept • uses specific and well-chosen details to create a convincing, compelling text.	The essay • demonstrates a solid understanding of the relationship between the chosen event and the thematic concept • uses specific details to provide support and create a convincing text.	The essay • demonstrates a superficial understanding of the relationship between the event and the thematic concept • underutilizes details, and those included do little to create a convincing text.	The essay • demonstrates no obvious understanding of the relationship between the event and the thematic concept • uses very few details or language to create an engaging or convincing text.
Structure	The essay • shows a perceptive understanding of the relationships among event, response, and reflection • uses transitions to enhance overall coherence and to connect ideas smoothly.	The essay • uses a form or structure that is appropriate to the purpose • uses transitional words, phrases, and clauses to link events and signal shifts between ideas.	The essay • uses a form or structure that shows little understanding of the relationships among event, response, and reflection • may contain minimal use of transitions.	The essay • uses a confusing form or structure that shows a lack of understanding of the relationships among event, response, and reflection • moves between ideas without use of transitions.
Use of Language	The essay • uses diction, syntax, and stylistic devices that are notable and appropriate for the subject, purpose, and audience • demonstrates strong command of the conventions of standard English capitalization, punctuation, spelling, grammar, and usage with few or no errors.	The essay • uses diction, syntax, and other stylistic devices that are appropriate for the subject, purpose, and audience • demonstrates adequate command of standard writing conventions; may contain minor errors that do not interfere with meaning.	The essay • uses vague diction, confusing syntax, and other stylistic devices less effectively for the subject, purpose, and audience • contains errors in standard writing conventions that interfere with meaning.	The essay • uses inappropriate diction, confusing syntax, and other stylistic devices that do not support the subject, purpose, and audience • contains multiple serious errors in standard writing conventions that interfere with meaning.

VISUAL PROMPT
How are people transformed through their relationships with others? Do people have a say in how they are perceived by others?

THE COLLECTIVE PERSPECTIVE

You see, really and truly, apart from the things anyone can pick up (the dressing and the proper way of speaking, and so on), the difference between a lady and a flower girl is not how she behaves, but how she's treated.

–from *Pygmalion*, by George Bernard Shaw

GOALS

- To understand and apply Archetypal, Marxist, and Feminist critical perspectives to drama, nonfiction, and narrative texts
- To use critical theories to analyze ideas in other texts and society at large
- To write an engaging script and an insightful analytical response using genre characteristics and craft
- To write a literary analysis that uses original commentary to support an evaluative response
- To engage in meaningful and respectful discussion with peers, asking questions and acknowledging the validity of other points of view

VOCABULARY

ACADEMIC
enfranchisement
faux pas
genre conventions
patriarchal
subtext

LITERARY
Archetypal Criticism
archetype
artistic license
Feminist Criticism
Marxist Criticism
mise en scène
motifs
myth
narrative arc
satire
subplot

ACTIVITY	CONTENTS	

Texts not included in these materials.

My Independent Reading List

Learning Strategies

Discussion Groups
Graphic Organizer
Marking the Text
Summarizing
Think-Pair-Share

My Notes

Learning Targets
- Preview the big ideas for the unit.
- Identify and analyze the skills and knowledge needed to complete Embedded Assessment 1 successfully.
- Create a plan for reading independently.

Preview
- In this activity, you will the explore the big ideas and tasks of the unit to come and make plans for your independent reading.

About the Unit

In this unit, you will focus on analyzing literary works through multiple critical perspectives. You will explore three theories: Archetypal Criticism, Marxist Criticism, and Feminist Criticism. The first half of the unit focuses on Archetypal Criticism and Marxist Criticism and the second half focuses on Feminist Criticism. Using these lenses, you will analyze the social and cultural implications of a variety of texts, including fiction and drama. As part of your study, you will write a script for a dramatic scene and a literary analysis of a short story, using a critical perspective.

Essential Questions

Based on your current knowledge, respond to the Essential Questions.

1. How do writers develop great characters?
2. How does a person's environment affect his or her identity?
3. How does power affect people's interactions and relationships?

Unpacking Embedded Assessment 1

Read the following assignment for Embedded Assessment 1.

Work with a partner to write a script that transforms a scene from *Pygmalion* so that it reflects one of the critical perspectives you have studied. You will also write a reflection analyzing and evaluating your process and product.

Summarize in your own words what you will need to know for this assessment. With your class, create a graphic organizer that represents the skills and knowledge you will need to complete the Embedded Assessment. To help you complete your graphic organizer, be sure to review the criteria in the Scoring Guide.

Planning Independent Reading

In this unit, you will read a play that has been adapted into a film. Collaborate with your peers to compile a list of texts that have also been made into film. For your independent reading, discuss how you might compare the original text and the film. Which narrative elements will you compare? Consider dialogue, exposition, and the interpretations of the characters. Consider the elements available to the filmmaker but not the author, such as music and special effects. How do these elements change the telling of the story?

A Closer Look: Archetypal Criticism

Learning Targets

- Collaborate with peers to understand and apply the definition of archetype.
- Analyze a series of photographs to draw conclusions about common archetypes and their universal meaning.

Preview

In this activity, you will learn about archetypes and collaboratively write definitions of common archetypes found in society. You then will identify recurring archetypes and motifs in photographs. Finally, you'll consider how archetypes shape perspective and give deeper meaning to texts.

How Is My Perspective Shaped?

Reading and viewing are not passive activities. You bring certain levels of engagement to your reading and viewing, just as you bring biases, experiences, and prior knowledge to any text you read.

Reading drama can be demanding because most often there is no narrative point of view to help the reader understand the action. To interpret meaning fully, readers and viewers have to pay attention to the usual literary elements, as well as dramatic elements such as stage directions, costume, and set design.

At the same time, you can layer on a critical perspective or lens through which to interpret and understand the larger ideas of the drama. In this way you can challenge and critique the ideas and opinions presented in the drama. Examining texts through multiple literary theories provides you the opportunity to sharpen your analytical skills as you consider alternative ways to view texts.

What Is an Archetype?

An archetype is a universal symbol, image, or character. Archetypal Criticism focuses on analyzing recurring archetypes found in the literature of widely diverse cultures. For example, most cultures have stories that present a hero's journey. Using Archetypal Criticism to analyze a text requires the reader or viewer to slow down and read closely. Using an archetypal critical lens, readers analyze and evaluate the following:

- recurring images that share a common interpretation across cultures, such as water, the sun, or fire, and settings such as a garden or a desert
- characters that recur across cultures, such as the hero, the trickster, the great mother, the sculptor, or the prodigal son
- motifs that recur across cultures, including creation stories, quests, journeys, initiations, and voyages to the underworld

Learning Strategies

Marking the Text
Note-taking
Quickwrite
Think-Pair-Share
Visual/Auditory Prompts

LITERARY

An archetype is a universal symbol that recurs in the myths, dreams, oral traditions, songs, literature, and other texts of peoples widely separated by time and place.

Motifs are words, characters, objects, images, or ideas that recur in a literary work or works. A motif is almost always related to the theme of a work of literature.

Archetypal Criticism deals with symbols and patterns that recur in the literature of widely diverse cultures.

VOCABULARY

WORD CONNECTIONS

Roots and Affixes
An archetype is an original pattern or prototype. It derives from the Greek word parts *arche*, meaning "first," and *type*, meaning "a mark."

Images as Archetypes

1. The use of archetypes in imagery can quickly convey a vast amount of information to an audience. Closely analyze the images to infer each photograph's meaning. Consider what you have learned about Archetypal Criticism and recurring images, symbols, and characters.

What universal symbols do you notice in this photo? What do these symbols mean to most viewers?

_____

_____

_____

What kinds of messages could be easily conveyed through this photo?

_____

_____

_____

What universal symbols do you notice in this photo? What do these symbols mean to most viewers?

_____

_____

_____

What kinds of messages could be easily conveyed through this photo?

_____

_____

_____

My Notes

What universal symbols do you notice in this photo? What do these symbols mean to most viewers?

What kinds of messages could be easily conveyed through this photo?

My Notes

What universal symbols do you notice in this photo? What do these symbols mean to most viewers?

What kinds of messages could be easily conveyed through this photo?

2. With your discussion group, share your observations of the four photographs. Be sure to use details from the photos to support your analysis.

On the Spot Research

3. Conduct research on the four archetypes your teacher has assigned to your group. Jot down key words relating to the archetypes in the notes column of the graphic organizer.

   Discuss your findings, and work collaboratively to add a list of examples of this archetype to your graphic organizer. Consider characters in movies and other works of fiction. Then use your notes and list of examples to write a definition of each archetype.

Notes	Examples	Definition

4. Share your definitions with the other groups in your class, so you have a complete list of 12 common archetypes.

5. Return to the photographs as you respond to the following questions. Use evidence from the photographs and apply your definitions to support your responses.

   - What archetype is presented in each photo?
   - How do the images diverge from or alter the archetype?
   - How do you think the creator of each image used knowledge of the archetype to make artistic choices?

☑ Check Your Understanding

Consider your initial analysis to each photograph. Were your inferences informed by universal symbols and archetypes? How does Archetypal Criticism provide you with a new understanding of each photograph that you have studied?

Introducing the Myth

Learning Targets

- Analyze and compare the key ideas and archetypes presented in two literary texts.
- Summarize the texts, concentrating on the most important elements.
- Examine how an author draws on and transforms ideas from other works.
- Integrate ideas from multiple texts to build knowledge and vocabulary about the concept of playing creator.

Preview

In this activity, you will analyze and compare two texts from different literary periods. You will read a myth and draw connections to the archetypes presented in the classic novel, *Frankenstein*. Then, you will summarize your new understanding of the texts in a written response.

As You Read

- Highlight words or phrases in the **myth** that reveal the main character's attributes.
- Circle unknown words and phrases. Try to determine the meaning of words by using context clues, word parts, or a dictionary.

About the Author

The Roman poet Ovid, born Publius Ovidius Naso (43 BC– AD 17) is best known for *Metamorphoses*, a collection of myths describing transformation. He was born into a well-to-do family in Sulmo, a small town near Rome, and was considered a great orator. Ovid worked for a time in a minor judicial post, honoring his father's wish for him to pursue a traditional career. He soon abandoned this life to pursue his interest in poetry full time. Ovid's early work centered on love, beauty, and amorous intrigue, reflecting the pleasure-seeking, sophisticated circles in which he moved. The humor, sympathy, and vividness of Ovid's writing, in particular *Metamorphoses*, influenced many writers and artists of Ovid's time period and beyond, including Geoffrey Chaucer, William Shakespeare, and George Bernard Shaw.

Learning Strategies

Drafting
Marking the Text
Note-taking
Paraphrasing
Summarizing
Visualizing

VOCABULARY

LITERARY
A **myth** is a traditional story, passed down from generation to generation, that explains beliefs, customs, or natural phenomena through the actions of gods or heroes. These stories often focus on supernatural beings or events.

My Notes

Myth

Orpheus Sings: Pygmalion and the Statue

by **Ovid**

from *Metamorphoses,* Book X

1 Pygmalion had seen them, spending their lives in wickedness, and, offended by the failings that nature gave the female heart, he lived as a bachelor, without a wife or partner for his bed. But, with wonderful skill, he carved a figure, brilliantly, out of snow-white ivory, no mortal woman, and fell in love with his own creation. The features are those of a real girl, who, you might think, lived, and wished to move, if modesty did not forbid it. Indeed, art hides his art. He marvels: and passion, for this bodily image, consumes his heart. Often, he runs his hands over the work, tempted as to whether it is flesh or ivory, not admitting it to be ivory. He kisses it and thinks his kisses are returned; and speaks to it; and holds it, and imagines that his fingers press into the limbs, and is afraid lest bruises appear from the pressure. Now he addresses it with compliments, now brings it gifts that please girls, shells and polished pebbles, little birds, and many-coloured flowers, lilies and tinted beads, and the Heliades'[1] amber tears, that drip from the trees. He dresses the body, also, in clothing; places rings on the fingers; places a long necklace round its neck; pearls hang from the ears, and cinctures[2] round the breasts. All are fitting: but it appears no less lovely, naked. He arranges the statue on a bed on which cloths dyed with Tyrian murex[3] are spread, and calls it his bedfellow, and rests its neck against soft down, as if it could feel.

2 The day of Venus's festival[4] came, celebrated throughout Cyprus, and heifers, their curved horns gilded, fell, to the blow on their snowy neck. The incense was smoking, when Pygmalion, having made his offering, stood by the altar, and said, shyly: "If you can grant all things, you gods, I wish as a bride to have …" and not daring to say "the girl of ivory" he said "one like my ivory girl." Golden Venus, for she herself was present at the festival, knew what the prayer meant, and as a sign of the gods' fondness for him, the flame flared three times, and shook its crown in the air. When he returned, he sought out the image of his girl, and leaning over the couch, kissed her. She felt warm: he pressed his lips to her again, and also touched her breast with his hand. The ivory yielded to his touch, and lost its hardness, altering under his fingers, as the bees' wax

Pygmalion working on Galatea, a beautiful statue of a woman, made out of ivory.

---

[1] The *Heliades* were daughters of Helios and turned into poplar trees.
[2] A *cincture* is a belt or sash.
[3] *Tyrian murex* is an expensive purple dye made often reserved for royalty.
[4] In Roman times, *Venus's festival* celebrated the goddess of love and desire.

of Hymettus[5] softens in the sun, and is molded, under the thumb, into many forms, made usable by use. The lover is **stupefied**, and joyful, but uncertain, and afraid he is wrong, reaffirms the fulfillment of his wishes, with his hand, again, and again.

3   It was flesh! The pulse throbbed under his thumb. Then the hero, of Paphos,[6] was indeed overfull of words with which to thank Venus, and still pressed his mouth against a mouth that was not merely a likeness. The girl felt the kisses he gave, blushed, and, raising her bashful eyes to the light, saw both her lover and the sky. The goddess attended the marriage that she had brought about, and when the moon's horns had nine times met at the full, the woman bore a son, Paphos, from whom the island takes its name.

⊘ Knowledge Quest

- What are your initial thoughts about Pygmalion's relationship with the statue?
- What emotions does Pygmalion convey toward Galatea in the image and the text?
- What do you notice in this myth that someone skimming over it might miss?

About the Author

Mary Shelley (1797–1851) is most known for her famous and enduring novel *Frankenstein, or The Modern Prometheus*. Mary Shelley met the well-known Romantic poet Percy Shelley when she was 16, and they married a year later. In the summer of 1816, Mary and Percy, along with friends, including the poet Lord Byron, gathered at the Villa Diodati on the shores of Lake Geneva in Switzerland. The weather was rainy and unpleasant, so they amused themselves by inventing ghost stories, providing the genesis for *Frankenstein*. Shelley published *Frankenstein* when she was 21 years old. Her novel is often considered the world's first science fiction novel and has become the inspiration for many 20th-century films.

WORD CONNECTIONS

Roots and Affixes
To be **stupefied** is to be shocked or stunned in amazement. The word derives from the Latin *stupere*, "to be stunned," and *facere*, "to make." Other related words are *stupefaction*, *stupid*, and *stupendous*.

My Notes

_____

_____

_____

_____

_____

_____

_____

_____

_____

_____

_____

_____

_____

_____

_____

_____

_____

_____

_____

_____

_____

stupefied: stunned

[5] *Hymettus* was a famous source of honey near Athens, Greece.
[6] *Paphos* is the mythical birthplace of Aphrodite.

KNOWLEDGE QUEST

Knowledge Question:
Why do people believe the price of playing creator outweighs the gains?

My Notes

WORD CONNECTIONS

Roots and Affixes

Traverse comes from a combination of the Latin words *trans*, meaning "across," and *versus*, meaning "turned." It shares a common root with the word *travel* and means "to move across or back and forth."

ardour: passion
traversing: moving across
lassitude: tiredness
livid: bluish gray

Novel Excerpt

from *Frankenstein, or the Modern Prometheus*

by **Mary Shelley**

excerpt from Chapter 5

1   It was on a dreary night of November that I beheld the accomplishment of my toils. With an anxiety that almost amounted to agony, I collected the instruments of life around me, that I might infuse a spark of being into the lifeless thing that lay at my feet. It was already one in the morning; the rain pattered dismally against the panes, and my candle was nearly burnt out, when, by the glimmer of the half-extinguished light, I saw the dull yellow eye of the creature open; it breathed hard, and a convulsive motion agitated its limbs.

2   How can I describe my emotions at this catastrophe, or how delineate the wretch whom with such infinite pains and care I had endeavoured to form? His limbs were in proportion, and I had selected his features as beautiful. Beautiful! Great God! His yellow skin scarcely covered the work of muscles and arteries beneath; his hair was of a lustrous black, and flowing; his teeth of a pearly whiteness; but these luxuriances only formed a more horrid contrast with his watery eyes, that seemed almost of the same colour as the dun-white sockets in which they were set, his shrivelled complexion and straight black lips.

3   The different accidents of life are not so changeable as the feelings of human nature. I had worked hard for nearly two years, for the sole purpose of infusing life into an inanimate body. For this I had deprived myself of rest and health. I had desired it with an **ardour** that far exceeded moderation; but now that I had finished, the beauty of the dream vanished, and breathless horror and disgust filled my heart. Unable to endure the aspect of the being I had created, I rushed out of the room and continued a long time **traversing** my bedchamber, unable to compose my mind to sleep. At length **lassitude** succeeded to the tumult I had before endured, and I threw myself on the bed in my clothes, endeavouring to seek a few moments of forgetfulness. But it was in vain; I slept, indeed, but I was disturbed by the wildest dreams. I thought I saw Elizabeth, in the bloom of health, walking in the streets of Ingolstadt. Delighted and surprised, I embraced her, but as I imprinted the first kiss on her lips, they became **livid** with the hue of death; her features appeared to change, and I thought that I held the corpse of my dead mother in my arms; a shroud enveloped her form, and I saw the grave-worms crawling in the folds of the flannel. I started from my sleep with horror; a cold dew covered my forehead, my teeth chattered, and every limb became convulsed; when, by the dim and

yellow light of the moon, as it forced its way through the window shutters, I beheld the wretch—the miserable monster whom I had created. He held up the curtain of the bed; and his eyes, if eyes they may be called, were fixed on me. His jaws opened, and he muttered some inarticulate sounds, while a grin wrinkled his cheeks. He might have spoken, but I did not hear; one hand was stretched out, seemingly to detain me, but I escaped and rushed downstairs. I took refuge in the courtyard belonging to the house which I inhabited, where I remained during the rest of the night, walking up and down in the greatest agitation, listening attentively, catching and fearing each sound as if it were to announce the approach of the demoniacal corpse to which I had so miserably given life.

4 Oh! No mortal could support the horror of that countenance. A mummy again **endued** with animation could not be so hideous as that wretch. I had gazed on him while unfinished; he was ugly then, but when those muscles and joints were rendered capable of motion, it became a thing such as even Dante[7] could not have conceived.

5 I passed the night wretchedly. Sometimes my pulse beat so quickly and hardly that I felt the palpitation of every artery; at others, I nearly sank to the ground through **languor** and extreme weakness. Mingled with this horror, I felt the bitterness of disappointment; dreams that had been my food and pleasant rest for so long a space were now become a hell to me; and the change was so rapid, the overthrow so complete!

⊘ Knowledge Quest

- What words of the narrator jump out at you?
- What details do you notice about the narrator playing creator?

---

[7] *Dante Alighieri* (1265–1321) was an Italian poet whose epic poem *The Divine Comedy* is considered the greatest poem of the Middle Ages and one of the greatest works of world literature in history. Dante's poem depicts the Christian conception of the afterlife and is especially known for its colorful and vivid depiction of hell.

endued: given or provided
languor: fatigue

Victor Frankenstein's scientific experiment produces life—but not in the way he had envisioned.

Returning to the Text

- Reread the myth and novel excerpt to answer these text-dependent questions.
- Write any additional questions you have about the text in your Reader/Writer Notebook.

Metamorphoses, Book X

1. In the first sentence, Ovid writes, "Pygmalion had seen them, spending their lives in wickedness ..." Whom is Ovid writing about when he uses the pronoun "them"? Use text evidence in your answer.

_____

_____

_____

_____

2. **KQ** Reread the description of Pygmalion's statue in lines 4–7. What is the dual meaning of "art hides his art"?

_____

_____

_____

_____

3. Describe Pygmalion at the beginning of the story. How has he changed or not changed by the end of the story?

_____

_____

_____

_____

4. **KQ** How does the main character's vanity as the creator drive the events of the plot?

_____

_____

_____

_____

Frankenstein, or the Modern Prometheus

5. What task is the narrator trying to complete in the first paragraph? What is his reaction once he achieves his goal?

_____

_____

_____

_____

6. What comparisons is the author making in paragraph 4? What purpose does it serve?

_____

_____

_____

_____

7. What is the significance of the narrator's dream? What "message" is the dream sending him?

_____

_____

_____

_____

8. KQ Which words or phrases in paragraph 3 show that the narrator is afraid of the moral and ethical consequences of his experiment? Cite the text and explain your answer.

_____

_____

_____

_____

9. KQ What connections might Shelley and Ovid be making to the concept of playing God?

_____

_____

_____

_____

Working from the Text

10. The myth of Pygmalion and the story of *Frankenstein* give us the opportunity to compare tales in which characters who represent similar archetypes experience drastically different outcomes for their behavior. Work with a partner to answer the questions. Refer to your notes on archetypes and the two texts as needed.

- What are the character's goals?
- What is the outcome of the story?
- Are both characters based on the same archetype? Why or why not?
- What are the character's positive qualities?
- What are the character's tragic flaws?

11. Use the graphic organizer to compare the characters of Victor Frankenstein and Pygmalion.

Character	Goal	Outcome of "experiment"	Positive personality traits	Tragic flaw	Possible archetypes
Pygmalion					
Victor Frankenstein (narrator)					

My Notes

_____

_____

_____

_____

_____

_____

_____

_____

_____

_____

_____

_____

_____

_____

_____

_____

_____

_____

_____

_____

_____

_____

_____

_____

_____

_____

_____

_____

_____

_____

_____

_____

_____

_____

_____

_____

_____

LANGUAGE & WRITER'S CRAFT: Summarizing

Good writers know how to express themselves concisely. When writing a summary of a literary or informational text, the goal is to condense the main idea and details into a concise paragraph or paragraphs. Use these guidelines for writing an effective summary:

- Begin the summary with a statement of the main idea.
- Include only the most significant details about the setting, characters, and events presented in the story.
- Keep the details in a logical order.
- Write in complete but concise sentences.
- Make no interpretive or analytical statements, and objectively report the main plot points.
- Paraphrase using your own words.

PRACTICE Using these guidelines, summarize Ovid's myth "Pygmalion and the Statue" in a single paragraph.

⊘ Knowledge Quest

Think about the two texts. Which was greater: the price of playing creator or the gains? Write an argumentative text answering this question. Be sure to:

- Cite evidence from both texts to support your argument.
- Use reasoning to develop your ideas and connect your claim to your evidence.
- Use precise language and topic-specific vocabulary.

INDEPENDENT READING LINK

You can continue to build your knowledge about the concept of playing creator by reading related fiction at ZINC Reading Labs.

Select the **fiction** filters and type *playing God* in the **Search all ZINC articles** field.

 ZINC

☑ Check Your Understanding

Many stories from different world cultures feature elements of Ovid's myth. Why do you think this myth exists in different cultures? How and why do you think authors draw inspiration from archetypes and modify them to tell new stories? Write a short paragraph explaining your ideas.

Learning Strategies

Brainstorming
Discussion Groups
Note-taking
Visual/Auditory Prompts

My Notes

© 2021 College Board. All rights reserved.

VOCABULARY

LITERARY

Mise en scène is a French expression used to describe a film or theater production's composition and setting. This includes everything presented to the viewer, such as the costumes, makeup, props, lighting, background scenery, and the actors' positioning, facial expressions, and behavior.

Learning Targets

- Analyze the composition and use of archetypes in a visual medium.
- Collaboratively make inferences about a story's plot and theme based on images.
- Analyze how setting, plot, and characterization work together to communicate a central theme.

Preview

In this activity, you will begin reading George Bernard Shaw's play, *Pygmalion*. Before reading, you will review the parts of a five-act play and make inferences about the play by closely analyzing film stills. Then you will read and reflect on Act I of the play, giving you an opportunity to confirm or correct your judgments and analyze the author's use of archetypes.

Reviewing the Five-Act Play

1. The structure pyramid depicts the traditional "dramatic arc" of a five-act play. This is often used to create an effective plot. In addition to drama, the pyramid is found in novels, short stories, films, television shows, and even individual scenes.

   With a partner, discuss how the major plot points of Ovid's myth can be broken into a five-act structure.

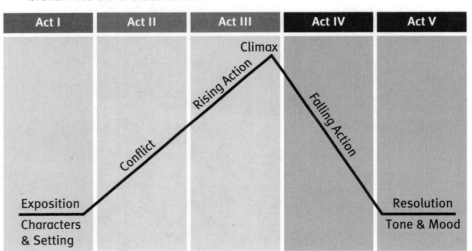

Making Inferences

2. Analyze the film stills from *My Fair Lady,* directed by George Cukor, and complete the descriptions of each image.

   - Describe the mise en scène (scene composition) of the photo. Consider where the characters are in relation to one another and within the setting.
   - Describe the subjects—the characters. Consider costume, facial expression, and body language. For example, look at the first photo. What additional context can you draw from the title, *My Fair Lady*? What time period do you think this film takes place in?

a.

Description of *Mise en Scène:*

_____

_____

_____

Description of Character:

_____

_____

_____

b.

Description of *Mise en Scène:*

_____

_____

_____

Description of Character:

_____

_____

_____

c.

Description of *Mise en Scène*:

_____

_____

_____

Description of Character:

_____

_____

_____

d.

Description of *Mise en Scène:*

_____

_____

_____

Description of Character:

_____

_____

_____

My Notes

3. Based on your observations of the photos, make inferences about elements of the play:

- Where might the play take place?
- What kind of characters might be in the play?
- What do you think is the relationship between the various characters?
- What do you think the play is about?

4. Ovid gives us a written version of the myth, which derives from the oral tradition of the early Greeks and Romans. Revisit the myth to look for archetypal characters: the creative person, the object of his affection, and the being who grants his wish. How are these characters represented in the images you viewed?

5. **Discussion Groups:** Share your preliminary ideas and discuss connections or differences between your inferences and the inferences of your peers. Based on the photos, what do you think the plot structure will be? Make sure to express your ideas clearly and build on others' ideas in a focused response.

Reading *Pygmalion*

As you read Act I, identify the characters, define the conflicts, and apply the archetypal perspective to gain understanding of the characters' relationships.

- Use sticky notes to identify textual evidence that will help you answer this question: Which archetypal characters do you recognize?
- Circle unknown words or phrases. Try to determine the meaning of the words by using context clues, word parts, or a dictionary.

GRAMMAR & USAGE

Idioms

An **idiom** is an expression that means something different from the literal meaning of the words. An idiom such as "throw one's hat into the ring" does not refer literally to throwing a hat into a ring; it can mean announcing you plan to enter a contest. With this and other idioms, context can help you understand the phrase. Many idioms are used only in informal English.

Notice how in Act I, line 11, Freddy states, "there's not one [cab] to be had for love or money." The idiom "for love or money" is always used in negative statements to indicate something that cannot be accomplished for anything. In this case, Freddy uses it to express how impossible it is to find a cab.

Try to find two more examples of idioms in *Pygmalion* and explain their meaning to a partner.

About the Author

George Bernard Shaw (1856–1950) was an Irish playwright and a cofounder of the London School of Economics. He was a prolific journalist, essayist, novelist, short story writer, and dramatist. He wrote more than 60 plays. Shaw often used wit and satire in writings about significant social issues such as education, marriage, religion, government, and class differences. He is the only person to have been awarded both a Nobel Prize in Literature (1925) and an Oscar (1938, for his work on the film *Pygmalion*).

Reflecting on Act I

6. Read the following lines from Act I, and then answer the following questions:

> THE NOTE-TAKER: You see this creature with her kerbstone English: the English that will keep her in the gutter to the end of her days. Well, sir, in three months I could pass that girl off as a duchess at an ambassador's garden party.

- What is the significance of language? Why does the note-taker believe that the flower girl's dialect hinders her ability to transform her station in life?
- Consider contemporary, real-life parallels to this idea. Can you think of a situation where people are judged by their accents, dialect, or style of speaking?

7. Revisit the film stills and compare the director's interpretation in *My Fair Lady* with *Pygmalion* after reading Act I. If you had been the director, what would you have done differently? Why?

Check Your Understanding

Now that you've read Act I, confirm or correct your ideas about the play's setting, characters, and major plot points. Use your revised notes to write a brief statement explaining the archetypes presented and the developing theme in Act I.

 INDEPENDENT READING LINK

Read and Research

Using your understanding of Archetypal Criticism, analyze the characters presented in the text you are reading. Which archetypes or universal symbols do you notice in your independent reading? How does identifying archetypes deepen your understanding of the text? Write a brief response in your Reader/Writer Notebook.

Ladies and Gentlemen

Learning Strategies

Discussion Groups
Graphic Organizer
Think-Pair-Share

Learning Targets

- Analyze the interactions between setting, dialogue, point of view and characterization.
- Evaluate and discuss how characters' motivations act as a driving force in advancing the plot.
- Write a comparative analysis of characters from two different texts

Preview

In this activity, you will read Act II of *Pygmalion*. As you reflect on this act, you will collect text evidence to inform your analysis of each character, and then you will discuss the traits of the various characters and what motivates them. Finally, you will complete a written response drawing connections between Shaw's *Pygmalion* and Ovid's *Metamorphoses*.

Reading *Pygmalion*: Act II

As you read Act II, identify each character's significant attributes. Jot down notes on how the playwright develops the characters in the play.

- Use sticky notes to identify elements of characterization: dialogue, dramatic action, or point of view.
- Circle unknown words or phrases. Try to determine the meaning of the words by using context clues, word parts, or a dictionary.

1. Based on your reading, list three to five adjectives that describe each of the characters and select evidence from the text to support your ideas.

Character	Characteristics	Textual Evidence
Eliza		
Higgins		
Pickering		
Mrs. Pearce		
Mr. Doolittle		

☑ Focus on the Sentence

Using what you know about the characters, turn the following fragments into complete sentences. Use correct punctuation and capitalization.

higgins treats

_____

_____

disagrees with

_____

_____

eliza's appearance

_____

_____

doolittle reveals

_____

_____

Reflecting on Act II

2. In your discussion groups, discuss your preliminary responses to the questions in preparation for a collegial discussion. Come to the discussion group prepared with relevant, insightful questions and well-reasoned ideas. Be sure to use evidence from the text to support your analysis and remain open to interpretations offered by your peers.

- How is Eliza made to conform at Professor Higgins's home?
- What will Eliza need to change about herself to be considered a "lady"?
- How does the setting of Victorian England influence the plot and character development?
- Does social class play a significant role in characterization? Explain.

☑ Check Your Understanding

Based on what you have read so far, what appears to motivate each of the characters?

My Notes

LANGUAGE & WRITER'S CRAFT: Organizing Information

When organizing a text that compares two literary works, an important step is identifying the points of comparison and creating a thesis statement to focus your writing. Then, for each point, cite textual evidence and explain the significance of the evidence. As you develop your ideas, use appropriate and varied transitions to link the major sections of the text.

Study this model text, which compares Ovid's character, Pygmalion, to Shaw's Professor Higgins. With your discussion groups, analyze the organizational structure.

- What is the thesis statement?
- What are the points of comparison?
- How does the writer use transitions to provide smooth links between these points?

Model Text

In Shaw's *Pygmalion*, Professor Higgins exhibits drive and passion for creating beauty just as Ovid's Pygmalion does. Both characters have rejected women. Professor Higgins proudly boasts in Act II that he is "a confirmed old bachelor," while Pygmalion, "offended by the failings that nature gave the female heart," lives as a bachelor. However, each takes on the task of shaping or transfiguring a woman. Higgins tells Colonel Pickering that the chore of transforming Eliza is "almost irresistible. She's so deliciously low—so horribly dirty." Like Higgins, Pygmalion desires to carve a beautiful figure that he can manipulate and beautify. In their actions, the two characters demonstrate their desires for control and manipulation. In addition, both characters dress and beautify their "works." Higgins tells Mrs. Pearce to take Eliza's clothes and burn them and to buy her new ones appropriate for her new station. Similarly, Pygmalion "dresses the body, also, in clothing; places rings on the fingers; places a long necklace round its neck." Both characters manipulate and control the women, perhaps to enhance their own feelings of power.

PRACTICE Find one other point of comparison the writer could have used in the model text. Write a sentence or two explaining the comparison, with text evidence, and mark the model text to show where you would add this information so it is logically organized.

Writing Prompt: Informational

Compare the character of Eliza with the statue in the original Pygmalion myth. How is each described by the author? What relationships do they have to the other main characters in the stories? In what ways are they acted upon, and in what ways are they the source of action? Be sure to:

- Begin with a concise comparative thesis statement.
- Develop the topic using direct quotations and specific examples to support your analysis.
- Use a coherent structure to organize information with appropriate transitions that highlight similarities and differences.
- Use precise vocabulary to convey your ideas in a clear and interesting way.
- Provide an engaging conclusion that summarizes your comparisons while examining their implications and significance.
- Maintain an engaging, formal, and objective tone, while using the standard English conventions of mechanics and usage.

INDEPENDENT READING LINK

Read and Recommend

Write a brief review and recommendation of your independent reading text based on what you have read so far. In your review, summarize what the text is about, explain how the author expresses ideas using archetypes, and provide commentary about why you would or would not recommend the text to your peers.

Learning Strategies

Discussion Groups
Marking the Text
Note-taking
Sharing and Responding
Skimming/Scanning
Think-Pair-Share

VOCABULARY

ACADEMIC
A **faux pas** is an embarrassing act or remark in a social situation.

WORD CONNECTIONS

Etymology
The term **faux pas** is an example of a "loan" phrase—one borrowed from another language that becomes, over time, adopted into common use. The literal translation of *faux pas* from French is "false step," but it has been used in English since the 17th century.

My Notes

Learning Targets

- Analyze how an author creates a satirical effect.
- Evaluate and discuss the significance of language, including diction and syntax, as a means of conveying tone and theme.
- Analyze the genre conventions and structure of a script and apply them by writing a scene.

Preview

In this activity, you will read Act III of *Pygmalion* and analyze how the author uses literary elements like tone to advance the plot and create a comedic effect. Then, you'll write a short script for a scene using characteristics of the genre.

Reading *Pygmalion*: Act III

In Act III, Eliza faces a challenge. The character undergoing a transformation must often face a test early in the training process and usually commits a significant mistake.

- Mark the text for evidence that helps you answer this question: What **faux pas** does Eliza commit, and how does this experience contribute to the plot and her development as a character?
- Circle unknown words or phrases. Try to determine the meaning of the words by using context clues, word parts, or a dictionary.

☑ Focus on the Sentence

Use information from the play to complete the sentences. Consult a dictionary to learn more about the term *faux pas*, if needed.

Eliza commits a faux pas because _____

_____

Eliza commits a faux pas, but _____

_____

Eliza commits a faux pas, so _____

_____

1. **Quickwrite:** Have you come across archetypal characters that undergo a transformation in any of the texts or films that you've encountered outside of class? Did the character commit a humorous faux pas? Compare their experience to Eliza's.

© 2021 College Board. All rights reserved.

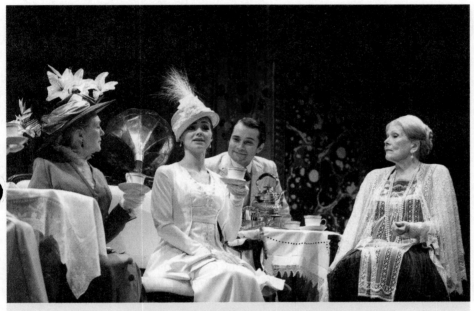

Pygmalion performance at the Garrick Theatre in London, 2011

Reflecting on Author's Craft in Act III

2. Shaw uses **satire** in his work to expose humanity's vices and shortcomings in a comedic way. Review a few writing techniques often found in satirical texts:

- **Exaggeration / Caricature:** to distort an individual's prominent characteristics to the point of making that individual appear ridiculous.
- **Parody:** to imitate a work with the intent of ridiculing the author, ideas, or work.
- **Irony:** to use words or events to convey a reality opposite to appearance or expectation. The recognition by the audience often produces a comic effect.

> **My Notes**

> **LITERARY**
> **Satire** describes a manner of writing that mocks social conventions, actions, or attitudes with wit and humor.

VOCABULARY

3. Skim Act III to identify the satirical techniques that Shaw employs. Notice his use of syntax and diction and the effects of these choices.

Satirical Technique	Text Evidence

4. Discuss with your group the specific character trait or flaw Shaw is satirizing in the scene. In your discussion, evaluate and answer the following:

   • What message is Shaw sending to the audience through his use of satire?
   • How does the social setting of Victorian England influence the plot?
   • How is Shaw making a statement about society through his use of satire?

☑ **Check Your Understanding**

Write a brief response explaining how Shaw uses satire throughout his play. What techniques does he primarily use and why might an audience find this funny?

Writing a Play Script

5. Writing a script for a play involves using certain conventions and dramatic elements, in order to give an audience context for the story that is taking place. Consider the following genre conventions of writing a play script.

   • **Title:** The name of the play
   • **List of Characters:** The people in the play; may include a brief description of each
   • **Setting:** Where and when the scene takes place; usually included at the beginning of each scene
   • **Dialogue:** The words spoken on stage, the primary vehicle through which the audience learns about the characters and conflicts. Writers use dialogue to advance the plot. Also, writers can add meaning or style through the language they choose.
   • **Conflict:** The problem that complicates the lives of the characters until the problem is resolved.
   • Narrative Arc: A clear and logical progression from one event or experience to the next.
   • **Stage Directions:** Language separate from dialogue that indicates the time and place of the action, entrances, exits, movement, and subtext. Stage directions also indicate what the characters are doing on stage as well as provide clues as to how actors should deliver their lines.

VOCABULARY

ACADEMIC

Genre conventions are the defining features of a specific type of writing, such as short story, poetry, or script.

LITERARY

The narrative arc is the story line of a text, which includes a beginning (the exposition), a middle (the rising action), a climax (the highest point of tension), and an end (the falling action and resolution). As part of the narrative arc, characters grow, change, and face conflicts.

☑ Check Your Understanding

Return to the beginning of *Pygmalion*, Act I. Annotate the text to identify the details from Act I that illustrate each of the conventions described here, and label the text accordingly.

✍ Writing Prompt: Literary

Think about a faux pas you have committed or can imagine someone committing. Write a one-scene script with at least two characters that satirizes the situation. Consider how you will incorporate the use of satire and archetypes. Be sure to:

- Include the conventions of a play script: setting, dialogue, conflict, narrative arc, and stage directions.
- Incorporate humor through word choice and diction.
- Incorporate one or more of the four elements of satire—exaggeration, incongruity, reversal, and parody.

Learning Strategies

Close Reading
Graphic Organizer
Note-taking
Oral Reading
Skimming / Scanning
Think-Aloud

VOCABULARY

ACADEMIC

Subtext is the unspoken meaning or context that can be inferred from what is directly stated. Written and spoken texts in many domains may include subtext. For example, a political speech may carry meaning in what is not stated as well as in what is stated. When studying drama, readers look for this implied meaning in order to understand a play on a deeper level.

Learning Targets

- Infer the subtext of dramatic dialogue by analyzing the impact of a speaker's delivery of lines.
- Analyze and annotate text to indicate how to present an oral reading of dialogue.
- Revise an original script to improve its impact on the audience.

Preview

In this activity, you discover how the delivery of lines can bring additional layers of meaning to a text. You will perform a dialogue using voice, tone, gestures, and other dramatic elements to bring different meanings and emotions to the text. With a group, you will analyze and discuss possible hidden meanings and different interpretations of a scene from *Pygmalion*. Finally, you will revise your script from the previous activity to include subtext.

Creating Subtext

1. This chart contains a dialogue between two characters, A and B. With your classmates, you will perform the dialogue with different scenarios in mind. During your performance, use your voice, facial expressions, and body language to give the dialogue a specific meaning. As you watch the other groups, try to identify the subtext.

   - What can you infer from the way a line is spoken?
   - Record notes about the way the tone of voice, pacing, body language and word emphasis provide clues.

My Notes

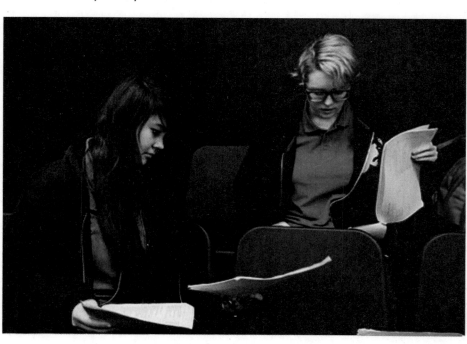

Text	Performance 1 (What clues help you figure out the subtext?)	Performance 2 (What clues help you figure out the subtext?)
A. Well, here it is.		
B. Is that what I think it is?		
A. I think so.		
B. Are you sure?		
A. See for yourself, if you don't believe me.		
B. Okay, what now?		

Analyzing Dialogue

Skim Acts II and III paying close attention to dialogue that implies meaning underlying the text. For example, consider the lines from Act I:

> THE DAUGHTER. If Freddy had a bit of gumption, he would have got one at the theatre door.

> THE MOTHER. What could he have done, poor boy?

INDEPENDENT READING LINK

Read and Respond

Infer the subtext in a scene from your independent reading text. What lines in the dialogue give clues to the subtext? Does the author provide stage directions or other commentary to clarify the subtext? Record your analysis in your Reader/ Writer Notebook.

Notice the absence of stage directions for these lines. When a playwright decides not to include stage directions, it is sometimes to emphasize the characters' words.

- Consider the effects of adding stage directions. How do the stage directions effect your understanding of these lines?

> THE DAUGHTER. *[snarling and growling]* If Freddy had a bit of gumption, he would have got one at the theatre door.

Snarling and growling adds the element of anger in the daughter's voice. She is obviously mad at Freddie.

- Now consider the line with this stage direction, which adds not only vocal but physical emphasis:

> THE DAUGHTER. *[speaking rapidly and eagerly; jumping up and down]* If Freddy had a bit of gumption, he would have got one at the theatre door.

Rapidly and eagerly and *jumping up and down* imply that the girl is agitated. How the mother responds might be to calm the daughter, and this would show in the mother's tone of voice.

- Read the next line aloud three times. The first time, emphasize the word *what*. Next, emphasize *could*. Then, emphasize *done*, and note how these three different ways of speaking influence your impression of how the mother is responding to the daughter.

> THE MOTHER. What could he have done, poor boy?

2. With your discussion group, consider these questions:
   - How does the addition of stage directions affect the delivery of lines?
   - Why do playwrights sometimes omit these directions, and why do they sometimes include them?
   - Choose a line or two of dialogue from the play that does contain stage directions. Why do you think stage directions were given here by the playwright?
   - What is the subtext created by each of the three readings of "What could he have done, poor boy?" Return to Act I, Scene 1. Reread this scene and think about what subtexts Shaw might have had in mind.

☑ Check Your Understanding

Return to the one-scene script about a faux pas that you wrote in the previous activity. Working with a partner, revise your script to show how you would direct actors to deliver the lines to convey the subtext.

Examining Eliza's Options

Learning Targets

- Analyze character development within a play to write an original script using genre characteristics and craft.
- Use logical arguments and text evidence to make a compelling argument, while acknowledging counterclaims.

Preview

In this activity, you will reflect on the character development in Act III of *Pygmalion*. You will collaboratively write and perform an original script based on what you have learned about the characters. Then you will read Act IV of the play and engage in a class debate.

Learning Strategies

Debating
Graphic Organizer
Sharing and Responding
Summarizing/Paraphrasing
Think-Pair-Share

My Notes

Reflecting on Act III

1. With a small group, summarize how Eliza, Higgins, or Pickering has evolved along with the plot. Compare the character's behavior before and after the ball.

The Character: _____

How does the character typically behave and speak? Use adjectives and adverbs to describe these behaviors. Cite textual evidence.	How does the character feel now that the ball is over? Cite textual evidence from Act III to support your position.

2. Now that you have discussed and taken notes on one of the characters with your small group, you will work with another group to create a dialogue among all three characters. Remember that the subtext is often even more important than the words that are spoken, so include any subtext that seems appropriate by noting it in parentheses at the end of the corresponding line.

My Notes

Reading *Pygmalion*: Act IV

Before reading Act IV, compare the dialogues your class has created. For your comparisons, consider the following and record notes in the My Notes area.

- Based on textual evidence of events of characters from Acts I–III, which imagined scene is the most plausible?
- What qualities of plot and character make your selection most authentic?

3. As you read Act IV:

- Mark the text for evidence that either supports or does not support your imagined scene.
- Circle any unknown words and phrases. Try to determine the meaning of the words by using context clues, word parts, or a dictionary.

Reflecting on Act IV

4. After you have read Act IV, compare how the conversation Shaw created is similar to and different from the one you and your group created.

5. How are Eliza's choices limited by the setting in Victorian England? How does this affect her behavior? How do Eliza's and Higgins' social classes impact their actions?

6. In Act IV, Eliza asks, "Where am I to go? What am I to do? What's to become of me?" What are Eliza's options, given the setting of the play? Using a T-graphic organizer, brainstorm Eliza's options and the pros and cons of each option.

☑ Check Your Understanding

Now that you have read Act IV, you have a clear picture of Higgins's and Pickering's attitudes toward their "project." Think about what Eliza should do next and jot down your ideas in the My Notes area. Keep the following in mind as you brainstorm ideas:

- The setting: Victorian England
- Eliza's personality
- Eliza's social class

Class Debate

7. Prepare for a class debate with your group. You will take on the persona of one of the characters in the play (Higgins, Pickering, or Eliza) and present an argument stating what you (the character) believe Eliza's next steps should be. Prepare to explain your reasoning using text evidence. Address counterarguments. Speak clearly and expressively in presenting your position. Prepare a well-organized presentation so that your viewpoint is clear to your audience.

   - Introduce a clear arguable claim as to what Eliza's next steps should be.
   - Logically present your reasoning and evidence.
   - Support your position with relevant evidence from Acts I–IV.
   - Acknowledge counterclaims made by others as part of the discussion.
   - Conclude by reminding the audience of how you proved your argument.

8. **Quickwrite:** Reflect on what you initially thought Eliza's next steps should be. Did the class debate present evidence that affects your opinion of what Eliza should do?

Learning Strategies

Close Reading
Graphic Organizer
Self-editing/Peer Editing

VOCABULARY

LITERARY

A **subplot** is a secondary plot in a fictional text, such as a play, short story, or television show. Authors often use this technique to support the main plot by driving part of the conflict, adding tension, or providing information or insight about the characters.

INDEPENDENT READING LINK

Read and Connect

Analyze how one or more characters change in your independent reading. How has the character evolved or transformed over time? What contributed to the change? How does the transformation affect the character's point of view and relationships with other characters? Create a two-column graphic organizer in your Reader/Writer Notebook to describe the changes that take place in characters.

Learning Targets

- Analyze how an author develops dynamic characters.
- Write an original script that reflects your working knowledge of critical theory and genre characteristics.
- Use the writing process to improve the clarity and organization of your writing.

Preview

In this activity, you will analyze how the main characters of a play undergo a transformation. You will discuss the parallels and differences between characters in order to anticipate the resolution of the play. Based on your new understanding, you will write an alternate ending for *Pygmalion*.

Reading *Pygmalion*: Act V

1. To begin your study of character transformations between Acts I and V, focus on two characters. For these two major characters—Eliza and Alfred Doolittle—create a two-column graphic organizer to list their characteristics in Act I. Try to include at least five adjectives to describe each character.

2. As you read Act V:
   - Draw a star any place you notice a transformation in Eliza or Alfred Doolittle.
   - Circle any unknown words and phrases. Try to determine the meaning of the words by using context clues, word parts, or a dictionary.

Reflecting on Act V

3. In Act V, Eliza's father, Alfred Doolittle resurfaces. Like Eliza, Doolittle has been transformed. Use a Venn diagram or other graphic organizer to compare these two transformations. You should consider these points, as well as any others that occur to you:
   - What, specifically, about each character has changed? Refer to the adjectives that you listed in Step 1. What comparisons to these adjectives can you identify? How did the transformation occur?
   - How might the transformation affect each character's future?
   - What is each character's attitude toward the transformation?
   - What role does social class play in each of their transformations?

4. Now that you have read Act V, discuss your Venn diagram with a partner.
   - How is Alfred Doolittle's transformation a **subplot** in *Pygmalion*?
   - How are the characters' transformations similar, and how do they differ?

5. Answer the questions after closely rereading the end of *Pygmalion* (beginning when Pickering and Doolittle exit for the wedding, leaving Higgins and Eliza alone).

	Henry	Eliza
Primary motivation at beginning of play/behavior:		
Primary motivation at end of play:		
Conflict:		

6. The play ends with Higgins laughing at the thought of Eliza marrying Freddy. Based on Shaw's portrayal of these characters, what do you imagine becomes of Eliza and of Higgins?

_____

_____

7. Review Reader Response Critical Theory, Cultural Criticism, and Archetypal Criticism. Select one of these critical perspectives and write three questions that will help you understand *Pygmalion*. You may use the questions here as models to craft your own questions:

- Reader Response: As a reader, what attitudes am I bringing to understanding this text?
- Cultural Criticism: What is Shaw saying about the differences in social customs and expectations in this play?
- Archetypal Criticism: Why does Higgins take on the role of the creator or transformer? What's in it for him?

☑ Check Your Understanding

Share your questions with a partner but do not reveal the critical perspective you chose. After reading the questions out loud, have your partner guess which critical perspective relates to the questions. Then take turns responding to the questions briefly.

My Notes

 Writing Prompt: Literary

Write an alternate ending that adheres to the conventions of a play script, addresses the changes in Eliza's character in the first half of Act V, and reflects one critical theory. Use well-chosen details and a well-structured event sequence to provide a logical conclusion for the story. You may want to review the elements of script writing in Activity 2.6. Be sure to:

- Use the genre characteristics of a script, including a narrative arc, subtext, and stage direction.
- Write dialogue that reflects your interpretation of the play through one critical perspective.
- Provide a conclusion that resolves the problem or situation of the story.
- Use consistent voice and purposeful vocabulary.

Self-Editing and Peer Editing

After you have responded to the writing prompt, use these questions to review your script.

- Which critical perspective is evident in this alternate ending?
- How has Eliza's transformation led to this alternate ending?

Share your draft with your writing partner. Using the checklist, jot down notes about your partner's script, recording your ideas in the My Notes section. Then expand your notes into clear and concise feedback. Be sure to use the feedback from your partner to revise your draft.

☐ **Form:** Are these elements present: title, act and scene numbers, list of characters, description of setting?

☐ **Dialogue:** Does the dialogue help create a logical resolution?

☐ **Problem:** Since this scene ends the play, how is the problem or conflict between Eliza and Professor Higgins resolved?

☐ **Stage Directions:** How do the stage directions suggest delivery of dialogue or movement of characters in a way that makes clear their final intentions?

What Does Eliza Do?

Learning Strategies

Brainstorming
Drafting
Note-taking
Visualizing

Learning Targets

- Draw on evidence from a source text to adapt a plot summary into a play script.
- Analyze how the structure of the play incorporates or departs from a traditional dramatic structure.
- Cite textual evidence in a discussion to evaluate an author's choices.

Preview

In this activity, you'll read Shaw's sequel to *Pygmalion* and evaluate and discuss the structure of the play. You then will transform Shaw's sequel into a cohesive script. You will complete a peer review activity with a partner to give and receive constructive feedback and improve the quality of your writing.

Analyzing the Plot Structure

1. Work with a partner to examine the dramatic arc in *Pygmalion*. Create a graphic organizer and jot down key details from each act. Does the play follow a traditional five-act structure? Review the structure of a five-act play in Activity 2.4 if needed.

2. Discuss the following with a partner to evaluate Shaw's decisions:

   - What elements does Shaw present to orient the reader to the story? How does the environment affect a person's identity?
   - Does the play have a clear rising and falling action? How do these elements advance the plot?
   - What message is Shaw conveying to his audience by omitting a detailed scene at the Ambassador's party?
   - What is the climax of the story? How does it advance the plot?
   - Is there a clear conclusion to the play's plot? Is it clear if the main characters achieve their goals?

   Why do you think Shaw chose to structure the play the way he did? What purpose does this allow him to achieve?

Reading *Pygmalion*: The Sequel

3. As you read the sequel to *Pygmalion*, visualize what Shaw is telling the readers.

   - Annotate with a star those lines you are able to visualize most easily.
   - Circle unknown words and phrases. Try to determine the meaning of words by using context clues, word parts, or a dictionary.

4. Consider the following quotation from Shaw's sequel to *Pygmalion*. Do you agree or disagree with Shaw's interpretation of what Eliza would do? With your discussion group, explain why you would defend or challenge Shaw's ending.

   "This being the state of human affairs, what is Eliza fairly sure to do when she is placed between Freddy and Higgins? ... Unless Freddy is biologically repulsive to her, and Higgins biologically attractive to a degree that overwhelms all her other instincts, she will, if she marries either of them, marry Freddy. And that is just what Eliza did."

GRAMMAR & USAGE

Commas
Writers often use commas to slow readers down, which leads them to pay closer attention to certain parts of the sentence. Reread this sentence from *Pygmalion*, focusing on Shaw's placement of commas: "Unless Freddy is biologically repulsive to her, and Higgins biologically attractive to a degree that overwhelms all her other instincts, she will ... marry Freddy."

Notice that the commas before "and" and after "instincts" are not required. Why does Shaw include them? Try reading the sentence again without those commas. How does the pacing change?

Find another example in *Pygmalion* that uses commas, and practice saying those lines out loud to see how the punctuation changes the pacing and emphasis of the words.

My Notes

_____
_____
_____
_____
_____
_____
_____

My Notes

✍ Writing Prompt: Literary

Think about the dialogue that would be shared during this scene. Using artistic license, write a script that reflects Shaw's version of the play's ending. Consider key points in the plot that would have an impact on the ending. How does Shaw's ending resolve the conflict of the story? Be sure to:

- Follow Shaw's version of the story's resolution.
- Structure the ending so that it follows from and reflects on what has been experienced by the characters in the story.
- Use appropriate diction and tone that reflect the characters' personalities and conditions.
- Correctly use subtext and genre characteristics of a play.

Use a separate paper to brainstorm ideas for your script. Consider the following elements of a script as you brainstorm ideas.

- Title and List of Characters
- Setting
- Problem/Dialogue
- Narrative Arc
- Stage Directions

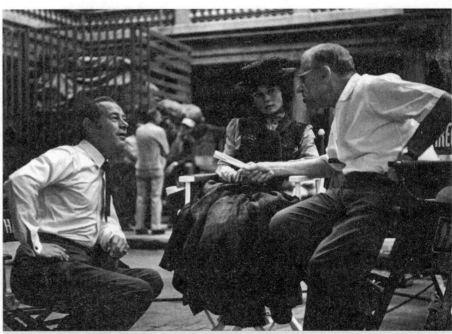

Director George Cukor coaches actors Audrey Hepburn and Rex Harrison during the musical production of *My Fair Lady*, 1964.

☑ Check Your Understanding

How can an author or director stay true to a source material while also using artistic license?

VOCABULARY

LITERARY

Artistic license describes the practice of rewording dialogue, alteration of language, or reordering of plot of a text created by another artist. The purpose of using artistic license is to give a different approach to a text or to enhance the text.

Examining the Archetypes

Learning Targets

- Draw connections between the key plot elements and archetypes presented in a myth and a play.
- Analyze how an author uses characterization, setting, and dialogue to communicate specific meanings and themes.
- Write an argument evaluating an author's interpretation of a myth.

Preview

In this activity, you will read excerpts from the play *Pygmalion* and make connections to archetypal elements found in Ovid's myth. You will then evaluate the effectiveness of the author's choices in the form of an argumentative essay.

Learning Strategies

Paraphrasing
Peer Editing
Rereading
Revising
Summarizing

My Notes

Appling Archetypal Criticism

1. Reread the excerpts from Shaw's *Pygmalion*, considering how each excerpt does or does not represent the archetypes present in Ovid's myth. As you read the excerpts, put a star next to lines that connect to the archetypal characters of the creator and the created.

Act I Excerpts:

- THE NOTE TAKER. You see this creature with her kerbstone English: the English that will keep her in the gutter to the end of her days. Well, sir, in three months I could pass that girl off as a duchess at an ambassador's garden party. I could even get her a place as a lady's maid or shop assistant, which requires better English.

- HIGGINS. Yes, you squashed cabbage leaf, you disgrace to the noble architecture of these columns, you incarnate insult to the English language: I could pass you off as the Queen of Sheba.

Act II Excerpts:

- HIGGINS. *[carried away]* Yes: in six months—in three if she has a good ear and a quick tongue—I'll take her anywhere and pass her off as anything. We'll start today: now! this moment! Take her away and clean her, Mrs. Pearce.

- HIGGINS. *[deftly retrieving the handkerchief and intercepting her on her reluctant way to the door]* You're an ungrateful wicked girl. This is my return for offering to take you out of the gutter and dress you beautifully and make a lady of you.

- HIGGINS. What! That thing! Sacred, I assure you. *[Rising to explain]* You see, she'll be a pupil; and teaching would be impossible unless pupils were sacred. I've taught scores of American millionairesses how to speak English: the best-looking women in the world. I'm seasoned. They might as well be blocks of wood. *I* might as well be a block of wood.

Act III Excerpts:

- HIGGINS. Oh, I can't be bothered with young women. My idea of a lovable woman is something as like you as possible. I shall never get into the way of seriously liking young women: some habits lie too deep to be changed. *[Rising abruptly and walking about, jingling his money and his keys in his trouser pockets]* Besides, they're all idiots.

2.11

GRAMMAR & USAGE

Compound Sentences

Compound sentences have two or more independent clauses. When Shaw writes, "I shall never get into the way of seriously liking young women: some habits lie too deep to be changed," he creates a compound sentence. In this case, a colon joins the two clauses. Independent clauses can also be joined by a semicolon or by a comma and a coordinating conjunction (e.g., *for*, *and*, *but*).

Find and underline two more examples of compound sentences in the text.

My Notes

Act V Excerpts:

* LIZA. *[continuing]* It was just like learning to dance in the fashionable way: there was nothing more than that in it. But do you know what began my real education?

    PICKERING. What?

    ELIZA. *[stopping her work for a moment]* Your calling me Miss Doolittle that day when I first came to Wimpole Street. That was the beginning of self-respect for me.

    [She resumes her stitching] And there were a hundred little things you never noticed, because they came naturally to you. Things about standing up and taking off your hat and opening doors—

* ELIZA. I know. I am not blaming him. It is his way, isn't it? But it made such a difference to me that you didn't do it. You see, really and truly, apart from the things anyone can pick up (the dressing and the proper way of speaking, and so on), the difference between a lady and a flower girl is not how she behaves, but how she's treated. I shall always be a flower girl to Professor Higgins, because he always treats me as a flower girl, and always will; but I know I can be a lady to you, because you always treat me as a lady, and always will.

* ELIZA. You never thought of the trouble it would make for me.

    HIGGINS. Would the world ever have been made if its maker had been afraid of making trouble? Making life means making trouble. There's only one way of escaping trouble; and that's killing things. Cowards, you notice, are always shrieking to have troublesome people killed.

* HIGGINS. *[wondering at her]* By George, Eliza, I said I'd make a woman of you; and I have.
    I like you like this.

Working from the Text

2. After reading the excerpts, respond to the following questions in your Reader/Writer Notebook:

    * Act I: What is Higgins's (the Note Taker's) opinion of himself and of Eliza? What textual clues reveal this opinion?

    * Act II: Through most of the myth, Pygmalion's ideal woman is ivory, not human. She fits the archetype of the created. How do Higgins's words echo this aspect of the myth?

    * Act III: How was Eliza's transformation different from what she expected?

    * Act V: How does Higgins's ego affect his point of view and perception of Eliza?

3. Return to the summary of Ovid's myth that you wrote for Activity 2.3. Review the text of the myth and your summary. Working with a writing partner, answer these reflective questions:

    * How has Shaw included the character of the creator?

    * How has Shaw included the character of the created?

    * How has Shaw defined the relationship between the creator and the creation?

    * How has Shaw defined the nature of the transformation?

☑ Check Your Understanding

How effectively does Shaw adapt or alter the original Pygmalion myth? Use text evidence to support your response.

✍ Writing Prompt: Argumentative

Review your summary of Ovid's version of the myth and your notes on these excerpts. To what extent does Shaw adhere to or depart from the Pygmalion archetype? How does recognizing the archetype advance or complicate the reading? Write an argumentative essay to defend your analysis of Shaw's use of the Pygmalion archetype. Be sure to:

- Introduce an analytical claim that is specific, clear, and compelling.
- Include convincing and relevant examples from both Ovid and Shaw to support your claim.
- Establish and maintain a formal style and objective tone.
- Observe the conventions of academic writing.
- Strategically use transitions to connect ideas and explain the relationship between the claim and the evidence.
- Provide a concluding statement that summarizes the argument presented.

Revising and Editing

After you have completed your draft, collaborate with a writing partner to enhance your drafts. Complete these next two steps of the writing process:

- REVISE: Review the content by considering the supporting evidence and logical organization of the essay. Evaluate the introduction, development, and conclusion of the argument based on the bullets in the writing prompt.
- EDIT: Correct any grammar, usage, mechanical, or spelling errors. Give special attention to syntax, correctly punctuating compound sentences.

Peer Review Checklist

You may want to use a checklist to guide your peer sharing and responding to produce a well-organized, well-supported essay demonstrating maturity of language and insight into Archetypal Criticism.

- ☐ Is the claim clearly stated in an engaging way?
- ☐ Is there plenty of convincing and relevant evidence, with multiple examples from both Ovid and Shaw?
- ☐ Is the relationship between the claim and the evidence logical and are ideas well-connected?
- ☐ Is the tone consistently interesting, formal, and impartial?
- ☐ Is the essay well-structured, with an effective introduction, well-developed claim, and a strong conclusion that summarizes the argument?

📖 INDEPENDENT READING LINK

Read and Discuss

Review your notes from your independent reading plan in Activity 2.1. Watch a film adaption of your independent reading text. Jot down how narrative elements are presented in the original text and film versions respectively. Compare how the author and filmmaker handled dialogue, character, exposition, and the interpretations of the characters. If you were the filmmaker, what might you have done differently? Discuss your observations with a peer and record notes of your discussion in your Reader/Writer Notebook.

From a Marxist Perspective

Learning Strategies

Discussion Groups
Graphic Organizer
Paraphrasing
SOAPSTone
Summarizing
Quickwrite

WORD CONNECTIONS

Etymology

Economics is the science that deals with the production, distribution, and consumption of wealth. The term came into usage in 1792, derived from the adjective *economic*. The word comes from the ancient Greek *oikonomos*, a combination of *oikos*, "house," and *nemein*, "to manage."

VOCABULARY

LITERARY

Marxist Criticism asserts that economics provides the foundation for all social, political, and ideological reality. Economic inequality is a power structure that drives history and influences differences in religion, race, ethnicity, and gender.

Learning Targets

- Conduct research and synthesize information from multiple sources to develop an understanding of Marxist Criticism.
- Analyze an author's message and draw connections to society's economic structures.

Preview

In this activity, you will read about Marxist critical theory and its influence on ideas about economics, culture, and society. You will then apply your understanding by analyzing song lyrics through a Marxist lens. Finally, you will collaboratively research the implications of social and economic class and share your findings with your peers.

Marxist Criticism

Karl Marx lived from 1818 to 1883. During his life, he was a philosopher, economist, political theorist, historian, and author whose work focused on how social classes struggle and how the accumulation of wealth and power enables an economic minority to dominate a working-class majority. He proposed that social conditions result from economic and political conditions. According to Marxist critics, economic conditions heavily influence a culture's literature.

Marxist Criticism asserts that economics is the foundation for all social, political, and ideological reality. Marxist critics would argue that economic inequalities create a power structure that drives history and influences differences in religion, race, ethnicity, and gender. The following are common principles of Marxist Criticism:

- Human relations are based on the struggle for economic power.
- The basic struggle in human society is between the "haves" and the "have nots."

Marxist Literary Criticism looks at ways in which a text reveals the oppression of the working class or poor by a dominant economic elite. Analyzing a text from a Marxist perspective helps the reader to evaluate how social class affects a story. Among questions that might be asked when analyzing a text through a Marxist Criticism lens are the following:

- Whose viewpoint is represented in the text (that of the poor, middle class, or wealthy)—that is, whose story gets told?
- What values are represented for each of the social classes (poor, middle class, wealthy)?
- What economic and social values do the main characters hold?
- Who is the audience, and what does the text suggest about their values?
- Who is the author and how might the author's own class or background influence the telling of the story?

☑ Focus on the Sentence

Write two complete sentences in response to what you have learned so far about Marxist Criticism. The first should be a statement that paraphrases the definition of Marxist Criticism in your own words. The second should be a question you have about Marxist Criticism.

Statement: _____

_____

Question: _____

Applying Marxist Criticism

1. To begin your study of Marxist Criticism, read the lyrics to Tracy Chapman's song "Talkin' 'bout a Revolution." As you use SOAPSTone to analyze the lyrics, try to keep in mind the principles of Marxist Criticism.

Speaker	
Occasion	
Audience	
Purpose	
Subject	
Tone	

2. Based on your analysis, how effective is the songwriter's message? Do you think her audience found her message to be compelling?

INDEPENDENT READING LINK
Read and Research

Apply your research from this activity to your independent reading text. Consider the economic values and attitudes of the characters in your independent reading. Add your notes to the chart you started in this activity to broaden your understanding of how such perspectives and attitudes are conveyed in literature.

My Notes

On the Spot Research

3. Marxist Criticism considers characters' perspectives in terms of economic and social status. It looks at the "hidden rules" that are characteristic of each economic and social class. With a partner, conduct research on the concept of "hidden rules" to describe attitudes of each of these groups toward the topics listed in the following graphic organizer.

	Poor	Middle Class	Wealthy
Money			
Use of Time			
Education			
Family Structure			
Language			

4. Respond to the following questions, using the information from your research.

   • What are the "hidden rules" for each social or economic class? Do you agree that these rules are hidden? Why or why not?

   • What connections can you make between these rules and Marxist Criticism?

   • Are these differences archetypal or stereotypical? Explain.

☑ Check Your Understanding

In your own words write a list of the key elements and considerations of Marxist Criticism. Use your Focus on the Sentence response as a starting point. Share your list with a partner.

Money, Power, and Class in *Pygmalion*

Learning Targets

- Analyze characterization and plot development through the Marxist perspective.
- Collaboratively analyze the effects of social class, power, and money on characters in the text.
- Explain how a critical perspective affects a reader's understanding of the meaning of a text.

Preview

In this activity, you will analyze and discuss the ways in which social class, wealth, and power dynamics impact the plot and character development of Shaw's *Pygmalion*. You will then reflect on the text from a Marxist critical perspective and explain your new understanding in the form of a written response.

Power

1. Create a graphic to illustrate the hierarchy of power in *Pygmalion*. In other words, visually represent a ranking of who has the most power to who has the least power. In addition to the major characters (Higgins, Pickering, and Eliza), be sure to include the minor characters, such as Mrs. Pearce, Mrs. Higgins, Mr. Doolittle, Freddy, Clara, and Mrs. Eynsford Hill. Include on your graphic an explanation as to why some of the characters have power while others do not.

Money

2. Create a graphic ranking the characters in *Pygmalion* according to their degree of power (highest to lowest), their social class (highest to lowest), and their wealth (richest to poorest). As you work to rank the characters, note whether the degree of wealth a character has correlates to their power. Does power always correlate with greater wealth and higher social class?

Social Class

3. With your discussion group analyze how social class, distribution of wealth, and power dynamics are represented through the characters in *Pygmalion*. Identify the social classes represented in *Pygmalion*.

- Who is in each class?
- What do you think Shaw thought of class divisions?
- What in the text makes you think this?
- If you need additional support, refer to your notes from the previous activity about how to apply Marxist Criticism.

Learning Strategies

Discussion Groups
Graphic Organizer
Think-Pair-Share

My Notes

2.13

☑ Check Your Understanding

Select one of the characters that you have analyzed and summarize the transformation the character undergoes over the course of the play. Consider how the following factors affect the character:

- external factors (money, historical context, and social class)
- internal factors (psychology, personality)

✍ Writing Prompt: Informational

In this activity, you analyzed *Pygmalion* from a Marxist perspective to evaluate how money, power, and social class are represented. How can applying critical perspectives create a new understanding of a literary work? Explain how using a critical lens changes or enhances a reader's understanding of the play. Be sure to:

- Introduce a clear thesis and continue to build on the thesis, using ideas, concepts, and information to create a unified whole.
- Organize your ideas clearly, using transitional words and phrases to connect the ideas.
- Use precise language to convey ideas and manage the complexity of the subject.
- Maintain an engaging, formal, and objective tone, while using the standard English conventions of mechanics and usage.
- Cite relevant textual evidence to support your explanation.
- Provide a logical conclusion that summarizes the new insights gained from applying Marxist Criticism.

⬡ Independent Reading Checkpoint

Review your independent reading and consider which critical perspective would provide the most interesting analysis of the reading (Reader Response Criticism, Cultural Criticism, Archetypal Criticism, or Marxist Criticism). How might you apply this perspective to transform your reading into a staged play? Record your ideas in your Reader/Writer Notebook.

Illuminating *Pygmalion*

 ASSIGNMENT

Work with a partner to write a script that transforms a scene from *Pygmalion* so that it reflects one of the critical perspectives you have studied. You will also write a reflection analyzing and evaluating your process and product.

Planning and Prewriting: Read and choose a scene to transform.	■ Which scene from *Pygmalion* gives the best opportunities to convey a clear and interesting interpretation of the text? ■ Which of the critical perspectives that you have encountered so far (Reader Response Criticism, Cultural Criticism, Archetypal Criticism, or Marxist Criticism) is the best choice for the scene you have selected? ■ What elements of the play will you change to emphasize the critical perspective, and how will it affect that scene? ■ What parts of using a critical lens to create a script are especially challenging?
Drafting: Write a draft of your script.	■ How will you approach your writing so that your script has both dialogue and subtext (two columns, for instance, or subtext in parentheses)? ■ How will you use dialogue to show new elements and perspectives that address your chosen critical perspective? ■ What can you include to help demonstrate the subtext of the scene (tone of voice, placement of actors, body language, and so on)? ■ How can you use your thinking as you plan and draft as part of your reflective analysis and evaluation? ■ How can you use technology to enhance your formatting and presentation of the script?
Evaluating and Revising Your Draft: Review and improve your draft.	■ How well do the changes that you made to the scene help to highlight your chosen critical perspective? ■ How can you work with peers and with the Scoring Guide to help you determine what needs to be added or changed?
Checking and Editing for Publication: Confirm that your final draft is technically accurate.	■ How will you review your work to make sure that you have followed the genre conventions of a play script? ■ What resources can you use to correct errors in spelling, conventions, grammar, style, and formatting?

Reflection

In this assignment, you were asked to transform a dramatic scene. Drama is a deeply interactive process between the writer and the audience; how effective is drama as a way to present ideas? How can different staging and acting choices create a new interpretation of a play? How does an audience's perspective mold and affect an interpretation or understanding of ideas?

SCORING GUIDE

Scoring Criteria	Exemplary	Proficient	Emerging	Incomplete
Ideas	The script • portrays a scene that lends itself well to the chosen critical perspective. • transforms the scene, revealing sophisticated understanding of the critical perspective. • offers thorough and well-considered reflection about choices made and insights into how the perspective affects the drama.	The script • portrays an appropriate scene for the chosen critical perspective. • transforms the scene in a way that shows adequate comprehension of the critical perspective. • includes some reflection that considers choices made and how the perspective affects the drama.	The script • portrays a scene that incompletely fits well with the chosen critical perspective. • changes the scene in ways that shows minimal understanding of the critical perspective. • includes a reflection that provides limited discussion of choices made and shows a vague grasp of how the perspective affects the drama.	The script • portrays a scene that does not fit well with the chosen critical perspective. • does not change the scene to show an understanding of the critical perspective and • does not include a reflection.
Structure	The script • follows an organization that clearly identifies dialogue, stage directions, and subtext. • smoothly incorporates new elements into the scene while maintaining an engaging plot. • includes an insightful reflection.	The script • follows an organization that adequately separates dialogue from stage directions and subtext. • incorporates new elements into the scene while maintaining a coherent plot. • includes some reflection.	The script • is not organized to show clear distinctions between dialogue, stage directions, and subtext. • includes changes that make the scene difficult to follow. • includes a weak or superficial reflection.	The script • is disorganized and does not show clear distinctions between dialogue, stage directions, and subtext. • is missing elements that make the scene difficult to follow • includes no reflection.
Use of Language	The script • crafts dialogue that maintains consistent character voice from the original text. • incorporates creative techniques to enhance meaning and add interest. • demonstrates strong control and mastery of standard writing conventions.	The script • includes dialogue that largely maintains character voice from the original text. • incorporates some creative techniques to add interest. • demonstrates control of writing conventions but may contain minor errors that do not interfere with meaning.	The script • includes dialogue that varies from the original text. • does not successfully incorporate creative techniques to add interest; techniques used may interfere with meaning. • contains frequent errors in standard writing conventions that interfere with meaning.	The script • includes dialogue that does not match the text or fit the scene. • does not creatively use techniques to add interest. • contains numerous errors in standard writing conventions that interfere with meaning.

Unpacking Embedded Assessment 2

Learning Targets

- Reflect on big ideas for the second half of the unit.
- Create a plan for reading independently.
- Identify and analyze the skills and knowledge needed to complete Embedded Assessment 2 successfully.

Preview

In this activity, you will review the Essential Questions and create an independent reading plan for the second half of the unit.

Learning Strategies

Close Reading
Graphic Organizer
Marking the Text
Summarize
Think-Pair-Share

My Notes

Making Observations

You have considered archetypes, power struggles, and wealth while examining and transforming a text. You have considered the social and cultural implications of presenting a text from a particular perspective. In the second half of this unit, you will expand your toolbox of critical theories by practicing analysis from another critical perspective: Feminist Criticism. In addition, you will encounter examples of how that theory is applied to a familiar story and a film, as models for applying that perspective to another work of literary merit.

Essential Questions

Review the Essential Questions for this unit. How would you answer them now?

1. How do writers develop great characters?

2. How does a person's environment affect his or her identity?

3. How does power affect people's interactions and relationships?

Unpacking Embedded Assessment 2

Closely read the assignment for Embedded Assessment 2: Applying a Critical Perspective and summarize the major elements in your Reader/Writer Notebook.

Your assignment is to write an analytical essay applying the Feminist Critical Perspective to a short story. You have two stories to read and choose from, "The Story of an Hour" by Kate Chopin and "The Chaser" by John Collier.

What knowledge must you have to succeed on Embedded Assessment 2? Summarize in your own words what you will need to know for this assessment. With your class, create a graphic organizer that represents the skills and knowledge you will need to accomplish this task. To help you complete your graphic organizer, be sure to review the criteria in the Scoring Guide.

Planning Independent Reading

Select a text for independent reading that lends itself to analysis from a feminist perspective. Authors for consideration might include Jane Austen, F. Scott Fitzgerald, Margaret Atwood, and Alice Walker, among others. Once you have selected a text, research the author's background and write a short reflection about how the author's circumstances may influence his or her writing.

From a Feminist Perspective

Learning Strategies

Activating Prior Knowledge
Discussion Groups
KWHL
Marking the Text
Quickwrite
Think-Pair-Share

Learning Targets

- Develop and apply an understanding of key concepts and vocabulary related to the study of Feminist Criticism.
- Conduct research to answer self-generated questions about Feminist Criticism.
- Deliver a logically structured oral presentation of research.

Preview

In this activity, you will learn about the feminist critical perspective. You will collaboratively develop questions for informal research and synthesize your findings in the form of a summary. Then you will share your response with your peers and reflect on how the feminist lens can be used to analyze texts.

VOCABULARY

LITERARY

Feminist Criticism focuses on relationships between genders. It examines the patterns of thought, behavior, values, enfranchisement, and power in relations between and within the sexes.

ACADEMIC

A **patriarchal** society is one in which men have greater power and influence than women.
Enfranchisement means having the rights of citizenship, such as the right to vote.

WORD CONNECTIONS

Word Relationships
Feminist is an adjective derived from the Latin word *femina*, meaning "woman." Other words derived from *femina* include *feminine, femininely, feminineness, femininity,* and *female.*

Feminist Criticism

The perspective that you will study in this half of the unit is Feminist Criticism, which focuses on relationships between genders. It evaluates the impact of patriarchy on both men and women. It also analyzes how the lack of enfranchisement may limit the role women play in public and economic life. Feminist criticism encourages an examination of the patterns of thought, behavior, values, and power in relations between and within the sexes. For example, a feminist reading of *Pygmalion* may emphasize the idea of power relationships between the men and women of the play. Following are some key concepts in Feminist Criticism:

- A pervasively patriarchal society conveys the notion of male dominance through the images of women in its texts.
- Many literary texts lack complex female figures, as they are written from a masculine point of view.
- Issues of gender and sexuality are central to artistic expression.
- Without enfranchisement, the choices open to women may be limited and narrow.
- Fictional portrayals of female characters often reflect and reinforce stereotypical attitudes toward women.
- The feminine point of view has often been devalued by society.
- Texts created by women may have different viewpoints than texts created by men.

1. **Quickwrite:** Briefly paraphrase the key concepts of Feminist Criticism in your own words.

2. Use the key concepts information and your prior knowledge to add notes to your KWHL chart.

- K: What do you know about feminist criticism? Add what you know based on your reading and prior knowledge to column "K."
- W: What do you want to know about feminist criticism? Add your questions to column "W." These will serve as preliminary research questions.

Feminist Criticism			
K: What Do I Know?	W: What Do I Want to Know?	H: How Can I Learn More?	L: What I Have Learned?

On the Spot Research

3. With your research group discuss your preliminary research questions. Discuss your questions and give one another feedback. Note how the feedback helps you revise or answer your questions. Collaborate with your group to identify at least one research question for each group member.

4. In the "H" column of your KWHL chart, list search terms that you might use and types of sources that you might find online to answer your question(s). As you compile your list note the following:

   - Where is this source located?
   - How reliable is the source?
   - Do you notice any explicit or implicit biases in the source?
   - How does the information drawn from various sources provide an answer to your question?
   - Is the information from various sources consistent and complementary?

5. Select the best resources based on your evaluation of their credibility.

6. Evaluate what you have learned from your research and decide how to best summarize your findings.

7. Share your findings with your research group. Prepare your findings in a brief summary to present to the class. When you present, be sure to:

   - Use information from your research to explain how Feminist Criticism is applied.
   - Use appropriate eye contact, adequate volume, clear pronunciation, and appropriate register.

☑ Check Your Understanding

Review your response to the quickwrite earlier in this activity. How would you revise your response, based on what you've learned about Feminist Criticism from your individual research and your classmates' presentations?

LANGUAGE & WRITER'S CRAFT:
Punctuating Lists

Notice that the first sentence in the second paragraph of Kolbenschlag's essay has a list introduced by a colon. When creating a list followed by a colon, you typically use commas to separate items. However, as seen in this list, it is necessary to separate items with a semicolon if the items already have commas within them.

For example, the first item in the list has a comma within it, which separates the descriptive clause ("who is forced to live by the hearth") from the word it modifies ("an ill-treated heroine"). In order to make the rest of the list clear, semicolons separate all the following items in the list.

PRACTICE Write a sentence that contains a list of other common elements in fairy tales. Be sure to practice proper placement of colons, commas, and semicolons.

Writing Prompt: Rhetorical Analysis

Write a response in which you explain how Kolbenschlag builds an argument to persuade her audience. As you write, consider how she uses persuasive elements to develop, support, and connect her ideas. Be sure to:

- Discuss how Kolbenschlag's feminist interpretation strengthens the logic and persuasiveness of her argument.
- Support your analysis by citing textual evidence.
- Use a clear and logical organizational structure.
- Use standard English conventions and proper punctuation.

My Notes

Learning Targets

- Identify essential and nonessential elements in sentences in order to improve sentence fluency.
- Use a style guide to determine how nonessential elements are set off correctly.
- Work with a partner to evaluate how well you convey both essential and nonessential elements in a sentence.

Preview

In this activity you will learn to distinguish between essential and nonessential information in your writing, and how to punctuate that information correctly. Then you will have the opportunity to practice your new knowledge on your own writing.

Identifying Essential and Nonessential Information

Words, phrases, and clauses that are not essential to the basic meaning of a sentence are nonrestrictive elements. Nonrestrictive elements are set apart from the rest of the sentence with punctuation. Words, phrases, and clauses that are essential to the basic meaning of a sentence are restrictive elements. Restrictive elements do not need any special punctuation.

Restrictive	Nonrestrictive
In most versions, Cinderella disappears into the realm **known as "the happily ever after."**	**Known all around the world**, the Cinderella story is a coming-of-age tale.
The version that **I read as a child** includes a fairy godmother.	I like Grimm's version, **which I read as a child**.

1. Read the following sentences and decide whether the bolded words are restrictive or nonrestrictive.

   In the Norse version of the tale, Aslaug, **the Cinderella character**, wields a good deal of power.

   In the Norse version of the tale, the character **Aslaug** wields a good deal of power.

2. With a partner, write a few sentences explaining how you decided whether the bolded words in each sentence are restrictive or nonrestrictive.

Punctuating Nonrestrictive Elements

Nonrestrictive elements are set off by punctuation (usually commas, parentheses, or dashes).

Punctuation	Examples
Comma: Most of the time, writers use commas to set off nonrestrictive elements. A nonrestrictive element in the middle of a sentence is set off with a comma before and after.	Madonna Kolbenschlag, **the writer of the essay,** discusses Cinderella. **Using fairy tales and myths,** she explores contemporary female psychology.
Parentheses: Using parentheses to set off nonrestrictive elements suggests that the information is extra or separate from the surrounding information.	One theme of the tale is social mobility **(the ability to move out of one class and into another).**
Dash: A dash or pair of dashes can be used to signal a pause that calls attention to information.	She changes her name, no doubt, and—**like so many women**—is never heard of again.

3. For each of the following sentences, underline the nonrestrictive element, and add punctuation to set it off from the rest of the sentence.

   One moral of the story that good fortune can be merited is a popular idea in Western countries

   Some versions have a gruesome finale birds pluck out the stepsisters' eyes.

4. Remember that restrictive elements do not have to be set off with punctuation. Extra punctuation can confuse readers. For the following sentence, delete any unnecessary punctuation around restrictive elements.

   Foot-binding, which disfigured many girls and women, began to die out as a result of a twentieth-century campaign, discouraging the practice.

Revising

Read the following student summary of part of "Cinderella, the Legend." Work with a partner to check whether restrictive and nonrestrictive elements are punctuated correctly. Mark the text to correct the mistakes.

[1] The essay, "Cinderella the Legend" was published as part of the book *Kiss Sleeping Beauty Goodbye.*[2] Madonna Kolbenschlag, the author, is a writer, educator, and activist.[3] Discussing and interpreting the Cinderella tale, Kolbenschlag covers a lot of ground.[4] The essay says that the story is very old and has hundreds of variants (at least 345 recorded ones. [5] The story's most prominent motifs, which include the young woman who sleeps near a hearth and who is treated as a servant, appear in many cultures.[6] Many versions also include the problematic symbol of the tiny slipper (how does anyone even walk in a glass slipper?) and the prince.[7] The main thing, that I will remember about this essay, is just how complex a "simple" fairy tale can be.

☑ Check Your Understanding

Imagine you are editing a classmate's writing and you notice this sentence:

Studying the fairy tale, Little Red Riding Hood I realized how strange how very, very strange a familiar story can be when you examine it closely.

Write a note to the writer describing why the original sentence is confusing. Help the writer understand how to correctly punctuate the sentence. Make sure your instructions are clear and your comments are succinct. After writing the note, add a question to your Editor's Checklist to remind yourself to check for correct punctuation of nonrestrictive elements.

Practice

Return to the essay you wrote in the previous activity, analyzing Kolbenschlag's argument. Check that you used punctuation correctly to set apart nonrestrictive elements. Consult a style guide if necessary. Be sure to:

- Use standard English conventions to punctuate nonrestrictive elements with commas, parentheses, or dashes.
- Revise any sentences that incorrectly use punctuation to improve sentence fluency.

Battle of the Sexes

Learning Targets

- Evaluate a folktale and literary critique through a feminist perspective.
- Collaboratively discuss an author's message and draw connections to your personal perspective.
- Synthesize your analysis of two texts in the form of an explanatory essay.
- Integrate ideas from multiple texts to build knowledge and vocabulary about gender equality.

Preview

In this activity, you will read a folktale using the ideas of Feminist Criticism to help you understand the author's message. With your discussion group, you will compare ideas about men and women presented in a folktale with the ideas presented in "Cinderella, the Legend," by Kolbenschlag. Finally, you will synthesize your understanding of the texts in a written response.

As You Read

- As you read, use metacognitive markers to monitor your comprehension and interact with the text.
- Circle unknown words and phrases. Try to determine the meaning of the words by using context clues, word parts, or a dictionary.

My Notes

About the Author

Zora Neale Hurston (1891–1960) is known for her powerful portrayals of African American life and culture in the rural South. An anthropologist, folklorist, novelist, civil rights activist, and journalist, she was a leading member of the Harlem Renaissance. Born in Florida, Hurston moved to New York in her twenties and studied anthropology at Barnard College and Columbia University. She became one of the first African American anthropologists to collect the folktales of the rural South and Haiti. These stories provided inspiration for her short fiction and novels. Her best-known work is the novel *Their Eyes Were Watching God* (1937). *Barracoon: The Story of the Last Black Cargo*, is based on her interviews with a survivor of the African slave trade. The manuscript was discovered by researchers among her papers in the Howard University Archives and published for the first time in 2018.

KNOWLEDGE QUEST

Knowledge Question:
Why is gender equality important?

Folktale

Why Women Always Take Advantage of Men

by **Zora Neale Hurston**

from *Mules and Men*

Chunk 1

1   "Don't you know you can't git de best of no woman in de talkin' game? Her tongue is all de weapon a woman got," George Thomas chided Gene. "She could have had mo' sense, but she told God no, she'd ruther take it out in hips. So God give her her ruthers. She got plenty hips, plenty mouf and no brains."

2   "Oh, yes, womens is got sense too," Mathilda Moseley jumped in. "But they got too much sense to go 'round braggin' about it like y'all do. De lady people always got de advantage of mens because God fixed it dat way."

3   "Whut ole black advantage is y'all got?" B. Moseley asked indignantly. "We got all de strength and all de law and all de money and you can't git a thing but whut we jes' take pity on you and give you."

4   "And dat's jus' de point," said Mathilda triumphantly. "You do give it to us, but how come you do it?" And without waiting for an answer Mathilda began to tell why women always take advantage of men.

Chunk 2

5   You see in de very first days, God made a man and a woman and put 'em in a house together to live. 'Way back in them days de woman was just as strong as de man and both of 'em did de same things. They useter get to fussin' 'bout who gointer do this and that and sometime they'd fight, but they was even balanced and neither one could whip de other one.

6   One day de man said to hisself, "B'lieve Ah'm gointer go see God and ast Him for a li'l mo' strength so Ah kin whip dis 'oman and make her mind. Ah'm tired of de way things is." So he went on up to God.

7   "Good mawnin', Ole Father."

8   "Howdy man. Whut you doin' 'round my throne so soon dis mawnin'?"

9   "Ah'm troubled in mind, and nobody can't ease mah spirit 'ceptin' you."

10   God said: "Put yo' plea in de right form and Ah'll hear and answer."

11   "Ole Maker, wid de mawnin' stars glitterin' in yo' shinin' crown, wid de dust from yo' footsteps makin' worlds upon worlds, wid de blazin' bird we call

© 2021 College Board. All rights reserved.

GRAMMAR & USAGE

Dialect
Languages change over time and spoken language can sound dramatically different according to geography. You might notice dialect in the ways people from different places and social backgrounds use words or phrases. Writers sometimes choose to write in dialect to provide authenticity when representing a certain time, place, or social group. Oftentimes dialect is spelled phonetically, or how the words sound when spoken aloud. For example, in the first paragraph of Chunk 3, the character uses words like *de*, *Heben*, *yo'*, *tole*, and *Ah' m*.

Find two more examples of the ways in which the author uses unconventional spelling to convey dialect and consider the impact it has on your understanding of the text.

de sun flyin' out of yo' right hand in de mawnin' and consumin' all day de flesh and blood of stump-black darkness, and comes flyin' home every evenin' to rest on yo' left hand, and never once in all yo' eternal years, mistood de left hand for de right, Ah ast you please to give me mo' strength than dat woman you give me, so Ah kin make her mind. Ah know you don't want to be always comin' down way past de moon and stars to be straightenin' her out and its got to be done. So give me a li'l mo' strength, Ole Maker and Ah'll do it."

12   "All right, Man, you got mo' strength than woman."

Chunk 3

13   So de man run all de way down de stairs from Heben till he got home. He was so anxious to try his strength on de woman dat he couldn't take his time. Soon's he got in de house he hollered "Woman! Here's yo' boss. God done tole me to handle you whichever way Ah please. Ah'm yo' boss."

14   De woman flew to fightin' 'im right off. She fought 'im frightenin' but he beat her. She got her wind and tried 'im agin but he whipped her agin. She got herself together and made de third try on him vigorous but he beat her every time. He was so proud he could whip 'er at last, dat he just crowed over her and made her do a lot of things she didn't like. He told her, "Long as you obey me, Ah'll be good to yuh, but every time yuh rear up Ah'm gointer put plenty wood on yo' back and plenty water in yo' eyes."

15   De woman was so mad she went straight up to Heben and stood befo' de Lawd. She didn't waste no words. She said, "Lawd, Ah come befo' you mighty mad t'day. Ah want back my strength and power Ah useter have."

16   "Woman, you got de same power you had since de beginnin'."

17   "Why is it then, dat de man kin beat me now and he useter couldn't do it?"

18   "He got mo' strength than he useter have. He come and ast me for it and Ah give it to 'im. Ah gives to them that ast, and you ain't never ast me for no mo' power."

19   "Please suh, God, Ah'm astin' you for it now. Jus' gimme de same as you give him."

20   God shook his head. "It's too late now, woman. Whut Ah give, Ah never take back. Ah give him mo' strength than you and no matter how much Ah give you, he'll have mo'."

Chunk 4

21   De woman was so mad she wheeled around and went on off. She went straight to de devil and told him what had happened.

22   He said, "Don't be **dis-incouraged**, woman. You listen to me and you'll come out mo' than conqueror. Take dem frowns out yo' face and turn round and go right on back to Heben and ast God to give you dat bunch of keys hangin' by de mantel-piece. Then you bring 'em to me and Ah'll show you what to do wid 'em."

WORD CONNECTIONS

Roots and Affixes
Dis-incouraged is not a word you'll find in the dictionary, but you can still decode it using roots and affixes. The Latin root *cur* means "heart" and is the base of the word courage. The prefix *en-* (here written *in-*) means "to make" or "to cause," and the prefix *dis-* means "to deprive." Hurston intentionally adds these two conflicting prefixes to create a word with complex meaning.

My Notes

23 So de woman climbed back up to Heben agin. She was mighty tired but she was more out-done that she was tired so she climbed all night long and got back up to Heben agin. When she got befo' de throne, butter wouldn't melt in her mouf.

24 "O Lawd and Master of de rainbow, Ah know yo' power. You never make two mountains without you put a valley in between. Ah know you kin hit a straight lick wid a crooked stick."

25 "Ast for whut you want, woman."

26 "God, gimme dat bunch of keys hangin' by yo' mantel-piece."

27 "Take 'em."

28 So de woman took de keys and hurried on back to de devil wid 'em. There was three keys on de bunch. Devil say, "See dese three keys? They got mo' power in 'em than all de strength de man kin ever git if you handle 'em right. Now dis first big key is to de do' of de kitchen and you know a man always favors his stomach. Dis second one is de key to de bedroom and he don't like to be shut out from dat neither and dis last key is de key to de cradle and he don't want to be cut off from his generations at all. So now you take dese keys and go lock up everything and wait till he come to you. Then don't you unlock nothin' until he use his strength for yo' benefit and yo' desires."

29 De woman thanked 'im and tole 'im, "If it wasn't for you, Lawd knows whut us po' women folks would do."

30 She started off but de devil halted her. "Jus' one mo' thing: don't go home braggin' 'bout yo' keys. Jus' lock up everything and say nothin' until you git asked. And then don't talk too much."

Chunk 5

31 De woman went on home and did like de devil tole her. When de man come home from work she was settin' on de porch singin' some song 'bout "Peck on de wood make de bed go good."

32 When de man found de three doors fastened what useter stand wide open he swelled up like pine lumber after a rain. First thing he tried to break in cause he figgered his strength would overcome all obstacles.

33 When he saw he couldn't do it, he ast de woman, "Who locked dis do'?"

34 She tole 'im, "Me."

35 "Where did you git de key from?"

36 "God give it to me."

37 He run up to God and said, "God, woman got me locked 'way from my vittles, my bed and my generations, and she say you give her the keys."

38 God said, "I did, Man, Ah give her de keys, but de devil showed her how to use 'em!"

39 "Well, Ole Maker, please gimme some keys jus' lak 'em so she can't git de full control."

40 "No, Man, what Ah give Ah give. Woman got de key."

41 "How kin Ah know 'bout my generations?"

42 "Ast de woman."

43 So de man come on back and submitted hisself to de woman and she opened de doors.

44 He wasn't satisfied but he had to give in. Way after while he said to de woman, "Le's us divide up. Ah'll give you half of my strength if you lemme hold de keys in my hands."

45 De woman thought dat over so de devil popped and tol her, "Tell 'im, naw. Let 'im keep his strength and you keep yo' keys."

46 So de woman wouldn't trade wid 'im and de man had to mortgage his strength to her to live. And dat's why de man makes and de woman takes.

47 You men is still braggin' 'bout yo' strength and de women is sittin' on de keys and lettin' you blow off till she git ready to put de bridle on you.

48 B. Moseley looked over at Mathilda and said, "You just like a hen in de barnyard. You cackle so much you give de rooster de blues."

49 Mathilda looked over at him archly and quoted:

50 Stepped on a pin, de pin bent.

51 And dat's de way de story went.

⌀ Knowledge Quest

• What emotions do you feel while reading the speech in this folktale?
• What is your first impression of the gender issues raised in this folktale?

My Notes

mortgage: hand over the rights of

INDEPENDENT READING LINK

You can continue to build your knowledge about gender equality by reading other articles at ZINC Reading Labs. Search for keywords such as gender equality.

 ZINC

 Knowledge Quest

Think about how Kolbenschlag and Hurston address gender equality. Choose "Cinderella, the Legend" or "Why Women Always Take Advantage of Men," and write a paragraph explaining how the conflict between men and women as explored in your reading is relevant today in gender equality issues. Be sure to:

- Clearly introduce the central idea and logically organize your ideas.
- Use significant and relevant examples, details, or quotations that thoroughly develop and explain the topic.
- Provide an engaging conclusion that supports the central idea and examines its implications.

Returning to the Text

- Reread the folktale to answer these text-dependent questions.
- Write any additional questions you have about the text in your Reader/Writer Notebook.

1. How does the author use the language and dialogue in Chunk 1 to reveal how men see the relative advantages of men and women? Use details from the text to support your answer.

_____

_____

_____

_____

2. How does the use of the word "triumphantly" to describe Mathilda's speech at the end of Chunk 1 create surprise and set up the folktale? How does this word shape the reader's anticipation of what will come next?

_____

_____

_____

_____

3. KQ Why does the man tell God he needs more strength than the woman at the end of Chunk 2? What does this reveal about his character and the power dynamics in the society in which he lives?

_____

_____

_____

_____

4. In Chunk 4, how does the Devil's explanation of the keys add irony to the folktale?

_____

_____

_____

_____

5. In Chunk 5, God says, "I did, Man, Ah give her de keys, but de devil showed her how to use 'em!" What does the image of the keys suggest? What does this statement show about how men see the power of women?

_____

_____

_____

_____

6. What is the cause of the conflict between the man and the woman in the folktale? How do the characters contribute to that conflict? What does this imply about men and women?

_____

_____

_____

_____

7. How does Hurston's choice to present the folktale as part of a conversation between men and a woman change the effect of the story and its impact on the reader?

_____

_____

_____

_____

8. **KQ** What themes are expressed in the last six paragraphs of the story? How do they interact to create a view of the power balance between men and women?

_____

_____

_____

_____

Gaining Perspectives

In the folktale, the woman has two interpersonal conflicts, which also happen in real life. In one instance, physical harm occurs, and in the other, there is a battle of wits. With a partner, discuss how the woman handles the situations she encounters. What other ways could someone in her situation prevent or resolve an interpersonal conflict where violence is involved? Based on your community, what options do people have if they need to ask for help? Who can a person reach out to if she or he is in this situation? Family? Friends? Healthcare workers? In your Reader/Writer notebook, write about some strategies for how to handle this situation.

Working from the Text

9. Think about the gender issues raised by the authors of the essay "Cinderella, the Legend" and the folktale "Why Women Always Take Advantage of Men." Use a Venn diagram to compare and contrast the issues raised by each author and those shared by both. As you fill out the diagram, make sure your commentary and summaries are supported by the texts. Share the information in your diagram with the rest of your group in a discussion.

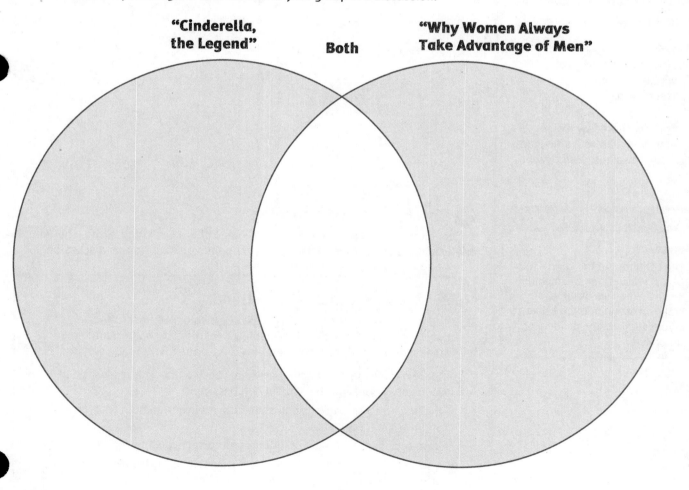

10. Consider some of the key ideas of Feminist Criticism. Based on your reading and discussion of "Cinderella, the Legend" and "Why Women Always Take Advantage of Men," decide whether Kolbenschlag and Hurston would tend to agree or disagree with the ideas here. Use evidence from the texts to support your views. Then decide whether you agree or disagree with the same statements and record your thinking in the last column.

Key Ideas Related to the Use of Feminist Critical Perspective	Kolbenschlag		Hurston		You	
	Agree	Disagree	Agree	Disagree	Agree	Disagree
The relationship between men and women has almost always been unequal.						
The female reader is an outsider who must assume male values.						
Gender issues are central in our society.						
Fictional portrayals of women are often stereotypical.						
Texts authored by women may have different viewpoints from those authored by men.						

WORD CONNECTIONS

Etymology

The Latin root of the word **assumption** is *sumere*, meaning "take." When we assume, or make an assumption, we take on a responsibility, an idea, or other item.

☑ **Check Your Understanding**

Reflect on the points that your group has made about each idea. Write a paragraph briefly summarizing some of the significant points of your group's discussion.

📝 **Writing Prompt: Informational**

Write a detailed response explaining a key idea of Feminist Criticism from the graphic organizer you completed in this activity. Evaluate how Kolbenschlag and Hurston explore this idea in their writing. Be sure to:

- Write a clear thesis that compares how each author addresses the key idea associated with the critical perspective.
- Include direct quotations and specific evidence from both texts to support your thinking.
- Introduce and punctuate all quotations correctly, using varied syntax.
- Use a coherent organizational structure and employ transitions effectively to highlight similarities and differences.

Feminist Critique: The Tree of Life

Learning Strategies

Activate Prior Knowledge
Discussion Groups
Graphic Organizer
Paraphrasing
Summarizing

Learning Targets

- Analyze a picture book through a feminist perspective.
- Develop claims and support them with textual evidence.

Preview

In this activity, you will review the general assumptions you have learned about Feminist Criticism. Then you will analyze character relationships presented in a picture book. Finally, you will write a literary analysis to reflect your new understanding of the text, viewed through a feminist perspective.

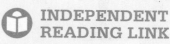

INDEPENDENT READING LINK

Read and Connect

Think about the analytical questions you have applied to your in-class reading. Use the questions to consider the perspective of Feminist Criticism in your independent reading. Create a Venn diagram in your Reader/Writer Notebook to explore the connections between the texts you have read independently and in class. How do the authors portray gender roles and relationships between men and women?

Feminist Criticism

1. Think about the description and definition of Feminist Criticism in Activity 2.15, then answer the following questions about the lens.

   - If a matriarchal society is the opposite of a patriarchal society, what is the basis of the difference?

   - What is one statement Feminist Criticism makes about patriarchal societies?

   - What assumption does Feminist Criticism make about the treatment of female characters in literary texts?

   - How can a literary character both reflect and reinforce stereotypes?

   - What perspective does Feminist Criticism present about texts authored by men versus those authored by women?

My Notes

My Notes

<table>
</table>

Opening Writing Prompt

Think about the phrase "the tree of life" and respond to the following question.

The tree of life is an archetype. What do you know about this phrase and its meaning? Are there any examples of this archetype that you can connect to texts, films, or artwork that you've read or viewed?

About the Author

Sheldon Allan "Shel" Silverstein (1930–1999) was an American author, cartoonist, songwriter, and playwright from Chicago. While Silverstein won multiple Grammy awards as a songwriter and musician, he is best known for his children's books and poetry collections. His first major poetry collection, *Where the Sidewalk Ends* (1974), is full of inventive characters and dark humor. His children's books, which he also illustrated, have been translated into more than 30 languages and have sold more than 20 million copies. Works including *The Giving Tree* and *Falling Up* are still cherished by children and adults alike.

The Giving Tree

You will read a picture book that allows you to analyze the phrase "the tree of life" from the perspective of Feminist Criticism. A cornerstone of Feminist Criticism is the examination of the portrayal of gender roles and relationships between men and women.

2. As your teacher reads aloud Shel Silverstein's *The Giving Tree*, listen for evidence that supports a feminist critique of the book, and record your ideas in the My Notes column. Consider the following:

   a. From whose point of view do we see this story?

   b. How are women presented in the text? How are men presented in the text?

   c. How does the author use imagery to convey ideas about men and women?

   d. How is the relationship between men and women presented?

   e. To what extent does the portrayal of men and women support a patriarchal view of the world?

   f. How do the characters' behaviors influence the theme?

3. Use the following graphic organizer to analyze the story. Write a quotation in the left column, and, using the questions from Step 2, write your analysis and commentary in the right column. Your teacher will model the completion of the first few passages.

Quotation	Answers and Analysis
a.	
b.	
c.	
d.	
e.	
f.	

My Notes

☑ **Check Your Understanding**

Based on your analysis and discussion of *The Giving Tree*, what is one new understanding that emerges when reading the story from a feminist perspective? How could you recast *The Giving Tree* as a feminist story?

✍ **Writing Prompt: Informational**

Consider the final line of the story: "And the tree was happy." Write an explanation of why the tree would or would not be happy. How could a feminist analysis of this story give the reader a new or different understanding? Consider the author's portrayal of men and women in the text and the relationship between them as you incorporate principles of Feminist Criticism in your explanation. Be sure to:

- Begin with a clear thesis statement.
- Include relevant quotations and examples from the text to support your analysis and commentary.
- Use a coherent organizational structure and employ transitions effectively to make connections between ideas.
- Use academic and purposeful vocabulary.

Seeing Beyond Your Own Perspective

Learning Targets

- Evaluate the author's craft in a short story and present your views in a collegial discussion.
- Compare multiple texts, from across genres, using a feminist perspective.
- Apply the feminist lens by writing a literary analysis of a short story.

Preview

In this activity, you will closely read a short story and develop analytical questions to actively participate in a Socratic Seminar. Then, using a feminist perspective, you will compare the short story to texts previously read in this unit. You will synthesize your new understanding in a written response.

As You Read

- As you read, underline instances where you feel the author is building a sense of foreshadowing or suspense.
- Circle unknown words and phrases. Try to determine the meaning of the words by using context clues, word parts, or a dictionary.

About the Author

Roald Dahl (1916–1990) was a prolific 20th-century writer who worked in a variety of genres. He is best known for his children's books, but he also wrote novels and short stories for adults, screenplays, and autobiographies. Born in Wales, UK, to Norwegian parents, Dahl was educated in Britain and became a British citizen. He joined the Royal Air Force during World War II and published his first short stories soon after the war in 1946. Dahl was known for his sense of irony and dark humor. His stories often end with a surprise twist. Among his most famous works are *Matilda*, *The Witches*, *James and the Giant Peach*, and *Charlie and the Chocolate Factory*.

Learning Strategies

Close Reading
Levels of Questions
Marking the Text
Socratic Seminar

My Notes

My Notes

Short Story

The Landlady

by **Roald Dahl**

1   Billy Weaver had travelled down from London on the slow afternoon train, with a change at Swindon on the way, and by the time he got to Bath it was about nine o'clock in the evening and the moon was coming up out of a clear starry sky over the houses opposite the station entrance. But the air was deadly cold and the wind was like a flat blade of ice on his cheeks.

2   "Excuse me," he said, "but is there a fairly cheap hotel not too far away from here?"

3   "Try The Bell and Dragon," the porter answered, pointing down the road. "They might take you in. It's about a quarter of a mile along on the other side."

4   Billy thanked him and picked up his suitcase and set out to walk the quarter mile to The Bell and Dragon. He had never been to Bath before. He didn't know anyone who lived there. But Mr. Greenslade at the Head Office in London had told him it was a splendid city. "Find your own lodgings," he had said, "and then go along and report to the Branch Manager as soon as you've got yourself settled."

5   Billy was seventeen years old. He was wearing a new navy-blue overcoat, a new brown trilby hat, and a new brown suit, and he was feeling fine. He walked briskly down the street. He was trying to do everything briskly these days. Briskness, he had decided, was the one common characteristic of all successful businessmen. The big shots up at Head Office were absolutely fantastically brisk all the time. They were amazing.

6   There were no shops on this wide street that he was walking along, only a line of tall houses on each side, all them identical. They had porches and pillars and four or five steps going up to their front doors, and it was obvious that once upon a time they had been very swanky residences. But now, even in the darkness, he could see that the paint was peeling from the woodwork on their doors and windows, and that the handsome white façades were cracked and blotchy from neglect.

7   Suddenly, in a downstairs window that was brilliantly illuminated by a street-lamp not six yards away, Billy caught sight of a printed notice propped up against the glass in one of the upper panes. It said BED AND BREAKFAST. There was a vase of yellow chrysanthemums, tall and beautiful, standing just underneath the notice.

8   He stopped walking. He moved a bit closer. Green curtains (some sort of velvety material) were hanging down on either side of the window. The chrysanthemums looked wonderful beside them. He went right up and peered through the glass into the room, and the first thing he saw was a bright

fire burning in the hearth. On the carpet in front of the fire, a pretty little dachshund was curled up asleep with its nose tucked into its belly.

9 The room itself, so far as he could see in the half-darkness, was filled with pleasant furniture. There was a baby-grand piano and a big sofa and several plump armchairs; and in one corner he spotted a large parrot in a cage. Animals were usually a good sign in a place like this, Billy told himself; and all in all, it looked to him as though it would be a pretty decent house to stay in. Certainly it would be more comfortable than The Bell and Dragon.

10 On the other hand, a pub would be more congenial than a boarding-house. There would be beer and darts in the evenings, and lots of people to talk to, and it would probably be a good bit cheaper, too. He had stayed a couple of nights in a pub once before and he had liked it. He had never stayed in any boarding-houses, and, to be perfectly honest, he was a tiny bit frightened of them. The name itself **conjured up** images of watery cabbage, **rapacious** landladies, and a powerful smell of kippers in the living-room.

11 After **dithering about** like this in the cold for two or three minutes, Billy decided that he would walk on and take a look at The Bell and Dragon before making up his mind. He turned to go. And now a queer thing happened to him. He was in the act of stepping back and turning away from the window when all at once his eye was caught and held in the most peculiar manner by the small notice that was there. BED AND BREAKFAST, it said. BED AND BREAKFAST, BED AND BREAKFAST, BED AND BREAKFAST. Each word was like a large black eye staring at him through the glass, holding him, compelling him, forcing him to stay where he was and not to walk away from that house, and the next thing he knew, he was actually moving across from the window to the front door of the house, climbing the steps that led up to it, and reaching for the bell.

12 He pressed the bell. Far away in a back room he heard it ringing, and then at once—it must have been at once because he hadn't even had time to take his finger from the bell-button—the door swung open and a woman was standing there.

13 Normally you ring the bell and you have at least a half-minute's wait before the door opens. But this dame was a like a jack-in-the-box. He pressed the bell—and out she popped! It made him jump.

14 She was about forty-five or fifty years old, and the moment she saw him, she gave him a warm welcoming smile.

15 "Please come in," she said pleasantly. She stepped aside, holding the door wide open, and Billy found himself automatically starting forward into the house. The **compulsion** or, more accurately, the desire to follow after her into that house was extraordinarily strong. "I saw the notice in the window," he said, holding himself back.

16 "Yes, I know."

17 "I was wondering about a room."

My Notes

_____

_____

_____

_____

_____

_____

_____

_____

_____

_____

conjured up: brought to mind
rapacious: extremely greedy
dithering about: pausing indecisively
compulsion: overwhelming urge

18 "It's all ready for you, my dear," she said. She had a round pink face and very gentle blue eyes.

19 "I was on my way to The Bell and Dragon," Billy told her. "But the notice in your window just happened to catch my eye."

20 "My dear boy," she said, "why don't you come in out of the cold?"

21 "How much do you charge?" "Five and sixpence a night, including breakfast."

22 It was fantastically cheap. It was less than half of what he had been willing to pay.

23 "If that is too much," she added, "then perhaps I can reduce it just a tiny bit. Do you desire an egg for breakfast? Eggs are expensive at the moment. It would be sixpence less without the egg."

24 "Five and sixpence is fine," he answered. "I should like very much to stay here."

25 "I knew you would. Do come in."

26 She seemed terribly nice. She looked exactly like the mother of one's best schoolfriend welcoming one into the house to stay for the Christmas holidays. Billy took off his hat, and stepped over the threshold.

27 "Just hang it there," she said, "and let me help you with your coat."

28 There were no other hats or coats in the hall. There were no umbrellas, no walkingsticks—nothing.

29 "We have it all to ourselves," she said, smiling at him over her shoulder as she led the way upstairs.

30 "You see, it isn't very often I have the pleasure of taking a visitor into my little nest."

31 The old girl is slightly dotty, Billy told himself. But at five and sixpence a night, who gives a damn about that?—"I should've thought you'd be simply swamped with applicants," he said politely.

32 "Oh, I am, my dear, I am, of course I am. But the trouble is that I'm inclined to be just a teeny weeny bit choosy and particular—if you see what I mean."

33 "Ah, yes."

34 "But I'm always ready. Everything is always ready day and night in this house just on the off-chance that an acceptable young gentleman will come along. And it is such a pleasure, my dear, such a very great pleasure when now and again I open the door and I see someone standing there who is just exactly right." She was half-way up the stairs, and she paused with one hand on the stair-rail, turning her head and smiling down at him with pale lips. "Like you," she added, and her blue eyes travelled slowly all the way down the length of Billy's body, to his feet, and then up again.

35 On the first-floor landing she said to him,

36 "This floor is mine."

37 They climbed up a second flight. "And this one is all yours," she said. "Here's your room. I do hope you'll like it." She took him into a small but charming front bedroom, switching on the light as she went in.

38 "The morning sun comes right in the window, Mr. Perkins. It is Mr. Perkins, isn't it?"

39 "No," he said. "It's Weaver."

40 "Mr. Weaver. How nice. I've put a waterbottle between the sheets to air them out, Mr. Weaver. It's such a comfort to have a hot water-bottle in a strange bed with clean sheets, don't you agree? And you may light the gas fire at any time if you feel chilly."

41 "Thank you," Billy said. "Thank you ever so much." He noticed that the bedspread had been taken off the bed, and that the bedclothes had been neatly turned back on one side, all ready for someone to get in.

42 "I'm so glad you appeared," she said, looking earnestly into his face. "I was beginning to get worried."

43 "That's all right," Billy answered brightly. "You mustn't worry about me." He put his suitcase on the chair and started to open it.

44 "And what about supper, my dear? Did you manage to get anything to eat before you came here?"

45 "I'm not a bit hungry, thank you," he said. "I think I'll just go to bed as soon as possible because tomorrow I've got to get up rather early and report to the office."

46 "Very well, then. I'll leave you now so that you can unpack. But before you go to bed, would you be kind enough to pop into the sitting-room on the ground floor and sign the book? Everyone has to do that because it's the law of the land, and we don't want to go breaking any laws at this stage in the proceedings, do we?" She gave him a little wave of the hand and went quickly out of the room and closed the door.

47 Now, the fact that his landlady appeared to be slightly off her rocker didn't worry Billy in the least. After all, she was not only harmless—there was no question about that—but she was also quite obviously a kind and generous soul. He guessed that she had probably lost a son in the war, or something like that, and had never got over it.

48 So a few minutes later, after unpacking his suitcase and washing his hands, he trotted downstairs to the ground floor and entered the living-room. His landlady wasn't there, but the fire was glowing in the hearth, and the little dachshund was still sleeping in front of it. The room was wonderfully warm and cosy. I'm a lucky fellow, he thought, rubbing his hands. This is a bit of all right.

My Notes

My Notes

49 He found the guest-book lying open on the piano, so he took out his pen and wrote down his name and address. There were only two other entries above his on the page, and, as one always does with guest-books, he started to read them. One was a Christopher Mulholland from Cardiff. The other was Gregory W. Temple from Bristol. That's funny, he thought suddenly. Christopher Mulholland. It rings a bell. Now where on earth had he heard that rather unusual name before?

50 Was he a boy at school? No. Was it one of his sister's numerous young men, perhaps, or a friend of his father's? No, no, it wasn't any of those. He glanced down again at the book. Christopher Mulholland, 231 Cathedral Road, Cardiff. Gregory W. Temple, 27 Sycamore Drive, Bristol. As a matter of fact, now he came to think of it, he wasn't at all sure that the second name didn't have almost as much of a familiar ring about it as the first.

51 "Gregory Temple?" he said aloud, searching his memory. "Christopher Mulholland? …"

52 "Such charming boys," a voice behind him answered, and he turned and saw his landlady sailing into the room with a large silver tea-tray in her hands. She was holding it well out in front of her, and rather high up, as though the tray were a pair of reins on a frisky horse.

53 "They sound somehow familiar," he said.

54 "They do? How interesting."

55 "I'm almost positive I've heard those names before somewhere. Isn't that queer? Maybe it was in the newspapers. They weren't famous in any way, were they? I mean famous cricketers or footballers or something like that?"

56 "Famous," she said, setting the tea-tray down on the low table in front of the sofa. "Oh no, I don't think they were famous. But they were extraordinarily handsome, both of them, I can promise you that. They were tall and young and handsome, my dear, just exactly like you."

57 Once more, Billy glanced down at the book.

58 "Look here," he said, noticing the dates.

59 "This last entry is over two years old."

60 "It is?"

61 "Yes, indeed. And Christopher Mulholland's is nearly a year before that—more than three years ago."

62 "Dear me," she said, shaking her head and heaving a dainty little sigh. "I would never have thought it. How time does fly away from us all, doesn't it, Mr Wilkins?"

63 "It's Weaver," Billy said. "W-e-a-v-e-r."

64 "Oh, of course it is!" she cried, sitting down on the sofa. "How silly of me. I do apologise. In one ear and out the other, that's me, Mr. Weaver."

My Notes

65 "You know something?" Billy said. 'Something that's really quite extraordinary about all this?"

66 "No, dear, I don't."

67 "Well, you see—both of these names, Mulholland and Temple, I not only seem to remember each one of them separately, so to speak, but somehow or other, in some peculiar way, they both appear to be sort of connected together as well. As though they were both famous for the same sort of thing, if you see what I mean—like … like Dempsey and Tunney, for example, or Churchill and Roosevelt."

68 "How amusing," she said. "But come over here now, dear, and sit down beside me on the sofa and I'll give you a nice cup of tea and a ginger biscuit before you go to bed."

69 "You really shouldn't bother," Billy said. "I didn't mean you to do anything like that." He stood by the piano, watching her as she fussed about with the cups and saucers. He noticed that she had small, white, quickly moving hands, and red finger-nails.

70 "I'm almost positive it was in the newspapers I saw them," Billy said. "I'll think of it in a second. I'm sure I will."

71 There is nothing more **tantalizing** than a thing like this which lingers just outside the borders of one's memory. He hated to give up.

72 "Now wait a minute," he said. "Wait just a minute. Mulholland … Christopher Mulholland … wasn't that the name of the Eton schoolboy who was on a walking-tour through the West Country, and then all of a sudden …"

73 "Milk?" she said. "And sugar?"

74 "Yes, please. And then all of a sudden …"

75 "Eton schoolboy?" she said. "Oh no, my dear, that can't possibly be right because my Mr. Mulholland was certainly not an Eton schoolboy when he came to me. He was a Cambridge undergraduate. Come over here now and sit next to me and warm yourself in front of this lovely fire. Come on. Your tea's all ready for you." She patted the empty place beside her on the sofa, and she sat there smiling at Billy and waiting for him to come over. He crossed the room slowly, and sat down on the edge of the sofa. She placed his teacup on the table in front of him.

76 "There we are," she said. "How nice and cosy this is, isn't it?"

77 Billy started sipping his tea. She did the same. For half a minute or so, neither of them spoke. But Billy knew that she was looking at him. Her body was half-turned towards him, and he could feel her eyes resting on his face, watching him over the rim of her teacup. Now and again, he caught a whiff of a peculiar smell that seemed to **emanate** directly from her person. It was not in the least unpleasant, and it reminded him—well, he wasn't quite sure what it reminded him of. Pickled walnuts? New leather? Or was it the corridors of a hospital?

tantalizing: fascinating
emanate: flow from

My Notes

trifle: little bit

78 "Mr. Mulholland was a great one for his tea," she said at length. "Never in my life have I seen anyone drink as much tea as dear, sweet Mr. Mulholland."

79 "I suppose he left fairly recently," Billy said. He was still puzzling his head about the two names.

80 He was positive now that he had seen them in the newspapers – in the headlines.

81 "Left?" she said, arching her brows. "But my dear boy, he never left. He's still here. Mr. Temple is also here. They're on the third floor, both of them together."

82 Billy set down his cup slowly on the table, and stared at his landlady. She smiled back at him, and then she put out one of her white hands and patted him comfortingly on the knee. "How old are you, my dear?" she asked.

83 "Seventeen."

84 "Seventeen!" she cried. "Oh, it's the perfect age! Mr. Mulholland was also seventeen. But I think he was a **trifle** shorter than you are, in fact I'm sure he was, and his teeth weren't quite so white. You have the most beautiful teeth, Mr. Weaver, did you know that?"

85 "They're not as good as they look," Billy said.

86 "They've got simply masses of fillings in them at the back."

87 "Mr. Temple, of course, was a little older," she said, ignoring his remark. "He was actually twenty-eight. And yet I never would have guessed it if he hadn't told me, never in my whole life. There wasn't a blemish on his body."

88 "A what?" Billy said.

89 "His skin was just like a baby's."

90 There was a pause. Billy picked up his teacup and took another sip of his tea, then he set it down again gently in its saucer. He waited for her to say something else, but she seemed to have lapsed into another of her silences. He sat there staring straight ahead of him into the far corner of the room, biting his lower lip.

91 "That parrot," he said at last. "You know something? It had me completely fooled when I first saw it through the window from the street. I could have sworn it was alive."

92 "Alas, no longer."

93 "It's most terribly clever the way it's been done," he said. "It doesn't look in the least bit dead. Who did it?"

94 "I did."

95 "You did?"

96 "Of course," she said. "And have you met my little Basil as well?" She nodded towards the dachshund curled up so comfortably in front of the fire.

Billy looked at it. And suddenly, he realised that this animal had all the time been just as silent and motionless as the parrot. He put out a hand and touched it gently on the top of its back. The back was hard and cold, and when he pushed the hair to one side with his fingers, he could see the skin underneath, greyish-black and dry and perfectly preserved.

97 "Good gracious me," he said. "How absolutely fascinating." He turned away from the dog and stared with deep admiration at the little woman beside him on the sofa. "It must be most awfully difficult to do a thing like that."

98 "Not in the least," she said. "I stuff all my little pets myself when they pass away. Will you have another cup of tea?"

99 "No, thank you," Billy said. The tea tasted faintly of bitter almonds, and he didn't much care for it.

100 "You did sign the book, didn't you?"

101 "Oh, yes."

102 "That's good. Because later on, if I happen to forget what you were called, then I can always come down here and look it up. I still do that almost every day with Mr. Mulholland and Mr ... Mr..."

103 "Temple," Billy said. "Gregory Temple. Excuse my asking, but haven't there been any other guests here except them in the last two or three years?"

104 Holding her teacup high in one hand, inclining her head slightly to the left, she looked up at him out of the corners of her eyes and gave him another gentle little smile. "No, my dear," she said. 'Only you.'

Making Observations

- What details do you notice about the landlady's living room?
- What emotions do you feel when reading this short story?

My Notes

GRAMMAR & USAGE

Complex Sentences

A complex sentence has one independent clause and one or more dependent clauses.

Independent Clause: *There were no shops on this wide street that he was walking along*

Dependent Clause: only a line of tall houses on each side

Dependent Clause: all them identical

Using a complex sentence structure enables a writer to show complex relationships between and among ideas.

Find one more example of a complex sentence in the story and note how it shows a complex idea.

My Notes

☑ **Focus on the Sentence**

Use details from the short story to complete the following sentences.

The landlady "seemed terribly nice" because

_____

_____

_____

The landlady "seemed terribly nice," so

_____

_____

_____

The landlady "seemed terribly nice," but

_____

_____

_____

Returning to the Text

- Reread the story to answer these text-dependent questions.
- Write any additional questions you have about the text in your Reader/Writer Notebook.

1. How is Billy described in the first few paragraphs of this story (paragraphs 1–5)? What does this reveal about his character? Use evidence to support your answer.

_____

_____

_____

_____

2. What does Billy observe about the Bed and Breakfast in paragraphs 8–9?

_____

_____

_____

_____

3. How does Billy feel about choosing between living in a boarding house and above a pub? What does this reveal about his perspective of men and women?

_____

_____

_____

_____

4. Describe the mood in paragraph 11. How does the author create this mood?

_____

_____

_____

_____

5. What is strange about the landlady when Billy rings the doorbell?

_____

_____

_____

_____

6. What juxtaposition does the author create to suggest to the reader that Billy's perception of the landlady is not quite accurate?

_____

_____

_____

_____

7. What can the reader infer, using evidence from the text, about the two boys that are missing? Based on this information, what conclusion can be drawn about Billy's fate?

_____

_____

_____

_____

8. What is the author implying when the landlady says, "... I stuff all my little pets myself when they pass away. Will you have another cup of tea?"

_____

_____

_____

_____

Working from the Text

9. Review your questions in the My Notes section. To prepare for a Socratic Seminar meet with your reading group. Share your list of questions with your group and work collaboratively to select 8–10 questions that deeply question the story from a Feminist perspective. Respectfully listen to your classmates' opinions. Record your group's questions in the chart.

Socratic Seminar Questions

10. Using the index cards provided by your teacher, write one question per card; on the reverse side, cite textual evidence that can support responses. Divide the cards among members of the group equally. Be prepared to refer to these cards during the seminar discussion.

11. Socratic Seminar: Listen closely to your peers' questions during the Socratic Seminar. Contribute relevant questions to the discussion and record notes from the discussion in the graphic organizer provided in step 12.

12. In previous activities, you have studied two texts written by women: "Cinderella, the Legend" and "Why Women Always Take Advantage of Men." You also have applied the feminist critical perspective to a text written by a man: *Pygmalion*. "The Landlady" is written by a man and the main character is a young man. To review how to apply Feminist Criticism, think about the works you have read, how you have applied the feminist perspective in each, and what attitudes and details you might expect to discover while applying this lens.

Work Studied	Plot Conflict, Character, or Values Commentary that Illustrate Feminist Perspective	Implications of Feminist Perspective
"Cinderella, the Legend"		
"Why Women Always Take Advantage of Men"		
Pygmalion		
"The Landlady"		

LANGUAGE & WRITER'S CRAFT: Citing Textual Evidence

For Embedded Assessment 2, you must include textual evidence and commentary to support your thesis statement. As you write the textual evidence on your index cards, practice three important skills of citing textual evidence:

- introducing the citation with a clearly written and appropriate lead-in.
- defining the source (In this case, cite paragraph or section number since the text is in your book)
- supporting the citation by providing original commentary and explanation

Examples:

Billy initially assumes the landlady is the stereotypical maternal older woman. He finds her to be warm and friendly and even thinks that she looks, "exactly like the mother of one's best schoolfriend welcoming one in the house to stay for the Christmas holidays" (paragraph 25).

Lead-in: Billy initially assumes the landlady is the stereotypical maternal older woman. He finds her to be warm and friendly and even thinks that she looks,

Textual evidence: "exactly like the mother of one's best schoolfriend welcoming one in the house to stay for the Christmas holidays"

Source: (paragraph 25)

In the parlor, Billy begins to wonder about other young men. His puzzlement and inability to remember make him a little unsure of himself in his surroundings. The landlady, on the other hand, begins to assert her control even further. When she tells him to come and sit by her, "He crossed the room slowly, and sat down on the edge of the sofa" (Paragraph 73).

Commentary: In the parlor, Billy begins to wonder about other young men. His puzzlement and inability to remember make him a little unsure of himself in his surroundings. The landlady, on the other hand, begins to assert her control even further

Lead-in: When she tells him to come and sit by her,

Textual evidence: "He crossed the room slowly, and sat down on the edge of the sofa"

Source: (Paragraph 73)

PRACTICE After finding your first piece of textual evidence to write on your index cards, follow the example to practice the skills mentioned for citing textual evidence: introduce with appropriate lead-in, define the source, and comment with an explanatory statement.

My Notes

📝 Writing Prompt: Argumentative

Write an analytical essay to explain the relationship between Billy and the landlady in "The Landlady," analyzing the story from a Feminist Perspective. In what ways do Billy and the landlady demonstrate characteristics stereotypical of men and women? In what way are the characters different? What is the balance of power between the sexes in this story and how is that power expressed? Use textual evidence to support and clarify your thinking. Be sure to:

- Begin with a clear thesis that states your primary interpretation of Dahl's story.
- Organize your analysis by logically sequencing your interpretation, counterclaims, reasons, and evidence.
- Use transitions strategically to link your ideas.
- Cite textual evidence to provide reasons to support your interpretation.
- Introduce and punctuate all quotations and nonrestrictive elements correctly.

📖 Independent Reading Checkpoint

Review your independent reading and any notes you have taken. What have you learned about Feminist Criticism and how to analyze a text from a feminist perspective? Discuss your learning with classmates, clarify your understanding of Feminist Criticism, and add new insight to your notes. How can this information help you complete the upcoming Embedded Assessment?

Applying a Critical Perspective

 ASSIGNMENT

Your assignment is to write an analytical essay applying the Feminist Critical Perspective to a short story. You have two stories to read and choose from, "The Story of an Hour" by Kate Chopin or "The Chaser" by John Collier. (Both stories are included.)

Planning and Prewriting: Read critically and collect your evidence.	▪ Which of the two stories resonates with you on a personal level? ▪ What questions are asked about a text when it is read from a feminist perspective? ▪ How will you collect your initial ideas to create a focus on feminist perspective of these stories? (e.g., brainstorming, a graphic organizer)? ▪ How will you determine which ideas should go into your draft? ▪ Who is the audience for your essay? How much do you think this audience knows about feminist issues and feminist criticism?
Drafting: Craft your analysis.	▪ How much summary is necessary to introduce the story to the audience? How can you summarize and paraphrase the text in a way that keeps the author's original meaning? ▪ How will you use both evidence from the text and your own words to support your feminist perspective? ▪ How can you make sure that your writing is clear and engaging to the reader (e.g., using appeals, sentence variety, transitions between ideas)?
Evaluating and Revising Your Draft: Review and improve to make your work the best it can be.	▪ How can you determine if your syntax and use of language helps the reader understand your feminist analysis? ▪ How will you determine if your sentence structure and transitions present your ideas in the best way? ▪ How can you use your peers' insights and the Scoring Guide to help evaluate your draft and guide your revision?
Checking and Editing for Publication: Confirm that your final draft is ready.	▪ How will you check for grammatical and technical accuracy? ▪ What tools are available to you to create a technically sound text (e.g., dictionary or format guide, spell check)?

Reflection

After completing this Embedded Assessment, think about how you went about accomplishing this assignment, and respond to the following:

• How did your understanding of Feminist Criticism shape your analysis of the short story?

SCORING GUIDE

Scoring Criteria	Exemplary	Proficient	Emerging	Incomplete
Ideas	The essay • demonstrates a thorough understanding of feminist issues in the short story. • perceptively applies the Feminist Critical perspective to the text. • uses well-chosen details that support the main ideas of the analysis.	The essay • demonstrates an understanding of the feminist issues in the short story. • appropriately applies the Feminist Critical perspective to the text. • analyzes the work with appropriate details that support the main ideas.	The essay • demonstrates a superficial understanding of the feminist issues in the short story. • contains an underdeveloped application of Feminist Criticism. • contains too few examples or details, possibly replaced by excessive and unorganized summary.	The essay • demonstrates little understanding of the feminist short story. • does not apply Feminist Criticism. • contains few examples or details and may repeat some details unnecessarily.
Structure	The essay • follows an exceptionally clear organization. • uses sentence structure and transitions effectively and creatively to move smoothly from one idea to the next.	The essay • organizes ideas clearly so that they are easy to follow. • uses sentence structure adequately and some transitions to move between ideas.	The essay • organizes ideas in ways that are difficult to follow. • uses weak sentence structure and few transitions or jumps too rapidly between ideas.	The essay • is disorganized or uses a confusing organization. • uses poor or awkward sentence structure and few or no transitions to move between limited ideas.
Use of Language	The essay • crafts language to enhance the analysis and consistently convey an academic voice. • successfully weaves in textual evidence from the story. • demonstrates strong control and mastery of standard writing conventions.	The essay • uses language clearly to communicate the analysis and demonstrate an appropriate academic voice. • accurately weaves in textual evidence from the story. • demonstrates control of standard writing conventions; may contain minor errors that do not interfere with meaning.	The essay • uses language that does not clearly communicate the analysis or demonstrate an academic voice. • awkwardly or inaccurately incorporates evidence from the story. • contains frequent errors in standard writing conventions that interfere with meaning.	The essay • does not clearly communicate the analysis or use an academic voice. • inaccurately uses a few details from the story. • contains numerous errors in standard writing conventions that seriously impede understanding.

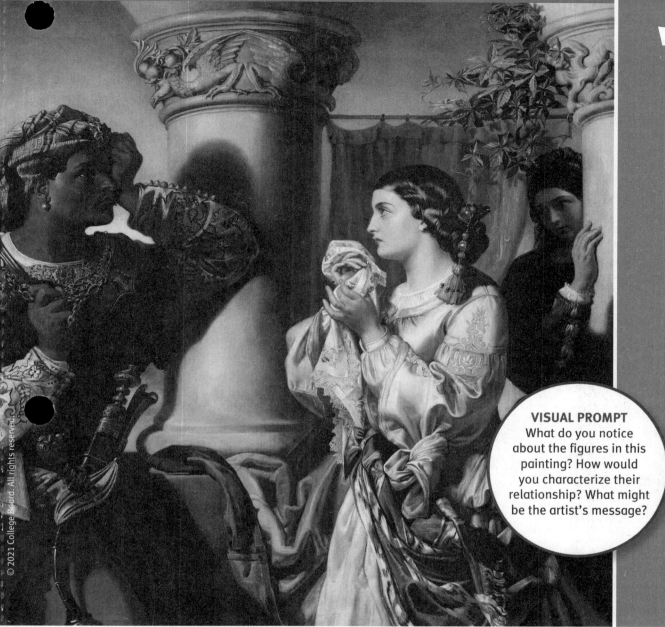

VISUAL PROMPT
What do you notice about the figures in this painting? How would you characterize their relationship? What might be the artist's message?

EVOLVING PERSPECTIVES

O! beware, my lord, of jealousy;
It is the green-ey'd monster which doth mock
The meat it feeds on.

—from *Othello*, by William Shakespeare

ACTIVITY	CONTENTS

CONTENTS

*Texts not included in these materials.

My Independent Reading List

Learning Strategies

Discussion Groups
Note-taking
Sharing and Responding
Visualizing

My Notes

Learning Targets

- Preview the big ideas for the unit.
- Create a plan for reading independently.
- Identify and analyze the skills and knowledge needed to complete Embedded Assessment 1 successfully.

Preview

In this activity, you will explore the big ideas and tasks of the unit and make plans for your independent reading.

About the Unit

In this unit, you will deepen your understanding of critical perspectives as you apply literary theories to Shakespeare's *The Tragedy of Othello, The Moor of Venice*. This play has been in continuous production for more than 400 years. In addition to its role as a drama, two operas, several ballets, and other plays have been derived from *Othello*. Shakespeare's works continue to be relevant today because they speak to universal themes that are still present in many people's lives. As you read *Othello* you will be introduced to Historical Criticism as a means to analyze the drama and the characters from a historical perspective.

Essential Questions

Based on your current knowledge, respond to the following Essential Questions.

1. What role does literature play in examining recurring social issues?

2. How can an original text be adapted for different audiences?

Unpacking Embedded Assessment 1

Closely read the following assignment for Embedded Assessment 1: Writing a Literary Analysis.

 Select a character from Othello and write a literary analysis about him or her using one of the critical lenses that you have studied (choose among Feminist, Marxist, Cultural, Historical, or Archetypal for this assignment). You will support your analysis with valid reasoning and sufficient evidence from your reading, observations, and previous written work.

With your class, create a graphic organizer that includes the skills and knowledge you will need to write an in-depth literary analysis. Summarize the major elements in your Reader/Writer Notebook.

🔵 Planning Independent Reading

The focus of this unit is the play *Othello* by William Shakespeare. For independent reading, consider a novel or play that connects to one or more themes from *Othello*, such as race, identity, jealousy, or deceit. Make a reading plan and decide which themes you'd like to explore. Discuss your plan and list of potential texts with a group of peers. Listen attentively and offer feedback on text selections and how to make your reading plans more effective.

Previewing Embedded Assessment 2

In this unit, you will be building skills and knowledge relevant to both Embedded Assessment 1 and Embedded Assessment 2 at the same time. Before diving in to study of *Othello*, it may be beneficial to also read the Embedded Assessment 2 assignment and Scoring Guide.

Learning Strategies

Discussion Groups

Marking the Text

Quickwrite

My Notes

Learning Targets

- Work collaboratively to examine the requirements for a staged interpretation of a scene from *Othello*.
- Examine scenes in the play to prepare a group performance.

Preview

In this activity, you will work with your group to create an acting company. You will familiarize yourself with the theatrical roles commonly found in a staged performance and collaborate to assign a role to each member of your group.

All the World's a Stage

1. In Shakespeare's day, acting companies named themselves, sometimes honoring their patron. Shakespeare belonged first to the Lord Chamberlain's Men and later to the King's Men. Choose a name for your acting company.

2. For the second Embedded Assessment, you and your acting group will stage an interpretation of a scene from *Othello* that you find demonstrates a critical perspective. Work with your acting company to make a preliminary scene selection from the list of suggested scenes on pages 255–256.

3. In Shakespeare's day, an acting company included a director, a dramaturge, and a company of actors. With the other members of your company, collaboratively assign roles for each member of the company for this activity. It is not absolutely necessary that gender dictate your casting choices. Make preliminary decisions about the following roles within your acting company:

   - **Director:** Leads rehearsals, working collaboratively with the group. Assumes responsibility for all of the theatrical elements: a set diagram, a plan for lighting and sound, props, and a complete script of the scene. Writes and memorizes an engaging introduction to the performance and delivers it to the audience on performance day.

   - **Dramaturge:** Conducts research to support the critical perspective the group has decided to apply to the scene and answers questions. Writes a concluding statement about the scene that explains how the group applied a critical perspective and how research supported the performance and recites this statement at the end of the performance.

   - **Actors:** Study the play, paying particular attention to their characters' motivations and relationships to other characters, and take notes. Collaborate with the director and the other actors to plan a performance. During the performance, use appropriate vocal delivery, tone, gestures, movement, props, and costumes to convey nuances of each character.

Scene	Description	Characters	First line and approximate length
Act I, Scene I	Iago and Roderigo awaken Brabantio and inform him that his daughter has eloped.	Iago Roderigo Brabantio	RODERIGO: Tush, never tell me! 206 lines (Companies could opt to do only part of the scene.)
Act I, Scene III Lines 197–335	Desdemona admits her love for Othello; the Duke dispatches them to Cyprus.	Duke Desdemona Othello First senator (only one line)	DUKE: I think this tale would win my daughter too. 139 lines
Act I, Scene III Lines 344–447	Iago continues to take advantage of Roderigo's affection for Desdemona.	Roderigo Iago	RODERIGO: Iago— IAGO: What say'st thou, noble heart? 104 lines
Act II, Scene I Lines 197–307	Desdemona welcomes Othello to Cyprus; Iago convinces Roderigo to attack Cassio.	Othello Desdemona Iago Roderigo	OTHELLO: O my fair warrior! 111 lines
Act II, Scene III Lines 14–124	With Iago's encouragement, Cassio gets drunk.	Cassio Iago Montano Gentleman (only one line, which could be given to Montano)	CASSIO: Welcome, Iago. We must to the watch. 111 lines
Act II, Scene III Lines 125–265	A drunken brawl ends with Othello demoting Cassio.	Iago Montano Cassio Roderigo	IAGO [*to Montano*]: You see this fellow that is gone before. 141 lines

Scene	Description	Characters	First line and approximate length
Act III, Scene III Lines 1–99	Desdemona tries to convince Othello to reinstate Cassio.	Desdemona Emilia Cassio Othello Iago	DESDEMONA: Be thou assured, good Cassio … 99 lines
Act III, Scene III Lines 100–240	Iago plants the seed of doubt in Othello's mind.	Othello Iago	OTHELLO: Excellent wretch! 141 lines
Act III, Scene IV Lines 39–115	Othello demands to see the handkerchief, while Desdemona tries to change the subject by pleading Cassio's case.	Othello Desdemona	OTHELLO: How do you, Desdemona? 77 lines
Act IV, Scene II Lines 128–201	Desdemona seeks advice from Iago, while Emilia curses the person who planted the thought of infidelity in Othello's mind.	Iago Desdemona Emilia	IAGO: What is your pleasure, madam? 74 lines
Act IV, Scene III Lines 11–117	Desdemona and Emilia discuss infidelity.	Desdemona Emilia	EMILIA: How goes it now? 107 lines
Act V, Scene I Lines 1–151	Roderigo attacks Cassio.	Iago Roderigo Cassio Gratiano Lodovico Bianca Emilia	IAGO: Here, stand behind this bulk. 151 lines
Act V, Scene II Lines 131–301	Emilia tells Othello the truth.	Emilia Othello Desdemona Montano	OTHELLO: What's the matter with thee now? 171 lines

4. Once you have come to an agreement, sign and turn in a contract to your teacher. You may use the following template:

We, the _____ (name of acting company),

pledge to plan, rehearse, and perform _____

(act and scene) **from William Shakespeare's *The Tragedy of Othello*.**

Cast:

(Name of student) **as** (name of character)

Director:

Dramaturge:

☑ Check Your Understanding

Quickwrite: Explain how you will help your troupe achieve the goal of interpreting a scene of *Othello*. How will your role impact the audience based on your understanding of the roles of a director, a dramaturge, and actors?

Learning Strategies

Graphic Organizer
Marking the Text
Summarizing

VOCABULARY

ACADEMIC

Components are the parts that make up a whole. They can be steps in a process, ingredients in a recipe, or aspects of a critical perspective.

WORD CONNECTIONS

Roots and Affixes

The word **components** contains the Latin prefix *com-*, which means "with" or "together." The Latin root of *component* is *ponere*, which means "to place." Related words include *comport*, *compose*, *composer*, and *composite*.

My Notes

_____

_____

_____

_____

_____

_____

_____

_____

_____

_____

_____

_____

Learning Targets

- Compare and contrast the development of a theme in song lyrics and a poem.
- Analyze two texts through a critical perspective to make connections to a social issue.
- Evaluate the use of meter and form in two texts.

Preview

In this activity, you will review the elements of Cultural Criticism and apply the lens to compare how two authors address similar themes. You will make pointed observations about the similarities and differences in how each writer has crafted their work to comment on a recurring social issue.

Cultural Criticism

1. Review the **components** of Cultural Criticism. Use this critical perspective as your lens as you carefully consider two texts that follow.

   Cultural Criticism examines how differing religious beliefs, ethnicities, class identifications, political beliefs, and individual viewpoints affect how texts are created and interpreted. What it means to be a part of—or excluded from—a specific group contributes to and affects our understanding of texts in relation to culture.

   Some common assumptions in the use of Cultural Criticism are as follows:

   - Ethnicity, religious beliefs, political beliefs, and customs are crucial components in formulating plausible interpretations of texts.
   - An examination or exploration of the relationship between dominant cultures and the marginalized groups is essential to understanding a text.

☑ Focus on the Sentence

Write two complete sentences in response to what you have learned so far about Cultural Criticism. The first should be a statement that paraphrases the definition of Cultural Criticism in your own words. The second should be a question you have about the lens.

Statement: _____

_____

Question: _____

2. Listen to the song "The Right to Love," written by Gene Lees and Lilo Schifrin in the 1960s. As you listen, follow along with the printed lyrics. After listening to the song, write a one-sentence summary of what the song is about. Then read the following poem.

© 2021 College Board. All rights reserved.

As You Read

- Underline words and phrases that connect to the song lyrics.
- Circle unknown words and phrases. Try to determine the meaning of the words by using context clues, word parts, or a dictionary.

About the Author

Born to a prosperous Catholic family in London at a time when anti-Catholic sentiment abounded, John Donne (1572–1631) had a promising career as a diplomat but spent most of his fortune on leisure and pleasure. He secretly married Anne More, much to the disapproval of her father, and she gave birth to 12 children, dying with the last birth. In 1615, at the king's order, he became an Anglican priest and was later dean of St. Paul's Cathedral. His life was influenced by spiritual conflict, and Donne is best known as a metaphysical poet whose writings are laden with rich religious symbolism, metaphor, and unexpected imagery.

Poetry

The Canonization

by **John Donne**

For God's sake hold your tongue, and let me love;
    Or **chide** my palsy, or my gout;
My five gray hairs, or ruin'd fortune **flout**;
    With wealth your state, your mind with arts improve;
5   Take you a course, get you a place,
        Observe his Honour, or his Grace;
Or the king's real, or his stamp'd face
    Contemplate; what you will, approve,
    So you will let me love.

My Notes

WORD CONNECTIONS

Etymology
The word **canonization**, in the Roman Catholic Church, refers to the act of formally recognizing a saint. The term comes from the Late Latin *canon*, meaning "church law," which later referred to a list of texts considered holy by the church. To *canonize* is to treat something as sacred.

chide: scold
flout: openly disregard

My Notes

10   Alas! alas! who's injured by my love?

        What merchant's ships have my sighs drown'd?

Who says my tears have overflow'd his ground?

        When did my colds a forward spring remove?

          When did the heats which my veins fill

15   Add one more to the plaguy bill?

Soldiers find wars, and lawyers find out still

        Litigious men, which quarrels move,

        Though she and I do love.

Call's what you will, we are made such by love;

20   Call her one, me another fly,

We're **tapers** too, and at our own cost die,

        And we in us find th' eagle and the dove.

          The phoenix riddle hath more wit

        By us; we two being one, are it;

25   So, to one neutral thing both sexes fit.

        We die and rise the same, and prove

        Mysterious by this love.

We can die by it, if not live by love,

        And if unfit for tomb or hearse

30   Our legend be, it will be fit for verse;

        And if no piece of chronicle we prove,

          We'll build in sonnets pretty rooms;

          As well a well-wrought urn becomes

The greatest ashes, as half-acre tombs,

35   And by these hymns, all shall approve

        Us **canonized** for love.

And thus **invoke us**, "You, whom reverend love

        Made one another's **hermitage**

You, to whom love was peace, that now is rage;

litigious: quarrelsome
tapers: candles
canonized: marked
invoke us: call upon us for help
hermitage: hideaway or retreat

40   Who did the whole world's soul contract, and drove

          Into the glasses of your eyes;

          So made such mirrors, and such spies,

     That they did all to you **epitomize**—

          Countries, towns, courts beg from above

45   A pattern of your love!"

Making Observations
- What is the speaker asking his audience?
- What imagery do you notice in the poem?
- How would you describe the speaker's relationship?

epitomize: represent

Returning to the Text

- Reread the poem to answer these text-dependent questions.
- Write any additional questions you have about the text in your Reader/Writer Notebook.

3. What clues in the poem indicate the message the author wishes to convey?

_____

_____

_____

_____

4. What context clues reveal the meaning of "the plaguy bill" in line 15?

_____

_____

_____

_____

5. How does the speaker use rhetorical questions in lines 10–15 to emphasize his point?

_____

_____

_____

_____

6. What images does Donne create in the lines "Call her one, me another fly, / We're tapers too, and at our own cost die" to compel his audience?

_____

_____

_____

_____

7. What does the title of the poem reveal about the speaker's descriptions of himself and his lover in lines 28–36?

_____

_____

_____

_____

8. What does the speaker say about the value of the criticisms leveled against his love by the end of the poem?

_____

_____

_____

_____

Working from the Text

9. Work with your discussion group to analyze the texts using Cultural Criticism. Respond to the questions in the following graphic organizer and conduct On the Spot Research, as needed, to learn more about the author or singer's background or the time period in which each text was written.

"The Right to Love"	Applying Cultural Criticism	"The Canonization"
	Who is the speaker? What is the situation? How might the cultural context affect the meaning of the text?	
	Is the point of view of the speaker from a marginalized or dominant perspective?	
	What does the author suggest about the experience of people who have been ignored, under-represented, or misrepresented in history (such as women, people of color)?	
	How does this literary work add to our understanding of the human experience of love in the time and place in which it is set?	
	How might this work be received differently by today's audience than it was by the audience of the time it was written?	
	Does the text have relevance to contemporary life?	

My Notes

☑ Check Your Understanding

How has Cultural Criticism provided you with insight into the authors' purposes and the circumstances surrounding the creation of "The Canonization" and "The Right to Love"?

LANGUAGE & WRITER'S CRAFT: Rhythm and Meter

Meter refers to a repeating pattern of stressed and unstressed syllables in spoken or written language. By placing an emphasis on certain syllables, an author is able to create rhythm. Look at these lines from the poem "The Canonization" by John Donne:

> Alas! Alas! Who's injured by my love?
>
> …
>
> Who says my tears have overflow'd his ground?
>
> When did my colds a forward spring remove?

These lines consist of a number of metrical feet, which in this case contain one unstressed and one stressed syllable. This pattern of unstressed-stressed creates iambic meter, the most common rhythm in English verse. Some say it sounds like a heartbeat:

> da-DUM, da-DUM, da-DUM, da-DUM, da-DUM

Much of *Othello* is written in blank verse, which is iambic pentameter (10 syllables to a line) that does not rhyme. Mark up the lines spoken by Othello to show meter. Write a symbol like this (˘) over each unstressed syllable and one like this (′) over each stressed syllable.

> She loved me for the dangers I had passed,
>
> And I loved her that she did pity them.
>
> This only is the witchcraft I have used.
>
> Here comes the lady; let her witness it.

Notice how the slight variations in the rhythm prevent the lines from becoming too singsong, even though most of the lines are in iambic pentameter.

PRACTICE Revisit a section of John Donne's poem of interest to you and mark the text to identify the meter.

My Notes

Writing Prompt: Informational

Write a comparative analysis paragraph that examines the rhythm and meter in the song lyrics and the poem. Be sure to:

- Identify the rhythm and meter of song lyrics.
- Support your analysis by providing examples from each text.
- Use the third-person point of view and a formal academic tone.

Building a Plot and Bringing It to Life: Irony

Learning Strategies

Drafting
Visualizing

VOCABULARY

ACADEMIC

Something **unconventional** does not follow the accepted ways of acting in a situation. Interracial marriages were uncommon in Shakespeare's time.

The word **scenario** refers to a hypothetical situation or specific possibility. As used here, it indicates the outline of a dramatic scene.

My Notes

Learning Targets

- Demonstrate your understanding of dramatic, situational, and verbal irony through preparation and performance of a scene.
- Interpret a scenario considering the characters' background and underlying motivations.

Preview

In this activity, you will examine the effects of verbal, situational, and dramatic irony. You will then collaborate with your group to present a scenario and one of the outcomes to the class. Then write an essay in a group describing how one of the other scenarios presented irony and subtext.

Analyzing the Plot and Themes

1. Although it is likely you have not encountered Shakespeare's *Othello* in your previous English classes, its plot and the theme—jealousy, leading to passion and betrayal—are universally appealing literary themes. In order to jump into the timeless story of an **unconventional** marriage and the jealousy that complicates it, visualize the **scenario** that follows and the outcome assigned to you by your teacher.

Scenario	Character 1 tells Character 2 that Character 2's romantic partner is cheating on him. Character 1 then produces "evidence." However, the story is untrue; Character 1 is actually lying.
Outcome A	Character 2 does not believe the story and turns on Character 1.
Outcome B	Character 2 considers the story as a possibility but then, after much investigation, decides it is not true.
Outcome C	Character 2 believes the story, is filled with jealousy, and wants revenge.

2. Review the definitions of the types of irony in the Literary Terms box. How is **dramatic**, **verbal**, or **situational irony** used in the scenario? How can you make irony a significant part of your plot?

- What is the character's motivation? Your identification of character backgrounds and motivations is an important aspect of the subtext of this scene.
- How will you use dialogue to advance the plot?
- What physical evidence will serve as "proof" of cheating? Knowledge of the truth by one character and not the other creates dramatic irony.

3. Work with your group to draft the scenario. As you review your draft, ask yourselves these questions:

- Is the language and word choice precise and engaging enough to keep listeners interested?
- Are your sentences varied?
- What adaptations have you made in order to present to your literary peers?

4. Rehearse and present the scenario to your classmates, employing eye contact, a reasonable speaking volume, and gestures that help your audience fully understand and appreciate your scenario. Think about the way your delivery of lines or the way you stand or move will enhance the performance.

5. Thoughtfully and respectfully attend the performances of the scenes developed by your classmates, and take note of how each scene makes use of the dramatic elements. Use the chart that follows to take notes on the performances you view.

© 2021 College Board. All rights reserved.

VOCABULARY

LITERARY

Dramatic irony is a situation in which the audience knows more about the circumstances or future events in a story than the characters within it; as a result, the audience can see a discrepancy between characters' perceptions and the reality they face.

Verbal irony occurs when a character says one thing but means something very different.

Situational irony is like a surprise ending—your audience expects one thing to happen, but something completely different takes place.

Performance Notes	
What clues were given to indicate the type of irony being displayed?	
What is the climactic aspect of the scene?	
How was subtext used to create irony?	

☑ **Check Your Understanding**

What did you learn about analyzing irony, writing dialogue, and performing a short scene?

📝 **Writing Prompt: Informational**

With your group, write a paragraph to analyze how one of the other groups conveyed irony and subtext in their performance. Be sure to:

- Identify the group and give a brief summary of its performance.
- Include specific examples from the performance that convey a particular type of irony.
- Use a coherent organizational structure and make connections between specific words, images, and ideas conveyed.

My Notes

✒ Writing Prompt: Informational

Write a paragraph that explains how Marxist Criticism can inform analysis of characters in the play. Take into consideration how each character interacts with others from the various social hierarchies. Be sure to:

- Begin with a topic sentence summarizing your understanding of the ways in which Marxist Criticism highlights the social hierarchy of characters.
- Cite relevant textual evidence to support your explanation.
- Use words, phrases, and clauses to link major sections of the text and explain relationships between your analysis and new understandings.
- Maintain an engaging, formal, and objective tone, while using the standard English conventions of mechanics and usage.
- Use precise, accurate language to explain your perspective on the topic.
- Consult a dictionary or other reference materials to clarify the meanings of unknown words.
- Provide a logical conclusion that summarizes the new insights gained from applying Marxist Criticism.

A Father's Reaction:
Performing and Defending an Interpretation

Learning Strategies

Drafting
Drama Games
Graphic Organizer
Marking the Text

ACADEMIC

A rationale is an explanation. A rationale can tell why a particular interpretation of a play is effective.

WORD CONNECTIONS

Roots and Affixes

The Latin root *notare*, meaning "note" or "mark," and the prefix *ad-*, meaning "to," form the base of the word **annotate**. A related noun is formed by adding the suffix *-tion*. Words from the same root include *notary*, *notable*, and *notation*.

Learning Targets

- Revise a scene with added subtext to convey an alternate tone in performance.
- Write a character analysis describing different, sometimes conflicting character traits.
- Analyze a performance of a Shakespearean scene using two critical perspectives.

Preview

In this activity, you will reread Act I, Scene I (lines 178–206). Then you will annotate the lines and perform the scene with your acting company. You will also write and share a rationale for your interpretation from a Marxist perspective.

As You Read

- Underline words and phrases that indicate Brabantio's emotional state.
- Circle unknown words and phrases. Try to determine the meaning of the words by using context clues, word parts, or a dictionary.

About the Author

British poet and playwright William Shakespeare (1564–1616) is perhaps the most famous writer of all time. Shakespeare began his theatrical life as an actor and writer. He eventually started an acting troupe and opened his own theatre, The Globe, in London. Shakespeare was a favorite playwright of many royals and noblemen, yet his work was also beloved by the common people. After his death, speculation grew as to whether or not one man could have written such eloquent and varied works. Nevertheless, Shakespeare has remained one of the most widely read, published, and studied authors of all time.

Play

My Notes

from *The Tragedy of Othello: The Moor of Venice*

by **William Shakespeare**

Enter Brabantio in his nightgown, with Servants and Torches.

  BRABANTIO: It is too true an evil. Gone she is;

  And what's to become of my despised time

180 Is naught but bitterness. Now, Roderigo,

  Where didst thou see her?—O, unhappy girl!—

  With the Moor, say'st thou?—Who would be a
   father?—

  How didst thou know 'twas she?—O, she deceives

185 me

  Past thought!—What said she to you?—Get more
   tapers.

  Raise all my kindred.—Are they married, think
   you?

190 RODERIGO: Truly I think they are.

  BRABANTIO: O heaven! How got she out? O treason of the blood!

  Fathers, from hence trust not your daughters' minds

  By what you see them act.—Is there not charms

  By which the property of youth and maidhood

195 May be abused? Have you not read, Roderigo,

  Of some such thing?

  RODERIGO: Yes, sir, I have indeed.

  BRABANTIO: Call up my brother.—O, would you had had her!—

  Some one way, some another.—Do you know

200 Where we may apprehend her and the Moor?

  RODERIGO: I think I can discover him, if you please

  To get good guard and go along with me.

GRAMMAR & USAGE

Complex Sentences

Even though the English of Shakespeare's day is somewhat different from the language we use today, much of the sentence structure remains the same.

Note Roderigo's sentence, "I think I can discover him, if you please to get good guard and go along with me."

This is a complex sentence, meaning that it begins with an independent clause (*I think I can discover him*) and ends with a dependent clause (*if you please to get good guard and go along with me*). This subordinate clause is introduced by the conjunction *if*, and since it modifies the verb *discover* it can be considered an adverbial clause. An adverbial clause gives details about the verb.

Find another complex sentence from *Othello* and annotate it for independent clause, dependent clause, conjunction, and adverbial clause where appropriate.

GRAMMAR & USAGE

Language Change

The English language has changed quite a bit in the 500 years since Shakespeare wrote his famous plays. Words such as *naught*, *hence*, *maidhood*, and *tapers* have dropped from common usage but can still be understood through **context**. Some usages are no longer modern, but people still understand them, as is the case with the word *treason* in "treason of the blood."

Other words such as *didst* and *say'st* can show us how verb forms have changed since Shakespeare's era. We have dropped the *-st* from our versions of these words.

Find two examples in the text of words that seem to have changed since Shakespeare's time and update them with modern language.

My Notes

_____
_____
_____
_____
_____
_____
_____
_____
_____
_____
_____
_____
_____
_____
_____

BRABANTIO: Pray you lead on. At every house I'll call.

I may command at most.—Get weapons, ho!

205 And raise some special officers of night.—

On, good Roderigo. I will deserve your pains.

They exit.

Iago and Roderigo inform Brabantio of Othello and Desdemona's marriage.

Making Observations

- What news does Roderigo share with Brabantio?
- What are your initial thoughts about Brabantio's reaction?
- What questions do you have about this scene?

☑ Focus on the Sentence

Use details from the passage to complete the sentences:

Brabantio is frantic because _____

_____

Brabantio is frantic, but _____

Brabantio is frantic, so _____

Returning to the Text

- Reread the play to answer these text-dependent questions.
- Write any additional questions you have about the text in your Reader/Writer Notebook.

1. What evidence in Brabantio's first speech shows how he is feeling?

_____

_____

_____

_____

2. What earlier phrase shows what Brabantio means when he says to "Call up my brother" the third time he speaks?

_____

_____

_____

_____

3. Speak aloud the sentence, "At every house I'll call" from Brabantio's last speech. How does the unusual sentence structure affect the emphasis?

_____

_____

_____

_____

4. Which details give clues to the meaning of the word *pains* in the last line of the excerpt?

_____

_____

_____

_____

5. What phrases in Brabantio's speech indicate his speed and urgency?

_____

_____

_____

_____

My Notes

Planning an Interpretation

6. Follow along as your teacher models how to annotate the text in order to guide an actor delivering Brabantio's lines. Consider how the delivery the can reveal Brabantio's characteristics.

7. Based on your assigned subtext, annotate the text to include how the actor should move on stage to convey the emotional tone of the scene.

> BRABANTIO: It is too true an evil. Gone she is,
>
> And what's to become of my despised time
>
> Is naught but bitterness.—Now, Roderigo,
>
> Where didst thou see her?—O, unhappy girl!—
>
> With the Moor, say'st thou?—Who would be a father?—
>
> How didst thou know 'twas she?—O, she deceives me
>
> Past thought!—What said she to you?—Get more tapers.
>
> Raise all my kindred.—Are they married, think you?
>
> RODERIGO: Truly, I think they are.
>
> BRABANTIO: O heaven! How got she out? O treason of the blood!
>
> Fathers, from hence trust not your daughters' minds
>
> By what you see them act.—Is there not charms
>
> By which the property of youth and maidhood
>
> May be abused? Have you not read, Roderigo,
>
> Of some such thing?
>
> RODERIGO: Yes, sir, I have indeed.
>
> BRABANTIO: Call up my brother.—O, would you had had her!—
>
> Some one way, some another.—Do you know
>
> Where we may apprehend her and the Moor?
>
> RODERIGO: I think I can discover him, if you please
>
> To get good guard and go along with me.
>
> BRABANTIO: Pray you lead on. At every house I'll call.
>
> I may command at most.—Get weapons, ho!
>
> And raise some special officers of night.—
>
> On, good Roderigo. I will deserve your pains.

8. With your acting company, rehearse the lines for a performance. Ensure that the performance includes strong stage presence, including eye contact and pacing.

Applying Critical Perspectives

9. Consider interpreting the text through the application of critical lenses. How might you adjust the scene so that it lends itself to a strong analysis from either a cultural or Marxist perspective? Review the assumptions of Cultural and Marxist Criticism as needed.

Critical Perspective	Delivery of Lines, Staging (characters' actions), Blocking (characters' movements)
Cultural	
Marxist	

3.6

☑ Check Your Understanding

Think about the decisions your acting company made about how to convey the scene onstage. How did you adapt the original text for your current audience? Explain the rationale—or reasons—behind those decisions.

📝 Writing Prompt: Literary Analysis

Write a brief character analysis of Brabantio from either a Cultural or a Marxist critical perspective. Choose the lens that best illuminates Brabantio's character in this scene, and state your claim at the beginning of your paragraph. Be sure to:

- Provide a well-reasoned claim that incorporates the critical lens.
- Establish the significance of your claim, distinguishing it from alternate or opposing choices made by others.
- Use varied syntax, such as adverb clauses, and proper grammar.

Learning Targets

- Examine and analyze how the descriptions of Othello reflect cultural and social attitudes of the time period.
- Write a character analysis based on the assumptions of Cultural Criticism.

Preview

In this activity, you will closely analyze the characters in Act I of *Othello*. Then you will use Cultural Criticism to write a character sketch about the main character.

Reflecting on *Othello*: Act I, Scene I

1. Whether endearing or irritating, the way others refer to us says a great deal about our culture—its values, beliefs, attitudes, and expectations. The use of an **epithet**, such as "so-and-so's daughter" or a "quarterback on team X," can reveal a culture's attitudes about family legacy or social expectations. With a partner, think of a few additional examples of epithets.

2. Skim and scan the first scene of *Othello*, paying particular attention to the ways in which the characters refer to Othello. Mark the text to indicate where epithets are used.

3. Throughout the first scene, no character uses Othello's name, although all three characters refer to him several times. Use your annotations to decide what each speaker is suggesting about Othello, and whether each term is complimentary or derogatory. Also, decide what the descriptive terms reveal about the speaker in each case. Use the graphic organizer on the following page to record your ideas.

Othello speaks before Brabantio and Venetian Senators.

Learning Strategies

Graphic Organizer
Quickwrite
Think-Pair-Share

VOCABULARY

LITERARY

An **epithet** is a descriptive word or phrase used in place of or along with a name. For instance, Shakespeare is sometimes simply called "the Bard." Detroit is known as "Motor City." Alexander III of Macedon is commonly called "Alexander the Great."

My Notes

_____

_____

_____

_____

_____

_____

_____

_____

_____

WORD CONNECTIONS

Word Relationships

A **derogatory** term conveys a lack of respect for a person or thing. Its synonym *belittling* describes making someone feel small, and to be *contemptuous* is to treat a person with hate or scorn. *Complimentary* is an antonym that describes speaking well about someone.

Reference to Othello	Who is speaking? (line number)	How does the phrase exhibit an attitude toward Othello?	How is the character of speaker revealed in his use of the phrase?
Example: "his Moorship's"	Iago (line 35)	He's ironically compared to royalty.	Iago uses verbal irony here; he doesn't think of Othello as royalty. Despite Othello's rank, Iago looks down on him.

Reading Othello: Act I, Scene II

4. As you read Act I, Scene II, make note of Othello's responses to the accusations against him.

Accusation	Accuser	Othello's Response	What does Othello's response indicate about him?

5. Discuss with a group how other characters' descriptions of Othello reveal the cultural attitudes of the time period. Why might they use derogatory phrases instead of referring to Othello by name or title?

☑ Focus on the Sentence

Given the subject, write a sentence using an appositive to describe the subject.

Brabantio

_____

_____

Desdemona

_____

_____

Othello

_____

_____

✐ Writing Prompt: Literary Analysis

Write a character analysis of Othello that describes him from the Cultural Criticism perspective. Consider your own observations and the insights from your group discussion. Use the following character analysis of Brabantio, Desdemona's father, as a model for your writing. Be sure to:

- Include a thesis statement that applies the perspective of Cultural Criticism.
- Include specific details and textual evidence about Othello that describe the character.
- Use correct punctuation, such as dashes and commas.

GRAMMAR & USAGE

Appositives

Appositives are nouns or noun phrases that rename, add emphasis to, clarify, or even contradict the meanings of other nouns; they are placed near to the nouns they are intended to qualify. An example of an appositive is given in the sentence, "Dan, the waiter, always gives us free dessert."

GRAMMAR & USAGE

Dashes

This sketch shows an example of how a writer can use dashes to amplify a point or to explain. Notice the writer's use of dashes in this sentence to offer an explanation:

Brabantio is unable to conceive of anything—aside from spells and witchcraft—that could move his dear Desdemona ...

Commas, parentheses, or colons can provide a similar effect, but here dashes slow the reader down enough to understand what the writer means by "anything."

Try revising another sentence from this sketch that uses dashes by replacing them with commas, parentheses, or a colon. Consider how your revision changes the way you read the sentence.

Brabantio, Desdemona's father in William Shakespeare's *Othello*, is a statesman and respected member of Venetian society. He disapproves of his daughter's marriage to the Moor. Brabantio is unable to conceive of anything—aside from spells and witchcraft—that could move his dear Desdemona to commit this "treason of the blood" (I.i.191). In spite of his having placed a great deal of trust in Othello—enough to honor Othello with frequent visits to his own home—Brabantio laments that "[Desdemona] is abused, stol'n from me, and corrupted" (I.iii.73). His views of his daughter as his property and of the valiant military man as an outlandish choice for his daughter's hand in marriage show Brabantio to be a nobleman who shares prejudices common in his culture. His inability to accept or honor the choices of others may help explain his grief at his daughter's elopement.

Learning Strategies

Activating Prior Knowledge
Drafting
Graphic Organizer
Oral Reading
SOAPSTone

VOCABULARY

LITERARY

A **monologue** is a speech that is delivered by a single character. This literary device is used to reveal a character's thoughts and underlying motivations. The character usually speaks directly to the audience, or to another character.

My Notes

_____

_____

_____

_____

_____

_____

_____

_____

_____

_____

_____

_____

_____

_____

_____

bade me: told me to
wherein: in which
imminent: approaching

Learning Targets

- Analyze the role of a monologue in advancing the action of a play.
- Evaluate and critique the effectiveness of delivery of the same monologue in two film adaptations.

Preview

In this activity, you will closely read and practice delivering lines from a monologue. Then you will compare two film adaptations of the text and evaluate the director's choices and how effectively the lines are delivered. Finally, you will write an analysis of the director's thematic and interpretive choices.

📝 Opening Writing Prompt

Analyzing literature and film is a specialized form of rhetorical analysis that requires critical analysis and evaluation. However, you have done this type of analysis if you have ever seen a movie version of a novel or short story you have read. Think of a time when you watched a film adaptation of a narrative that you had read, and then respond to the Essential Question: How can an original text be adapted for different audiences?

As You Read

- Underline the claims Othello makes about other characters in the play.
- Circle unknown words and phrases. Try to determine the meaning of the words by using context clues, word parts, or a dictionary.

Monologue

from **Act I, Scene III**

Her father loved me; oft invited me,

150 Still questioned me the story of my life

From year to year—the battles, sieges, fortunes

That I have passed.

I ran it through, even from my boyish days

To th' very moment that he **bade me** tell it,

155 **Wherein** I spake of most disastrous chances:

Of moving accidents by flood and field;

Of hairbreadth 'scapes i' th' **imminent** deadly

breach,

Of being taken by the insolent foe

160 And sold to slavery; of my redemption thence

And portance[1] in my travel's history,

Wherein of antres[2] vast and deserts idle,

Rough quarries, rocks, and hills whose heads

　　touch heaven

165 It was my hint to speak—such was the process—

And of the Cannibals that each other eat,

The Anthropophagi[3] and men whose heads

Do grow beneath their shoulders. This to

　　hear

170 Would Desdemona seriously incline:

But still the house-affairs would draw her thence,

Which ever as she could with haste dispatch

She'd come again, and with a greedy ear

Devour up my discourse. Which I, observing,

Took once a **pliant** hour, and found good means

To draw from her a prayer of earnest heart

That I would all my pilgrimage **dilate**,

Whereof by parcels she had something heard,

But not intentively. I did consent,

180 And often did **beguile** her of her tears

When I did speak of some distressful stroke

That my youth suffered. My story being done,

She gave me for my pains a world of sighs.

She swore, in faith, 'twas strange, 'twas passing

185　strange,

'Twas pitiful, 'twas wondrous pitiful.

She wished she had not heard it, yet she wished

That heaven had made her such a man. She thank'd

　　me,

---

[1] *portance*: bearing or carriage; figuratively, behavior
[2] *antres*: caves
[3] *Anthropophagi* is a Greek word that means "cannibals."

pliant: flexible
dilate: expand
beguile: charm

My Notes

190 And bade me, if I had a friend that loved her,

I should but teach him how to tell my story.

And that would woo her. Upon this hint I spake.

She loved me for the dangers I had passed,

And I loved her that she did pity them.

195 This only is the witchcraft I have used.

Here comes the lady: let her witness it.

COMÉDIE-FRANÇAISE
OTHELLO, LE MORE DE VENISE
Othello, M. Mounet-Sully.

An illustration of French actor Mounet-Sully as Othello, 1899

Making Observations
- What details about Othello's life stand out to you?
- How would you describe Othello's relationship with Desdemona?

Returning to the Text

- Reread the monologue to answer these text-dependent questions.
- Write any additional questions you have about the text in your Reader/Writer Notebook.

1. What tone does Othello take to defend himself? What words or phrases at the beginning of the monologue contribute to this tone?

_____

_____

_____

_____

2. How do Othello and Desdemona's differences in background contribute to them falling in love? Provide support from the text.

_____

_____

_____

_____

3. What does Shakespeare reveal about Othello's character through this monologue? Use text evidence to support your answer.

_____

_____

_____

_____

My Notes

Working from the Text

4. With a partner, use the SOAPSTone graphic organizer provided by your teacher to analyze how the monologue builds. Use your notes from the first reading of the text to help support your answers.

Introducing the Strategy: Oral Interpretation

An **oral interpretation** is reading aloud a literary text with expression. The purpose is to share with an audience the reader's personal insight into a text through voice, fluency, and tone. The oral interpretation requires careful analysis of a text to determine appropriate rate (speed), inflection (emphasis on specific words for effect), and tone (speaker's attitude toward the subject).

5. Discuss how you would have Othello deliver these lines in a performance by your acting company. As you discuss the planning of your performance, highlight lines that you find particularly important in conveying how Othello's past experiences led him to his present circumstances.

6. Use the lines that you have highlighted to practice giving an oral interpretation of Othello's monologue with your acting company. Listen attentively and provide feedback on each other's use of enunciation, volume, rate, tone, pauses, and gestures.

☑ Check Your Understanding

How will your performance of this scene differ according to the chosen critical perspective? Highlight a few lines from Othello's speech and perform them based on your chosen lens.

7. As you view different interpretations of Othello's speech, take notes in the graphic organizer that follows. Evaluate the elements listed to analyze the effectiveness of each adaptation.

Film version 1	Film version 2
Delivery of lines	
Actions/gestures/facial expressions	
Interactions among characters	
Props/costumes	
Set	
Dramatic/ Theatrical elements	

INDEPENDENT READING LINK

Read and Discuss

Based on what you've read so far, discuss with a partner the aspects of your text that would lend themselves to a film interpretation. How would you convey narrative elements visually? Would modifying the original text enhance or diminish the audience's ability to comprehend and appreciate the text?

My Notes

8. Discuss with a partner which film adaptation you find more effective. Use your notes from the graphic organizer and the following questions to guide your discussion:

- How do the set, costumes, and theatrical elements affect the viewer?
- Which film adaptation evokes an emotional response from the viewer?
- How effective is the actor's delivery of the lines in helping the audience connect to Othello's life story?
- Which film adaption best illuminates Othello's honor and nobility?

LANGUAGE & WRITER'S CRAFT: Language Change

Language changes over time because of shifts in culture, geography, and trends. Although we can still read and understand Shakespeare, we can also see that certain words from his era are not in use anymore or that they are used in different ways. We also know that there are many words and usages that have evolved since Shakespeare's time. As language changes, rules about how to use language change, too.

For example, read the following sentence from Act I:

Her father loved me; oft invited me;

Still questioned me the story of my life

Oft has the same usage as our modern *often*, indicating a language change. Another difference appears in the structure of "still questioned me the story of my life," which is not how someone might say it today, though we still understand its meaning.

Who gets to decide what usage is correct, or **standard**? As new words and usages appear to fill new communication needs, they may become more popular. People who create dictionaries and usage guides then decide which new usages to include and which to get rid of. Over time, a consensus arises about what the new words and usages mean and how to use them effectively. This means that standard usage is largely a matter of cultural consensus, or convention.

PRACTICE Skim a few scenes from *Othello*. In your Reader/Writer notebook, list a few words that are not commonly used today or that are used differently now. Look them up in a dictionary of etymology such as the *Oxford English Dictionary* or etymonline.com. Then create a chart with the categories *then* and *now* to show how the meanings have shifted.

Writing Prompt: Rhetorical Analysis

Think about the film interpretations of *Othello* you have viewed. Evaluate how the features of each clip affect how the audience experiences the drama. Write a paragraph comparing the directors' thematic and interpretive choices to the scene. Be sure to:

- Include a comparative statement in your thesis.
- Identify the interpretive approach of each film and explain how it conveys the character of Othello.
- Support your commentary by citing examples of imagery and cinematic techniques used in each film.

A Historical Look at the Moor

Learning Targets

- Closely read and analyze an author's claims in a literary criticism text.
- Participate in a discussion to analyze a character through the lens of Historical Criticism.
- Integrate ideas from multiple texts to build knowledge and vocabulary about stereotypes and racial prejudice.

Preview

In this activity, you will learn about Historical Criticism and then closely analyze an excerpt from a book of literary criticism. You will work collaboratively to generate discussion questions to participate in a Socratic Seminar.

Learning Strategies

Levels of Questions
Marking the Text
Paraphrasing
Sketching
Socratic Seminar

LITERARY

Using **Historical Criticism**, the reader recognizes the significance of historical information in interpreting literature. This perspective assumes that texts both influence and are influenced by the times in which they were created.

VOCABULARY

Historical Criticism

1. Previously, you learned about critical theories and used them to understand and interpret various texts. Review the critical perspectives with a partner, taking turns to identify and define the perspectives until you have reviewed all those you have studied. In your Reader/Writer Notebook, sketch a picture suitable to represent each critical perspective.

2. Another critical perspective is **Historical Criticism**. Historical Criticism considers the time period in which a work was created and how that time period may have influenced the work. For example, an interpretation of *Things Fall Apart* by Chinua Achebe may be enhanced by an understanding of the effects of colonialism in present-day African life. Likewise, an interpretation of *The Crucible*, which is set in 17th-century New England, may be enhanced by an understanding of political developments in the 1950s, when Arthur Miller wrote the play. The major principles of Historical Criticism are as follows:

   - A text cannot be separated from its historical context, which is a web of social, cultural, personal, and political factors.
   - An understanding of a text is enhanced by the study of cultural norms and of artifacts such as diaries, films, paintings, and letters in existence when the text was created.

   Historical Criticism suggests that we examine how the historical context in which a text is created or set might influence the text's themes, characters, events, ideas, and structure. With drama, the time period in which a drama is reimagined and performed adds another layer of interpretation of historical significance. For instance, in South Africa under apartheid, producing *Othello*—a drama about an interracial marriage—was an act of social, cultural, and historical significance.

   Historical performances of *Othello* give modern audiences a peek into the minds of people in generations past and inspire us to imagine how future generations might perform and receive this play.

3. Add Historical Criticism to your list of critical theories. In your Reader/Writer Notebook, sketch a symbol or picture suitable to represent this critical perspective.

My Notes

My Notes

☑ **Focus on the Sentence**

Use what you have learned about Historical Criticism to turn the following fragments into complete sentences.

Historical Criticism interprets a text based on

_____

_____

to study *Othello* with Historical Criticism

_____

_____

can shed light on the historical context of the play

_____

_____

As You Read

- Use **metacognitive markers** to annotate the text to help you monitor your own understanding of the author's argument.

    ?   Use a question mark to signal confusion or question an idea.

    *   Use an asterisk for comments about the text.

    !   Use an exclamation point for reactions to the text.

    _   Underline the key idea or topic sentence in each paragraph.

- Circle unknown words and phrases. Try to determine the meaning of the words by using context clues, word parts, or a dictionary.

About the Author

Jack D'Amico (b. 1939) was born the son of a musician in Buffalo, New York, and earned his PhD from the State University of New York in 1965. He served as the English Department Chair of Canisius College in Buffalo, New York, from 2000–2002. In addition to *The Moor in English Renaissance Drama* (1991), D'Amico has written *Shakespeare and Italy: The City and the Stage* (2001).

Literary Criticism

from The Moor in English Renaissance Drama

by Jack D'Amico

Chunk 1

1   Relations between England and Morocco were extremely complex, and the opinions generated by those relations were as varied. What we find is not one image of the Moroccan, but many images, from the dangerously **inscrutable** alien to the exotically attractive ally. I have reviewed the experiences of these men in this chapter because, it seems to me, theater has the ability to re-create for its audience the encounter with an alien culture and to force an imaginative assessment of likeness and difference. Through this kind of experience some prejudices may be confirmed, while in other ways spectators may come to see themselves and their world differently.

2   The positive and negative characterizations that emerge from the first fifty years of trade and diplomacy can with ease be related to the specific historical perspectives of trade, war, and diplomacy. But traditional images of the Moor as black devil, Islamic infidel, or oriental **despot** were certainly drawn on to articulate what the traders and diplomats experienced. Optimistic prospects, disappointment and frustrations, and strong prejudices against Catholic Spain were by turn equally strong. Dramatic contexts, too, reflect a give-and-take of opinion, a frequent counter-balancing of prejudices, the interplay of abstract stereotypes and the more complex shadings of experience.

3   The theatrical representation of the Moor, while shaped in part by the traditional anti-Islam **polemic**, or the characterization of the black man as devil, also reshapes those traditions. Along with the stereotypes we will find subtler explorations of the problems that beset individuals from different cultures as they attempt to judge one another. Stereotypes often provide a convenient mask the dramatist can use to identify a character. But under the pressure of dramatic experience that character will move often closer to the context of the observer's world, exhibiting the same needs, frustrations, and perceptions that shape "our" experience. As with the diversity of opinion about Moors and Morocco represented by the reports of traders and diplomats, we must follow the complex, and at times tangled, dramatic interplay of ideas, opinions, stereotypes, and fresh characterizations within the plays. Even if the spectator does not come away from the dramatic experience with a fuller understanding of another culture and its people, in most instances seeing the familiar world set in a different perspective leads to an expansion of imaginative experience.

****

KNOWLEDGE QUEST

Knowledge Question:

How do stereotypes affect the social issue of racial prejudice? In Activity 3.9, you will read literary criticism that examines the topic of stereotypes. While you read and build knowledge about the topic, think about your answer to the Knowledge Question.

GRAMMAR & USAGE

Modifiers

A **free modifier** is a phrase or clause that modifies the main clause. Pay attention to the bolded part of the following sentence, which is a free modifier: *But under the pressure of dramatic experience that character will often move closer to the context of the observer's world, **exhibiting the same needs, frustrations, and perceptions that shape 'our' experience.***

Notice how this **participial phrase** modifies the subject, "character."

Find another example of a free modifier in this text, and diagram how it modifies the subject.

inscrutable: mysterious
despot: tyrant
polemic: argument

My Notes

Chunk 2

4   Yet the representation of the Moor could also lead the dramatist and the audience beyond a comfortable sense of **superiority** or the superficial **titillation** provided by a darkly alien villain. The Moor could become a dramatic symbol of the many stereotypes and masks that divide society and alienate the individual. The process by which a character is reduced to a type and the consequences of that reduction became a central dramatic issue. The representation of the Moor, whether motivated by a desire to make theatrical capital of a famous event, such as the Battle of Alcazar, or by a desire to discover and explore difference, opened up the question of what resulted from the contact between different cultures, religions, and races.

5   Dramatic interest also seemed naturally to focus on the question of the kind of power the isolated individual sought within a society of others. Power could mean destroying or mastering that society, controlling its women and tricking its men into acts of blind self-destruction. Or power could be sought in ways acceptable to society, as was the case for Othello, who could seem "fair" both within his dark exterior and within the Venetian state because of his military **prowess**. Audiences and dramatists were drawn to the Moor as a type because the character provided a way to examine some of the most difficult questions of division and alienation. The audience that witnessed the struggle for self-control and the **insidious** powers that transform Othello would confront the destructiveness of its own collective perceptions of race, religion, and cultural difference. In this case, the audience would engage in an exchange of something other than a coin for the sight of a dead Indian; the living character required that the audience engage in an emotional and intellectual exchange. And that giving, which is the life of theater, certainly drew the audience into some understanding of the tragic divisions within their own world as mirrored in the story of a character such as Othello, the Moor of Venice.

6   Our imaginative journey into the dramatic world of these plays fosters respect for the willingness and ability of Renaissance dramatists to do more than trade in dead stereotypes. Most of the plays created for their audience a complex dramatic encounter with the Moor. The audience identified the otherness of the type and to the extent that individual members of that audience saw difference as essential to human experience, they were connected to the outsider. Working within the conventions of Western theater and poetry, the dramatist could use the open stage of Shakespeare's age to explore inner perspectives and challenge easy assumptions about difference and inferiority. The poet-dramatist was provided with a further connection between the Moor, or the alien, and the role of the artist within society.

****

Chunk 3

7   Shakespeare more than any other dramatist of the English Renaissance used theater to create an important political perspective that framed the

superiority: thinking themselves better than others

titillation: excitement

prowess: skill and accomplishments

insidious: sneakily harmful

encounter between different cultures. On the Moor he focused the problems that any state would face when it moved from a relatively closed condition to the open expansion that generates contact and conflict with other civilizations. Around the Moor he built those conflicts which test a society's sense of the natural rightness of its particular cultural traditions. He saw that with the kind of political expansion that characterized Renaissance Venice and ancient Rome came the problem of absorbing the outsider and the fear of being absorbed. The opposition between Roman reason and the darkly feminine otherness and fertility of Egypt is but one variation on this conflict between different **conceptions** of power and order. Shakespeare could also identify with a Moor of military virtú who is fearful of the erotic femininity of Venice, a European city as exotic for him as Alexandria was for the Romans. For the modern, cosmopolitan state that thrives on the exchange of goods and images with other nations and cultures, this conflict persists in the struggle between a closed national identity and the need for intercourse with others.

8 … Shakespeare wrote for a society that saw its contact with other people increase, while it struggled to define for itself the kind of government and religion it would have. Traditional definitions of Western norms and of the others who deviated from those norms provided a groundwork for curiosity, or a base of operations for exploration and **exploitation**. But the ground was and always is shifting as experience and traditional values interact. What may have seemed strange turns out to be familiar, as when Clem finds that courts in Morocco and England are much the same; and what is native may, upon closer examination, turn out to be more monstrous than the strangest alien. As we have seen with Tamburlaine[1], an outsider who became a projection of new political ambition, the imaginative contact with the outsider became a way of dramatizing the need to create new categories. The Moor's difference was something established by tradition, and the Moor was a sign of **spatial** distance, a creature from a distant place. But for the English Renaissance stage the Moor could also be identified with the newness of discovery, exploration, and trade. This experience, real or theatrical, might confirm or challenge the tradition. Since the Moor was often portrayed as isolated and in rebellion against Western society, the type might conveniently channel opposition to traditional structures. If the old definitions fixed the character in safe inferiority, the new experience created an emotionally and intellectually charged encounter with a figure who required the audience to reflect on and to question its own values.

9 The plays certainly trade in what were, and still are, trusted assumptions about the Moor, Islam, and cultural difference. And they also draw upon our fascination with how another culture can make the familiar world seem strange. It is unsettling and also exciting to feel the ground of assumptions shift, as is the case in travel, when the norm is not your norm, when dress, speech, food, and the details of life reflect a difference that places you at the margin, reduced to a sign of **deviation** from the norm. That sense of

---

[1] *Tamburlaine* is a character who had high political aspirations, from the play of the same name by Christopher Marlowe.

WORD CONNECTIONS

Roots and Affixes
The word **cosmopolitan** contains the Greek prefix *cosmo-*, meaning "world" or "universe." Someone who is *cosmopolitan* is not bound by any local or national customs or prejudices. Other words beginning with this prefix include *cosmonaut, cosmology,* and *cosmopolis.*

My Notes

conceptions: ideas
exploitation: using for their own benefit
spatial: physical
deviation: departure

My Notes

disorientation was projected into an Eleazar[2] who speaks of the finger of scorn pointed at him, or Othello who fears the accusing gesture that will destroy his reputation. What is most disturbing for the outsider is the sense that the secret, unwritten codes are being used to degrade one's true image. As a group, sharing language, a national and racial identity, and an inherited set of theatrical conventions, the audience would have been like those Venetians or Spaniards who share a culture the Moor can never understand. And yet the individual spectator might retain a sense of separateness and know what it is like to be the object of open scorn, or what is worse, to feel the unspoken isolation of one who is reduced to a mere sign of the abnormal.

Ⓩ Knowledge Quest

- Which of the author's claims stand out to you the most?
- What questions do you have after reading this essay?
- What are your first thoughts about the relationship between stereotypes and racial prejudice after reading the essay?

---

[2] *Eleazar* is a villainous Moor in an English Renaissance drama called *Lust's Dominion*.

Returning to the Text

- Reread the literary criticism to answer these text-dependent questions.
- Write any additional questions you have about the text in your Reader/Writer Notebook.

Chunk 1

4. What historical connection does the author focus on in Chunk 1? How are the two cultures connected? What differences separate them?

_____

_____

_____

_____

5. KQ What two stereotypes of Moroccans (or Moors) does the author give in the first paragraph? Which stereotype most closely applies to the character of Othello?

_____

_____

_____

6. KQ In paragraph 3, what two points does the author make about stereotypes in theatrical presentations? How can stereotypes lead to a richer theater experience?

_____

_____

_____

_____

Chunk 2

7. How does the author introduce and develop a key idea in paragraph 4?

_____

_____

_____

_____

8. **KQ** What clues to the meaning of "dead stereotype" does the author provide at the end of paragraph 5? Does Othello fit this description?

_____

_____

_____

_____

9. In paragraph 6, what opinion does the author express about Renaissance dramatists?

_____

_____

_____

_____

Chunk 3

10. In paragraph 7, what historical changes do Shakespeare's plays reflect? How are the conflicts that arise from changes reflected in modern cultural exchanges?

_____

_____

_____

_____

11. What character in *Othello* could fit the description "what is native may ... turn out to be more monstrous than the strangest alien"?

_____

_____

_____

_____

12. How can traditional themes of being a cultural outsider, such as those described by the author, connect with people watching plays today?

_____

_____

_____

_____

Knowledge Quest

The author of this essay explores the way theater can lead "the individual spectator" to look closer at stereotypes and re-examine prejudices. Think about a contemporary film and write an informative text explaining how the film uses stereotypes to affect racial prejudice. Be sure to:

- Provide a well-reasoned claim that is clearly stated.
- Use significant and relevant examples, details, or quotations from the film that thoroughly develop and support your claim.
- Provide an engaging conclusion that supports the claim and examines its implications.

 INDEPENDENT READING LINK

You can continue to build your knowledge about the effects of stereotypes and racial prejudice by reading other articles at ZINC Reading Labs. Search for keywords such as *stereotypes* and *racial prejudice*.

 ZINC

Working from the Text

13. Your teacher will assign chunks of the excerpt from *The Moor in English Renaissance Drama* to various individuals in your group. Reread your assigned chunk to write levels of questions in preparation for a Socratic Seminar. Locate textual evidence from Act I of Othello that helps address your questions, or that confirms or counters D'Amico's assertions.

14. Using the lens of Cultural Criticism, write Levels of Questions to explore the preceding text. Choose at least one question for each chunk to pose during the Socratic Seminar. With your group, review the levels of questions for each chunk.

Literal: _____

_____

_____

Interpretive: _____

_____

_____

Universal: _____

_____

_____

My Notes

15. Participate in a Socratic Seminar, making sure to address the following questions:

   - How do English Renaissance poets and playwrights represent the Moors in their literature?
   - What evidence from Act I of the play supports or contradicts D'Amico's assertions about Othello as a character?

   Remember to listen attentively, evaluating evidence and reasoning that may modify or change your own understanding of the text.

☑ Check Your Understanding

Use your new understanding of Historical Criticism to respond to the following question in the form of a quickwrite: How can a playwright impact an audience's perspective of social and cultural stereotypes?

Desdemona: From a Feminist Perspective

Learning Targets

- Analyze the portrayal of women in a scene from *Othello*.
- Research the historical and social context of a play to analyze character development.
- Explain various interpretations of a scene based on differing critical perspectives.

Preview

In this activity, you will analyze the character of Desdemona through a feminist lens. You will also conduct research to better understand how cultural and historical context influence character development. Finally, you will join your acting company to interpret and perform a scene through a feminist critical perspective.

Learning Strategies

Double-Entry Journal
Quickwrite
Revisiting Prior Work

My Notes

Revisiting Feminist Critical Perspective

1. Review the principles of Feminist Criticism. In what light has Desdemona's character been cast in Act I of *Othello*? How does she fulfill or resist societal and familial expectations?

On the Spot Research

How different are the rules of courtship, marriage, and filial duty to one's parents, in Shakespeare's time (1600s) from those of today?

Conduct research into how women of different social strata were expected to perform their duties in society. Use print and digital information from reputable sources, such as academic journals or established encyclopedias. Remember that a Wiki source is not guaranteed to be reliable or authoritative. However, one way to use it is to search key words and access the bibliography for titles of books or articles that touch on your topic of interest.

2. Quickwrite: What are the most striking differences in the expectations of marriageable noble women in Shakespeare's Elizabethan England (such as Desdemona) and young women of today?

Othello and Desdemona in Venice, by Théodore Chassériau (1850)

3. As you read Act II, Scene I, pay attention to the ways women are referred to in the text. When you encounter a character's perception of women in lines 108–179, record the quotation and your response in the following double-entry journal. Include the line numbers.

Quotation	Response

4. How might someone view this scene from a Feminist critical perspective?

5. How do Desdemona and Emilia simultaneously "comply and defy" restrictions on their lives and behaviors?

6. In what ways do you find Feminist Criticism overlaps considerations inherent in Historical, Cultural, or Marxist critical perspectives?

Interpreting the Lines

7. Choose a few lines to perform as an acting company. Discuss how you would interpret the lines through a feminist lens, taking into considering your research on courtship. As a group, determine the tone of each of the characters and of the conversation as a whole.

INDEPENDENT READING LINK

Read and Discuss

With a partner discuss the main or supporting female characters in your text. Explain how someone might analyze the characters from a Feminist critical perspective. Work together to list the similarities and differences between how the two authors' portrayals of women.

8. Pay attention to how tone of voice, body language, timing, and setting complement the relationships women have with men in the scene.

My Notes

9. Now select a different critical perspective through which to examine the scene. Describe how the dramatic elements of the scene change when performed through a different lens.

☑ Check Your Understanding

How can a critical perspective be conveyed in a dramatic performance? How has this lesson strengthened your understanding of the way literary theories can shape a staged scene?

Honest Iago: The Dramatic Speech

Learning Strategies

Graphic Organizer
Marking the Text
Paraphrasing
Think-Pair-Share

My Notes

Learning Targets

- Analyze a character's motivations and traits by closely reading a soliloquy.
- Interpret a scene and evaluate how the delivery of lines can be used to amplify dramatic irony.

Preview

In this activity, you will review three dramatic elements and evaluate how they can be used to convey a specific message to an audience. You will then conduct a close reading of a character's speech and work with your acting group to interpret and deliver the lines.

Dramatic Elements

1. Revisit the definition of dramatic irony from Activity 3.4. How is dramatic irony already evident in *Othello*?

2. What do you recall about the dramatic elements known as soliloquies and monologues from your previous study of plays? Refer to print or digital sources for examples and definition of a soliloquy to sharpen your understanding of this dramatic device.

Soliloquies and monologues are speeches given by an actor on stage. Soliloquies are directed to the character, voicing his or her own thoughts. Sometimes the character is aware of the audience, and sometimes the viewers are an "omniscient witness" to the internal, secret thoughts of the character. Monologues, by contrast, are directed to other characters. Monologues may reveal the character's secret thoughts, but other characters, whether or not the speaker is aware, overhear those voiced ideas.

An aside also allows a character to reveal his or her thoughts to the audience. However, asides are much shorter and are spoken while others are on stage, often in reaction to another character's words or actions. An aside lets the audience in on information that the other characters are not able to hear, so the audience is in a privileged position of knowing something hidden from others. For this reason, asides are a good set up for dramatic irony. Asides and soliloquies can be used as dramatic devices in three ways:

- directly to the audience, or to the camera (if filmed)
- as if the character is simply talking to himself
- as a voice-over, while the actor appears to be lost in thought

VOCABULARY

LITERARY

A **soliloquy** is a long speech delivered by a character alone on the stage. The audience hears the character's internal thoughts.

An **aside** is a short speech spoken by an actor directly to the audience and unheard by other actors on stage.

Reading *Othello*: Act II

3. With your acting company, conduct a close reading of one of Iago's asides or soliloquies. As you read, annotate the places that reveal Iago's motivations and emotions and convey the tone and mood of the speech. Choose one of the following scenes:

Scene A: Act II, Scene I, lines 182–193 ("He takes her by the palm ...")

Scene B: Act II, Scene III, lines 49–66 ("If I can fasten but one cup ...")

Scene C: Act II, Scene III, lines 356–382 ("And what's he, then, that says ...")

- Set the scene: what has happened before this speech?

- How does the aside or soliloquy use irony?

- What phrases and words in the speech reveal Iago's secret motivations leading to his actions?

- How does the speech advance the plot of the drama?

WORD CONNECTIONS

Roots and Affixes

The word **soliloquy** comes from the Latin for "talking to oneself," from the roots *solus* ("alone") and *loqui* ("speak"). Other words from the roots *solus* include *sole*, *solitary*, and *desolate*, and *loqui* forms words such as *eloquence* and *ventriloquist*.

My Notes

Interpreting the Lines

4. Now that you have annotated the text, work as a group to decide how to best represent Iago's character traits. Each member of the group will deliver the speech and provide feedback to one another on the delivery. Take these questions into consideration as you reread the text and plan your presentation:

   • What do you want the audience to understand about the play and about Iago?

   • How will the character's vocal delivery, staging (gestures, acting choice), and blocking (movement) convey an interpretation of Iago's character?

   • Are any other actors on the stage? If so, what are they doing?

   • Do you see the opportunity for staging to enhance irony in the speech? How could you prepare the delivery or setting to optimize the impact of the irony?

Comparing Interpretations

5. Listen to the audio recording of the same three scenes performed by each acting company in your class. As you listen, compare and contrast each recording with the interpretation presented by your peers. Then evaluate both performances against the original play. Jot down your ideas and observations in the My Notes section.

☑ Check Your Understanding

Reflect on the dramatic elements your acting company incorporated. How did these elements affect the meaning and delivery of the lines?

Demystifying Emilia: Questioning Through a Critical Lens

Learning Strategies

Discussion Groups
Graphic Organizer
Jigsaw
Levels of Questions
Summarizing
Web Organizer

Learning Targets

- Analyze how a minor character in *Othello* influences the plot.
- Apply a critical perspective to gain new insights about a minor character.

Preview

In this activity, you will analyze how one character's actions and motives influence the moral dilemmas and advance the plot of *Othello*. You will then use your analysis to write a short story from the character's point of view.

Reading *Othello*: Act III

1. Though Emilia is a minor character in *Othello* and her marriage to the antagonist Iago is secondary to that of Othello and Desdemona, the drama unfolds around and in some ways because of her.

    Where does Emilia's loyalty lie—to her honest lady, Desdemona, or to her husband, Iago? As you read Act III, consider Emilia's duty to Iago and Desdemona.

2. Preview the following graphic organizer, and then read closely the short scene assigned to your group. What does the scene reveal about Emilia? You may begin to make your determinations about this character by questioning the text. How is she characterized? What is her relationship to other characters? What are her motivations? Use the graphic organizer for your notes.

Scene	What the Scene Reveals About Emilia	Textual Evidence
Act III, Scene I, lines 46–64, Emilia & Cassio (Begins with EMILIA: Good morrow ... and goes to the end of Scene I)		
Act III, Scene III, lines 344–368, Emilia & Iago (Begins with IAGO: How now? What do you here alone? and ends when Emilia exits)		

Scene	What the Scene Reveals About Emilia	Textual Evidence
Act III, Scene IV, lines 23–34, Emilia & Desdemona (Begins with DESDEMONA: Where should I lose that handkerchief, Emilia? and ends when Othello enters)		

3. With a partner, choose one critical perspective (Archetypal, Marxist, Feminist, Reader-Response, Cultural, or Historical). Draft one literal, one interpretive, and one universal question through that lens to explore the character of Emilia. For example, using a Cultural critical lens:

- **Literal:** Why does Emilia give Iago the handkerchief?
- **Interpretive:** Is Emilia torn between her duty to Desdemona and Iago?
- **Universal:** How can the powerless be coerced into other people's schemes?
- You should focus your questions on the character of Emilia. When you have checked your work with another group, repeat the process for a different critical perspective, this time on your own.

Act/Scene/Lines: _____

    Critical Perspective: _____

    Literal: _____

    Interpretive: _____

    Universal: _____

Act/Scene/Lines: _____

    Critical Perspective: _____

    Literal: _____

    Interpretive: _____

    Universal: _____

✒️ Writing Prompt: Literary

Write a short story from the perspective of Emilia talking to a close friend in person. Explain the moral dilemma that you, the character, are having and how you feel about it. Use your analysis of the character and your assigned scene to inform how you shape the character's point of view. Be sure to:

- Summarize conflict in the play and clearly present Emilia's point of view.
- Use narrative techniques, such as dialogue and pacing, to develop the story.
- Organize the events in your story so the relationship between them is evident.
- Use appropriate register and tone to reflect the moral dilemma.
- Develop descriptive details that convey a realistic picture of Emilia and what she thinks and experiences.
- Provide a conclusion that reflects on the resolution.

INDEPENDENT READING LINK

Read and Respond

Think about the reading you are doing independently. Jot a few notes in your Reader/Writer Notebook about which critical perspective best illuminates your reading, and why.

Staging Iago's Lies: Blocking for Effect

Learning Strategies

Drafting
Drama Games
Graphic Organizer
Revisiting Prior Work
Sketching
Summarizing

Learning Targets

- Evaluate two directors' use of dramatic elements in their interpretations of a scene.
- Apply a critical interpretation to the staging of a scene.
- Make informed decisions about blocking to convey a particular effect on the audience.

Preview

In this activity, you will compare, evaluate, and critique how the same scenarios—and even the same characters and lines—can change based on the setting, the staging strategies, and the actors' approaches to the material.

Reading *Othello*: Act IV, Scene I

1. Revisit your work from Step 1 in Activity 3.4. The scenario and outcomes in that activity reflect the events in *Othello*. Discuss your scenario with your acting company and take notes on connections between it and Shakespeare's play.

Scenario: Character 1 tells Character 2 that Character 2's romantic partner is cheating on him. Character 1 then produces "evidence." However, the story is untrue; Character 1 is actually lying.

Outcomes	How my acting company (or another company in my class) presented the outcome	How Shakespeare presents the situation in *Othello*
Outcome A Character 2 does not believe the story and turns on Character 1.		
Outcome B Character 2 considers the story as a possibility but then, after much investigation, decides it is not true.		
Outcome C Character 2 believes the story, is filled with jealousy, and wants revenge.		

Reflecting on *Othello*: Act IV, Scene I

2. Summarize the key events of Act IV, Scene I, in the space provided.

3. Summarize lines 91 (IAGO: Stand you awhile apart) to 120 (IAGO: How do you, lieutenant?).

My Notes

4. The moment when Othello falls into a trance is important, but it can be challenging to stage. How would your acting company present Othello's trance in a way that would not create an inadvertently humorous effect? With your acting company, read Act IV, Scene I, lines 1–89 on your feet, pausing to discuss and determine the most effective way to **block** this scene. In the space that follows, describe how you will stage the scene.

5. Working with a partner, choose one of the critical perspectives (Archetypal, Feminist, Marxist, Cultural, or Historical) and develop a literal question, an interpretive question, and a universal question about Act IV, Scene I.

6. The conversation that follows in Act IV, Scene I (lines 120–180) can be tricky to stage. Othello must be visible to the audience but not to Cassio. The audience needs to see how Othello could misinterpret Cassio's comments about Bianca, knowing all the while, of course, how Iago has orchestrated this misunderstanding.

Block this scene by using paper as the set and X's and arrows to indicate characters and blocking. Or use trinkets to represent characters in a "shoebox" set, with arrows to show blocking. Be prepared to explain your choices regarding blocking and the effects you intend to create through characters' movements on stage.

Film Study: Evaluating Act IV, Scene I

You will view two versions of this scene: one a filmed version and the other a stage production. How effective are the filmed and staged productions?

- What advantages might a film version have?
- What advantages might a stage version have?

Film version—Director: Miller, Parke, or Welles	How is it presented?	What is the effect?
Dialogue between Iago and Othello, up to the trance		
The trance		
Dialogue between Iago and Cassio, observed by Othello		
Dialogue between Cassio and Bianca, observed by Othello		
Dialogue between Othello and Iago, after Cassio and Bianca exit		
Othello striking Desdemona		

Filmed stage version—Director: Burge, Milam, or Suzman	How is it presented?	What is the effect?
Dialogue between Iago and Othello, up to the trance		
The trance		
Dialogue between Iago and Cassio, observed by Othello		
Dialogue between Cassio and Bianca, observed by Othello		
Dialogue between Othello and Iago, after Cassio and Bianca exit		
Othello striking Desdemona		

7. With your peers, discuss the effectiveness of the scenes in the film and staged productions. Evaluate the directors' use of dramatic or cinematic elements.

Gaining Perspectives

You have learned that Iago is a master at manipulating people, especially Othello, and people like Iago often create interpersonal conflicts between people for their own personal gain or enjoyment without worrying about the consequences. With a partner, imagine that Othello and Desdemona are a real-life modern couple that you know. What types of conflict resolution skills would help a contemporary Othello and Desdemona resolve the problem in an effective way? What strategies would help a modern Othello work effectively with a twenty-first century Iago?

☑ Check Your Understanding

In discussion groups, determine which film interpretation of the scene creates the strongest effect on the viewer. Then, explain your selection in a quickwrite with appropriate examples to support your opinion.

One Scene, Many Perspectives

Learning Strategies

Graphic Organizer
Note-taking
Oral Interpretation
Rehearsing

Learning Targets

- Analyze a scene through multiple critical perspectives and evaluate how each lens affects the interpretation of the scene.
- Rehearse and perform a dramatic interpretation of a text while using a critical perspective.

Preview

In this activity, you will analyze a scene from *Othello* from multiple critical perspectives. You will then work with your acting company to present the scene from a specific critical perspective. Then you will write an essay stating which critical lens provides the strongest insight into the scene.

Reading *Othello*: Act IV

1. Now that you have read through Act IV, Scene III, select a quotation from scene II or III that you find to be especially interesting or significant. Share the quote and your commentary with your acting company. Be sure to use evidence from the text to support your comments.

2. Examine Scene II (lines 1–110) through each critical perspective. Use evidence from the text to support your analysis through the different lenses.

Critical Perspective	What is revealed by analyzing the text through this Critical Perspective?
Archetypal Criticism might suggest that an archetype such as the temptress (a woman who uses her power—intellect, magic, or beauty—to make men weak) is essential to understanding this scene.	
Feminist Criticism might suggest that the male-female power relationships that come into play in this scene are the most important influence on our understanding of it.	
Marxist Criticism might suggest that we must examine the issues of class or social standing in order to fully understand this scene.	
Reader response Criticism might suggest that what you bring to the scene will determine its significance.	
Cultural Criticism might suggest that we must consider such issues as ethnicity, religious beliefs, and customs to understand this scene.	
Historical Criticism might suggest that the historical context plays a significant role in a modern reader's understanding the scene.	

Interpreting the Scene

3. Your teacher will assign you one of the critical perspectives from the list. With your acting company, determine how the interpretation of Act IV, Scene II, lines 1–110 from this perspective would translate into staging this scene. Record your ideas in the space that follows. Also add some notes, with support and references from your previous responses to convey how your ideas reflect the perspective your company has been assigned.

Critical Perspective: _____

Vocal Delivery (rate, volume, and the general tone this character should convey):

Othello: _____

_____

_____

Emilia: _____

_____

_____

Desdemona: _____

_____

_____

Staging (gestures, mannerisms each character will use):

Othello: _____

_____

_____

Emilia: _____

_____

_____

Desdemona: _____

_____

_____

Blocking (the position of the actors on stage in relation to one another, the set, and the props): Illustrate your plan for blocking on separate paper.

INDEPENDENT READING LINK

Read and Respond

Write a paragraph analyzing one of the key themes presented in your independent reading. Be sure to include a thesis statement that makes an assertion about that theme, a direct quotation from the text, and a strong concluding sentence.

4. Assign roles and rehearse the scene according to your notes. Choose one individual to play the role of director to guide speaking and moving and to ensure that actors are conveying the assigned interpretation. Rehearse your scene before presenting it to the class.

 Check Your Understanding

Reflect on the vocal, staging, and blocking choices that your acting company made. How did your assigned critical perspective inform your decisions? Did the critical perspective lend itself to a rich interpretation of the text?

✍ Writing Prompt: Argumentative

Write an argumentative paragraph about the critical lens that provides the most interesting perspective for the scene. Explain how interpreting the scene through this lens provides the most compelling understanding of the scene. Be sure to:

- Include a claim that states which critical lens provides the best insight into Othello.
- Include relevant evidence from the stages interpretations and the text demonstrating how of critical lenses can help shape dramatic elements.
- Provide a concluding statement that supports your key claim.

"Talk You of Killing?": Defending a Perspective

Learning Targets

- Make predictions about how the plot and subplots of the play will be resolved.
- Evaluate and critique the dramatic elements used in two film interpretations of *Othello*.
- Defend one film interpretation and the corresponding critical perspective it uses in an argumentative essay.

Preview

In this activity, you will read Act V of *Othello* and watch two film adaptions of the final act of the play. After comparing the dramatic elements in the films, you will write an argument stating which version best expresses the themes of the play through the use of a critical perspective.

Learning Strategies

Drafting
Graphic Organizer
Levels of Questions
Note-taking

My Notes

Reading *Othello*: Act V

1. **Quickwrite:** It is no surprise that a Shakespearean tragedy ends … tragically. Now that you have read Act V, Scene I, predict the action in the final scene. Will Othello learn the truth? Will Iago be brought to justice? How will the conflict ultimately be resolved?

2. Act V, Scene II of *Othello* is the climax of the tragedy. As you read Desdemona's last conversation with her husband, visualize the set, costumes, actions, lighting, and music. Make notes in your Reader/Writer Notebook.

3. Now that you have completed the play, reflect on your predictions about the final scene. How accurate were your predictions? Why do you think Shakespeare chose to end the play this way?

4. Using the same critical lens you chose in the last activity, write one literal, one interpretive, and one universal question about Act V. Be sure your interpretive and universal questions are written in a way that requires literary analysis as well as support from the text. Here are some examples written from the cultural perspective:

    Literal: What is Desdemona's fate?

    Interpretive: What drives Othello to commit such an act?

    Universal: How can jealousy and revenge cloud a person's judgement?

Film Study

5. Your class will watch two versions of the final act of *Othello*. As you view two versions of the film, take notes in the following graphic organizer.

Dramatic Element:	Film Version 1 Director: Year:	Film Version 2 Director: Year:
The set (Consider use of space, etc.)		
Sound (Think about how music and other sounds influence the production.)		
Delivery (What is the impact of the actors' delivery of the line?)		
Mood (Consider how elements including lighting, props, costumes, and more work together to create mood.)		
Critical perspective reflected in the film adaptation		

Write your own caption: _____

☑ Check Your Understanding

Which interpretation of the final scene best conveys the tragic themes of the play? What dramatic elements does your chosen version use most effectively to communicate with the audience and bring the play to a close?

📝 Writing Prompt: Argumentative

Select one of the themes presented in *Othello*. Write an argumentative essay explaining which film adaptation of *Othello* best illuminates your selected theme through its use of dramatical elements. Consider using your Check Your Understanding response as a starting point. Be sure to:

- Include a clear claim about a theme and critical perspective/interpretation.
- Use specific evidence from the text and one or more film interpretations to reinforce your claim about the connection between the play and film.
- Provide a concluding statement that supports your key claim.

A Minor Folly: Analyzing Roderigo

© 2021 College Board. All rights reserved.

Learning Strategies

Marking the Text
Note-taking
Rereading
Skimming/Scanning

VOCABULARY

LITERARY

A **subplot** is a feature in a work of fiction, especially in a drama, that comments on the main plot of the story. Subplots may either complement or present an opposition to the main plot in a narrative.

Learning Targets

- Closely analyze a scene from a play to summarize a character's underlying motives and actions.
- Identify, evaluate, and critique a subplot in *Othello*.
- Collaboratively create a pictorial timeline that illustrates a subplot found in *Othello*.

Preview

In this activity, you will evaluate and critique Shakespeare's use of subplot in *Othello*. You will work collaboratively to summarize how Roderigo's actions and words contribute to plot and subplot within the play.

Reviewing Subplot

1. A **subplot** is a secondary or minor story that unfolds in a narrative text. Authors often use a subplot to add complexity to characters and conflicts within a story. Think of a novel you've read or a film that you have watched. Did it have a subplot? How did the subplot contribute to the action in the story?

My Notes

2. Reread your assigned scene and mark the text to indicate how the subplot contributes to or advances the plot in the play. Consider the following questions as you read:

- What is Roderigo's motivation?
- How is he persuaded by Iago?
- What is the result of Roderigo's actions?
- What conflict or dilemma does he create?

"Othello. Act V, Scene I" by Felix Octavius Carr Darley (1895)

3. With your group, write a brief summary of Roderigo's actions and the impact on the overall action in the play. As you complete the graphic organizer, include text evidence to strengthen your summary.

Scene	Summary	Impact on the Plot
Act I, Scene I–II		
Act II, Scene III		
Act IV, Scene II		
Act V, Scene II		

4. Be prepared to share your summary in a group discussion. Listen to your classmates' summaries of the remaining scenes and jot down notes in your graphic organizer. Ask insightful questions to capture the following information about each scene:

- What happens in the scene?
- What motivates Roderigo in each scene?
- How do Roderigo's actions in the scene contribute to or advance the main plot of the play?

5. With your group, create a timeline of the scenes you have discussed. Use drawings, symbols, and words to demonstrate the action in each scene. In addition, consider how you can show the scene's impact on the overall plot.

6. As a group, critique and evaluate how these subplots contribute to and advance the action in the play. How effective are the scenes in making the play move forward? Which of Roderigo's actions is most critical to driving other action in the play?

☑ Check Your Understanding

Write a paragraph explaining how Shakespeare uses a subplot to advance the action in *Othello*. What does this technique add to the play?

Evolving Perspectives

Learning Strategies

Discussion Groups
Drafting
Graphic Organizer
Note-taking

Learning Targets

- Review characteristics of various critical perspectives and apply those characteristics to the plot and other elements of a text.
- Work collaboratively to present your analysis of a character.

Preview

In this activity, you will work in groups to apply a specific critical perspective to a character in *Othello*. Then you will create a class presentation to share your findings with your peers.

My Notes

Applying Critical Perspectives

1. You will complete a matching activity to review the critical perspectives and how each one might apply to *Othello*. Once you receive a card from your teacher, you will need to find two classmates with cards that have the same critical perspective. Of the three cards, one will have the name of the critical perspective, another will have a brief note about that critical perspective, and the third card will show a statement about one of the main characters that has been filtered through that critical perspective. Once you find the other members of your group, you will be asked to focus on the critical perspective you have on your cards. See the example cards.

> ### HISTORICAL CRITICISM

> Text cannot be separated from its historical context; situating a text in its time period helps the reader understand the text.

> Othello feels isolated from Venetian society because of prevailing views about race and culture at that time and place in history.

2. With your group, complete the graphic organizer on the following page as you use the perspective on your cards to analyze *Othello*.

Critical Perspective:	
Paraphrase the definition and position of this critical perspective.	
How does this perspective provide insight into a particular theme?	
How does thinking about this perspective affect your understanding of the characters' behaviors?	
How does thinking about this perspective affect your understanding of the setting?	
Which aspects of the plot best lend themselves to an interpretation from this critical perspective? Explain.	

3. Each group will present its findings. In planning the presentation, assign roles within your group or divide the group's notes from the graphic organizer to ensure everyone is actively involved in the presentation.

4. As you view other groups' presentations, use the following graphic organizer to take notes and record questions or comments about their presentations in your Reader/Writer Notebook.

Notes on the Play
Which critical perspective lends itself to a deep analysis of *Othello*?

What does the critical perspective reveal about the themes, characters, setting, and plot?	Textual support for your ideas:

5. Be prepared to use your notes on your own and your classmates' presentations in a class discussion of the way an examination of a text through multiple perspectives can impact understanding of the character.

☑ Check Your Understanding

After listening to your classmates' presentations, identify the most compelling new idea to emerge from the analysis. Draft a thesis statement to sum up the idea.

Learning Strategies

Close Reading
Graphic Organizer
Quickwrite
Revisiting Prior Work

My Notes

Learning Targets

- Collaboratively construct a rubric that effectively evaluates the ideas, organizational structure, and style of a written response.
- Closely evaluate and critique the characteristics of your own argumentative writing and that of your peers.

Preview

In this activity, you will prepare for Embedded Assessment 1 by analyzing the Assignment and Scoring Guide. With your group, you will create a rubric and use it to evaluate previous writing assignments you and your classmates have completed, paying close attention to the quality of the thesis statements, supporting evidence, and conclusions.

Revisiting Prior Work

1. **Quickwrite:** Review some of the essays you wrote earlier in the year. What kind of feedback did you receive? Write some of the comments about your writing in the following space.

2. In relying on the teacher to assess written work, you may not have considered your own ability to assess your writing. The process of writing is ongoing, and getting in the habit of planning your writing will strengthen your ability to make an effective argument.

   In order to create a standard for evaluating your writing, you need to be fully aware of the criteria. With your acting company or discussion group, closely read the Assignment and Steps for Embedded Assessment 1: Writing a Literary Analysis. Identify the key categories in column 1 that, according to the Assignment and Steps, need to be mastered in this assessment.

Rubric

Key Categories			

Key Categories			

How to Write a Literary Analysis

3. Writing a literary analysis requires you to break down a text into smaller components and carefully examine these different elements of a literary text to reach new understandings about the text and its significance. Read the following standards for writing a literary analysis. Is there anything missing from your rubric?

Standard for Writing a Literary Analysis: A literary analysis examines how elements such as setting, characters, plot, literary devices, and theme come together to tell a story. There are many ways to approach writing an analytical essay, but here are some elements all literary analyses should include:

- A thesis statement that makes some sort of assertion about one or more of the literary elements of the text.

- Body paragraphs that each begin with a topic sentence and contain evidence and details from the text and other relevant sources that support the topic sentence and the essay's overall thesis. Your body paragraphs should address specific literary elements such as theme, plot, and characters.

- Transitional words, phrases, and clauses as well as varied syntax that link the major sections of the text, create cohesion, and clarify the relationships between the thesis, topic sentences, and supporting details and evidence.

- A formal style and use of an appropriate tone for your purpose, audience, and topic.

- A concluding statement or section that follows from and supports the argument presented.

4. Your teacher will distribute your essays from a previous activity. Skim the essays, noting the apparent strengths and weaknesses of each. Use the sample papers to guide you as you construct the scoring guidelines for your essay. What constitutes the highest-quality paper in each of the key categories?

5. Write a thorough explanation of the level of mastery for each category, quoting examples from the sample essays where possible and appropriate.

My Notes

6. Using your established guidelines, evaluate at least two sample essays. If you do not have multiple copies of the rubric, use abbreviations and a number system to score each essay on a separate sheet of paper. In addition to giving a score, answer the following questions about each:

   • Does this paper have a clear thesis?
   • What is the strongest sentence in the paper? Why?
   • What is the writer's most effective argument in support of his or her thesis?
   • How does this paper's conclusion give it a sense of closure?
   • One suggestion for improvement to this essay is...

7. After your teacher has collected and redistributed essays to their owners, evaluate your essay using the rubric and questions **before** viewing others' feedback about your writing.

🎲 Independent Reading Checkpoint

Write a paragraph analyzing one of the characters in your text using one of the critical lenses that you have studied. Using your rubric as a guide, include a clear thesis statement, supporting evidence from the text and a conclusion that provides a sense of closure.

Writing a Literary Analysis

ASSIGNMENT

Select a character from *Othello* and write a literary analysis about him or her using one of the critical lenses that you have studied (choose Feminist, Marxist, Cultural, Historical, or Archetypal for this assignment). You will support your analysis with valid reasoning and sufficient evidence from your reading, observations, and previous written work.

Planning and Prewriting: Take time to plan ideas and structure.	■ How will you evaluate the different critical perspectives and decide which will provide a strong analysis of one of the characters? ■ How will you go about collecting textual evidence that supports your thesis? ■ How will you analyze the character's behaviors and motivations? ■ What sorts of tools will you use to record your ideas and structure the essay (for instance, an outline or a graphic organizer)?
Drafting: Select evidence to support your thesis and develop body paragraphs that analyze the literary elements of the play while supporting your thesis.	■ How can you craft a single thesis statement so that it makes a clear assertion about a character through a specific critical lens? ■ How will you use the evidence you selected to support your thesis and clarify your thinking? ■ Which literary elements will you analyze and how will they contribute to supporting your thesis? ■ How can you conclude your work in a way that follows naturally from the ideas while avoiding unnecessary repetition?
Evaluating and Revising: Get feedback from peers and revise to improve structure, transitions, and coherence.	■ How will you make sure that the evidence you include clearly and consistently supports your position? ■ How will you make sure you avoid oversimplifying the critical perspective you are using to analyze your character? (For example, "from a Feminist critical perspective, all men are bad")? ■ What kinds of feedback from peers and the Scoring Guide can you use to guide your revision?
Checking and Editing for Publication: Make your work the best it can be.	■ How will you ensure that your essay maintains an academic, formal tone; that it seamlessly embeds quotations within the text; and that it uses varied syntax? ■ How will you check for grammatical and technical accuracy? ■ What sort of outside resources can help you to check your draft? ■ How will you publish and present your essay to its intended reader or readers in a format that reflects its content and purpose?

Reflection

After completing this Embedded Assessment, think about how you went about accomplishing this assignment, and respond to the following:

- How were you able to consider your audience when crafting your thesis, anticipating what information they would need, and what potential questions they might have?

SCORING GUIDE

Scoring Criteria	Exemplary	Proficient	Emerging	Incomplete
Ideas	The essay • offers a clear thesis statement supported by strong evidence and provides valuable insight into the text • offers an insightful and thorough analysis of the chosen critical perspective • demonstrates a sophisticated understanding of the perspective and the dramatic elements of the play • offers in-depth analysis of a specific character, considering that character in light of the theme and plot.	The essay • provides a solid thesis statement that is supported by adequate evidence and shows some level of analysis of the text • offers a reasonable analysis of the chosen critical perspective • demonstrates an adequate understanding of the perspective and of the dramatic elements used in the play • offers analysis of a specific character that extends beyond summary of the text.	The essay • struggles to articulate a clear thesis and support, often relying on summary or paraphrase instead of specific evidence • offers a less-than-thorough understanding of the task and an inadequate treatment of the chosen critical perspective • overlooks or understates the complexity of the perspective and the text's use of dramatic elements • offers analysis of a specific character that relies on summary and generalization.	The essay • does not articulate a clear thesis and support, often relying on summary or paraphrase instead of specific evidence • offers a tenuous understanding of the task and an inadequate treatment of the chosen critical perspective • does not address the complexity of the perspective or adequately analysis any dramatic elements in the play • offers little or no analysis of a specific character.
Structure	The essay • is organized exceptionally, so that ideas move smoothly • uses transitions effectively to enhance the essay's coherence.	The essay • has an organization that is clear and easy to follow • includes transitions that help readers move between ideas.	The essay • is difficult to follow and may jump too rapidly between ideas • lacks transitions between ideas.	The essay • is confusing and difficult to follow, moving back and forth among different ideas • lacks transitions between ideas.
Use of Language	The essay • uses diction, syntax, and other stylistic devices that are notable and appropriate for the subject, purpose, and audience • demonstrates command of standard English conventions, with few or no errors.	The essay • uses diction, syntax, and other stylistic devices that are appropriate for the subject, purpose, and audience • contains few errors in standard writing conventions; minor errors do not interfere with meaning.	The essay • uses diction, syntax, and other stylistic devices inconsistently for the subject, purpose, and audience • contains errors in standard writing conventions that seriously interfere with meaning.	The essay • uses diction, syntax, and other stylistic devices ineffectively or inappropriately for the subject, purpose, and audience • contains numerous errors in standard writing conventions that seriously interfere with meaning.

Unpacking Embedded Assessment 2

Learning Strategies

Close Reading
Graphic Organizer
Paraphrasing
Summarizing
Think-Pair-Share

Learning Targets

- Reflect on and make connections between literature, performance, and critical perspectives.
- Identify and analyze the skills and knowledge needed to complete Embedded Assessment 2 successfully.

Preview

In this activity, you will explore the big ideas and tasks of the second half of the unit and make plans for your independent reading.

Making Connections

Think about the events in *Othello* and how you might perform them. In this part of the unit, you will deliver a dramatic interpretation of a scene from *Othello*. Staging a scene will make the play come alive for you and your classmates. As part of the assessment, you will also craft a note to your audience explaining the reasons your company chose to interpret the material through a specific critical lens.

Essential Questions

Review your answers to the essential questions based on your current knowledge.

1. What role does literature play in examining recurring social issues?

2. How can an original text be adapted for different audiences?

INDEPENDENT READING LINK

Read and Respond

Reflect on the plot of your independent reading and the unit's Essential Questions. Write a paragraph explaining what aspects of your text connect to recurring social issues. What is the social issue? What message is the author trying to convey to his or her audience about this issue? Use textual evidence to support your response.

Unpacking Embedded Assessment 2

Closely read the assignment for Embedded Assessment 2: Staging an Interpretation.

 Your assignment is to interpret a scene from *Othello* to emphasize the principles of one of the critical perspectives you have studied, then plan, rehearse, and perform the scene. With your acting company write a letter to the audience explaining the message your interpretation is trying to convey.

With your classmates, identify the skills and knowledge you will need to complete this assessment successfully. With your class, create a graphic organizer to represent the skills and knowledge you will need to complete the tasks identified in the Embedded Assessment.

My Notes

Learning Strategies

Close Reading
Discussion Groups
Marking the Text
Paraphrasing
Skimming/Scanning
Summarizing

My Notes

Learning Targets

- Trace the use of critical perspectives in an essay.
- In an argumentative essay, apply one's own perspective to a contemporary staging of *Othello*.
- Integrate ideas from multiple texts to build knowledge and vocabulary about changing interpretations of *Othello* over time.

Preview

In this activity, you will read an essay that traces multiple interpretations of *Othello* over time. Then, after listening to your peers' opinions, you will consider how the interpretation of the character of Othello has changed over time. Finally, you will write more broadly about the merits of modifying an original text.

As You Read

- Highlight phrases that help answer the guiding question, *How has the lead character of* Othello *been portrayed throughout history?*
- Circle unknown words and phrases. Try to determine the meaning of the words by using context clues, word parts, or a dictionary.

About the Author

Sylvan Barnet (1926–2016) was a professor of English and former director of writing at Tufts University. Barnet served as general editor for the Signet Classic Shakespeare series, aimed at making the writer's work more accessible to college students. Barnet's writing remains significant in the field of English literature. This essay was first published in 1963.

KNOWLEDGE QUEST

Knowledge Question:

What do differences in the interpretations of Othello's character over time express about culture and society?

In Activity 3.20 you will read an essay that traces multiple interpretations of *Othello* over time. The author explains how society and culture impact the way the character of Othello is interpreted. As you read and build knowledge about the topic, think about your answer to the Knowledge Question.

Essay

Othello on Stage and Screen

by **Sylvan Barnet**

1   The earliest mention of a performance of *Othello*, in an account of 1604, reports only that the play was acted before James I at Whitehall Palace. Next come two references to performances in 1610, one telling us that it was acted at the Globe in April, the other telling us that it was acted in September at Oxford. The reference to the Oxford production is especially valuable, since it provides one of the very few glimpses we have of early seventeenth-century acting and of an audience's response to a performance. The relevant passage, in Latin, may be translated thus:

> In their tragedies they acted with appropriate decorum; in these they caused tears not only by their speaking, but also by their action. Indeed

Desdemona, although greatly successful throughout, moved us especially when at last, lying on her bed, killed by her husband, she implored the pity of the spectators in her death with her face alone.

2 This may not seem like much, but it is more than we have for all but a few of Shakespeare's other plays, and it is especially valuable as a reminder that the Renaissance boy actors—a boy played Desdemona—were highly skilled performers.

3 There are only a few additional references to performances in the first half of the seventeenth century, but a very large number of rather general references to the play (as opposed to specific performances) allows us to conclude that the play must have been popular on the stage. From 1642 to 1660 the theaters were closed by act of Parliament, but when the theaters reopened in 1660, *Othello* was staged almost immediately. Samuel Pepys saw it in 1660:

> To the Cockpit to see *The Moor of Venice*, which was well done. [Nathaniel] Burt acted the Moor: by the same token, a very pretty lady that sat by me called out, to see Desdemona smothered.

4 He saw it again in 1669, this time with less pleasure:

> To the King's playhouse, and there in an upper box … did see *The Moor of Venice*: but ill acted in most parts; [Michael] Mohun which did a little surprise me not acting Iago's part by much so well as [Walter] Clun used to do … nor, indeed, Burt doing the Moor's so well as I once thought he did.

5 During this period, the great interpreter of the title role was Thomas Betterton, who performed it from 1684 to 1709. Although he was the leading Othello of the period and was much praised, the only informative contemporary account of his performance in the role tells us little more than that his

> aspect was serious, **venerable**, and majestic. … His voice was low and grumbling, though he could lime it by an artful climax, which enforced attention. … He kept this passion under, and showed it most.

6 Betterton's successor as Othello was James Quin, who played the part from 1722 to 1751. Wearing a white wig and the white uniform (including white gloves) of a British officer, he was said to have presented an impressive appearance, but his acting was characterized as statuesque, even stiff, lacking in tenderness, pathos, fire, and any suggestion of inner pain. Quin was eclipsed in 1745 by David Garrick, whose Othello was quite different: the complaint now was that this Othello lacked dignity. The accusation was not merely a glance at Garrick's relatively short stature (he sought to compensate for his height by adding a turban to the costume of an officer in the British army), or even at his bold restoration of the fainting episode (4.1.45), which had been cut by his predecessors. Rather, it was directed at Garrick's violent gestures, which suggested to one critic that Othello seemed afflicted with St. Vitus' dance. Garrick defended his interpretation by arguing that Shakespeare

My Notes

venerable: worthy of respect

had shown us white men jealous in other pieces, but that their jealousy had limits, and was not so terrible. … [In] Othello he had wished to paint that passion in all its violence, and that is why he chose an African in whose being circulated fire instead of blood, and whose true or imaginary character could excuse all boldness of expression and all exaggerations of passion.

7 Garrick's rival, Quin, was not convinced. Of Garrick's Othello, Quin said: "Othello! … psha! no such thing. There was a little black boy … fretting and fuming about the stage; but I saw no Othello."

8 A reader can scarcely overlook the racism in these remarks, and something should be said about attitudes toward Moors. There is no doubt that most Elizabethans regarded Moors as vengeful—largely because they were not Christians. That Moors were black—the color of the devil—was thought to be a visible sign of their capacity for endless evil. (In fact, Shakespeare specifies that Othello is a Christian, and this is only one of several ways in which Othello departs from the stereotype.) Othello's physical blackness, by the way, seems not to have been doubted until the early nineteenth century. Certainly Quin and Garrick played him in blackface, and presumably so did their predecessor Betterton. And there is no doubt that on the Elizabethan stage Othello was very black. The only contemporary illustration of a scene from Shakespeare shows another of Shakespeare's Moors, Aaron in *Titus Andronicus*, as having an inky complexion. But in the early nineteenth century one finds expressions of distinct discomfort at the thought that Othello is black rather than, say, bronzed, or (to use an even loftier metaphor) golden. Even the best critics were not exempt from the racist thinking of their times. Thus, in 1808 Charles Lamb, picking up Desdemona's assertion that she judged Othello by his mind rather than by his color, argued that although we can share her view when we read the play, we cannot do so when we see a black Othello on the stage:

She sees Othello's color in his mind. But upon the stage, when the imagination is no longer the ruling faculty, but we are left to our poor unassisted senses, I appeal to every one that has seen Othello played, whether he did not, on the contrary, sink Othello's mind in his color; whether he did not find something extremely revolting in the courtship and wedded caresses of Othello and Desdemona, and whether the actual sight of the thing did not over-weigh all that beautiful compromise which we make in reading. …

9 At about the time that Lamb offered his comment on Othello, Lamb's friend Coleridge made some notes to the effect that Shakespeare could not possibly have thought of Othello as a black:

Can we suppose [Shakespeare] so utterly ignorant as to make a barbarous *negro* plead royal birth? Were negroes then known but as slaves; on the contrary, were not the Moors the warriors? … No doubt Desdemona saw Othello's visage in his mind; yet, as we are constituted, and most surely as an English audience was disposed in the beginning of the seventeenth century, it would be something monstrous to conceive this beautiful Venetian girl falling in love with a veritable negro. It would argue a disproportionateness, a want of balance in Desdemona, which Shakespeare does not appear to have in the least contemplated.

10 Given Coleridge's certainty that Othello could not possibly have been black, it is well to reiterate that the Elizabethans thought of Moors as black. True, there are a few references in Elizabethan literature to "tawny" Moors, but there is no evidence that the Elizabethans distinguished between tawny and black Moors, and in any case, if they did, various passages in *Othello* indicate that the protagonist is surely a black Moor. Admittedly, most of the references to Othello's Negroid features are made by persons hostile to him—Roderigo calls him "the thick-lips" (1.1.63), for instance, and Iago speaks of him as "an old black ram" (1.1.85)—but Othello himself says that his name "is now begrimed and black / As mine own face" (3.3.384–5). Of course "black" is sometimes used in the sense of brunette, but there really cannot be any doubt that Othello is black in the most obvious modern sense, and to call him tawny or golden or bronzed, or to conceive of him as something of an Arab chieftain, is to go against the text of the play.

11 When Spranger Barry, the actor who displaced Garrick as Othello in the middle of the eighteenth century (he was said to have not only the passion of Garrick but also the majesty that in Quin was merely stiffness), the question of color seems not to have come up, nor did it come up when the role in effect belonged to John Philip Kemble, the chief Othello at the turn of the eighteenth century (he played his first Othello in 1785, his last in 1805). Kemble, tall and stately, acted in what can be called a classic rather than romantic manner, a style suited more to, say, Brutus than to Othello. His interpretation of the role was criticized for its superabundance of dignity and for its lack of variety and fire, but not for its blackness. But when Edmund Kean played the role in 1814 he is said to have used a light brown makeup in place of the usual burnt cork. Oddly, there is some uncertainty about this—most critics of the period did not comment on the novelty—but putting aside the question of who made the change, and exactly when, about this time the color changed. By 1827 Leman Thomas Rede's *The Road to the Stage* (a book on makeup) could report that "A tawny tinge is now the color used for the gallant Moor." Here it is evident that the makeup no longer uses burnt cork. Most of the Othellos of the rest of the century were tawny, their bronze skin suggesting that they were sons of the desert, but Henry Irving's Othello of 1881 was conspicuously dark (darker than his "bronze" Othello of 1876), and, as we shall see, in the twentieth century dark Othellos have been dominant, especially in our own generation, when American blacks have often played the part.

12 Putting aside the point that Kean's Othello was lighter than usual, it was exceptional for its power and its pathos. If Kemble is the paradigm of classical acting, Kean—passionate, even spasmodic—is the paradigm of romantic acting. Coleridge wrote: "Seeing [Kean] act was like reading Shakespeare by flashes of lightning." Another great romantic writer, William Hazlitt, at first found Kean too passionate. In the following passage Hazlitt complains that the fault in the performance is not in the color of Kean's face, or in Kean's relatively short stature:

> Othello was tall, but that is nothing; he was black, but that is nothing. But he was not fierce, and that is everything. It is only in the last agony of human suffering that he gives way to his rage and despair. … Mr. Kean is in general all passion, all energy, all relentless will. … He is too often in the highest key of passion, too uniformly on the verge of extravagance, too constantly on the rack.

13 Kean later moderated the passion, perhaps under Hazlitt's influence, but, curiously, Hazlitt regretted the change, remarking: "There is but one perfect way of playing Othello, and that was the way … he used to play it." Equally compelling is the tribute to Kean offered by the American actor Junius Brutus Booth, who in England in 1817–18 played Iago to Kean's Othello. Booth said that "Kean's Othello smothered Desdemona and my Iago too." Kean's triumph in the role was undoubted, but in 1825, two weeks after he had been proved guilty of adultery, public opinion turned against him, denouncing the hypocrisy of an adulterer who dared to play the outraged husband lamenting his wife's infidelity. Still, he continued in the role, playing Othello almost to the day of his death. His last performance was in this role, in 1833, when he collapsed on the stage and died a few weeks later.

14 Other nineteenth-century actors have made their mark in the role—for instance William Macready (he sometimes played Iago against Kean's Othello) and Samuel Phelps—but here there is space to mention only four, Ira Aldridge, Edwin Booth, Tommaso Salvini, and Henry Irving. Aldridge, a black, was born in New York in 1807. As a very young man he determined to be an actor, but seeing no possibility of a career as an actor in America, he went to London in 1824 and never returned to the United States. At least one black actor, James Hewlett, had already played Othello in America, but that was with the all-black African Company, and Aldridge's ambition was to be accepted as an actor, not as a black actor, an ambition impossible to fulfill in the United States, where there were no interracial companies. He performed throughout the British Isles and also on the Continent, playing not only Othello but also (with white makeup) such roles as Richard III, Shylock, Hamlet, Macbeth, and Lear.

15 In America, Edwin Booth (son of Junius Brutus Booth) acted Othello almost annually from 1826 to 1871. From time to time he changed his performance, sometimes working in the violent style associated with Tommaso Salvini, hurling his Iago to the ground, but sometimes he played with

restraint—occasionally he even omitted striking Desdemona at IV.i.240—and he was especially praised for his tender passion. Most critics, however, preferred his Iago, which seemed genial, sincere, and terrifyingly evil; he was widely regarded as the greatest Iago of the later nineteenth century. (Among the performers with whom he alternated the roles of Othello and Iago were Henry Irving and James O'Neill, Eugene O'Neill's father; and he played Iago to Salvini's Othello. Here is his advice on how to play Iago:

> Don't *act* the villain, don't *look* it or *speak* it (by scowling and growling, I mean), but *think* it all the time. Be genial, sometimes jovial, always gentlemanly. Quick in motion as in thought; **lithe** and sinuous as a snake. A certain **bluffness** (which my temperament does not afford) should be added to preserve the military flavor of the character; in this particular I fail utterly, my Iago lacks the soldierly quality.

16 Henry Irving played Othello only in 1876 and 1881. Although he had already achieved success in the roles of Hamlet, Macbeth, and Lear, his Othello did not find equal favor. It was not especially violent, but it was said to lack dignity (apparently there was much lifting up of hands and shuffling of feet), and after the attempt in 1881 Irving decided to drop the role. Still, some things about the 1881 performance should be mentioned. The makeup was very black, the costume exotic (a white jeweled turban, an amber robe), and the killing of Desdemona very solemn—until Desdemona tried to escape, at which point he flung her on the bed. The play ended with Othello's suicide, the curtain descending as he fell at Gratiano's feet. Iago (played by Booth) stood by, smiling malignantly.

17 By common consent the greatest Othello of the later nineteenth century was Tommaso Salvini, who acted in Italian—even when in England or the United States, with the rest of the company speaking English. Some Victorians regarded Salvini as too savage, too volcanic, too terrifying to arouse pity—he seized Iago by the throat and hurled him to the floor, and put his foot on Iago's neck, and of course he did not hesitate to strike Desdemona—but most audiences were deeply moved as well as terrified by his performance. We are told that especially in the first three acts, where some of the love play seemed almost to be high comedy, his Othello was "delightful" and "delicate." Still, the overall effect was that of enormous energy, though not of mere barbarism. Henry James was among Salvini's greatest admirers:

> It is impossible to imagine anything more living, more tragic, more suggestive of a tortured soul and of generous, beneficent strength changed to a purpose of destruction. With its tremendous force, it is magnificently quiet, and from the beginning to the end has not a touch of rant or crudity.

18 Actors of note who played Othello or Iago in the early twentieth century include Johnston Forbes-Robertson, Oscar Asche, and Beerbohm Tree, but none of these was widely regarded as great. Indeed, the standard opinion is

lithe: moving easily
bluffness: frankness

WORD CONNECTIONS

Roots and Affixes
The verb **obliterate** originates from the Latin root *littera*, meaning "letter," combined with the prefix *ob-*, meaning "against" or "in the way of." *Obliterating* something means removing it or obscuring it so it cannot be seen or understood. Other words from *littera* include *literature*, *alliteration*, *literal*, and *letter*.

My Notes

that the twentieth century did not have a great Othello until Paul Robeson, an African American, played the role in 1943. But Robeson was not primarily an actor. As a college student at Rutgers he distinguished himself not to theatrics but in athletics (all-American end in football in 1918, and letters in several varsity sports) and in scholarship (Phi Beta Kappa). He next prepared for a career in the law, taking a law degree at Columbia University, but while at Columbia in 1921 he performed in his first amateur production. He soon began to appear in some professional productions, including *Showboat*, where his singing of "Ol' Man River" led to a career as a concert singer, especially of spirituals and work songs, though he returned to the stage to play Othello in 1930 in England, in 1942 in Cambridge, Boston, and Princeton, in 1943 in New York, and in 1959 at Stratford-upon-Avon. Observers agree that the 1959 performance was poor; Robeson had been weakened by an attack of bronchitis, his political beliefs had been shaken (earlier he had praised Stalin, but now the crimes of the Stalin era were evident), and, perhaps worst of all, the director's presence was too strongly felt, for instance in a distracting fog that supposedly was the result of the storm at Cyprus. Many scenes were so dark that spectators could not see the actors' faces, and there seems no reason to doubt the accuracy of those reviewers who accused the director of obliterating the principal actors.

19 Robeson's first Othello—indeed, his first performance in a play by Shakespeare, in 1930—was much more enthusiastically received. The London *Morning Post* said: "There has been no Othello on our stage for forty years to compare with his dignity, simplicity, and true passion." But not all of the reviewers were entirely pleased. James Agate, the leading theater critic of the period, said that Robeson lacked the majesty that Shakespeare insists on early in the play, for instance in such lines as

I fetch my life and being

    From men of royal siege,   (I.ii.20–21)

and

    Were it my cue to fight, I should have known it

    Without a prompter,   (82–83)

and

    Keep up your bright swords, for the dew will

    rust them.   (58)

20 The majesty displayed in such passages, Agate said, tells us how Othello must behave when he puts down Cassio's drunken brawl, but according to Agate, Robeson (despite his height—six feet, three inches) lacked this majesty. Thus, when Robeson's Othello said "Silence that dreadful bell! It frights the isle/ From her propriety" (II.iii.174–75), he showed personal annoyance rather than the "passion for decorum" (Agate's words) that the line reveals. Agate found Robeson best in the third and fourth acts, where he captured the jealousy of the part, but weak (lacking in dignity) in the last act, where he failed to perform the murder with a solemn sense of sacrifice.

21 Despite the reservations of Agate and others, there was some talk of bringing the production to the United States, but nothing came of it, doubtless because of uncertainty about how American audiences (and perhaps performers?) would respond to a company that mixed whites and blacks. In 1938 Margaret Webster again raised the topic, but she was discouraged by the Americans with whom she talked. It was acceptable for a black actor—a real black man, not a white man in blackface—to kiss a white girl in England, but not in the United States. Fortunately, however, Webster later persuaded the Theatre Guild to invite Robeson to do *Othello* in the United States in 1942, if not on Broadway at least as summer stock, with José Ferrer as Iago and Uta Hagen as Desdemona. The production was enthusiastically received, but Robeson's concert commitments prevented it from going to New York until the fall of 1943. When it did open in New York, the reviews were highly favorable, but some of them contained reservations about Robeson's ability to speak blank verse and to catch the grandeur of the role. In any case, the production was an enormous success, running for 296 continuous performances. The previous record for a New York *Othello* had been 57.

22 Robeson inevitably was asked to discuss his conception of the role; equally inevitably, he said different things at different times, and perhaps sometimes said what reporters wanted to hear—or perhaps the reporters heard only what they wanted to hear. Sometimes he was reported as saying that the matter of color is secondary, but on other occasions he is reported as saying: "The problem [of *Othello*] is the problem of my own people. It is a tragedy of racial conflict, a tragedy of honor, rather than of jealousy."

23 Until Robeson, black actors in the United States were in effect limited to performing in all-black companies. With Robeson, a black actor played Othello with an otherwise white company. His appearance as Othello in 1943 was an important anticipation of the gains black actors were to make in later decades. Earle Hyman, Moses Gunn, Paul Winfield, William Marshall, and James Earl Jones are among the black actors who have played impressive Othellos in mixed-race companies. More important, however, as the careers of these actors show, a black may now also play a role other than Othello, as Ira Aldridge did a hundred and fifty years ago, though he had to cross the Atlantic to do it.

24 Before looking at Laurence Olivier's Othello in 1964, mention should be made of Olivier's Iago in a production of 1937, directed by Tyrone Guthrie at the Old Vic. Olivier and Guthrie talked to Ernest Jones, friend of Sigmund Freud, and came away with the idea that Iago's hatred for Othello was in fact based on a subconscious love for Othello. That Iago protests "I hate the Moor" means nothing, for he is unaware of his true emotions. Ralph Richardson was Othello in this production, but Guthrie and Olivier decided not to shock him (remember, this was 1937) by any such unconventional idea, and so, the story goes, Richardson could never quite understand what Olivier was making out of the role. (What Olivier apparently made out of it was something like this: Iago is manic because he cannot face his true feelings.) The critics, like Richardson

Paul Robeson and Uta Hagen as Othello and Desdemona on Broadway, 1943

My Notes

My Notes

and the general public, were in the dark, and the production was poorly reviewed. Guthrie himself later called the production "a ghastly, boring hash," and Olivier has said that he no longer subscribes to Jones's interpretation.

25 In 1964 Olivier played Othello, with Frank Finlay as Iago, and Maggie Smith as Desdemona, in a production directed by John Dexter. (This production was later filmed, and most of what is true of the stage production is true also of the film.) Far from suggesting that Othello was some sort of desert chief, Olivier emphasized the Negroid aspects, or at least the white man's stock ideas of Negroid aspects. Thus, Othello's skin was very dark, his lips were red and sensuous, and his lilting voice had something of a West Indian accent. He rolled his eyes a good deal, and he walked (barefooted and adorned with ankle bracelets) with a sensuous sway. More important (worse, some viewers felt), was the idea behind this Othello, which was indebted to some thoughts by T. S. Eliot and F. R. Leavis. For Eliot (in an essay called "Shakespeare and the Stoicism of Seneca," first published in 1927) and for Leavis (in an essay first published in a journal in 1937 but more readily available, in reprinted form, in Leavis's *The Common Pursuit*), Othello is not so much a heroic figure—the noble Moor who gains our sympathy despite the terrible deed he performs—as a **fatuous** simpleton, a man given to egotistical self-dramatizing. The playbill included some passages from Leavis's essay, which the director in effect summarized when he told the cast that

> Othello is a pompous, word-spinning, arrogant black general. … The important thing is not to accept him at his own valuation. … He isn't just a righteous man who's been wronged. He's a man too proud to think he could ever be capable of anything as base as jealousy. When he learns he can be jealous, his character changes. The knowledge destroys him, and he goes berserk.

26 Thus, Olivier delivered "Farewell the tranquil mind" (3.3.345)—a speech customarily delivered reflectively—in a frenzy. It's probably fair to say that the gist of the idea underlying this production is fairly odd: Othello is a barbarian with a thin veneer of civilization. Thus, the early speeches were delivered with easy confidence because Othello had no understanding of how simple and how volatile he really was. The change from civilized man to barbarian was marked by Othello tearing off a crucifix he wore, an effective enough bit of business but one at odds with two aspects of the end of Shakespeare's play: Othello (who just before he kills Desdemona is careful to urge her to make her peace with God; "I would not kill thy soul" (5.2.32) murders Desdemona partly because he believes she has been false to the highest ideals. Second, when he comes to understand the horror of his action he executes justice upon himself. Still, although much in the conception could be faulted, it was widely agreed that Olivier's acting was a triumph—a triumph won, among other things, at the expense of an **unprepossessing** Iago and a **negligible** Desdemona.

fatuous: foolish
unprepossessing: unappealing
negligible: unimportant

My Notes

27 The film with Olivier (1965), directed by Stuart Burge, was made in a sound studio, using sets that were essentially those of the stage production—even for scenes set out-of-doors—but it was not simply a filmed version of what a spectator sitting in the third row center would have seen. For instance, because close-ups are used for all of Iago's soliloquies, Iago becomes considerably more prominent in the film than he was on the stage.

28 Olivier said that the backgrounds in the film were minimal because he was concerned with "offering as little visual distraction as possible from the intentions of Shakespeare—or our performance of them." For a film of the opposite sort, a film that does not hesitate to introduce impressive visual effects not specified in the text, one should look at Orson Welles's *Othello*, a black and white film begun in 1951 and completed and released in 1955, with Welles in the title role. The film was shot on location, chiefly in Morocco and Venice, but what especially strikes a viewer is not that the camera gives us a strong sense of the real world, but that the camera leads us into a strange, shadowy world of unfamiliar and puzzling appearance. The film begins with Welles reading a passage from Shakespeare's source while we see a shot of the face of the dead Othello. The camera rises above the bier, which is carried by pallbearers, and we then see Desdemona's body, also being borne to the grave. We see the two funeral processions converge, and then we see Iago, in chains, thrust into a cage and hoisted above the crowd. From above—Iago's viewpoint—we look down on the bodies of Othello and Desdemona. All of this is presented before we see the credits for the film. The film ends with a dissolve from the dying Othello to a shot of the funeral procession and then to shots of the fortress at Cyprus, the cage, and Venetian buildings and ships. Between this highly cinematic beginning and ending, other liberties are taken with the text. The murder of Roderigo, for instance, is set in a steamy bathhouse. Welles had intended to shoot the scene in a street, but because he had run out of money and didn't have costumes, he set it in a steam bath, where a few towels were all the clothing that was needed. In short, Welles's *Othello* is not for the Shakespeare purist (too much is cut and too much is added), but it is imaginative and it often works. Admirers will want to see also *Filming "Othello,"* a film memoir (1978) in which Welles and others discuss the work.

29 The BBC television version of *Othello*, directed by Jonathan Miller and released in 1981, is, like Olivier's film, somewhat in the Eliot-Leavis tradition. In the introduction to the printed text of the BBC version, Miller says that the play does not set forth "the spectacle of a person of grandeur falling." Rather,

> what's interesting is that it's not the fall of the great but the disintegration of the ordinary, of the representative character. It's the very ordinariness of Othello that makes the story intolerable.

30 Miller is insistent, too, that the play is not about race. "I do not see the play as being about color but as being about jealousy—which is something we are all vulnerable to." In line with this emphasis on the ordinary, Othello (Anthony

Hopkins) is relatively unheroic, though he is scarcely as commonplace as Miller suggests, since he is full of energy and rage. More successful is Iago (Bob Hoskins), a bullet-headed hood who delights in Othello's anguish. The sets, in order to reduce any sense of heroism or romance, are emphatically domestic; no effort was made to take advantage of the camera's ability to record expansive space. Interestingly, however, the domestic images on the screen are by no means ordinary; notably beautiful, they often remind us of Vermeer.

31 During the course of this survey it has been easy to notice racist implications in the remarks of certain actors and critics. And it was racism, of course, that kept blacks from acting in *Othello* and in other plays) along with whites. One point that has not been raised till now is this: Does it matter if a black plays Othello? When Robeson played the part, some theatergoers found that the play made more sense than ever before, partly because Robeson (whatever his limitations as an actor) was a black [man]. Others found that it was distracting for a black to play the part; it brought into the world of *Othello* irrelevant issues of twentieth-century America. Jonathan Miller, holding the second position, puts it thus:

> When a black actor does the part, it offsets the play, puts it out of balance. It makes it a play about blackness, which it is not. … The trouble is, the play was hijacked for political purposes.

32 Many things can be said against this view, for instance that when the white actor Olivier played Othello he expended so much energy impersonating a black that a spectator was far more conscious of the performer's blackness than one is of, say, James Earl Jones's. In any case, Miller has not said the last word on this topic, which will continue to be debated.

> *Bibliographic Note*: For a modern edition of *Othello* prefaced with a long stage history, and equipped with abundant footnotes telling how various actors delivered particular lines, see Julie Hankey, *Othello* (1987), a volume in a series entitled Plays in Performance.

33 For a survey of *Othello* on the stage, see Marvin Rosenberg, *The Masks of "Othello"* (1961); for a brief study of five recent productions (including Robeson in 1943, Olivier in 1964, and the BBC television version of 1981), see Martin L. Wine, *"Othello": Text and Performance* (1984). Errol Hill's *Shakespeare in Sable* (1984), a history of black actors of Shakespeare, contains much information about *Othello*. Other items especially relevant to the productions discussed above include: Arthur Colby Sprague, *Shakespearian Players and Performances* (1953), for Kean's Othello and Edwin Booth's Iago; Daniel J. Watermeier, "Edwin Booth's Iago," *Theatre History Studies* 6 (1986): 32–55; Kenneth Tynan, ed., *"Othello" by William Shakespeare: The National Theatre Production* (1966), on Olivier; *The BBC TV Shakespeare: "Othello"* (1981), on the version directed

by Jonathan Miller. On Robeson, see Susan Spector, "Margaret Webster's *Othello*," *Theatre History Studies* 6 (1968): 93–108. For film versions, see Jack J. Jorgens, *Shakespeare on Film* (1977), and, for Welles's film only, see Michael MacLiammoir, *Put Money in Thy Purse* (1952).

Laurence Fishburne and Irene Jacob as Othello and Desdemona, in the 1995 film adaptation

⌀ Knowledge Quest

- What example of staging *Othello* can you picture most vividly as you read Barnet's essay?
- Which interpretation of *Othello* stands out to you the most as being influenced by society and culture? Why?

Returning to the Text

- Return to the essay as you respond to the following questions. Use text evidence to support your responses.
- Write any additional questions you have about the text in your Reader/Writer Notebook.

1. Shakespeare died in 1616. What can the reader infer about his vision for *Othello* from the performance described in paragraph 1?

_____

_____

_____

2. KQ What inference can a reader make about society's views on race based on the quoted passage at the end of paragraph 6?

_____

_____

_____

3. KQ How do cultural attitudes toward black people change between Shakespeare's time and Coleridge's (paragraphs 6–10)?

_____

_____

_____

4. KQ What details from paragraph 8 explain what the author means by "bronzed, (or to use an even loftier metaphor) golden"?

_____

_____

_____

5. What might be the author's purpose behind mentioning aspects of Kean's personal life in paragraph 13?

_____

_____

_____

6. Based on Edwin Booth's advice on how to play Iago in paragraph 15, why was his Iago more "terrifyingly evil" than others'?

_____

_____

_____

_____

7. In paragraph 16, the author says that "some things about the 1881 performance should be mentioned." What are they and why are they noteworthy?

_____

_____

_____

_____

8. Based on context clues and word parts, what is the meaning of *malignantly* at the end of paragraph 16?

_____

_____

_____

_____

9. KQ How did the circumstances in which black actors portrayed Othello change over time?

_____

_____

_____

_____

10. In paragraph 20, how do Agate's criticisms of Robeson's performance suggest a critical lens?

_____

_____

_____

_____

11. Based on the description of Robeson's 1943 New York production of *Othello* at the end of paragraph 21, did the audience agree with the critics? How do you know?

_____

_____

_____

_____

12. In paragraph 24, how did Freud inspire the new interpretation of Iago in the 1930s? What is the effect of this interpretation, and how was the performance received?

_____

_____

_____

_____

13. KQ In paragraph 25, what two cultural influences were reflected in Eliot's and Leavis's new interpretation of Othello? What evidence shows these influences?

_____

_____

_____

_____

14. In paragraphs 29 and 30, what clues show what Miller means by "It's the very ordinariness of Othello that makes the story intolerable"?

_____

_____

_____

_____

15. What organizational pattern does Barnet use in his essay? How does it aid his purpose?

_____

_____

_____

_____

Knowledge Quest

In analyzing the staging of *Othello* over time, the author connects artistic choices to the prevailing social and cultural perspectives regarding race at various times. Imagine a contemporary production of *Othello* in a particular American city. What do you believe are the prevailing social and cultural perspectives regarding race that would affect the production? With your small group, discuss the context in which a contemporary staging of *Othello* would be presented. How might this influence the decisions of the director and actors working on a modern production? Be sure to:

- Prepare by reviewing what you have learned about how society and culture have influenced the way the character of Othello has been interpreted to date.

- Ask and respond to questions to clarify details, evidence, and ideas.

- Acknowledge perspectives and reasoning that are different from your own.

INDEPENDENT READING LINK

You can continue to build your knowledge about changing interpretations of *Othello* over time by reading other articles at ZINC Reading Labs. Search for keywords such as *Othello* or *Shakespeare*.

 ZINC

My Notes

Working from the Text

16. Through today's critical lens of Cultural Criticism, do you think the answers to "Does it matter if a black plays Othello?" (paragraph 31) would be different? Why or why not?

My Notes

17. **Quickwrite:** Answer the following questions then discuss your responses with your acting company. Use evidence from the text to support your claims:

   - What is Barnet's primary claim in his essay?
   - Does he make that claim convincingly, or do you challenge any of his points?
   - What questions does he leave unanswered?
   - Do Barnett's thesis, evidence, commentary, and conclusion all support his purpose?

☑ Check Your Understanding

Sylvan Barnet's review pointed out that observers of one production noted "the director's presence was too strongly felt." What is the proper role of a director in a performance? How can you use this information to guide your staging of a scene from *Othello*?

▣ Writing Prompt: Argumentative

At this point, you have seen or read about various stage and screen interpretations of *Othello*. Combining what you've learned about *Othello* with your prior knowledge about stage and screen adaptations, explain how modifying an original text can affect the audience's perception. Be sure to:

- Begin a clear thesis to present your position.
- Support your claims with engaging details and examples.
- Include a conclusion that reinforces your thesis in a convincing way without introducing any new ideas.

Language Checkpoint: Understanding Verb Voice and Mood

Learning Targets

- Understand verb voice and mood.
- Revise writing to correct inappropriate shifts in verb voice and mood.

Preview

In this activity you will learn about appropriate use of voice and mood to enhance your writing. Then you will practice revising for consistency in voice and mood.

Reviewing Verb Voice and Mood

Verbs are the engines of sentences. They express action (run, jump, think) or a state of being (is, was). Verbs have qualities called **voice** and **mood** that provide additional information.

Verb voice refers to whether the verb is active or passive. In a sentence using active voice, the subject of the sentence performs the action expressed by the verb. In a sentence using passive voice, the subject of the sentence receives the action.

Passive Voice: The title role was performed by Tim Betterton from 1684 to 1790.

Active Voice: Thomas Betterton performed the title role from 1684 to 1709.

Active voice is more direct and less wordy than passive voice, so you should use active voice in most cases. In some cases, though, the passive voice may be preferable. For instance, a writer might want to emphasize the recipient of the action or may want to avoid naming who or what performs an action.

Verb mood expresses a writer's or speaker's attitude. Indicative mood, the most common mood, is used to make statements or ask questions. Imperative mood is used to give a command or make a request. Subjunctive mood is used to express doubt or discuss hypothetical situations.

Indicative Mood: The performance is popular in several major cities.

Imperative Mood: Take me to go see the performance!

Subjunctive Mood: If I were you, I would be excited to watch the performance.

Exploring Verb Voice

1. Writers use active voice most of the time. Read the following sentence, which uses active voice. Then briefly describe why you think the writer chose the active voice.

   I wrote a negative review of the play.

2. Now read this sentence, which is written in passive voice. How does the passive voice change the meaning and effect of the sentence?

   The play was negatively reviewed.

Avoiding Unnecessary Shifts in Voice

Writers may choose to use active and passive voice for different effects, but they should avoid unnecessary shifts in voice.

3. Look at this sentence from a student's essay about *Othello*. Underline the verbs.

   The critic recalls the play, and Salvini's terrifying portrayal of Othello is remembered.

4. What do you notice about the verbs in these two clauses? With a partner, look at the sentence, and make an observation about the verbs' voice.

Exploring Verb Mood

5. The indicative mood is used most often. But there are specific situations when other verb moods are useful. Read the following sentence, which is in the imperative mood, and describe briefly when you would use this mood.

   Go watch the play!

6. Now read this sentence, which is in the subjunctive mood. Describe briefly when you would use this mood.

If I were you, I would have played the part of Iago.

Avoiding Unnecessary Shifts in Mood

7. Look at this sentence from "Othello on Stage and Screen." Underline the verbs.

The critic is entertained, but he does not understand Othello's complexity.

8. Continue examining the same sentence from the text, and determine the mood of the verbs you identified. With a partner, write a new sentence that uses the same mood.

9. Look at this sentence from a student's essay about "Othello on Stage and Screen." Underline the verbs.

Think about the critic's review. Imagine his perspectives.

10. What mood are these verbs in? With a partner, write a new sentence that uses the same mood.

Editing

Read the following passage and revise the underlined words as needed to correct inappropriate shifts in voice or mood. If the sentence has no unnecessary shifts, write "no change."

11. The audience <u>watched</u> the play and warmly receives Robeson's performance.

_____

_____

12. If the survey <u>were</u> correct, American audiences would not have welcomed a black actor playing Othello in the United States.

_____

_____

13. Surprisingly, Robeson's Othello is a success and the audience <u>watched</u> the performance.

_____

_____

☑ Check Your Understanding

Imagine you are editing a classmate's writing, and you notice these sentences:

> What would you do if you are cast as Iago in the play? You could act like a villain, or acting friendly.

Write an explanation so that your classmate understands how to correct the unnecessary shifts. Add an item to your Editor's Checklist to help you remember to check for verb voice when revising your own work.

Practice

Using what you have learned about verb usage in this lesson, revisit what you wrote for the writing prompt in Activity 3.19. Be sure to:

- Check for appropriate verb voice and mood.
- Revise any inappropriate shifts between voices and moods.

Staging a Performance

Learning Targets
- Determine the theme of a play from its dramatic structure.
- Apply dramatic elements to a performance to reveal theme and reflect a critical perspective.

Preview
In this activity, you will identify a universal theme found in *Othello* and analyze it through multiple critical perspectives. Then you will prepare for Embedded Assessment 2 by planning and rehearsing your staged interpretation of a scene from the play.

Learning Strategies
Graphic Organizer
Note-taking
Rehearsal
Think-Pair-Share
Visualizing
Visual Response

My Notes

Staging a Dramatic Scene

1. What do you know about the dramatic structure of a play? Share your ideas about this term with a partner.

2. Thinking back to one of the stage or film versions of *Othello*, how does this structure and other dramatic elements such as the actors' and director's use of space advance the plot of the play? Be sure to consider secondary characters like Emilia when sharing thoughts with a partner or your acting company.

3. How would you map the plot of *Othello*? Think back to the events that took us from Othello and Desdemona's marriage to the tragic ending. Create mental images of Othello's transformation throughout the play. Plot the key events with your acting company. Be prepared to share your visual with the class.

Timeless Themes

A text conveys meaning in multiple ways. Consider, for example, how theme is developed through dramatic structure. Sometimes, determining the theme of a work is easier when you simplify the plot. Suppose you were to wrap up the plot of *Othello* in as few as nine words (three 3-word sentences). For *Romeo and Juliet*, a literal 3 x 3 might look like this:

> Montague loves Capulet.
>
> Feud complicates love.
>
> Miscommunication brings death.

In order to derive theme from the literal events, let's substitute thematic ideas for the specific ones in the previous 3 x 3.

> Adolescents defy boundaries.
>
> Emotions go unchecked.
>
> Interference complicates reality.

Our "literary 3 x 3" now leads us to some general truths about life. What is Shakespeare saying about the unchecked emotions of adolescence, or of the unchecked emotions of adults engaged in an ancient quarrel? Could we also safely infer from the text that adults' interference in the lives of young people invites— rather than prevents—complications that are a natural part of growing up?

My Notes

4. Work with your acting company to "wrap up" the dramatic structure of *Othello* in a literal 3 x 3.

5. Write your class's combined "best" in the space provided.

6. Now move from the literal to capture the themes at work in *Othello* in a literary 3 x 3.

7. Write a thematic statement from your 3 x 3 in the space provided.

Make It Work for You

8. Keeping in mind the theme that you identified from your work with 3 x 3s, now consider your assigned scene for Embedded Assessment 2: Staging an Interpretation. Where does your scene fit in the dramatic structure of the play? Revisit your dramatic structure visual from the beginning of this activity, and plot it on your "map." Then, apply the theme from your 3 x 3 to your assigned scene.

9. How does your acting company's scene connect to the themes of the work? How would the themes of the work impact how the actors in your company portray the characters? Explain the relationship in a quickwrite.

10. How can you apply a critical perspective to the scene? Considering the scene's place in the dramatic structure and its connection to a theme of the work as a whole, what are some lenses through which you can view the scene? Begin with Marxist, Cultural, and Feminist Criticism, and add any others that offer a suitable lens for viewing the scene.

Marxist:

Cultural:

Feminist:

11. As an acting company, come to an agreement about the critical perspective that offers the most engaging interpretation of the scene for a staged performance.

12. Now it's time to consider how to blend the play's literary elements and the dramatic elements you will use while staging your assigned scene to reflect a specific critical perspective in a performance. The dramatic and literary elements will vary depending on your scene. For example, if your scene includes a soliloquy, you might need to consider how the actor who delivers the lines can stand or act apart from the other actors onstage to maintain the audience's focus. Use the graphic organizer to plan your presentation. Use the additional rows for other categories/characters.

Scene:

_____

_____

Connection to Theme:

_____

_____

Critical Perspective:

_____

_____

	Creating the Desired Effect	Notes Create notes and suggest changes during rehearsal.
Timing	Work with the actors and the director to plan out movements and gestures to increase the impact of dialogue.	
Mood	Decide on the appropriate mood for the scene and adjust sound, music, props, etc. to evoke the desired mood.	
Space	Work together to block the scene in a way that uses the space effectively. How will the movement on stage enhance your interpretation?	
Language	Consider how the actors will deliver their lines. How will they use body language and tone of voice? Will you adjust the script or deliver the lines as written?	
Other	Consider props, use of music, lighting, etc. How will the props and music enhance your interpretation?	

Make Final Preparations

13. Print your script and annotate the scene for your vocal delivery, gestures, use of space, etc. Rehearse your scene and accept constructive criticism from your director to help you convey a convincing performance. Be sure to keep in mind the critical perspective you are applying to the scene and adjust your character's performance to reflect that interpretation.

☑ Check Your Understanding

Review the Assignment, Steps, and Scoring Guide from Embedded Assessment 2 with your acting company. Discuss which components of the assignment may need further preparation. How will you work together as a group to complete any remaining steps?

INDEPENDENT READING LINK

Read and Discuss

Select a point in your independent reading in which a character or the narrator experiences feeling like an outsider. Discuss with a partner or a group how the character reflects on this incident.

Close Reading
Round Table Writing
Sketching
Skimming/Scanning

My Notes

Learning Targets

- Research, plan, and produce a playbill that follows formatting and writing conventions.
- Contribute to the creation of a performance guide for a staged performance.
- Collaboratively write a playbill, or theatre program, that explains the use of a critical perspective

Preview

In this activity, you will analyze the graphics and textual content in a variety of playbills, and then work with your acting company to create a playbill for your interpretation of *Othello*. Collaboratively, you will write a letter to your audience about your acting company's use of a specific critical perspective to drive your interpretation.

Planning a Playbill

1. Use the Internet and your school's library to research playbills used for theater performance. You can view playbills online at playbill.com. To help you plan your company's playbill, jot down notes to answer the following questions:

   - How is a playbill typically structured?
   - What kind of information is included in a playbill based on the examples you viewed?

2. Playbills generally include the background and acting experience of the performers. Take the time to closely read a description of a cast member.

   - What information is included in the description?
   - What point of view is used in the description?
   - What does the actor or production company want a reader to know?

3. A synopsis is another staple of a playbill.

   - How is it structured?
   - How much detail does it provide?

4. Share the notes from your research with your acting company. Then make a list of the key sections that are consistent to all playbills. Note special sections that appear for a single production. As you make your observations, discuss the possible reasons the creator of the playbill chose to include the information and place it accordingly.

5. With your group, complete the graphic organizer to plan the basic structure of your company's playbill.

Key sections	Notes on each section	New ideas and additions to your playbill

6. Next, look at the graphics and/or artwork incorporated in the playbill.

_____

_____

7. What images from the play did the artist choose to represent? Why?

_____

_____

8. What message might the production company want to send through the print and graphics used in the publication?

Do you think the purpose was achieved? Why or why not?

_____

_____

If you have more than one playbill, what differences do you notice in design, artwork, and (copy) text? If you were to choose one of the performances to attend, which would it be? Why?

_____

_____

9. How are advertisements incorporated into the playbill?

_____

_____

Designing the Playbill

10. Your group is responsible for creating a playbill to accompany your performance of *Othello*. Your playbill should enhance your performance and your audience's understanding of the critical perspective that informs your interpretation. Imitate the playbills you viewed in class to guide your content and structure.

As you design your playbill, be sure to:

- Include a creative design with the artwork, graphics, and advertisements presented.
- Adhere to the message and literary theory pursued through the staged performance.
- Use a computer program to produce a visually appealing and technically sound publication.
- Share the responsibilities of designing the playbill by listing all of its components and then assigning an individual to each task.

11. Sketch a plan for the playbill's design in the space provided. Then, have each member of the group develop a brief, written plan to complete the task. Share plans among the company and make any constructive suggestions that could help others improve their plan and accomplish the task in the most effective way.

Playbill design for the 1943 Broadway production of *Othello*, featuring Paul Robeson

☑ Check Your Understanding

In the form of quickwrite, explain how an author can strategically use organizational design and graphic elements when creating a playbill to inform and engage the audience.

✍ Writing Prompt: Informational

With your acting company, draft a professional letter to the audience explaining the interpretation of the scene you will produce. In your letter, describe the message the adaptation is trying to convey by interpreting the work through a specific critical lens. You will finalize your letter for Embedded Assessment 2. Be sure to:

- State which cultural perspective is providing the framework for your production and explain the lens in a way that will clarify its impact on the presentation.
- Follow the formatting conventions and structure of professional letters.
- Use appropriate register and vocabulary.

⬡ Independent Reading Checkpoint

Review your independent reading. Suppose you were going to design a playbill for your text. What kind of information would you include? What design elements would you make or use that reflect aspects of your text? Which actors might you choose as performers? Share your ideas with a group.

My Notes

Staging an Interpretation

 ASSIGNMENT

Your assignment is to interpret a scene from *Othello* to emphasize the principles of one of the critical perspectives you have studied, and then plan, rehearse, and perform the scene. With your acting company, write a letter to the audience explaining the message your interpretation is trying to convey.

Planning and Prewriting: Take time to plan ideas and the structure of your scene.	■ How will you determine which critical perspective will best apply to your scene? ■ What message is your production planning to convey? How explicitly will you state this message in your communication to the audience? ■ How can your acting company bring to life the principles or core ideas of the critical perspective you've chosen? ■ How will you divide the various tasks among group members?
Drafting: Create all elements needed for an effective performance.	■ How can you integrate dramatic elements into your scene? ■ What changes do you need to make to your scene (delete or change lines, alter the setting or gender of characters) in order to apply your selected critical perspective? Will you detail some or all of these changes in your letter to the audience? ■ How can you ensure that the group works successfully to maintain its purpose and achieve its goals?
Evaluating and Revising: Obtain feedback and revise to make your work the best it can be.	■ How can you use practice and rehearsal to prepare and evaluate your presentation (videotape a rehearsal, ask another group to provide feedback)? ■ How can you use the Scoring Guide as a resource to evaluate your draft? ■ Are you being faithful to Shakespeare's original within your interpretation?
Checking and Editing for Performance: Polish your written materials and your vocal delivery.	■ How will you check for grammatical and technical accuracy in your written materials? ■ Are you prepared to provide feedback to other acting companies as well as to accept constructive criticism for your own performance? ■ How will you structure the feedback to ensure it is fair and useful?

Reflection

After completing this Embedded Assessment, think about how you went about accomplishing this assignment, and respond to the following:

- The goal of applying a critical perspective to a text is to bring out a new, deeper understanding of the work. How did you manage the challenge of making changes to your scene in order to highlight the chosen critical perspectives without completely altering the scene's original meaning?

SCORING GUIDE

Scoring Criteria	Exemplary	Proficient	Emerging	Incomplete
Ideas	The interpretation • reveals an insightful analysis and mature understanding of the scene • insightfully interprets the scene and applies the critical perspective • shows strong understanding of the historical context of the play and the critical lens of the interpretation • clearly communicates the intended effect through dramatic elements • (the letter) effectively explains how a critical lens is reflected in the performance.	The interpretation • demonstrates clear analysis and understanding of the scene • plausibly interprets the scene and applies the critical perspective • shows understanding of the historical context of the play and the critical lens of the interpretation • communicates the intended effect through dramatic elements • (the letter) adequately explains how a critical lens is reflected in the performance.	The interpretation • reveals a limited analysis and understanding of the scene • interprets the scene and applies the critical perspective with limited success • shows limited understanding of the historical context of the play and the critical lens of the interpretation • inadequately communicates the intended effect; dramatic elements are ineffective • (the letter) inadequately explains how a critical lens is reflected in the performance.	The interpretation • reveals little analysis or understanding of the scene • attempts to interpret the scene but does not successfully apply a critical perspective • does not show understanding of the historical context of the play and the critical lens of the interpretation • does not communicate the intended effect; dramatic elements are absent or ineffective • does not explain how a critical lens is reflected in the performance.
Structure	The interpretation • skillfully uses dramatic elements and effective vocal delivery • demonstrates equal and appropriate sharing of responsibility.	The interpretation • uses adequate dramatic elements and vocal delivery • demonstrates mostly balanced sharing of responsibility.	The interpretation • offers few dramatic elements and vocal delivery that detract from the quality of the scene • demonstrates an unequal division of responsibilities.	The interpretation • offers a disorganized scene with few to no dramatic elements and vocal delivery that detracts from the performance • demonstrates an unequal division of responsibilities that affects the performance.
Use of Language	The interpretation • includes written materials that advance the group's ideas • demonstrates command of oral and written English with few or no errors.	The interpretation • includes written materials that adequately support the group's ideas • demonstrates good usage of oral and written English with few errors.	The interpretation • ineffectively supports the group's ideas in written material • attempts to use appropriate oral and written language but contains errors that interfere with meaning.	The interpretation • contains inadequate support in written materials • contains serious errors in language use or inappropriate language.

VISUAL PROMPT
Think about the individuals who lived in the homes flooded during a hurricane. What different experiences, stories, and perspectives might they have? How does the media distill a multitude of stories into a single narrative?

CREATING PERSPECTIVES

In the online environment where information comes as a steady linear stream, where it's not divided up with a front page, an opinion page, and different specialized news sections (that prioritize news information according to prominence, urgency, civic importance, or local, national, and international orientation), it's all just mixed together.

—from "How News Has Changed," by Michael Griffin

GOALS

- To develop and support inferences and analyses by synthesizing information from a variety of informational texts
- To work collaboratively with a team, offering ideas, judgments and insightful questions, while working toward common research goals
- To critique and evaluate how authors present information and organize ideas based on purpose
- To write an argumentative text that cites credible academic sources to support claims
- To formulate and present a persuasive argument using elements of classical speeches
- To analyze how different critical perspectives shape the reporting and interpreting of events

VOCABULARY

ACADEMIC
agenda
archival footage
annotated bibliography
conventions
documentary
media
media channel
primary footage
rhetorical context

LITERARY
logical fallacy
rhetorical slanters

CONTENTS

CONTENTS

Texts not included in these materials.

My Independent Reading List

Learning Strategies

Close Reading
Graphic Organizer
Marking the Text
Summarizing

VOCABULARY

ACADEMIC

The word **agenda** may refer to a list of items to be discussed during a meeting. As used here, however, it refers to an underlying, often ideological, plan or program that guides behavior and opinion.

My Notes

Learning Targets

- Preview the big ideas for the unit.
- Identify and analyze the skills and knowledge needed to complete Embedded Assessment 1 successfully.
- Create a plan for reading independently.

Preview

In this activity, you will explore the big ideas and tasks of the unit, identify the skills and knowledge you will need to be successful on the first Embedded Assessment, and make plans for your independent reading.

About the Unit

We are not passive consumers of media; rather, as active participants we bring our own sets of interests, experiences, assumptions, and biases to what we read, see, and hear, as do those who produce what we read, see, and hear. When we care about an event, we want to know how to determine what is true about the event and how to get close to that truth. However, it is important to recognize our own filters—those personal interests, experiences, assumptions, and biases—and how they influence our ability to discern the truth. Media and government reports, like literary texts, need to be read or "decoded" carefully. In this unit, you will use critical perspectives to analyze informational texts.

Essential Questions

Based on your current knowledge, write answers to these questions in the My Notes space.

1. How do media sources influence our understanding of the truth and significance of an issue?

2. How are media texts constructed to cater to media consumers' interests, experiences, assumptions, and biases or to promote a particular **agenda**?

Unpacking Embedded Assessment 1

Read the following assignment for Embedded Assessment 1 and summarize the major elements in your Reader/Writer Notebook.

 Your assignment is to write an argumentative essay that argues for the use of a particular critical lens to interpret an event. Your essay must include an annotated bibliography and evidence from at least five texts gathered alone or with your group members.

Summarize in your own words what you will need to know for this assessment. With your class, create a graphic organizer that represents the skills and knowledge you will need to accomplish this task, and strategize how you will complete the assignment. As you complete your graphic organizer, be sure to review the criteria in the Scoring Guide.

⊕ Planning Independent Reading

During this unit, you will read a variety of information texts, including a series of texts on the topic of Hurricane Katrina. For your independent reading during the first part of this unit, consider choosing nonfiction relating to the media, such as a biography about a prominent journalist or books about the experiences of journalists reporting from the front lines. Later in the unit, find independent reading texts that will deepen your understanding about Hurricane Katrina and its long-term effects. Discuss your selections with a small group. Explain why you would or would not recommend your choices to your classmates.

My Notes

The Evolution of Media

Learning Strategies

Discussion Groups
Graphic Organizer
Note-taking

ACADEMIC

Media, collectively, refers to the organizations that communicate information to the public. A **media channel** is one method an organization uses to communicate, such as radio, television, website, newspaper, or magazine.

Learning Targets

- Explain how informational texts reflect or reveal critical perspectives.
- In collaborative groups, develop criteria and strategies for selecting supporting evidence from texts.
- Write an argument citing evidence from an informational text.

Preview

In this activity, you will read an article that traces the history of the media industry since the advent of television news. Through discussion and writing, you will analyze some of the article's key ideas through various critical perspectives.

What Is the Media?

1. Take a minute to consider how you gather information about events that take place in the world around you, using **media**. Complete the following graphic organizer with information about current events and the **media channels** that you use.

School/Local Event	Details/Facts I Know About Event	Media Channel
State/National Event	**Details/Facts I Know About Event**	**Media Channel**
International Event	**Details/Facts I Know About Event**	**Media Channel**

Returning to the Text

- Return to the article as you respond to the following questions. Use textual evidence to support your responses.
- Write any additional questions you have about the article in your Reader/Writer Notebook.

2. According to the article, what were some of the factors that contributed to the quality of network news in the middle of the 20th century?

_____

_____

_____

_____

3. How does the author characterize the quality of television news in the 1980s and 1990s? Use details from the text to paraphrase the description of news media during this period.

_____

_____

_____

_____

4. What effects did the changes to television news and the move toward online news in the middle of the 20th century have on newspapers?

_____

_____

_____

_____

5. What is the effect of the organizational structure used in Griffin's article?

_____

_____

_____

6. What is the effect of the author's use of rhetorical questions in his article?

_____

_____

_____

_____

7. What is the author's purpose? What is he trying to achieve by writing this article?

_____

_____

_____

_____

Working from the Text

8. Consider this sentence from the last paragraph of the article:

> "As a result, more and more young people don't have a clear notion of the distinction between something that's a news article and something that's just an opinion piece."

Do you agree or disagree with the author's claim? With a partner, share your opinion, making sure to support it with examples from your personal experience that either refute or back up the ideas in the article.

9. Use the guiding questions to analyze Griffin's article through three different critical lenses (cultural, historical, and Marxist). Skim the article again and focus on gathering claims and evidence that fit each lens.

Guiding Question 1: What do changes in media coverage reveal about changing cultural perspectives of the news?

Guiding Question 2: How have historical developments influenced the role of news in America?

Guiding Question 3: How have economic or market factors affected news coverage in America?

10. In a group, share your observations based on one of the three lenses you used to analyze the text. Then write a concise thesis statement in your Reader/Writer Notebook that explains the change in how news is delivered and consumed, interpreted through one specific lens.

11. Read the following quotations. Use three colors to highlight the quotations by type: cultural, historical, Marxist. Then, in the second column on the left, rank the quotes within each color category based on their potential usefulness as evidence. Which would best serve as evidence to support your interpretive take on "How the Media Has Changed"? Why?

Quotes	Lens	Reasoning
In the middle of the 20th century, television network leadership believed that providing news was a public service. News wasn't expected to make money for national broadcasters.		
Whenever a big entertainment company or conglomerate came in, the news divisions had to answer to shareholders and improve the bottom line. For the first time, there was an expectation that the news divisions had to make money, just like the entertainment divisions.		
Right after that came cable television. Instead of three channels (ABC, CBS, and NBC) dividing up a big, diversified national audience, cable TV came along and targeted narrow niche audiences.		
If you believe the polls, there's now a real lack of trust in the media among the public. Some polls show that more than half of Americans don't trust the media to tell them the truth.		
Everything about the way the web works—and the algorithms that track the patterns of your internet activity—reinforces the idea that there's a feedback loop that constantly redirects us toward what we're already interested in.		
In the early 2000s, newspapers weren't experiencing a significant readership dropoff yet, but they were starting to lose advertising money.		
When their ad and classified revenues dropped, the only recourse in their view at the time was to cut costs. By 2005–06, this was leading to massive layoffs in the newsroom.		
... there's no longer a model that most citizens in our country share for standards that news should meet.		
As a result, more and more young people don't have a clear notion of the distinction between something that's a news article and something that's just an opinion piece.		

My Notes

LANGUAGE & WRITER'S CRAFT: Citing Quotations

Documentaries, research papers, and other kinds of nonfiction often incorporate direct quotations to provide specifics about the topic. Direct quotations use a speaker's or writer's exact words, enclosed in quotation marks:

> **Example:** The author explains, "[The 24-hour news cycle] meant newsrooms didn't have longer periods of time to prepare content, check it, edit it, vet it, and then present it to audiences."

Notice the term in brackets. When quoting a sentence with a pronoun that would be unclear to readers without context, you may replace the pronoun with its antecedent, and use brackets to indicate this small change to the original text. While this approach is acceptable, it should not be used very often.

Writers can also paraphrase speakers, citing sources while making the words their own:

> **Example:** The author explains that newsrooms needed to produce content much more quickly, and with looser editorial standards, to keep up with the pace of the 24-hour news cycle.

Adding quotations to your writing is a great way to add color and alternate voices to make your writing more compelling and persuasive. They also help make nonfiction writing seem more authentic and less filtered through an author's voice.

PRACTICE Add support to your thesis statement from the previous page by citing one quotation and one paraphrase from the article.

☑ Check Your Understanding

What are some criteria for selecting quotations to support an interpretive claim?

✍ Writing Prompt: Argumentative

Use one of the critical perspectives to argue which of the following developments was most instrumental in catalyzing the changes in the news industry since the middle of the 20th century: conglomerates buying out media companies, the rise of cable news, the increase of target marketing, the decline of newspapers, or the rise of the internet as a news source. Develop the topic thoroughly by selecting the most significant and relevant examples from the text and citing them properly. Be sure to:

- Include a clear arguable thesis statement.
- Smoothly incorporate quotations and paraphrased details from the article to support your ideas.
- Create cohesion by using an appropriate organizational structure and transitions.
- Write a conclusion that follows from your arguments and evidence.

Constructing Public Opinion

Learning Targets

- Evaluate and critique two texts that present competing arguments.
- Form an argument and communicate your claim and supporting evidence effectively in a debate.
- Address a counterclaim in your argumentative writing.
- Integrate ideas from multiple texts to build knowledge and vocabulary about perspective and media.

Preview

In this activity, you will read and analyze two texts that present different perspectives on the root cause of media bias. Then you will present your own perspective in classroom debate and complete a written response.

Media Study

1. Working with a partner, write definitions for the following terms in relation to media study in your Reader/Writer Notebook. Leave space to add to or revise your definitions later. Consult references—either print or online—to clarify and validate your understanding, and then find or write a sentence that uses the term in what you believe to be the proper context.

Term	Definition
Target Audience	
Objectivity	
Perspective	
Agenda	
Bias	

Quickwrite: Keeping your definitions in mind, to what extent do you think media coverage shapes and influences our perception of issues and events?

Learning Strategies

Debate
Graphic Organizer
Marking the Text
Quickwrite
Think-Pair-Share

My Notes

My Notes

Opening Writing Prompt

Read the first few sentences of the article "How Headlines Change the Way We Think," and answer the following question in a quickwrite.

How Headlines Change the Way We Think

"Why Headlines Matter." "Misleading Headlines Can Lead You Astray." "How What You Read Affects What You See." "How Bad Headlines Make Bad Memories." "Eleven Reasons Headlines Are Important." "You'll Never Believe How Important an Accurate Headline Is."

Those are all possible titles for this piece that I discussed with my editor. And, actually, the one that we picked may be the most important part of this article.

Why do you think the Konnikova suggests that the headline might be the most important part of her article? What purpose do headlines serve in an informational text?

As You Read

- Put a star next to each specific example of a headline used to support the author's thesis.
- Circle unknown words and phrases. Try to determine the meaning of the words by using context clues, word parts, or a dictionary.

About the Author

Maria Konnikova (b. 1984) is an author and journalist whose work has appeared in publications including *The Smithsonian*, *The Atlantic*, and *The New Yorker*, where she is a contributing writer. Following graduation from Harvard University, she went on to Columbia University to earn her Ph.D. in psychology in 2013. Konnikova's first book, *Mastermind: How to Think Like Sherlock Holmes*, is a New York Times bestseller and has been translated into 17 languages.

Article

How Headlines Change the Way We Think

by **Maria Konnikova**

December 17, 2014

1   "Why Headlines Matter." "Misleading Headlines Can Lead You Astray." "How What You Read Affects What You See." "How Bad Headlines Make Bad Memories." "Eleven Reasons Headlines Are Important." "You'll Never Believe How Important an Accurate Headline Is."

2   Those are all possible titles for this piece that I discussed with my editor. And, actually, the one that we picked may be the most important part of this article. By now, everyone knows that a headline determines how many people will read a piece, particularly in this era of social media. But, more interesting, a headline changes the way people read an article and the way they remember it. The headline frames the rest of the experience. A headline can tell you what kind of article you're about to read—news, opinion, research, LOLcats—and it sets the tone for what follows.

3   Psychologists have long known that first impressions really do matter—what we see, hear, feel, or experience in our first encounter with something colors how we process the rest of it. Articles are no exception. And just as people can manage the impression that they make through their choice of attire, so, too, can the crafting of the headline subtly shift the perception of the text that follows. By drawing attention to certain details or facts, a headline can affect what existing knowledge is activated in your head. By its choice of phrasing, a headline can influence your mindset as you read so that you later recall details that coincide with what you were expecting. For instance, the headline of this article I wrote—"A Gene That Makes You Need Less Sleep?"—is not inaccurate in any way. But it does likely prompt a focus on one specific part of the piece. If I had instead called it "Why We Need Eight Hours of Sleep," people would remember it differently.

4   As a result of these shifts in perception, problems arise when a headline is ever so slightly misleading. "Air pollution now leading cause of lung cancer," ran a headline last year in the U.K. paper Daily Express. The article, however, said no such thing, or, rather, not exactly. Instead, it reported that pollution was a leading "environmental" cause; other causes, like smoking, are still the main culprits. It is easy to understand a decision to run that sort of opening. Caveats don't fit in single columns, and, once people are intrigued enough to read the story, they'll get to the nuances just the same. But, as it turns out, reading the piece may not be enough to correct the headline's misdirection.

KNOWLEDGE QUEST

Knowledge Question:

How does the media shape our view of the world, or how does our view shape our perception of the media?

In Activity 4.3 you will read two articles about how we frame the media and how the media frames us. As you read and build knowledge about the topic, think about your answer to the Knowledge Question.

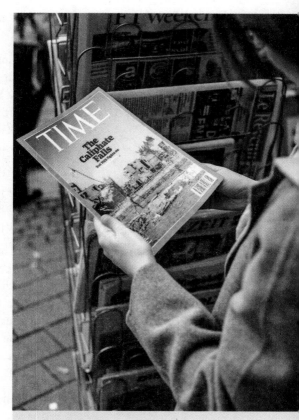

Headlines quickly grab readers' attention and help steer them from story to story.

GRAMMAR & USAGE

Sentence Variety

Varying the length and syntax of your sentences helps maintain the interest of your readers. Too many long sentences can wear your reader out, and too many short sentences can feel dull.

However, you can use a series of short sentences to grab the readers' attention. Notice how short the eighth paragraph of this article is compared to all the other paragraphs. It contains only two sentences that slow the reader down and help focus attention on the information that the writer is presenting.

As you write, think about how you can vary the length of your sentences to create variety, power, and emphasis.

My Notes

anomalous: unusual

5 It's these sorts of misleading maneuvers that Ullrich Ecker, a psychologist and cognitive neuroscientist at the University of Western Australia, was pondering when he decided to test how slight—and slightly misleading—shifts in headlines can affect reading. In Ecker's prior work, he had looked at explicit misinformation: when information that's biased influences you, no matter what you're subsequently told. This time around, he wanted to see how nuance and slight misdirection would work.

6 In a series of studies, out this month in the Journal of Experimental Psychology: Applied, Ecker had people in Australia read either factual or opinion pieces, where the only shifting variable was the headline. (He had his subjects read a total of four articles—two factual, two opinion.) One factual article, for instance, talked about a change in burglary rates over the last year—a rise of 0.2 percent—that ran counter to a ten percent decline over the past decade. The slight rise, the article pointed out, was an anomalous side note; the longer trend was what was important. The accompanying headline highlighted either the smaller or the larger of the two trends: "Number of burglaries going up" and "Downward trend in burglary rate," respectively. The opinion pieces pitted the thoughts of an expert against those of a layperson—for instance, one piece contrasted a citizen's concerns about the safety of genetically modified food with the opinion of a scientist from the fictional company Organic Food Science Australia. The headline focused on one of the two sides. In this case, it read either "GM foods may pose long-term health risks" or "GM foods are safe." Each participant read all four articles.

7 Ecker's goal was to test whether the degree of the slant would matter. With the factual piece, the misdirection was obvious—the entire piece was about a broader trend, with one tiny deviation. In the opinion piece, it was much more subtle. The article was, first of all, opinion, and each voice was given its own space; it was up to the reader to judge how the opinions should be considered.

8 After reading each article, the University of Western Australia students rated it on five different scales, to gauge things like interest and ease of reading. Once a student had read the complete set of pieces, she was given a surprise six-question quiz, with questions concerning both recollection and inference.

9 The headline, it turns out, had done more than simply reframe the article. In the case of the factual articles, a misleading headline hurt a reader's ability to recall the article's details. That is, the parts that were in line with the headline, such as a declining burglary rate, were easier to remember than the opposing, non-headlined trend. Inferences, however, remained sound: the misdirection was blatant enough that readers were aware of it and proceeded to correct their impressions accordingly. According to the study, "No matter which headline they saw, they predicted that, next year, the crime rate would go down."

10 In the case of opinion articles, however, a misleading headline, like the one suggesting that genetically modified foods are dangerous, impaired a reader's ability to make accurate inferences. For instance, when asked to predict

the future public-health costs of genetically modified foods, people who had read the misleading headline predicted a far greater cost than the evidence had warranted.

11 Ecker and his colleagues then replicated the results in a second study—this time, the discrepancies were between the headline and the image, rather than between the headline and the text. ...

12 For conscientious readers and editors, Ecker's findings across the two studies give cause for concern. First, misinformation appears to cause more damage when it's subtle than when it's blatant. We see through the latter and correct for it as we go. The former is much more insidious and persistent. It is also, unfortunately, much more likely to be the result of sloppiness or inconsideration rather than a deliberate effort to lead readers astray. Take this article from the Times in May. "Selling a Fake Painting Takes More Than a Good Artist," reads the headline. Alongside it: a photograph of a gallery owner who is not actually one of the culprits. A criminal implication is paired with a photograph, and the photograph may **inadvertently** be tainted as well.

13 Here's the other thing: almost every journalist has experienced the aggravation of having readers give aggrieved, enraged, dismissive, or, really, any other type of negative reaction to an article based solely on a headline. "Read the article!" the writer often wants to scream...What Ecker's work shows, though, is that with the right—or, rather, wrong—headline, reading the article may not be enough. Even well-intentioned readers who do go on to read the entire piece may still be reacting in part to that initial formulation.

14 If I had titled this column "Why Headlines Matter," I would be picking the broadest possible option. Next week, you might be able to remember that headlines are important but not be able to tell your friend exactly why. If I had called it "Misleading Headlines Can Lead You Astray," you might have forgotten the details of the study showing that we can actually overcome factually misleading headlines. "Eleven Reasons Headlines Matter"? More people might have clicked, but they might not have retained the information. It's not always easy to be both interesting and accurate, but, as Ecker's study shows, it's better than being exciting and wrong.

GRAMMAR & USAGE

Integrating Quotations

Notice how Konnikova integrates quoted headlines and other quoted material in a variety of ways by varying the placement of the quoted portion in sentences:

For instance, the headline of this article I wrote—"A Gene That Makes You Need Less Sleep?"—is not inaccurate in any way. But it does likely prompt a focus on one specific part of the piece. If I had instead called it "Why We Need Eight Hours of Sleep," people would remember it differently.

"Read the article!" the writer often wants to scream...

According to the study, "No matter which headline they saw, they predicted that, next year, the crime rate would go down."

Varying the ways quotations are integrated keeps the writing from being dull or repetitive. Highlight each integrated quote on this page, and discuss how this variety in syntax affects the flow of the writing.

⊘ Knowledge Quest

• What is the author's main idea in this article?
• Which details from Ullrich Ecker's study capture your interest?
• What is your immediate impression about whether or not headlines can affect how you think?

inadvertently: accidentally

My Notes

As You Read

- Underline the claim and star examples that the writer uses throughout the article.
- Circle unknown words and phrases. Try to determine the meaning of the words by using context clues, word parts, or a dictionary.

About the Author

Matthew C. Nisbet is a professor of communication studies at Northeastern University and serves as editor-in-chief of the journal *Environmental Communication* and senior editor of *ORE Climate Science*. Nisbet studies and writes about the role of communication, journalism, and advocacy in shaping discourse and debates over meaningful policy issues including climate change and income inequity.

KNOWLEDGE QUEST

Knowledge Question:

How does the media shape our view of the world, or how does our view shape our perception of the media?

Article

Why Partisans View Mainstream Media as Biased and Ideological Media as Objective

by **Matthew C. Nisbet**

July 21, 2011

1   We've reached a unique paradox in American political culture today: Both liberals and conservatives view the mainstream media as biased, yet tend to believe that their own ideologically-like minded outlets and commentators provide objective coverage. Claims of media bias have long been the lingua franca[1] of the conservative movement with the creation of rival outlets first in the form of magazines such as the *National Review*, then political talk radio, and culminating with Fox News and right-wing blogs.

2   Yet over the past decade, harsh criticism of the mainstream media has also increasingly **emanated** from the left with claims of biased coverage a fundamental core belief of progressive advocates working on issues ranging from climate change to social policy. In turn these same progressives tend to prefer the "objective" coverage at magazines like the *Nation*, blogging platforms

---

[1] A *lingua franca* is a common language used between people who speak different native languages.

emanated: originated

like the *Huffington Post*, and most prominently MSNBC which has positioned itself as the liberal counter-weight to Fox News.

3 Research in the field of communication has tracked the psychological under-pinning of this societal trend, explaining why partisans view mainstream coverage as biased but perceive their preferred ideological outlets as fair and balanced. In a recently published book chapter on the social psychology of political communication, my colleague Lauren Feldman and I review and explain this research, drawing in part on Feldman's own work in the area.

4 Here is an excerpt on media bias, from that chapter.

5 Across national settings, there is an ever **pervasive** belief in various forms of media bias. In the U.S., over the past two decades, the dominant belief regarding media bias is that the mainstream news media favor liberal causes and political candidates. Yet, when researchers conduct content analyses to search for systematic patterns of partisan bias in coverage of elections, across studies they are unable to find definitive evidence (D'Alessio D. & Allen, 2000). If social scientists using the best tools available to them find it difficult to observe hard evidence of liberal bias, why are beliefs among the public so widespread? Moreover, across country settings and issues, what explains the difference between subjective perceptions of media bias and objective indicators relative to coverage?

6 In research on perceptions of the news media, credibility is understood as a subjective assessment, influenced by the partisan or ideological background of the audience and the claims about bias that might emanate from trusted sources such as political commentators or like-minded friends. In the U.S. context, these claims are typically focused on a liberal bias charged by conservative elites and reinforce a widespread belief among conservative-leaning audiences (Watts, Domke, Shah, & Fan, 1999). Audiences, then, do not typically assess story content on its own merits but rather on the basis of preconceived notions about the news media—often stemming from journalists' tendency in many stories to cover and reflect on their own potential liberal bias. A number of other studies have also suggested that individuals' expectations for bias in a news source or in the media, more generally, are likely to influence their perceptions of bias in news coverage (Arpan & Raney, 2003; Baum & Gussin, 2007).

7 Perhaps the most crucial determinant of perceptions of bias in the news, however, is the extent to which news coverage is seen as disagreeing with one's own views. Individuals who feel most strongly about an issue tend to see their own side's views as being more a product of objective analysis and **normative** concerns, and less influenced by ideology, than the other side's views (Robinson, Keltner, Ward, & Ross, 1995). This human tendency translates directly to judgments about the media. In a range of studies, when news

pervasive: widespread
normative: standard-setting

My Notes

audiences who **hew** to opposing sides on an issue are given the same news coverage of the topic to evaluate, both view this identical coverage as biased in favor of the other side (Gunther & Schmitt, 2004; Vallone et al., 1985). The phenomenon is commonly referred to as the "hostile media effect." Researchers believe that the explanation for this hostile media effect is selective categorization: opposing partisans attend to, process, and recall identical content from a news presentation but mentally categorize and label the same aspects of a story differently—as hostile to their own position (Schmitt, Gunther, & Liebhart, 2004).

8   The original hostile media effect assumes that news coverage is inherently balanced. The relative hostile media perception (Gunther, Christen, Liebhart, & Chia, 2001) relaxes this assumption, making it applicable to news that is slanted in favor of or against a particular issue. In the presence of the relative hostile media effect, supporters and opponents of a given issue perceive bias in a consistent direction (i.e., leaning toward one side), but each group perceives coverage as significantly more unfavorable to their own position relative to those in the other group. In other words, partisans perceive less bias in news coverage slanted to support their view than their opponents on the other side of the issue.

9   Interestingly, then, whereas the implication of the original hostile media effect is a partisan public perceiving media bias where none was present and thus potentially rejecting useful information, the implications of the relative hostile media effect are somewhat different. Of consequence here is that partisans will fail to recognize bias in news that is in fact biased, in instances when that bias is **congruent** with their pre-existing views. This bias against news bias is troubling. Americans' trust in news sources has become deeply **polarized** in recent years—with Republicans, for example, attributing more credibility to the conservative Fox News and less to most other news organizations than Democrats (Pew Research Center, 2008). In other countries, similar perceptions of a left or right bias to news or alternatively a bias relative to national or ethnic identity exist.

10 In each context, as news—particularly on cable TV and online—is infused with increasing amounts of opinion and ideology, this may make it even easier for partisans to validate their personal political beliefs—by accepting at face value information that comports with their views while rejecting information that advocates for the other side. Thus, the relative hostile media effect may not only reflect partisan divides in news perceptions but may also contribute to the further polarization of political attitudes and knowledge across political systems.

hew: adhere
congruent: in agreement
polarized: divided into sharply opposing sides

After reading the articles in this activity, respond to the Essential Question: How are media texts constructed to cater to an audience or to promote a particular agenda?

Knowledge Quest
- What are your first thoughts about partisan bias versus media bias?
- What questions do you have after reading the excerpt the first time?

Returning to the Text

- Reread the articles to answer these text-dependent questions.
- Write any additional questions you have about the texts in your Reader/Writer Notebook.

"How Headlines Change the Way We Think"

2. Is the use of short sentences, in the form of a list of rejected titles for the article, effective in the opening paragraph? Why might the author have opened her article this way?

_____

_____

_____

_____

3. **KQ** According to Konnikova's arguments, how does the headline frame the rest of the reader's experience? Cite details from the text to support your answer.

_____

_____

_____

_____

4. What does Konnikova mean by the phrase "Caveats don't fit in single columns"?

_____

_____

_____

_____

5. According to the article, why was the misdirection in the headline easier to detect for the factual pieces used in the Ullrich Ecker study than in the opinion pieces?

_____

_____

_____

_____

6. **KQ** What is the author's purpose for including the Ecker study in this article?

_____

_____

_____

_____

7. What is Konnikova's purpose for repeating the rejected titles for her article that she used at the beginning of the article in her conclusion?

_____

_____

_____

_____

8. Konnikova writes, "It's not always easy to be both interesting and accurate, but, as Ecker's study shows, it's better than being exciting and wrong." Apply this to what the article is trying to say about headlines.

_____

_____

_____

_____

"Why Partisans View Mainstream Media as Biased and Ideological Media as Objective"

9. KQ What is the difference between "mainstream" and "ideological" media? Why is their difference a paradox?

_____

_____

_____

_____

10. What is the meaning of *progressive* as it is used in paragraph 2? Use an online or print dictionary and thesaurus to confirm your understanding.

_____

_____

_____

_____

11. KQ According to the text, what is the "hostile media effect"?

_____

_____

_____

_____

12. **KQ** Compare the opinions of Konnikova and Nisbet toward the news media. Do they view journalists as generally responsible?

_____

_____

_____

_____

 INDEPENDENT READING LINK

You can continue to build your knowledge about the media by reading other articles at ZINC Reading Labs. Search for keywords such as *media bias*, *confirmation bias*, and *hostile media effect*.

 ZINC

 Knowledge Quest

Think about how both authors explore media bias: the way media can shape a reader's perception and the way the reader's perception can shape how media is interpreted. Which do you think is more influential? Write an argumentative paragraph about whether the media or the reader's interpretation is more powerful. Be sure to:

- Provide a well-reasoned claim that is clearly stated.
- Use significant and relevant examples, details, or quotations from one or both articles that thoroughly develop and support your claim.
- Provide an engaging conclusion that supports the claim and examines its implications.

Working from the Text

13. Use a two-column graphic organizer to evaluate and critique the arguments made in each article. For the purposes of framing your thinking, it is worth noting that Konnikova's article focuses more on journalists' role in the news process while Nisbet focuses more on the readers' role.

"How Headlines Change the Way We Think"	"Why Partisans View Mainstream Media as Biased and Ideological Media as Objective"
Claim:	Claim:
Reasons/Evidence:	Reasons/Evidence:
Structure:	Structure:
Evaluation and Critique:	Evaluation and Critique:

14. Review your response to the Opening Writing Prompt about the importance of headlines as well as your answer to the final "Returning to the Text" question about Nisbet's article. Based on those responses and the information from your graphic organizer, respond to the following questions: Who holds responsibility for avoiding media bias in the news: the creators of the news or the consumers of the news?

15. Outline your position to prepare for a classroom debate on the question. Your outline should include:

    • A concise statement of your claim

    • Three points of evidence, taken from the text, to support your claim

    • A concluding statement that includes a call to action

16. Share your opinion in a class debate. Be sure to:

    • Listen and respond to your classmates' points before adding a new point to the discussion.

    • Cite textual evidence to support your claim. (Refer to your graphic organizer when responding to other students' points.)

17. After discussing the two articles, reflect on the following questions.

    • How much did your existing personal opinions influence your perspective on which author was more persuasive regarding media bias?

    • How much did your existing personal opinions influence your perspective on which author was more correct regarding media bias?

    • What's the difference between being persuasive and being correct?

    • In general, to what extent does our perspective on what is correct influence our perspective on what is persuasive and vice versa?

☑ Check Your Understanding

Write one sentence in which you agree with another student's argument or present a counterargument in response to another student's claim.

✍ Writing Prompt: Argumentative

Who holds more responsibility for media bias, the journalist or the reader? Write a brief argument defending your position. Weave in at least one counterargument made by your peers in the class debate. Be sure to:

• Include a clear claim, supporting evidence from the text, and a conclusion.

• Address counterarguments and use evidence from the texts to support your point of view.

• Include a conclusion with a call to action.

Bias in News Reports

Learning Targets

- Evaluate media texts for credibility, bias, accuracy, and faulty reasoning.
- Craft a written argument that fairly and accurately identifies an example of biased reporting.

Preview

In this activity, you will watch two reports of a news event, noting any reporting and filming techniques that indicate bias. Then you will write an argument exposing the bias and logical fallacies evident in one of the news reports.

Learning Strategies

Discussion Groups
Graphic Organizer
Visual Prompt

LITERARY

A logical fallacy is an error in reasoning that weakens an argument.

Rhetorical slanters are words that put a negative or positive spin on what the speaker or writer is saying.

VOCABULARY

Slanting the News

Writers and directors can influence our perspective on a subject through the use of selection and omission, source control, and other manipulations of content, but rhetoric itself may be the most powerful tool through which our perceptions can be influenced. The following rhetorical slanters (adapted from Brooke Noel Moore and Richard Parker's *Critical Thinking*, 8th ed., 2007) identify key techniques often used to influence readers and viewers:

Rhetorical Slanter	Example
Rhetorical Analogy: the use of a figurative comparison (sometimes a simile or a metaphor) to convey a positive or negative feeling toward the subject	"The environment needs this candidate like farmers need a drought."
Rhetorical Definition: the use of emotionally charged language to express or elicit an attitude about something	"Capital punishment is government-sanctioned murder."
Rhetorical Explanation: expressing an opinion as if it were fact, and doing so in biased language	"Joe didn't have the guts to fight back," as compared to "Joe did not take a swing."
Innuendo: the use of language to imply that a particular inference is justified, as if saying "go ahead and read between the lines"	"Think carefully about whom you choose; you want a mayor who will be ready to do the job on day one."
Downplayers: the use of qualifier words, phrases, or punctuation to make someone or something look less important or significant	"She's a 'reporter' for a blog that hardly anyone reads."
Hyperbole: the use of extravagant overstatement	"The building quivered from the audience's momentous applause."
Truth Surrogates: hinting that proof exists to support a claim without actually citing that proof	"There's every reason to believe that …"
Ridicule/Sarcasm: the use of language that suggests the subject is worthy of scorn	"The news media themselves are oh-so-clearly impervious to the predispositions and prejudice that afflict their audience."

News anchors earn credibility by having a record of presenting factual and objective information.

My Notes

1. As you watch the two video clips, complete the graphic organizers. Closely evaluate the information presented for bias and credibility.

News Source 1

Facts	Example of Bias
Bias by headline?	
Bias by photos, captions, camera angles?	
Bias through omission?	
Bias by source selection? Who is the information supplied by?	
Bias through statistics/ number inflation?	
Bias through labels/titles/ word choice?	

News Source 2

Facts	Example of Bias
Bias by headline?	
Bias by photos, captions, camera angles?	
Bias through omission?	
Bias by source selection? Who is the information supplied by?	
Bias through statistics/ number inflation?	
Bias through labels/titles/ word choice?	

☑ Check Your Understanding

How does bias affect the credibility of a source?

Finding the Logical Fallacy

2. A logical fallacy is an error in reasoning. Some authors use such faulty reasoning intentionally in an effort to convince readers without adequate evidence. Other writers might use it unintentionally. Whether used purposefully or accidentally, logical fallacies negatively impact the accuracy and credibility of the information or ideas being presented. Here are three common types of flawed reasoning and an example of each:

Faulty Analogy

Assuming that if two things are alike in one or more ways, they are automatically alike in other respects.

Example: Buying a stock is just like betting on a horse race. You can never be sure of picking a winner.

Slippery Slope

Assuming that one event will lead to another or to a chain of events that lead to an undesirable result.

Example: If a high school student doesn't study for one test, they are sure to fail it and eventually drop out of school.

Straw Man

Distorting or oversimplifying your opponent's argument, and then building your counterargument against the distorted argument.

Example: Opponents of capital punishment think the lives of victims are less valuable than the lives of criminals.

☑ Focus on the Sentence

Write two sentences about logical fallacies, one in the form of a statement and one in the form a question. Be sure to use correct capitalization and punctuation.

Statement (.) _____

_____

Question (?) _____

_____

✍ **Writing Prompt: Argumentative**

Write an argument exposing the bias evident in the way one of the news stories reports the event. In addition to using the information from your graphic organizer, identify any use of logical fallacies in the story. Be sure to:

- Develop a precise and arguable claim.
- Cite details and quotes from the news story to support your claim.
- Acknowledge and refute counterclaims fairly and thoroughly.
- Conclude by evaluating how the bias affects the credibility and accuracy of the text.
- Check for correct spelling, punctuation, grammar, and usage.

Framing the Investigation

Learning Targets

- Investigate how critical lenses can both shape and reveal perspectives about real-world events and issues.
- Use different critical lenses to frame research questions.
- Ask questions to evaluate the effectiveness of structural characteristics in nonfiction texts related to the same topic.

Preview

In this activity, you will begin exploring the ways the media, public figures, and government organizations shape or construct the meaning of a historical event: Hurricane Katrina. You will start by reading several texts that help frame and contextualize the event.

As You Read

- Put a star next to actions Congress will take and put a dash next to actions Congress expects individuals, state governments, and local governments to take.
- Circle unknown words and phrases, including legal language used in the document. Try to determine the meaning of the words by using context clues, word parts, or a dictionary.

Law

The Robert T. Stafford Disaster Relief and Emergency Assistance Act, Section 101

Sec. 101. Congressional Findings and Declarations (42 U.S.C. 5121)

a. The Congress hereby finds and declares that

1. because disasters often cause loss of life, human suffering, loss of income, and property loss and damage; and

2. because disasters often disrupt the normal functioning of governments and communities, and adversely affect individuals and families with great severity; special measures, designed to assist the efforts of the affected States in expediting the rendering of aid, assistance, and emergency services, and the reconstruction and rehabilitation of devastated areas, are necessary.

Learning Strategies

Discussion Groups
Marking the Text
Note-taking
Quickwrite
Think-Pair-Share

My Notes

⬡ **INDEPENDENT READING LINK**

Read and Connect

Much has been written about Hurricane Katrina and its massive effects on the people, environment, government, and history of the Gulf Region. Find and read an informational or fiction text about Hurricane Katrina that interests you. Take notes as you read it to help you develop contextual understandings about the event. Record your notes in your Reader/Writer Notebook.

My Notes

b. It is the intent of the Congress, by this Act, to provide an orderly and continuing means of assistance by the Federal Government to State and local governments in carrying out their responsibilities to **alleviate** the suffering and damage which result from such disasters by

3. revising and broadening the scope of existing disaster relief programs;

4. encouraging the development of comprehensive disaster preparedness and assistance plans, programs, capabilities, and organizations by the States and by local governments;

5. achieving greater coordination and responsiveness of disaster preparedness and relief programs;

6. encouraging individuals, States, and local governments to protect themselves by obtaining insurance coverage to supplement or replace governmental assistance;

7. encouraging hazard **mitigation** measures to reduce losses from disasters, including development of land use and construction regulations; and (6) providing Federal assistance programs for both public and private losses sustained in disasters.

Making Observations

- What stands out about the document's structure?
- What are your initial thoughts on Congress's plan?

alleviate: relieve
mitigation: lessening

Returning to the Text

- Reread the legal document to answer these text-dependent questions.
- Write any additional questions you have about the text in your Reader/Writer Notebook.

1. According to this document, why and how does the federal government step in to assist state and local governments in the event of a disaster?

_____

_____

_____

_____

2. What is the primary purpose of this document? Who is the intended audience?

_____

_____

_____

_____

3. According to subsection (b), what is the government's responsibility in times of disaster?

_____

_____

_____

_____

4. How do subsections (a) and (b) differ in purpose? What is the overall effect of using these text features?

_____

_____

_____

_____

As You Read

- As you read "Day Long Efforts to Repair Levee Fail," underline words and phrases that help you visualize the scene.
- Circle unknown words and phrases. Try to determine the meaning of the words by using context clues, word parts, or a dictionary.

WORD CONNECTIONS

Etymology

Levee is a noun derived from the French word *lever*, "to raise." A levee is a wall or raised ridge of soil alongside a river, built to prevent flooding. Other words derived from the word *lever* include alleviate, elevate, elevator, leverage, levity, and relieve.

About the Author

Dan Shea (b. 1963) is the publisher of *The Advocate*. Prior to this role, Shea served as the managing editor of *The Times-Picayune* for 19-years. At *The Times-Picayune*, Shea supervised newsroom operations, presentations, photography, and copyediting. He also played a pivotal role in the continued print and online coverage of the harrowing days after Hurricane Katrina. The reporting under Shea's leadership led *The Times-Picayune* to win the Breaking News Pulitzer Prize in 2006.

My Notes

Article

Daylong Efforts to Repair Levee Fail

by **Dan Shea**

The Times-Picayune, **August 31, 2005**

1   New Orleans became an unimaginable scene of water, fear and suffering Tuesday after a levee breach in the 17th Street Canal sent billions of gallons of Lake Pontchartrain coursing through the city.

2   As the day wore on, the only dry land was a narrow band from the French Quarter[1] and parts of Uptown, the same small strip that was settled by Bienville[2] amid the swamps.

3   On Tuesday night, it appeared the city was returning to swamp when a daylong effort to shore the levee near the Hammond Highway failed. Mayor Ray Nagin said pumps were being overwhelmed and warned that a new deluge would bury the city in up to 15 feet of water.

4   With solid water from the lake to the French Quarter, the inundation and depopulation of an entire American city was at hand.

5   "Truth to tell, we're not too far from filling in the bowl," said Terry Ebbert, the city's director of homeland security. The waters were still rising at 3 inches per hour, and eventually could move close to the French Quarter levee.

6   Although the breach occurred on the Orleans side of the canal, it did not spare the Jefferson side. Water found its way into much of the east bank, meeting the flow that came in from the west from Hurricane Katrina's storm surge Monday.

---

[1] The French Quarter is New Orleans's oldest neighborhood.
[2] Jean-Baptiste Le Moyne de Bienville was governor of Louisiana and founder of New Orleans.

7 An accurate tally of death was hard to determine. Five deaths related to Katrina have been confirmed in Jefferson Parish[3], officials said. There also are seven people missing who decided to ride out Katrina on Grand Isle.

…

8 As to the living, with the absence of cars and electric motors in the powerless city, a sad tableau played itself out in an eerie quiet.

9 All day, a weary army of storm victims trudged through waist-deep muddy water toward the Superdome, where more than 20,000 people took refuge. The next problem is what to do with them. Late Tuesday Gov. Blanco ordered them out, saying the facility was too damaged to house people and the atmosphere too dangerous. Officials said the National Guard soon would begin driving them out to dry ground, then airlift them out of southeast Louisiana.

10 In other areas, lawlessness took hold.

11 The giant new Wal-Mart in the Lower Garden District was looted, after a limited distribution of supplies broke down in chaos. The entire gun collection was taken.

12 "There are gangs of armed men in the city moving around the city," Ebbert said.

13 One looter shot a New Orleans police officer, who was in critical condition with a head wound.

14 Although local police focused solely on rescue, a call for help was answered by swarms of deputies from western Louisiana parishes.

15 But cops on the street, cut off from their superiors by a failure of the communications system, complained of chaos.

16 "Put this in your paper," one officer on Canal Street said. "They told us nothing. We were unprepared. We are completely on our own."

17 If it wasn't coordinated, the rescue was heroic.

18 Firefighters, police and Coast Guardsmen waded through water and climbed to roofs.

19 "We've got boats everywhere," said Capt. Tim Bayard of the New Orleans Police Department. "We're going to try and get who we can get and take them to higher ground. We may have to come back for some."

20 They were joined by an armada of Louisiana sportsmen in flat-bottomed boats, who responded to an appeal for help.

21 Ferdinand Emory rescued about 100 people, ten at a time in his boat.

22 Ebbert estimated 1,500 to 2,000 people were saved in Lakeview and Mid-City.

My Notes

A woman is carried out of floodwaters after being trapped in her home after Hurricane Katrina.

---

[3] Jefferson Parish is one of 64 parishes (rather than counties) into which Louisiana is divided.

23 But rescue from the water didn't mean an end to misery. They were simply dropped off at the few stretches of dry ground, overpasses and parking lots along Metairie Ridge.

24 Aleck Scallan, 63, a paraplegic, was ferried in a boat from his Lakeview home. But he had been sitting for more than six hours on an overpass, with no clear indication when he and scores of others would be picked up.

25 Along the Metairie Road railroad embankment, the only passage through two parishes, people wandered aimlessly, along with dogs and cats that headed for high ground.

26 After the rescue effort, the next priority is trying to heal the breach. Ebbert said plans called for giant panels to be dropped in place by helicopter, accompanied by 50, 3,000-pound sandbags. Next the Interstate 10 underpass under the railroad trestle would have to be drained, after the giant new pumping station utterly failed its first test. That would give disaster recovery teams open access to the city from the west.

27 The failure of the Industrial Canal levee created massive flooding in St. Bernard and the 9th Ward[4] on Monday.

28 Estimates on when the city would become habitable again ranged from two weeks to months.

People wade through high water in front of the Superdome August 30, 2005 in New Orleans, Louisiana, days after Hurricane Katrina.

Making Observations

- What images come to mind while reading this article?
- What emotions do you feel after reading this article?

---

[4] The 9th Ward is the largest of 17 wards, or areas, into which New Orleans is divided.

Returning to the Text

- Reread the article to answer these text-dependent questions.
- Write any additional questions you have about the text in your Reader/Writer Notebook.

5. Which major levee breach is the focus of this article? At the time of printing, what were the plans for repairing it? How will this help rescue efforts?

_____

_____

_____

_____

6. What is the implied connection between the events in paragraphs 11 and 12?

_____

_____

_____

_____

7. Summarize paragraphs 10–16. Whom does the officer blame for the chaotic rescue effort? Use details to support your inference.

_____

_____

_____

_____

8. Why do Aleck Scallan and others have no idea when they will be picked up from the overpass?

_____

_____

_____

_____

As You Read

- Underline the priorities that President Bush mentions in his speech.
- Circle unknown words and phrases. Try to determine the meaning of the words by using context clues, word parts, or a dictionary.

ACADEMIC

Rhetorical context refers to the subject, purpose, audience, occasion, or situation in which writing or speaking occurs.

My Notes

About the Author

George W. Bush (b. 1946) was the 43rd president of the United States. Before becoming president, Bush served as Governor of Texas from 1995–2000. His presidency was shaped by the terrorist attacks on September 11, 2001, which occurred eight months into his presidency. After his presidency, Bush founded the George W. Bush Presidential Center in Dallas, Texas and created a collection of paintings, *Portraits of Courage: A Commander in Chief's Tribute to America's Warriors*, to honor American veterans.

Speech

President Outlines Hurricane Katrina Relief Efforts

by **President George W. Bush**

August 31, 2005

1   I've just received an update from Secretary Chertoff and other Cabinet Secretaries involved on the latest developments in Louisiana, Mississippi, and Alabama. As we flew here today, I also asked the pilot to fly over the Gulf Coast region so I could see firsthand the scope and magnitude of the devastation.

2   The vast majority of New Orleans, Louisiana, is under water. Tens of thousands of homes and businesses are beyond repair. A lot of the Mississippi Gulf Coast has been completely destroyed. Mobile is flooded. We are dealing with one of the worst natural disasters in our nation's history.

3   And that's why I've called the Cabinet together. The people in the affected regions expect the federal government to work with the state government and local government with an effective response. I have directed Secretary of Homeland Security Mike Chertoff to chair a Cabinet-level task force to coordinate all our assistance from Washington. FEMA[5] Director Mike Brown is in charge of all federal response and recovery efforts in the field. I've instructed them to work closely with state and local officials, as well as with the private sector, to ensure that we're helping, not hindering, recovery efforts. This recovery will take a long time. This recovery will take years.

4   Our efforts are now focused on three priorities: Our first priority is to save lives. We're assisting local officials in New Orleans in evacuating any remaining citizens from the affected area. I want to thank the state of Texas, and particularly Harris County and the city of Houston and officials with the Houston Astrodome, for providing shelter to those citizens who found refuge

---

[5] The acronym FEMA stands for Federal Emergency Management Agency.

in the Super Dome in Louisiana. Buses are on the way to take those people from New Orleans to Houston.

5   FEMA has deployed more than 50 disaster medical assistance teams from all across the country to help the affected—to help those in the affected areas. FEMA has deployed more than 25 urban search and rescue teams with more than a thousand personnel to help save as many lives as possible. The United States Coast Guard is conducting search and rescue missions. They're working alongside local officials, local assets. The Coast Guard has rescued nearly 2,000 people to date.

6   The Department of Defense is deploying major assets to the region. These include the USS *Bataan* to conduct search and rescue missions; eight swift water rescue teams; the Iwo Jima Amphibious Readiness Group to help with disaster response equipment; and the hospital ship USNS *Comfort* to help provide medical care.

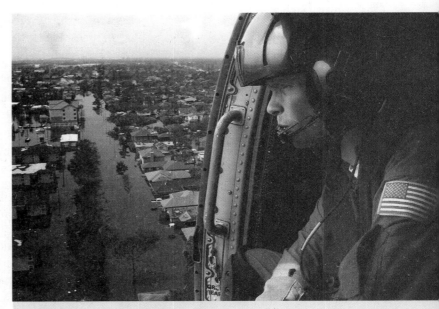

A U.S. Coast Guard Petty Officer and a rescue crew sent from Clearwater, Florida, look for survivors near the Louisiana bayou town of Buras.

My Notes

7   The National Guard has nearly 11,000 Guardsmen on state active duty to assist governors and local officials with security and disaster response efforts. FEMA and the Army Corps of Engineers are working around the clock with Louisiana officials to repair the breaches in the levees so we can stop the flooding in New Orleans.

8   Our second priority is to sustain lives by ensuring adequate food, water, shelter and medical supplies for survivors and dedicated citizens—dislocated citizens. FEMA is moving supplies and equipment into the hardest hit areas. The Department of Transportation has provided more than 400 trucks to move 1,000 truckloads containing 5.4 million Meals Ready to Eat—or MREs, 13.4 million liters of water, 10,400 tarps, 3.4 million pounds of ice, 144 generators, 20 containers of pre-positioned disaster supplies, 135,000 blankets and 11,000 cots. And we're just starting.

9   There are more than 78,000 people now in shelters. HHS and CDC are working with local officials to identify operating hospital facilities so we can help them, help the nurses and doctors provide necessary medical care. They're distributing medical supplies, and they're executing a public health plan to control disease and other health-related issues that might arise.

10   Our third priority is executing a comprehensive recovery effort. We're focusing on restoring power and lines of communication that have been knocked out during the storm. We'll be repairing major roads and bridges and other essential means of transportation as quickly as possible.

My Notes

11 There's a lot of work we're going to have to do. In my flyover, I saw a lot of destruction on major **infrastructure**. Repairing the infrastructure, of course, is going to be a key priority.

12 The Department of Energy is approving loans from the Strategic Petroleum Reserve to limit disruptions in crude supplies for refineries. A lot of crude production has been shut down because of the storm. I instructed Secretary Bodman to work with refiners, people who need crude oil, to alleviate any shortage through loans. The Environmental Protection Agency has granted a nationwide waiver for fuel blends to make more gasoline and diesel fuel available throughout the country. This will help take some pressure off of gas price. But our citizens must understand this storm has disrupted the capacity to make gasoline and distribute gasoline.

13 We're also developing a comprehensive plan to immediately help displaced citizens. This will include housing and education and health care and other essential needs. I've directed the folks in my Cabinet to work with local folks, local officials, to develop a comprehensive strategy to rebuild the communities affected. And there's going to be a lot of rebuilding done. I can't tell you how devastating the sights were.

14 I want to thank the communities in surrounding states that have welcomed their neighbors during an hour of need. A lot of folks left the affected areas and found refuge with a relative or a friend, and I appreciate you doing that. I also want to thank the American Red Cross and the Salvation Army and the Catholic Charities, and all other members of the armies of compassion. I think the folks in the affected areas are going to be overwhelmed when they realize how many Americans want to help them.

. . .

15 The folks on the Gulf Coast are going to need the help of this country for a long time. This is going to be a difficult road. The challenges that we face on the ground are unprecedented. But there's no doubt in my mind we're going to succeed. Right now the days seem awfully dark for those affected—I understand that. But I'm confident that, with time, you can get your life back in order, new communities will flourish, the great city of New Orleans will be back on its feet, and America will be a stronger place for it.

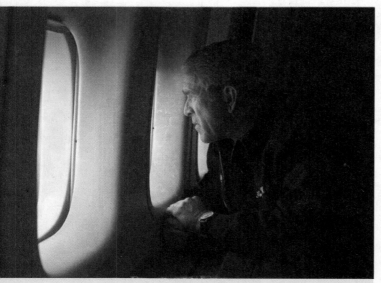

President George W. Bush looks out the window of Air Force One as he flies over New Orleans, Louisiana, surveying the damage left by Hurricane Katrina.

infrastructure: buildings, roads, and utility systems

Making Observations

- What details from this speech stand out to you?
- What are your thoughts on the priorities that the President lays out in his speech?

Returning to the Text

- Reread the speech to answer these text-dependent questions.
- Write any additional questions you have about the text in your Reader/Writer Notebook.

9. Based on details in the text, infer the rhetorical context of this speech.

_____

_____

_____

_____

10. According to President Bush, what are the federal government's three priorities? How would you categorize them?

_____

_____

_____

_____

11. What does President Bush mean by "major assets" in paragraph 6? What examples does he provide?

_____

_____

_____

_____

12. What does President Bush compare charitable relief agencies to in paragraph 14? How might this comparison appeal to his audience?

_____

_____

_____

_____

13. How does President Bush structure paragraph 15 to appeal to his audience?

_____

_____

_____

_____

My Notes

Gaining Perspectives

When a natural disaster happens, local, state, and federal governments provide disaster relief to the community; however, these events don't happen every day. With a partner, pick one topic that affects the daily lives of the people living in your community, such as education, transportation, or crime prevention. How does the government provide for your community at the local, state, and federal levels? Are there problems that are related to your topic where you think the government could be taking a more active or proactive role? What would happen if the government, at any level, wasn't involved? Summarize your discussion in your Reader/Writer Notebook.

Working from the Text

14. Based on the texts that you've read, respond to the Essential Question: How do media sources influence our understanding of the truth and significance of an issue? Write a one-paragraph response in your Reader/Writer Notebook.

15. Revisit either the news article, "Daylong Efforts to Repair Levee Fail," or President Bush's Rose Garden address, and briefly annotate evidence that links to any of the critical lenses you have studied. Then use the following questions to analyze how the lenses might connect to bias in the text.

    • What is being reported (the who, what, where, when, why, and how of the event)?

    • How is it being reported? How objective is the coverage? Identify textual details (slanters, titles, labeling, omission, and so forth) that reveal bias.

    • Who is the target audience for the publication/broadcast? How does the text's rhetorical context affect what it talks about and its language and tone? What inferences can you draw about the writer's or speaker's expectations about the audience's perspective?

    • If you read only this article or heard only this speech, what would you think is the key issue? In other words, how does the article frame the truth and significance of the event?

    • What critical lens or lenses can be seen in how the text approaches the issue? What specific language reveals the lens(es)?

Guiding Questions

Guiding questions are questions about a specific aspect of a topic that you can research in order to learn more about that facet of the topic and the topic as a whole. If you are writing a research paper, good guiding questions should be:

• Focused enough that it is possible for you to search for, gather, and analyze information that will give you new knowledge about a topic

• Significant enough to have been addressed in reputable research materials

• Complex enough to require in-depth research and analysis

16. In preparation for further investigation of Hurricane Katrina, use guiding questions to develop focus questions to guide your research. Use the following steps and questions to narrow your thinking down to guiding questions that are more specific to what you have read about Hurricane Katrina:

- Review your understanding of the critical perspectives (archetypal, cultural, feminist, historical, Marxist, reader response). Which ones seem relevant to this topic? Why? Which ones do not? Why not?

- Based on background knowledge and your preliminary investigation of the topic, brainstorm connections between each relevant lens and the topic.

My Notes

17. Draft an initial closed (yes/no) question linking the lens to the subject.

18. Modify the question to make it open-ended by using one of the following stems:

    • To what extent did X influence Y?

    • In what ways did ...?

    • What does the controversy surrounding (this topic) reveal about attitudes toward the (underlying issue)?

    • What recurring story patterns are evoked by ...?

☑ **Check Your Understanding**

Quickwrite: Choose a lens you think applies to the event, and briefly explain what elements of the story may be most relevant through this lens.

Exploring Media Sources

Learning Targets

- Analyze ideas and details in informational material to gain an understanding of the aftermath of Hurricane Katrina.
- Closely examine and evaluate a film trailer, infographic, and podcast for credibility and bias.
- Use details in a series of visual and audio texts to make inferences about the creators' perspective.

Preview

In this activity, you will examine a variety of media. You will evaluate the texts to determine their value as research sources, considering credibility and bias in forming your judgments.

Learning Strategies

Graphic Organizer
Note-taking
Visual/Audio Prompts

My Notes

Viewing the Photographs

1. With your group, analyze the images from Hurricane Katrina by discussing your observations and making inferences. Evaluate the captions by using the critical perspective questions that follow:

   Cultural Criticism: How might issues of race, age, or power be at play?

   Feminist Criticism: What are some ways in which gender and gender roles represented in the photos?

   Historical Criticism: What contemporary trends, conflicts, or developments might provide important context for understanding the images today?

   Marxist Criticism: To what extent might questions of class be relevant for the viewer to consider?

A mother feeds her 9-day-old baby as she awaits evacuation from the Superdome in New Orleans, Louisiana. A riot erupted, and shots were fired outside of the arena as thousands fought to board buses heading to Houston, Texas.

Dillion Chancey, seven years old, is amongst those who have lost everything that they had in the wake of Hurricane Katrina. He and his parents endured the hurricane in Biloxi, Mississippi.

President George W. Bush boards Air Force One after delivering a speech to the nation about Hurricane Katrina's damage from Jackson Square in New Orleans, September 15, 2005. In his speech Bush calls for the nation to prepare for a long-term effort to rebuild New Orleans.

A firefighter helps evacuate a man out of toxic flood waters as homes burn in the 7th Ward of New Orleans during the aftermath of Hurricane Katrina. The mixture of toxic chemicals and human waste in the New Orleans floodwaters increased the environmental toll of this natural disaster.

My Notes

Evaluating Multimedia Sources

2. Analyze and discuss initial impressions of the multimedia texts with your group. Evaluate the infographic, podcast, and video for any initial signs of bias or other flaws that could compromise their credibility as research sources.

Viewing the Infographic

3. Analyze the details in the infographic that follows, taking note of the data and sources presented in your Reader/Writer Notebook.

   - Based on the information presented, what might be the creator's main purpose?
   - How does the use of print and graphic features impact the data presented?
   - What critical perspectives can you use to analyze this infographic?
   - In your view, are the sources credible? How can you determine their validity?
   - In your opinion, were the authors successful in achieving their goals? How did you arrive at that point of view?
   - Does this infographic appear to be a credible source of information? Are there rhetorical slanters or biases present in the infographic?

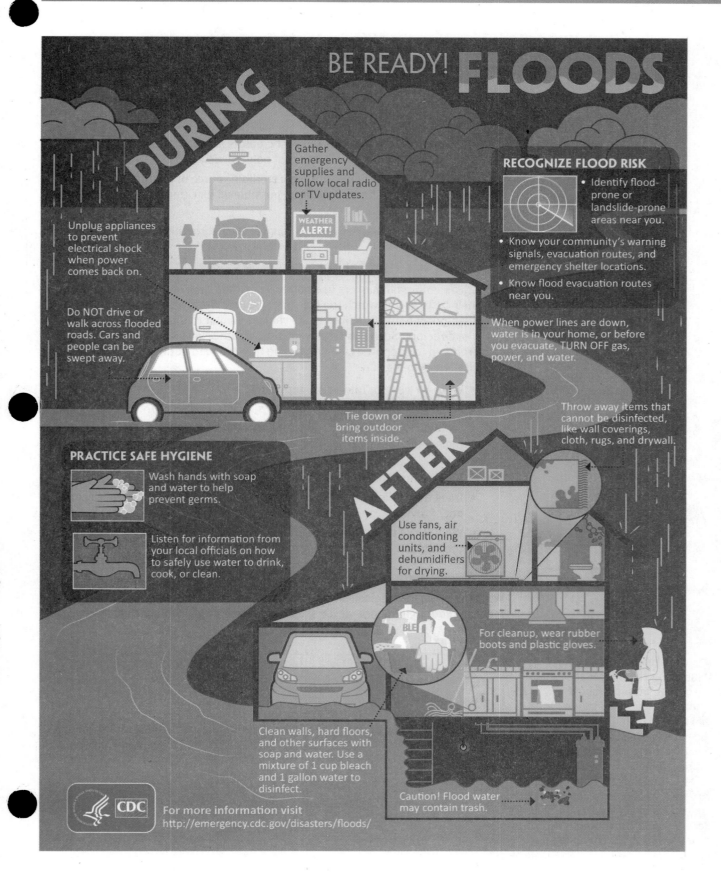

My Notes

_____
_____
_____
_____
_____
_____
_____
_____
_____
_____
_____
_____
_____

VOCABULARY

ACADEMIC

A **documentary** film is based on factual events. **Primary footage** refers to footage shot by the filmmaker for the text at hand. **Archival footage** is footage taken from another, previously recorded source.

INDEPENDENT READING LINK

Read and Respond

If you are reading nonfiction, think about the choices that the author has made about what information to include and what to omit. Do you sense the ways in which the author's opinions and preference create a filter through which you take in the information? What do you observe about the author's take on his or her subject? Record your observations in your Reader/Writer Notebook.

Listening to the Podcast

4. As you listen to the podcast, jot down notes in preparation for your group discussion in your Reader/Writer Notebook.

- How would you summarize the theme or message of this podcast?
- How do the additional sounds (music, etc.) contribute to the theme?
- In your opinion, were the podcast creators successful in expressing their theme? How did you arrive at that point of view?
- Does this podcast appear to be a credible source of information? Why or why not? Try to be as specific as possible when citing details to support your answer.
- What critical perspectives can you use to analyze this infographic?

Watching the Film Trailer

5. **Documentary** filmmakers use both **primary** and **archival footage** to present their case. As you watch the trailer for _Trouble the Water_, remember that directors of nonfiction films make choices similar to those made by fiction film directors. Such choices reveal bias, whether in subtle or blatant ways. Be prepared to support a claim regarding the level and nature of bias in the text after viewing the clip.

- What do we hear (dialogue, narration)?
- What do we read (subtitles, graphics, labels, and so on)?
- What do we see (primary or archival footage, interviews, still images, the filmmaker, cinematic techniques, narrative elements)?
- In your opinion, were the directors successful in expressing their theme? Provide textual details to support your answer.
- Does this trailer appear to be a credible source of information? Why or why not? Provide textual details to support your answer.
- What is the theme/message of the film? What "truth" does it convey about the subject? What lenses are most helpful?

☑ Check Your Understanding

What are some key choices photographers, directors, and graphic designers can make in order to influence viewers' understanding of the truth and significance of an event?

✐ Writing Prompt: Informational

After discussing the infographic, podcast, and video in groups, write a brief essay explaining how producers of media can select information–interviews, statistics, images, or sounds–to frame the information they present through a particular critical lens. Cite a specific critical lens and examples from your analysis and discussion to support your argument. Be sure to:

- Use the guiding questions to inform your thesis and analysis.
- Support your claims by using vivid descriptions of elements of one or more of the media sources discussed.

Throwing Light on the Situation

Learning Targets

- Closely read and analyze an informational text in order to present key information to peers.
- Evaluate different organizational options to choose the clearest structure for information you plan to present.
- Integrate ideas from multiple texts to build knowledge and vocabulary about the effects of Hurricane Katrina.

Preview

In this activity, you will closely read and analyze a text, and then you will work together with your peers to synthesize evidence from multiple texts in a presentation and a written analysis.

As You Read

- Use metacognitive markers to annotate important, surprising, confusing, or key details in the text.
- Circle unknown words and phrases. Try to determine the meaning of the words by using context clues, word parts, or a dictionary.

Editorial

An Editorial: It's Time for a Nation to Return the Favor

The Times-Picayune

November 20, 2005

1   The federal government wrapped levees around greater New Orleans so that the rest of the country could share in our bounty.

2   Americans wanted the oil and gas that flow freely off our shores. They longed for the oysters and shrimp and flaky Gulf fish that live in abundance in our waters. They wanted to ship corn and soybeans and beets down the Mississippi and through our ports. They wanted coffee and steel to flow north through the mouth of the river and into the heartland.

3   They wanted more than that, though. They wanted to share in our spirit. They wanted to sample the joyous beauty of our jazz and our food. And we were happy to **oblige** them.

4   So the federal government-built levees and convinced us that we were safe.

5   We weren't.

6   The levees, we were told, could stand up to a Category 3 hurricane.

7   They couldn't.

Learning Strategies

Close Reading
Marking the Text
Think-Pair-Share

My Notes

KNOWLEDGE QUEST

Knowledge Question:

What are the major challenges in responding to natural disasters, both immediately and in the long term?

In Activity 4.7 you will read articles and reports that each interpret the impact and aftermath of Hurricane Katrina differently. As you read and build knowledge about the topic, think about your answer to the Knowledge Question.

oblige: allow

GRAMMAR & USAGE

Rhetorical Devices

Writers use a number of rhetorical devices to make their writing more persuasive. In this editorial, the authors use anaphora, or repetition, to emphasize a point. Notice how the authors repeat the phrase "they wanted" to emphasize how much the rest of the nation demanded from New Orleans.

Find one more example of a rhetorical device in this text, and compare your findings with a partner.

My Notes

8   By the time Katrina surged into New Orleans, it had weakened to Category 3. Yet our levee system wasn't as strong as the Army Corps of Engineers said it was. Barely anchored in mushy soil, the floodwalls gave way.

9   Our homes and businesses were swamped. Hundreds of our neighbors died.

10   Now, this metro area is drying off and digging out. Life is going forward. Our heart is beating.

11   But we need the federal government—we need our Congress—to fulfill the promises made to us in the past. We need to be safe. We need to be able to go about our business feeding and fueling the rest of the nation. We need better protection next hurricane season than we had this year. Going forward, we need protection from the fiercest storms, the Category 5 storms that are out there waiting to strike.

12   Some voices in Washington are arguing against us. We were foolish, they say. We settled in a place that is lower than the sea. We should have expected to drown.

13   As if choosing to live in one of the nation's great cities amounted to a death wish. As if living in San Francisco or Miami or Boston is any more logical.

14   Great cities are made by their place and their people, their beauty and their risk. Water flows around and through most of them. And one of the greatest bodies of water in the land flows through this one: the Mississippi.

15   The federal government decided long ago to try to tame the river and the swampy land spreading out from it. The country needed this waterlogged land of ours to prosper, so that the nation could prosper even more.

16   Some people in Washington don't seem to remember that. They act as if we are a burden. They act as if we wore our skirts too short and invited trouble.

17   We can't put up with that. We have to stand up for ourselves. Whether you are back at home or still in exile waiting to return, let Congress know that this metro area must be made safe from future storms. Call and write the leaders who are deciding our fate. Get your family and friends in other states to do the same. Start with members of the Environment and Public Works and Appropriations[1] committees in the Senate, and Transportation and Appropriations in the House. Flood them with mail the way we were flooded by Katrina.

18   Remind them that this is a singular American city and that this nation still needs what we can give it.

⊘ Knowledge Quest

- Which of the authors' claims stand out to you the most?
- What captures your attention about the government's response to Hurricane Katrina?

---

[1] *Appropriations:* House and Senate Appropriations Committees pass bills that set aside money for specific federal agencies and programs.

Returning to the Text

- Reread the editorial to answer these text-dependent questions.
- Write any additional questions you have about the text in your Reader/Writer Notebook.

1. What is the "favor" in the editorial's title?

   _____

   _____

   _____

   _____

2. According to the text, how has the federal government failed to uphold its promises? What does it need to do to make up for that failure? Cite evidence to support your answer.

   _____

   _____

   _____

   _____

3. **KQ** What does describing displaced New Orleanians as "in exile" suggest about how they view themselves?

   _____

   _____

   _____

   _____

4. What counterarguments do the writers present? How do they respond to them?

   _____

   _____

   _____

   _____

5. What comparison is implied by the sentence, "They act as if we wore our skirts too short and invited trouble." Is this an effective analogy?

_____

_____

_____

_____

6. **KQ** What was the purpose of this editorial? Cite details to support your answer.

_____

_____

_____

_____

Article

Looters Leave Nothing Behind in Storm's Wake:

Police officers seen joining in on free-for-all

by **Mike Perlstein and Brian Thevenot**

The Times-Picayune, **August 31, 2005**

1   Law enforcement efforts to contain the emergency left by Katrina slipped into chaos in parts of New Orleans Tuesday—with some police officers and firefighters even joining looters in picking stores clean.

2   At the Wal-Mart on Tchoupitoulas Street, an initial effort to hand out provisions to stranded citizens quickly disintegrated into mass looting. Authorities at the scene said bedlam erupted after the giveaway was announced over the radio.

3   While many people carried out food and essential supplies, others cleared out jewelry racks and carted out computers, TVs and appliances on handtrucks.

4   Some officers joined in taking whatever they could, including one New Orleans cop who loaded a shopping cart with a compact computer and a 27-inch flat screen television.

5   Officers claimed there was nothing they could do to contain the anarchy, saying their radio communications had broken down and they had no direction from commanders.

6   "We don't have enough cops to stop it," an officer said. "A mass riot would break out if you tried."

7   Inside the store, the scene alternated between celebration and frightening bedlam. A shirtless man straddled a broken jewelry case, yelling, "Free samples, free samples over here."

8   Another man rolled a mechanized pallet, stacked six feet high ... Perched atop the stack was a bewildered toddler.

9   Throughout the store and parking lot, looters pushed carts and loaded trucks and vans alongside officers. One man said police directed him to Wal-Mart from Robert's Grocery, where a similar scene was taking place.

10   A crowd in the electronics section said one officer broke the glass DVD case so people wouldn't cut themselves.

KNOWLEDGE QUEST

Knowledge Question:
What are the major challenges in responding to natural disasters, both immediately and in the long term?

WORD CONNECTIONS

Etymology
Bedlam is a noun used for a scene of noise and confusion. The word can be traced back to the Hospital of Saint Mary of Bethlehem in London, which became an institution for people with mental illnesses in 1402. It soon became known as *Bedlam*, a Middle English corruption of *Bethlehem*. Later the word came to be used for any chaotic scene similar to conditions found in early hospitals for people with mental illnesses.

My Notes

GRAMMAR & USAGE

Appositives

An appositive is a word, phrase, or clause that is in apposition to, or side by side with, a noun or pronoun. The purpose of an appositive is to identify or describe the noun or pronoun.

Appositives are either essential or nonessential. If an appositive is nonessential, containing supplemental rather than essential information, it should be set off by commas. Find a nonessential appositive in this example from the article:

Toni Williams, 25, packed her trunk with essential supplies, such as food and water, but said mass looting disgusted and frightened her.

My Notes

11 "The police got all the best stuff. They're crookeder than us," one man said.

12 Most officers, though, simply stood by powerless against the tide of law breakers. One veteran officer said, "It's like this everywhere in the city. This tiny number of cops can't do anything about this. It's wide open."

13 At least one officer tried futilely to control a looter through shame.

14 "When they say take what you need, that doesn't mean an f-ing TV," the officer shouted to a looter. "This is a hurricane, not a free-for-all."

15 Sandra Smith of Baton Rouge walked through the parking lot with a 12-pack ... under each arm.

16 "I came down here to get my daughters," she said, "but I can't find them."

17 The scene turned so chaotic at times that entrances were blocked by the press of people, shopping carts and traffic jams that sprouted on surrounding streets.

18 Some groups organized themselves into assembly lines to more efficiently cart off goods.

19 Toni Williams, 25, packed her trunk with essential supplies, such as food and water, but said mass looting disgusted and frightened her.

20 "I didn't feel safe. Some people are going overboard," she said.

21 Inside the store, one woman was stocking up on make-up. She said she took comfort in watching police load up their own carts.

22 "It must be legal," she said. "The police are here taking stuff, too."

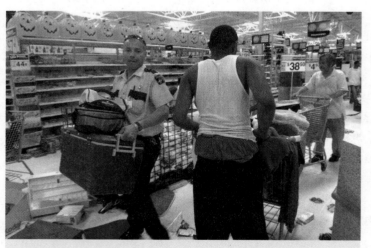

An unidentified official takes part in looting a K-Mart on August 30, 2005 after Hurricane Katrina devastated Louisiana.

⊘ Knowledge Quest

• Which details in the article help you envision the scene?

• Which quotes are particularly striking about people's attitudes toward the situation?

Returning to the Text

- Reread the article to answer these text-dependent questions.
- Write any additional questions you have about the text in your Reader/Writer Notebook.

7. What is the writers' purpose for this article and who is their likely audience?

_____

_____

_____

_____

8. How were police responding to the emergency? Cite details from the article to support your answer.

_____

_____

_____

_____

9. KQ What effect does describing the looters as "a tide of law breakers" have on readers?

_____

_____

_____

_____

10. KQ What is the key idea of the text? How does this text complement the message in the editorial "It's Time for a Nation to Return the Favor"?

_____

_____

_____

_____

KNOWLEDGE QUEST

Knowledge Question:

What are the major challenges in responding to natural disasters, both immediately and in the long term?

My Notes

Article

Who's a Looter? In Storm's Aftermath, Pictures Kick up a Different Kind of Tempest

by **Tania Ralli**

New York Times, **September 5, 2005**

1   Two news photographs ricocheted through the Internet last week and set off a debate about race and the news media in the aftermath of Hurricane Katrina.

2   The first photo, taken by Dave Martin, an Associated Press photographer in New Orleans, shows a young black man wading through water that has risen to his chest. He is clutching a case of soda and pulling a floating bag. The caption provided by the A.P.[2] says he has just been "looting a grocery store."

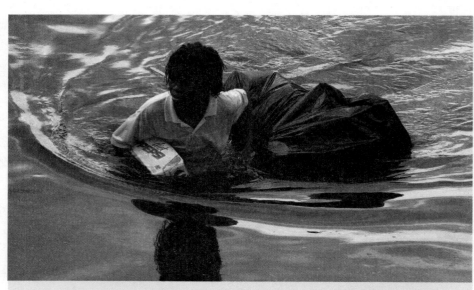

"A young man walks through chest deep flood water after looting a grocery store in New Orleans on Tuesday, Aug. 30, 2005. Flood waters continue to rise in New Orleans after Hurricane Katrina did extensive damage when it made landfall on Monday." (AP Photo/Dave Martin)

3   The second photo, also from New Orleans, was taken by Chris Graythen for Getty Images and distributed by Agence France-Presse. It shows a white couple up to their chests in the same murky water. The woman is holding some bags of food. This caption says they are shown "after finding bread and soda from a local grocery store."

---

[2] A.P. stands for Associated Press.

4 Both photos turned up Tuesday on Yahoo News, which posts automatic feeds of articles and photos from wire services. Soon after, a user of the photo-sharing site Flickr juxtaposed the images and captions on a single page, which attracted links from many blogs. The left-leaning blog Daily Kos linked to the page with the comment "It's not looting if you're white."

5 The contrast of the two photo captions, which to many indicated a double standard at work, generated widespread anger toward the news media that quickly spread beyond the Web.

6 On Friday night, the rapper Kanye West ignored the teleprompter during NBC's live broadcast of "A Concert for Hurricane Relief," using the opportunity to **lambaste** President Bush and criticize the press. "I hate the way they portray us in the media," he said. "You see a black family, it says they're looting. You see a white family, it says they're looking for food."

7 Many bloggers were quick to point out that the photos came from two different agencies, and so could not reflect the prejudice of a single media outlet. A writer on the blog BoingBoing wrote: "Perhaps there's more factual substantiation behind each copywriter's choice of words than we know. But to some, the difference in tone suggests racial bias, implicit or otherwise."

8 According to the agencies, each photographer captioned his own photograph. Jack Stokes, a spokesman for the A.P., said that photographers are told to describe what they have seen when they write a caption.

9 Mr. Stokes said the A.P. had guidelines in place before Hurricane Katrina struck to distinguish between "looting" and "carrying." If a photographer sees a person enter a business and emerge with goods, it is described as looting. Otherwise the A.P. calls it carrying.

10 Mr. Stokes said that Mr. Martin had seen the man in his photograph wade into a grocery store and come out with the sodas and bag, so by A.P.'s definition, the man had looted.

11 The photographer for Getty Images, Mr. Graythen, said in an e-mail message that he had also stuck to what he had seen to write his caption, and had actually given the wording a great deal of thought. Mr. Graythen described seeing the couple near a corner store from an elevated expressway. The door to the shop was open, and things had floated out to the street. He was not able to talk to the couple, "so I had to draw my own conclusions," he said.

"Two residents wade through chest-deep water after finding bread and soda from a local grocery store after Hurricane Katrina came through the area on August 29, 2005, in New Orleans, Louisiana. Katrina was downgraded to a Category 4 storm as it approached New Orleans." (Photo by Chris Graythen/Getty Images)

lambaste: harshly criticize

My Notes

12 In the extreme conditions of New Orleans, Mr. Graythen said, taking necessities like food and water to survive could not be considered stealing. He said that had he seen people coming out of stores with computers and DVD players, he would have considered that looting.

13 "If you're taking something that runs solely from a wall outlet that requires power from the electric company—when we are not going to have power for weeks, even months—that's inexcusable," he said.

14 Since the photo was published last Tuesday Mr. Graythen has received more than 500 e-mail messages, most of them supportive, he said.

15 Within three hours of the photo's publication online, editors at Agence France-Presse rewrote Mr. Graythen's caption. But the original caption remained online as part of a Yahoo News slide show. Under pressure to keep up with the news, and lacking the time for a discussion about word choice, Olivier Calas, the agency's director of multimedia, asked Yahoo to remove the photo last Thursday.

16 Now, in its place, when readers seek the picture of the couple, a statement from Neil Budde, the general manager of Yahoo News, appears in its place. The statement emphasizes that Yahoo News did not write the photo captions and that it did not edit the captions, so that the photos can be made available as quickly as possible.

17 Mr. Calas said Agence France-Presse was bombarded with e-mail messages complaining about the caption. He said the caption was unclear and should have been reworded earlier. "This was a consequence of a series of negligences, not ill intent," he said.

18 For Mr. Graythen, whose parents and grandparents lost their homes in the disaster, the fate of the survivors was the most important thing. In his e-mail message he wrote: "Now is no time to pass judgment on those trying to stay alive. Now is no time to argue semantics about finding versus looting. Now is no time to argue if this is a white versus black issue."

⌀ Knowledge Quest

- What are your first thoughts about how the people in both photos were affected by Katrina?
- How does Ralli's knowledge of the aftermath of Hurricane Katrina compare with the authors of the previous article?

Returning to the Text

- Reread the article to answer these text-dependent questions.
- Write any additional questions you have about the text in your Reader/Writer Notebook.

11. **KQ** Based on this article, what made the two photos controversial?

_____

_____

_____

_____

12. Who do you think would be the most likely audience for this article? Support your answer with evidence from the text.

_____

_____

_____

_____

13. What different perspectives on the photographs are introduced in the first three paragraphs? How does the author frame the issue?

_____

_____

_____

_____

14. **KQ** Define *objective coverage* in your own words and apply your definition to the article. Does it provide objective coverage? What evidence supports your conclusion?

_____

_____

_____

_____

_____

_____

_____

_____

_____

_____

KNOWLEDGE QUEST

Knowledge Question:

What are the major challenges in responding to natural disasters, both immediately and in the long term?

_____

_____

_____

_____

_____

_____

_____

_____

_____

_____

_____

_____

_____

_____

WORD CONNECTIONS

Cognates

The word **palpable** is a cognate in Spanish and English. In both languages, the word is an adjective meaning "able to be touched or felt" or "easy to perceive."

About the Author

Madison Gray is a seasoned editor and writer who has contributed to online publications such as Ebony.com, CBSNews.com, Time.com, and TheRoot.com over the past decade. Gray served as chief producer for _Time Magazine_ from 2006–2014, where he created quality content for the website's homepage and recorded podcasts for TIME's Assignment Detroit project. Currently, his reporting is focused on urban issues affecting the New York area.

Article

The Press, Race, and Katrina

_by_ **Madison Gray**

Time Magazine, **August 30, 2006**

1   If you watched any television, listened to any radio, picked up a newspaper or visited a news website in the days that followed Hurricane Katrina last year, you probably were witness to the result of dozens of on-the-spot editorial decisions made by news managers around the country.

2   As much as we may have wanted to avoid the issue in those first confusing days, because New Orleans was 67% African American prior to the storm, race played a significant role in criticisms of government, both local and federal, humanitarian aid and not surprisingly, the media. Fortunately, the fourth estate3 has its own self-policing mechanisms and is much faster than government and other industries at evaluating and scrutinizing itself. But it is only in recent years that the media has taken a look at how it relates to the country's racial divisions, and Katrina provided an opportunity to do just that.

3   Keith Woods, faculty dean of the Poynter Institute, a St. Petersburg, Fla.-based journalism training organization, said many mistakes were made by the media, but in bringing attention to the crisis, the press got it right.

4   "The media brought a palpable sense of outrage with the coverage from the very beginning," said Woods. "If you looked at NPR, CNN and scattered sightings of the networks and newspapers, where they did well was to recognize the size of the story and the need to stay with it."

---

3 The fourth estate refers to the press.

5   But where race comes in is more difficult, he told me. Where journalism failed is not in any lack of emphasis on how disproportionately blacks were affected, but in how "too many people were making the surface observation that there were lots of blacks affected without spending the time parsing the facts that would make it meaningful or informative."

6   In fact, many journalists who monitored the coverage felt in hindsight that African Americans caught in Katrina's wake were misrepresented in the press.

7   "I don't think African Americans were portrayed in the best light," said Camille Jackson, a staff writer for the Southern Poverty Law Center's Tolerance. org website. "It came out just how uncomfortable the media is when it comes to race, with the exception of a few."

8   Jackson authored a series of articles for the website that spoke to media outlets referring to victims as "hoodlums," "animals" and "thugs." But she said it comes from cultural insensitivity in the media, which led to false news reports and eventually to a curtailing of emergency response.

9   She warned that the important lesson to be learned is "to be an honest journalist, to tell the whole story, and be aware of your own personal biases. I know it's scary, but we're going to have to start talking about race so that we can get at the fear."

10   Buttressing criticisms of the press response to Katrina was a bipartisan Congressional report released in February that outright accuses the media of making a bad situation worse. It does not specify race in its pages, but its accusations implicate press reports that it says contributed to the confusion. The report from the bipartisan House committee investigated preparations for and responses to Katrina and found that media reports of gunshots fired at rescue helicopters, rapes and murders in the Superdome, and mass rioting in the streets were unsubstantiated at best, and many were simply false. "It's clear accurate reporting was among Katrina's many victims," the report says. "If anyone rioted, it was the media."

11   But Margaret Engel, managing editor of the Newseum, an Arlington, Va.-based interactive news museum said there are more important things to consider, like images that seemingly cast a divide between black and white survivors. Two in particular were now-infamous captions placed with Agence France-Presse and Associated Press photos. The AFP photo caption described two whites as "finding" food, while the AP caption described a black youth as "looting" a store.

12   "That to me is much more troubling than reporters quoting cops who didn't really know," said Engel. "I think you'll find that some of the stories on that day of looting were wildly overstated. It's not good that the press reported that, but it is a footnote to the overall coverage which riveted the nation over the lack of response." She added: "I think for Congress to cast the media response as rumor-mongering is to miss the forest for the trees."

13 Despite the varied points of view, two things are clear. First, mistakes were made. As Woods pointed out, there has never been a how-to book on covering a disaster that nearly wipes out a whole city. Secondly, and most importantly, if African Americans in New Orleans are to be fairly served, the story must be told. "Now that the initial event has passed, the problem is maintaining people's attention," said Richard Prince, chairman of the National Association of Black Journalists' Media Monitoring Committee. "People are desperate for media attention because they fear the country will forget them. While a lot of reporters have covered the follow-up, it has not been compelling enough."

14 Prince said that the way to learn from what happened is for journalists to continually go to the Gulf Coast Region and find new stories, which are abundant. "They call it one of the worst natural disasters in the history of the country. So many people have a story to tell; somehow those stories have to be told."

Knowledge Quest
- Whose perspective does this article present?
- What aspect of Hurricane Katrina's aftermath stands out to you the most after reading this article?

Returning to the Text

- Reread the article to answer these text-dependent questions.
- Write any additional questions you have about the text in your Reader/Writer Notebook.

15. How does the article frame the issue in the first two paragraphs? What does the author mean by "self-policing mechanisms"?

_____

_____

_____

_____

16. KQ What impact does the author's use of words like *hoodlums*, *animals*, *thugs*, and *looting* have on the tone of the article?

_____

_____

_____

17. KQ Apply Gray's critique to the editorial, "It's Time for a Nation to Return the Favor." How would you evaluate the editorial in its treatment of the aftermath of Hurricane Katrina and issues of racial division?

_____

_____

_____

_____

KNOWLEDGE QUEST

Knowledge Question:
What are the major challenges in responding to natural disasters, both immediately and in the long term?

My Notes

Report

A Failure of Initiative: Report by the Select Bipartisan Committee to Investigate the Preparation for and Response to Hurricane Katrina

Union Calendar No. 205
109th Congress
2nd Session
Report 109–377

1 On September 15, 2005, the House of Representatives approved H. Res. 437, which created the Select Bipartisan Committee to Investigate the Preparation for and Response to Hurricane Katrina ("the Select Committee").

2 According to the resolution, the Committee was charged with conducting "a full and complete investigation and study and to report its findings to the House not later than February 15, 2006, regarding—(1) the development, coordination, and execution by local, State, and Federal authorities of emergency response plans and other activities in preparation for Hurricane Katrina; and (2) the local, State, and Federal government response to Hurricane Katrina."

3 The Committee presents the report narrative and the findings that stem from it to the U.S. House of Representatives and the American people for their consideration. Members of the Select Committee agree unanimously with the report and its findings. Other members of Congress who participated in the Select Committee's hearings and investigation but were not official members of the Select Committee, while concurring with a majority of the report's findings, have presented additional views as well, which we offer herein on their behalf.

4 First and foremost, this report is issued with our continued thoughts and prayers for Katrina's victims. Their families. Their friends. The loss of life, of property, of livelihoods and dreams has been enormous. And we salute all Americans who have stepped up to the plate to help in any way they can.

5 It has been said civilization is a race between education and catastrophe. With Katrina, we have had the catastrophe, and we are racing inexorably toward the next. Americans want to know: what have we learned?

6 Two months before the Committee was established, former Speaker of the House Newt Gingrich testified before a Government Reform subcommittee

about the need to move the government to an "entrepreneurial" model and away from its current "bureaucratic" model, so that we can get government to move with Information Age speed and effectiveness.

7 "*Implementing* policy effectively," Speaker Gingrich said, "is ultimately as important as *making* the right policy."

8 The Select Committee first convened on September 22, 2005, understanding, like Speaker Gingrich, that a policy that cannot be implemented effectively is no policy at all.

9 The Select Committee was created because, in the tragic aftermath of Katrina, America was again confronted with the vast divide between policy creation and policy implementation. With the life-and-death difference between theory and practice.

10 The Select Committee has spent much of the past five months examining the aftermath of this catastrophic disaster. It has become increasingly clear that local, state, and federal government agencies failed to meet the needs of the residents of Louisiana, Mississippi, and Alabama. It has been our job to figure out why, and to make sure we are better prepared for the future.

11 Our mandate was clear: gather facts about the preparation for and response to Katrina, at all levels of government.

12 Investigate aggressively, follow the facts wherever they may lead, and find out what went right and what went wrong. Ask why coordination and information sharing between local, state, and federal governments was so dismal.

- Why situational awareness was so foggy, for so long.
- Why *all* residents, especially the most helpless, were not evacuated more quickly.
- Why supplies and equipment and support were so slow in arriving.
- Why so much taxpayer money aimed at better preparing and protecting the Gulf coast was left on the table, unspent or, in some cases, misspent.
- Why the adequacy of preparation and response seemed to vary significantly from state to state, county to county, town to town.
- Why unsubstantiated rumors and uncritically repeated press reports—at times fueled by top officials—were able to delay, disrupt, and diminish the response.
- And why government at all levels failed to react more effectively to a storm that was predicted with unprecedented timeliness and accuracy.

13 We agreed early on that the task before us was too important for **carping**. This was not about politics. Katrina did not distinguish between Republicans and Democrats.

14 This was about getting the information we need to chart a new and better course for emergency preparation and response. The American people want the

carping: petty complaining

My Notes

facts, and they've been watching. They alone will judge whether our review has been thorough and fair. Our final exam is this report.

…

15   Our investigation revealed that Katrina was a national failure, an abdication of the most solemn obligation to provide for the common welfare. At every level—individual, corporate, philanthropic, and governmental—we failed to meet the challenge that was Katrina. In this cautionary tale, all the little pigs built houses of straw.

16   Of all we found along the timeline running from the fictional Hurricane Pam to the tragically real devastation along the Gulf coast, this conclusion stands out: A National Response Plan is not enough.

17   What's needed is a National Action Plan. Not a plan that says Washington will do everything, but one that says, when all else fails, the federal government must do something, whether it's formally requested or not. Not even the perfect bureaucratic storm of flaws and failures can wash away the fundamental governmental responsibility to protect public health and safety.

18   Still, no political storm surge from Katrina should be allowed to breach the **sovereign** boundaries between localities, states, and the federal government. Our system of federalism wisely relies on those closest to the people to meet immediate needs. But faith in federalism alone cannot **sanctify** a dysfunctional system in which DHS and FEMA simply wait for requests for aid that state and local officials may be unable or unwilling to convey. In this instance, blinding lack of situational awareness and disjointed decision making needlessly compounded and prolonged Katrina's horror.

19   In many respects, our report is a **litany** of mistakes, misjudgments, lapses, and absurdities all cascading together, blinding us to what was coming and hobbling any collective effort to respond.

20   This is not to say there were not many, many heroes, or that some aspects of the preparation and response were not, by any standard, successful. We found many examples of astounding individual initiative that saved lives and stand in stark contrast to the larger institutional failures. Nor do we mean to focus on assigning individual blame. Obtaining a full accounting and identifying lessons learned does not require finger pointing, instinctively tempting as that may be.

21   There was also an element of simple bad luck with Katrina that aggravated the inadequate response. The hurricane arrived over a weekend, at the end of the month. People on fixed incomes had little money for gas or food or lodging, making them more likely to remain in place and wait for their next check. Communicating via television or radio with families enmeshed in their weekend routines was difficult at best, as was finding drivers and other needed volunteers.

22   Over the past several months, we have become more than familiar with the disaster declaration process outlined in the Stafford Act. We understand

sovereign: independent
sanctify: redeem or save
litany: long list

the goals, structure and mechanisms of the National Response Plan. We've digested the alphabet soup of "coordinating elements" established by the Plan: the HSOC (Homeland Security Operations Center) and RRCC (Regional Response Coordination Center); JFOs (Joint Field Offices) and PFOs (Principal Federal Officials); the IIMG (Interagency Incident Management Group); and much more.

23 But the American people don't care about acronyms or organizational charts. They want to know who was supposed to do what, when, and whether the job got done. And if it didn't get done, they want to know how we are going to make sure it does the next time.

…

24 What this Select Committee has done is not rocket science.

25 We've gathered facts and established timelines based on some fairly rudimentary but important questions posed to the right people in both the public and private sectors.

- What did you need and what did you get?
- Where were you in the days and hours right before, during, and after the storm?
- Who were you talking to?
- What were you doing?
- Does that match what you were *supposed* to be doing? Why or why not?

26 In other words, the Select Committee has matched what was *supposed* to happen under federal, state, and local plans against what *actually* happened.

27 Our findings emerged from this process of matching.

28 Too often there were too many cooks in the kitchen, and because of that the response to Katrina was at times overdone, at times underdone. Too often, because everybody was in charge, nobody was in charge.

29 Many government officials continue to stubbornly resist recognizing that fundamental changes in disaster management are needed. This report illustrates that we have to stop waiting for the disaster that fits our response plan and instead design a scalable capacity to meet whatever Mother Nature throws at us. It's not enough to say, "We wouldn't be here if the levees had not failed." The levees *did* fail, and government and other organizations failed in turn—in many, many ways.

30 It remains difficult to understand how government could respond so ineffectively to a disaster that was anticipated for years, and for which specific dire warnings had been issued for days. This crisis was not only predictable, it was predicted.

31 If this is what happens when we have advance warning, we shudder to imagine the consequences when we do not. Four and a half years after 9/11, America is still not ready for prime time.

My Notes

...

32 With Katrina, there was no shortage of plans. There were plans, but there was not enough plan-*ning*.

33 Government failed because it did not learn from past experiences, or because lessons thought to be learned were somehow not implemented. If 9/11 was a failure of imagination, then Katrina was a failure of initiative. It was a failure of leadership.

Tom Davis

Harold Rogers

Christopher Shays

Henry Bonilla

Steve Buyer

Sue Myrick

Mac Thornberry

Kay Granger

Charles W. "Chip" Pickering

Bill Shuster

Jeff Miller

✎ Knowledge Quest

- What stands out about Congress's grasp of the aftermath of Hurricane Katrina?
- Which of Congress's claims is the most striking to you?

Returning to the Text

- Reread the report excerpt to answer these text-dependent questions.
- Write any additional questions you have about the text in your Reader/Writer Notebook.

18. How does the use of bulleted lists and questions enhance the main argument of the report?

_____

_____

_____

_____

19. KQ What is the point of view of the authors of this report on the preparation and response to Hurricane Katrina? Use evidence in the text to support your answer. Compare their view to that expressed in the editorial, "It's Time for a Nation to Return the Favor." Would these writers agree?

_____

_____

_____

_____

20. KQ Based on the context, what is the meaning of the word *dismal* in paragraph 12?

_____

_____

_____

_____

KNOWLEDGE QUEST

Knowledge Question:

What are the major challenges in responding to natural disasters, both immediately and in the long term?

My Notes

About the Author

Simone Bruni is a Louisiana native and founder of Demo Diva. After losing her home and career during Hurricane Katrina, Bruni began a demolition business on the campus of Xavier University in 2005. With no prior experience in demolition, Bruni has created a highly successful business that is based in New Orleans.

Article

'Attitude of Resilience' Helped Create Demo Diva

by **Simone Bruni**

Chicago Tribune, **September 3, 2015**

1   How many times in life do we have to start over? How many times do we have to reinvent ourselves just to survive?

2   Hurricane Katrina washed through my house, my city and my life. In the blink of an eye, the comfortable routine I had known was over. The high-heeled world of a party planner came crashing down. My home was flooded. I lost my job. No neighbors. No friends nearby. Everyone had evacuated elsewhere. My city was devastated. Everything was turned upside down.

3   I fell to my knees in grief.

4   As a corporate event planner, I sold parties, petals and pretties. I showcased and show-boated all the best of New Orleans: restaurants, hotels, musicians, plantations and bayous. The sounds of clinking china and crystal, the laughter and revelry were now drowned out by the National Guard and heavy machinery rolling through our streets. Blanketed in a film of mud and toxicity, the city was grey and lifeless.

5   Oh my gosh, I'm single. Who is going to protect me? Who is going to put my shelter back together? How am I going to survive? What other type of work can I do? Do I have any other skills? These are the most basic questions we ask ourselves in the middle of any type of disaster: divorce, death, unemployment, and loss of relationships. This is when our survival instincts give us options: morph or die!

6   My answer came from the most unlikely source one afternoon. Two Brazilian brothers were gutting the mildewed walls of my little house. I was sitting on a 5-gallon paint can watching them and holding my head in despair. I seemed to be in my own trance, mumbling to myself, "What am I going to do? What am I going to do?" They spoke an epiphany, "You are an American. You have every right to own your own business. You have

opportunities that we do not have in our country. You don't know how lucky you are. Go start a business."

7   In that moment, I received the greatest lesson of my life. Two simple, down-to-earth boys showed me the way. When catastrophe hit, it didn't matter that I was a doctor's daughter; that I had private-school education; or that I knew the best concierges, restaurant owners and all those other meaningless things. I had a choice of how I was going to react to my circumstances. I had to choose my attitude. I chose to be hopeful. I chose to humble myself. I chose to be positive and it paid off: The Demo Diva Co. was born.

8   Equipped with hot pink business cards and yard signs, I sold my demolition services across the city. Door to door. Flyers on windshields. At first, I knew nothing about the demolition equipment but I assured my customers that they could trust me to help them. I would solve their problem. It worked.

9   Six years later, I own a fleet of hot pink dumpsters, dump trucks and excavators. Our equipment is all over the city. I can't go into a grocery store or gas station around town without a young or old person singing the jingle from my commercial. "Who fights the Blight, Demo Diva fights the Blight!" Demo Diva isn't just a demolition company. It's an attitude of resilience. It's the personification of us—the people of New Orleans and we, Americans!

10   It took immigrants to show me the light. It took my passion to help my community. But I have influenced a male-dominated industry with a little pink flair and emerged with a successful small business.

Simone Bruni's demotion company has gained recognition for using a fleet of hot pink dumpsters and dump trucks.

⊘ Knowledge Quest

- How do you feel after reading about Bruni's experience from her own perspective?
- Which line in the article best shows the resilience of survivors affected by a natural disaster?

WORD CONNECTIONS

Cognates
The English word **catastrophe** and the Spanish word *catástrofe* are cognates. Both words mean a sudden, unexpected disaster. Many English words spelled with the letters *ph* are spelled with the letter *f* in Spanish: *metamorfosis*, *teléfono*, and *foto* are a few examples.

My Notes

Returning to the Text

- Reread the article to answer the text-dependent questions.
- Write any additional questions you have about the text in your Reader/Writer Notebook.

21. The author opens her essay with questions. What effect does this have on readers? How does she begin to answer those questions in the next three paragraphs?

_____

_____

_____

_____

22. KQ What is the author's point of view regarding how the aftermath of the hurricane affected her life? How would her account be different if it were told objectively rather than subjectively?

_____

_____

_____

_____

23. KQ Compare Bruni's actions to the ideas expressed in the editorial, "It's Time for a Nation to Return the Favor." In what ways would she agree with the editorial? In what ways might she disagree?

_____

_____

_____

_____

Report

The Need for Science in Restoring Resilience to the Northern Gulf of Mexico

from *Science and the Storms: the USGS Response to the Hurricanes of 2005*

by **Gregory J. Smith**

KNOWLEDGE QUEST

Knowledge Question:
What are the major challenges in responding to natural disasters, both immediately and in the long term?

> …thousands of people had to chop their way through rooftops or cling to trees waiting for rescue…thousands are camped upon broken levees…this is a pitiable plight of a lost battle…

Description of the human tragedy following the 1927 Mississippi River flood in Rising Tide by John M. Barry

> …thousands of people being rescued from their rooftops and attics…there's a lot more people who need assistance…

Description of the human tragedy following the 2005 Hurricane Katrina landfall broadcast by WWL-AM New Orleans radio following the post hurricane levee breaches

Unprecedented Events

1   No recent events in the history of the United States have so highlighted the discord between the human landscapes (development patterns) and natural landscapes of coastal America as did the hurricanes of 2005. Hearing the news of stranded citizens after Hurricane Katrina made many recall the plight of those stranded by the 1927 Mississippi River flood. In the nearly 80 years following the great Mississippi River flood of 1927, the U.S. population, indeed the world's population, has migrated to coastal areas. During Hurricane Katrina, the Mississippi River and delta, the coastal habitats, the urban environments, and the massive storm came together on August 29, 2005, in coastal Louisiana. This storm produced a massive loss of life and property as well as an economic impact along the Gulf Coast that was unprecedented in U.S. history. Hurricanes Dennis, Rita, and Wilma were also powerful hurricanes that affected the Gulf Coast in 2005 and were among the record 27 named storms of that year. The most intense storms took people's lives, homes, property, livelihoods, and futures as the world witnessed in disbelief, via sophisticated satellite technology, the raw, massive forces of nature. Of the record number of cyclonic storms in 2005, Katrina and its aftermath stand as perhaps the best example of the critically urgent need to harmonize and integrate scientific, social, and economic coastal planning on a scale that has never before been attempted.

My Notes

My Notes

USGS Response to the Storms

2   The geological and geographic setting, the hydrologic[4] regime, and the biological landscapes of the northern Gulf of Mexico coast have intersected with human coastal development, creating a vulnerable coast. In many ways science, engineering, and technology played a role in the development of this situation; it is these same enterprises that offer the greatest opportunity for transforming our coasts from ones that are vulnerable, like those impacted in 2005, to ones that are resilient…

A Valuable Coast

3   The benefits of the Gulf Coast to the Nation's economy are numerous. For example, in Louisiana alone, the Port of South Louisiana handles more tonnage than any other port in the Nation; nearly 34 percent of the U.S. natural gas supply and over 29 percent of the Nation's crude oil supply moves through the State (U.S. Army Corps of Engineers, 2004). Additionally, the Mississippi River Delta is the gateway to the Nation's lifeline for moving goods and materials to and from the heart of the United States and the rest of the world. The Gulf Coast region accounted for the largest U.S. commercial fish and shellfish landings, by weight, in the lower 48 States, in 200304 (National Oceanic and Atmospheric Administration, 2004).

4   Beyond the stark economic figures, the Gulf Coast provides important natural benefits, such as the critical coastal habitat for wintering waterfowl and birds migrating from North America to South and Central America. Additionally, these valuable habitats of marshlands and barrier islands are critical to buffering human populations and property from the winds and flood waters of storms.

5   The economic and ecological benefits of the coast are considerable and are critical to America. Harmonizing economic and ecological processes and recovering the human landscape while restoring the natural landscapes are formidable tasks. Scientists, engineers, and resource managers, working together and using an adaptive management approach, offer the greatest promise of transforming a vulnerable coast to a resilient coast for the future. Adaptive management is a type of natural resource management in which decisions are made as part of an ongoing science-based process. It involves testing, monitoring, and evaluating applied strategies and incorporating new knowledge based on scientific findings and the needs of society. Results are used to modify management policy, strategies, and practices (Unified Federal Policy for Watershed Approach to Federal Land and Resource Management, 2000).

. . .

Science and a Resilient Coast

6   In the aftermath of the storms of 2005, there was an increase in the already active efforts for coastal restoration and planning that have involved biologists, hydrologists, geologists, engineers, planners, and the public. Previously, virtually all of the coastal restoration efforts and programs had cited hurricane protection

---

[4] *Hydrologic* relates to the study of water, its properties, and its movements on earth.

as a key benefit to restoring coastal Louisiana (Coastal Wetlands Planning, Protection and Restoration Act, 1990; Louisiana Coastal Wetlands Conservation and Restoration Task Force, 1998; U.S. Army Corps of Engineers, 2004). Following the 2005 storm season, it has become obvious not only that coastal restoration efforts are urgently needed but also that these efforts must be completely harmonized with hurricane protection, flood control, navigation, river and hydrological management, and ultimately with human development and activities. Restoration of the coast affords the opportunity to integrate and harmonize the diverse activities and ecological benefits provided by a resilient coast ecosystem. Integrating these massive enterprises will require that goals transcend each of these independent endeavors beyond the interests of any single stakeholder group. Maintaining navigation of the Mississippi and Atchafalaya Rivers, flood control structures, hurricane levees, and storm protection—while simultaneously restoring land lost to the northern Gulf of Mexico to an ecologically functional system—will be a massive and complex challenge for the future. The hurricanes of 2005, with their dramatic impact on lives and property, have clearly brought a new sense of urgency to this challenge in which the entire Nation holds a stake.

7   Two major efforts that pointed to the need for integrated, harmonized planning across human and natural landscapes were focused on a new planning framework and a new vision for the future of the Gulf Coast (Working Group for Post-hurricane Planning for the Louisiana Coast, 2006; Technical Group, 2006). These efforts have built consensus and recommendations for approaches to building a resilient coast.

8   One such recommendation focuses on retaining Mississippi River sediments in coastal wetlands instead of allowing them to bypass the Continental Shelf. This retention of sediments would emulate the historical geological and hydrological processes on the coast that once built land and sustained the wetlands that are now critically needed to protect coastal communities. Such recommendations focus on restoring the coast as opposed to simply armoring the coast (with levees, barriers, and other hard structures). The diversity of factors that drive recovery and restoration will certainly include hard structures and will deal with both flood control and hurricane protection. Scientific studies, however, have made it clear that the restoration of natural coastal wetlands and ecosystem function must be a part of this equation if we are to achieve a sustainable coastal landscape.

USGS Science and the Storms

9   This volume contains a **synoptic** overview of the immediate scientific assessments that were conducted by USGS throughout the Gulf Coast region. The science addressed issues as they arose, since establishing a research design and specific study area prior to the occurrence of a hurricane is unrealistic. While post-storm science tends to focus on impacts and rely less on experimental methods, there is a great deal to be learned through assessing the changes caused by these storms in relation to the human landscape. These studies provide important understandings and point to additional scientific work that is needed to produce further knowledge critical in transforming our coast from a state of vulnerability to one that is resilient and sustainable.

synoptic: general

Knowledge Quest

- Which groups of people are mentioned in the report that haven't been mentioned in the previous texts?
- What is one new detail you learned about long-term recovery after a natural disaster?

Returning to the Text

- Reread the report to answer these text-dependent questions.
- Write any additional questions you have about the text in your Reader/Writer Notebook.

24. KQ What clues does the title of this report give about its overall purpose?

_____

_____

_____

_____

25. Why did the author begin the report with descriptions of two disasters?

_____

_____

_____

26. What effect does the author hope to achieve by including such specific figures in the report's third paragraph? How effective is it?

_____

_____

_____

_____

27. KQ Through which lens does the author approach the issue of Hurricane Katrina? Is it an objective or subjective article? How do you know?

_____

_____

_____

_____

Knowledge Quest

Think about how the articles and reports explore all elements of Hurricane Katrina, including the aftermath. Within your small group, discuss which article or report makes the most compelling claim about what needs to change in the aftermath of future, similar disasters. Be sure to:

- Prepare by analyzing and evaluating what you have learned about how New Orleanians and other people and organizations view Hurricane Katrina's initial impact and aftermath.
- Ask and respond to questions to clarify details, evidence, and ideas.
- Acknowledge perspectives and reasoning that are different from your own.

 INDEPENDENT READING LINK

You can continue to build your knowledge about how different people and organizations respond to natural disasters by reading other articles at ZINC Reading Labs. Search for keywords such as *natural disaster* and *natural disaster relief*.

 ZINC

Working from the Text

28. Based on the text you have read, respond to your assigned Essential Question. Once you have listened to each group's presentation, respond to the other Essential Question based on the information you learned about one of the other informational texts.

Article Read	Essential Question
"Looters Leave Nothing Behind in Storm's Wake," by Mike Perlstein and Brian Thevenot "Who's a Looter? In Storm's Aftermath, Pictures Kick Up a Different Kind of Tempest," by Tania Ralli "'Attitude of Resilience' Helped Create Demo Diva," by Simone Bruni "The Need for Science in Restoring Resilience to the Northern Gulf of Mexico," by Gregory J. Smith	How do media sources influence our understanding of the truth and significance of an issue?
"An Editorial: It's Time for a Nation to Return the Favor," from The Times-Picayune "The Press, Race, and Katrina," by Madison Gray "A Failure of Initiative," by the Select Bipartisan Committee to Investigate the Preparation for and Response to Hurricane Katrina	How are media texts constructed to cater to media consumers' interests, experiences, assumptions, and biases or to promote a particular agenda?

29. Revisit the Text: With your reading group, reread the text to locate evidence as you answer the following questions in a small group discussion. Record notes from your discussion in your Reader/Writer Notebook.

30. Summarize the information covered in the text and connect it to the original news event.

31. How objective is the coverage? Identify and list (or highlight in the article) specific textual details (titles, labeling, omissions, and so on) that reveal any bias in the text.

32. What is the target audience for the publication/broadcast? How does the text's rhetorical context affect the language and tone used?

33. What is the writer's point of view? How do the evidence and the rhetoric support that point of view?

34. If you read only this article or report, what would you think is the key issue? In other words, how does the text frame the truth and/or significance of the event?

35. Which critical lenses are evident in how the text approaches the issue? Provide examples to support your answer.

Planning Your Presentation: Now that you have completed your analysis, come up with a plan for preparing and presenting the article or report to the class. Your group's presentation to your peers should include the following:

- **The most significant information from your text:** Be sure that your presentation summarizes the text in a way that allows classmates to understand its main ideas.

- **A discussion of how the text frames the event and its aftermath:** What issue(s) does it focus on? How slanted is the language? Does it include obvious examples of faulty reasoning? Be ready to cite specific examples to support your evaluation of the text.

- **An analysis of what lens(es) connect to the text:** Which quotations from the text support your claims about its perspective? If needed, use the following stem:

  When we read this text through a _____ lens, we notice that _____.

36. Consider the information from your presentation plan. Brainstorm different organizational strategies your group could use to present your article to your classmates. Once you've identified the strengths and weaknesses of each approach, it might be helpful to try to outline the presentation using a few of the approaches that seem to fit best. Evaluate the results as a group to choose the approach you plan to take in the final draft.

Organizational Approach	Strengths and Weaknesses of This Approach

37. Based on your evaluation of your options, which approach will you use to present your article and why?

My Notes

Analyzing Presentations

38. As you listen to the presentations of the other groups, use the space to create a concept map. Record titles, ideas, and page numbers as you make connections between your guiding question and the information presented in the other groups' presentations.

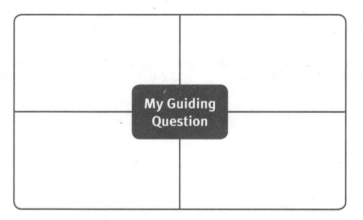

My Guiding Question

39. In addition to listening for the ideas each group shares, observe and evaluate each group's presentation techniques. Use your Reader/Writer Notebook to record observations and questions you might like to ask after each presentation, as well as any relevant insights you think the class might find interesting or helpful. When listening, be sure to evaluate the following:

- Is the speaker's reasoning sound and well supported by evidence?
- What specific rhetorical strategies are used in the presentation? Are they effective?
- How does the speaker link ideas and make connections to the premise of the piece?
- What points does the speaker emphasize, and how do they support the overall premise?

☑ Check Your Understanding

When writing or presenting a critical interpretation, what key questions should guide your decision about what to include and how to organize it?

📝 Writing Prompt: Informational

Write a brief essay using evidence from the various articles you have discussed to answer your guiding question. Be sure to:

- Choose an organizational approach that will engage your audience.
- Integrate quotations in different ways to create syntactic variety in your writing.
- Tailor your rhetoric to your target audience.
- Punctuate your paper correctly and check for spelling errors.

Language Checkpoint: Writing Logical Comparisons

Learning Targets

- Recognize the structure of a logical comparison.
- Understand what makes a comparison illogical.
- Revise in order to maintain logical comparisons in writing.

Preview

In this activity you will learn and practice using logical comparisons. After reading some examples and completing some exercises, you will demonstrate your new knowledge in a paragraph about how illogical comparisons can weaken your writing.

Understanding Logical Comparisons

Writers frequently use comparisons to help their audience understand their ideas. Comparisons are usually made between two nouns. For example:

Hurricane Katrina caused more financial damage than Hurricane Sandy.

Two similar things are being compared—the financial damage caused by two storms. This comparison is logical, and a reader will clearly understand what the writer is trying to say.

A couple of different mistakes are common when making comparisons:

Error	Example	Why It Is an Error
Illogical Comparison	I like the restaurants in New Orleans better than Houston.	The things being compared are not actually similar. Because of the way this sentence is written, restaurants are being compared with a city.
Comparing one specific thing to all things of that type	Hurricane Katrina was worse than any natural disaster.	The comparison doesn't acknowledge that Hurricane Katrina is a natural disaster and can't, logically, be worse than itself.

1. **Quickwrite:** Why might a writer accidentally make an illogical comparison? Why might a reader be able to understand the comparison even though it is illogical?

2. What is the illogical comparison in the following sentence?

The music scene in New Orleans in more robust than Houston.

3. Revise the sentence to make the comparison logical.

4. What is the illogical comparison in the following sentence?

New Orleans is the most fascinating city.

5. Revise the sentence to make the comparison logical.

Fixing Illogical Comparisons

Revising illogical comparisons is important for ensuring that the meaning of the writing is clear to readers. There are a few ways that illogical comparisons can be revised and made logical.

Rewrite a sentence's noun phrases so that each is parallel with the other.

I found **Maria Konnikova's arguments** about the effect of headlines more convincing than **Matthew C. Nisbet's arguments** about partisan readers' biases.

Konnikova's writing style was more conversational than **Nisbet's writing style**.

When two phrases are parallel, they have a similar construction that makes clear which things are being compared. For example, in the sentences provided, the noun phrases—in bold—are parallel. So it is clear that the authors' writing styles and techniques are what are being compared.

Rewrite the noun phrases so that each uses a possessive noun, or a noun that shows ownership.

> **Government report writers'** word choice is more complex than **newspaper reporters'** word choice.

> **Academics'** writing style is also more complicated than most **news reporters'** style.

In the first sentence, both *government report writers* and *newspaper reporters* are possessive, so the sentence implies that both groups have a writing style and that is what is being compared. In the second sentence, both *academics* and *reporters* are possessive, so the sentence implies that the groups are being compared.

Add a determiner to the sentence.

> The damage caused by Hurricane Katrina was more widespread than <u>that</u> of Hurricane Sandy.

> Hurricane Katrina's highest wind speeds were faster than <u>those</u> measured during Hurricane Sandy.

A determiner is a kind of pronoun that shows ownership. The determiner *that* agrees with a singular antecedent and the determiner *those* agrees with a plural antecedent. In the first sentence, the antecedent of *that* is *damage*, which is singular. In the second sentence, the antecedent of *those* is *speeds*, which is a plural.

6. Work with a partner to make each of the following comparisons logical.

 a. The audiences in New York were larger than San Francisco.

 b. The president's approval ratings were lower than her opponent.

 c. The United States swim relay team was faster than the Italians.

Revising

Read the following paragraph. It includes some illogical comparisons. Mark each illogical comparison, and then rewrite it.

[1] Edward R. Murrow was the best journalist. [2] He reported many stories that were better than Walter Cronkite. [3] His reporting was more thorough than Cronkite. [4] However, they were both excellent and well-respected journalists. [5] And Cronkite's stories had impact, as did Murrow. [6] Today's journalists could learn from them both.

Practice

Write a short paragraph explaining why illogical comparisons can be confusing to readers. In your paragraph, be sure to include one original example of each type of faulty comparison explained in the table. In your paragraph, include advice and information on how writers can avoid faulty comparisons.

☑ Check Your Understanding

Take a few minutes to think about why illogical comparisons creep up in writing and how you can keep your eye out for them in the future. Are there any words that often occur in comparisons that you can look out for?

Creating a Research Plan

Learning Targets

- Work collaboratively to generate a list of potential research topics.
- Use your preliminary topic as a starting point for developing a guiding research question, investigating it, and synthesizing relevant information from multiple sources.

Preview

In this activity, you will collaborate to select a topic and generate a research question to explore for the remainder of the unit. Your group research will inform your argumentative essay.

Learning Strategies

Activating Prior Knowledge
Brainstorming
Discussion Groups

My Notes

Preparing for Research

Before selecting a preliminary topic for your individual and group assessments, work with your group members to complete the following steps.

1. Based on the different ways in which you have been thinking about Hurricane Katrina in this unit, work with your classmates to generate a list of potential issues and topics. Consider topics that will:

   - provide opportunities to analyze the subject through various critical perspectives
   - change over time as cultural perspectives change
   - appear in a range of print and nonprint media texts
   - reveal contrasting values and beliefs
   - reveal differing representations of the truth of what happened

2. Brainstorm a list of potential topics or issues. Write your ideas in your Reader/Writer Notebook.

3. With your group members, explore the possible topics and issues you generated. When a specific topic seems interesting to the group, brainstorm about what a research plan and report might include. Use this graphic organizer to take notes.

Topic	Key Research Points	Advantages/Disadvantage of Topic	Group members' views on topic
Response to Katrina vs. other hurricanes	Compare federal responses across time Look at changes in federal policy	Broad topic that would require lots of background research Hard to compare hurricanes that caused different amounts of damage	

4. When you narrow down your group's ideas to a few potential topics, brainstorm resources you might be able to use to conduct your research. Draw on your knowledge of the different sources you've already read in this unit to generate ideas in the graphic organizer. Assign each member a potential topic to brainstorm.

Topic	Resource	Contribution to Research
		(Sum up how the resource relates to the topic.)

5. Work to come to an agreement on your group's issue and event. Offer ideas to help the group develop a strong research topic. For example, is it possible to include relevant aspects of more than one topic to address the interest areas of everyone in the group? Review the information gathered in the first two steps to decide on a topic.

6. How did your group select an issue and event? For instance, did the group vote on an issue and choose the one favored by the majority? Write your issue in the space that follows and provide a brief rationale for how the group chose it.

Issue and Rationale:

7. Apply your knowledge about guiding questions and formulate a strong guiding question that stems from the issue your group selected and reflects your specific critical lens. Then, work as a group to collect information from the texts you've read that could help answer the question. Make notes in your Reader/Writer Notebook.

8. Use the chart that follows to consider what approaches each of you might take to complete your individual essay for Embedded Assessment 1. How will you support each other in crafting guiding questions?

Criticism	Can you analyze the issue through this lens?	What elements of the issue does the critical perspective link to?	What could be the guiding question?
Archetypal			
Cultural			
Feminist			
Historical			
Marxist			

Refining Your Research Question

9. Using the insights from the chart, how might you revise your guiding question to make it a stronger foundation for a research paper?

10. Is the question focused enough that it is possible for you to search for, gather, and analyze information that will give you new knowledge about a topic? Add to the graphic organizer created by the group by individually conducting on-the-spot research using online sources to locate one additional resource that could be used to gather information on your group's chosen topic. Be sure to include a sentence on the resource's possible contribution to knowledge.

11. Collect all the charts and other notes from the group and use the information to craft a single guiding question that will be the backbone of your group research paper.

12. A research proposal informs the reader about your research question and how you intend to answer it. Organizing your thoughts before writing your research proposal will help you to synthesize your ideas in a logical way.

Research Proposal Notes
Issue/Event: What issue and event has the group chosen?
Review of the Issue: Write a summary of what you currently know about your chosen issue.
Critical Perspective: Which lens will you apply while exploring the issue? How will you apply the critical lens to your group's issue?
Research Question: What question will you use to guide your research?
Research Plan: How will you further explore the issue through your research?

✍ Writing Prompt: Informational

Use your notes to write a one-page research proposal that explains your topic, briefly notes any information you have already learned, states which critical perspective you plan to use to examine the issue, and defines your guiding question. Mention any sources you have identified and plan to include in your final research report. Lastly, indicate where and how you will continue to conduct research to answer your guiding question. Be sure to:

- Identify your guiding question.
- Include significant details related to your critical perspective.
- Review your notes on what you already know about the issue and identify additional research needed to find supporting evidence for your group's ideas.
- Read and revise your research proposal draft to make sure your proposal demonstrates a command of standard English conventions.

Evaluating Sources

© 2021 College Board. All rights reserved.

Learning Targets

- Locate and evaluate sources for credibility, bias, accuracy, and evidence of faulty reasoning or other issues that might make them unsuitable for research.
- Use sources accurately and cite them adequately to avoid plagiarism.

Preview

In this activity, you will use a checklist to determine whether specific sources are relevant to your research question and are suitable as references based on their accuracy and other factors critical to collecting high-quality information.

Learning Strategies

Graphic Organizer
Note-taking

My Notes

Researching Your Topic

Locating reliable sources is a central part of the research process. Remember that sources are generally classified as primary or secondary.

Primary Source: Provides direct evidence or testimony about an event and is created as the event is happening. Primary sources include articles written soon after an event takes place or reporting events as they happened, as well as video footage taken during an event.

Secondary Source: Analyzes and/or interprets an event, often through the use of primary sources, after it has occurred. As an example, a documentary about the Vietnam War could use wartime footage but, as a whole, would be considered a secondary source. Newspaper or magazine articles that offer opinions, historical perspective, or reflection on past events are also secondary sources.

1. Revisit the sources you have read in the unit. What kind of sources are they?

Criteria for Evaluating Sources

2. It is important to be able to identify if sources will help to strengthen your argument. Think about which search engines and terms you will use and how you will know that sources are credible and accurate. This task requires you to examine each source for credibility, accuracy, bias, and relevance. Use the following questions to evaluate sources for use for Embedded Assessment 1. Keep in mind that you should be able to analyze each source through one or multiple critical lenses.

Credibility

3. Who is the identified author?

_____

_____

4. What is the reputation of the author, publisher, or sponsor of the information?

_____

_____

5. What is the author's research technique?

_____

_____

6. Does the author cite sources that highlight different points of view?

_____

_____

7. Does the author address counterarguments?

_____

_____

8. How does the author's use of the following features impact his or her credibility?
- Multiple sources
- Headlines or captions
- Photos or other visuals

_____

_____

Bias

9. Are any of the following logical fallacies or rhetorical slanters evident in the source? How do these impact the reliability of the source?
- Emotional language
- Political leanings
- Missing information or selective use of facts
- Other (straw man, slippery slope, faulty analogy)

_____

_____

10. What does the text's publication context reveal about the author's agenda?

_____

_____

11. What might be the effect of this bias?

_____

_____

Accuracy

12. How does this source cover the content?
    - statistics and similar evidence that support the author's claims
    - relevant examples to support claims (from a peer-reviewed scientific study, for example)
    - experts cited or quoted to support the author's position
    - relevant information taken directly from primary sources

13. What quotations might you cite as support for your claims?

_____

_____

Relevance

14. Is the information relevant to your research?

    Is yes, then how?

    If no, then why not?

_____

_____

15. Has the information on this subject changed since the publication date?

_____

_____

16. How can you analyze the text through a critical lens?

_____

_____

☑ Check Your Understanding

Make a list of the resources you plan to use for your research paper. Do they pass the test for relevancy, accuracy, credibility, and absence of bias?

Ethical Use of Sources

When you paraphrase, summarize, or quote other people's work in your own, it is important to cite that work using the appropriate academic style. Not only does citing your sources help you avoid plagiarism, but it also gives your work credibility because it adheres to ethical standards of academic writing. This shows you have consulted experts to join a scholarly conversation.

Creating an Annotated Bibliography

17. An annotated bibliography is a list of references used in a work in which each reference includes a paragraph, or annotation, in order to provide readers additional information about the sources used to produce a piece of research. Use the samples that follow as models for the annotations you write for your sources. The following models show the MLA standard format for citing bibliographic information. Note that the examples include a summary of the source, an assessment of the usefulness of the source in providing information about a topic, and a reflection on how the source might be used to address the research question.

Magazine or Newspaper Article

Author(s). "Title of Article." *Title of Periodical*, Day Month Year: pages. Medium of publication.

Smith, Gregory J. "Science and the storms—the USGS response to the hurricanes of 2005." *U.S. Geological Survey Circular 1306*, 1 October 2007: 1–4. Web.

Smith provides a comprehensive assessment of the impacts of the 2005 hurricanes in the Gulf of Mexico as well as the important role of science in landscape restoration and community recovery. This work is relevant because it provides extensive information about the effects of Hurricane Katrina and comes from a reputable government source.

Website Entry

Author(s). "Article Title." *Name of Site*. Name of institution/organization affiliated with the site, date of resource creation (if available). Medium of publication. Date of access.

Blumberg, Alex. "After the Flood: Social Studies Lesson." *ThisAmericanLife.org*. WBEZ Chicago, 9 September 2005. Web. 4 May 2016.

In the days after the storm, radio producer Alex Blumberg interviews Ashley Nelson, an 18-year-old resident of one of New Orleans' many flooded neighborhoods. After listening to a clip from a news program claiming that the aftermath of Hurricane Katrina had more to do with class than race, Ashley reflects on the effect of socioeconomic status on residents' actions before and during the storm and their ability to survive after.

Film or Video Recording

Title of Film. Director, Distributor, Release year. Medium.

Trouble the Water. Directed by Carl Deal, Zeitgeist Films, 2008. DVD.

New Orleans residents record their efforts to weather Hurricane Katrina and their struggles to rebuild their lives in the aftermath of its devastation. The film provides a unique insiders' look into the city after the storm and examines how one community banded together to survive.

Independent Reading Checkpoint

Review the independent reading you have completed so far. Read any notes you took about how the texts discuss or explain the role of the media. Reflect on how you might use the information from these selections as you begin working on the Embedded Assessment. Share your observations with a group of peers.

Examining How an Issue Is Presented in Media Texts

 ASSIGNMENT

Your assignment is to write an argumentative essay that argues for the use of a particular critical lens to interpret an event. Your essay must include an annotated bibliography and evidence from at least five texts gathered alone or with your group members.

Planning and Prewriting: Take time to make a plan for your essay.	■ Which insights gained from learning about this event from multiple viewpoints can help you form a critical interpretation? ■ Which evidence from your sources will you need to support your interpretation and show the different ways the event is represented in the media?
Drafting: Determine the structure and how you will incorporate your evidence.	■ How will you craft a thesis so that your audience will understand your critical perspective and see how that perspective influences your response to the texts you are analyzing? ■ How can you use evidence to support your analysis of the event and how it is depicted? ■ How can you weave together engaging analysis and support to make your ideas and writing flow in a logical order? ■ How can you use varied and appropriate diction and syntax to enhance the rhetorical effectiveness of your claims?
Evaluating and Revising the Draft: Make your work the best it can be.	■ How will you use the Scoring Guide and peer responses to help guide your revision? ■ How can examining another writer's essay help you evaluate your own use of evidence and analysis?
Checking and Editing for Publication: Confirm that your final draft is ready.	■ How will you check for grammatical and technical accuracy? ■ What sort of outside resources can help you to check your citations and annotated bibliography? ■ How can you complete an effective final read-through of your essay?

Reflection

After completing this Embedded Assessment, think about how you went about accomplishing this assignment, and respond to the following:

- How did your own perspective on your chosen issue affect your work on this essay? Consider how you responded to each of the sources and their varied interpretations of the event.

SCORING GUIDE

Scoring Criteria	Exemplary	Proficient	Emerging	Incomplete
Ideas	The essay • effectively combines the sources and the writer's position to argue for using a particular lens to interpret a single event discussed in multiple texts • contextualizes the event and presents the critical lens in a clear thesis • includes a conclusion that suggests the larger significance of the writer's position on the event.	The essay • adequately combines the sources and the writer's position to argue for using a particular lens to interpret a single event discussed in multiple texts • briefly contextualizes the issue and identifies the critical lens in a straightforward thesis • concludes logically but repeats the thesis somewhat.	The essay • inadequately argues how a particular lens can be used to interpret a single event discussed in multiple texts • presents a weak thesis or one that is lost in a summary of sources • concludes by returning directly to the attempted thesis, or offers no conclusion.	The essay • provides a confusing argument on how a particular lens can be used to interpret a single event discussed in multiple texts • presents an incomplete thesis that summarizes rather than describes a position • offers no conclusion.
Structure	The essay • sequences material to reinforce the ideas of the argument • paraphrases and summarizes information from sources in a way that provides strong support for its claims. • uses transitions that enhance the essay's coherence • includes an extensive annotated bibliography.	The essay • sequences material to support the ideas of the argument • paraphrases and summarizes information from sources in a way that provides adequate support for its claims • uses transitions to move between ideas • includes a complete annotated bibliography.	The essay • organizes ideas ineffectively or jumps too rapidly between ideas • paraphrases and summarizes information from sources in a way that provides inadequate support for its claims • lacks effective transitions • includes an incomplete or inaccurate annotated bibliography.	The essay • organizes ideas ineffectively or jumps too rapidly between ideas • does not paraphrase or summarize information from sources to support its claims • does not use transitions • does not include an annotated bibliography.
Use of Language	The essay • demonstrates a mature style that advances the writer's ideas • employs precise diction and a skillful use of syntax and punctuation to create an authoritative and engaging voice • follows standard writing conventions, including accurate citation of sources.	The essay • demonstrates a style that adequately supports the writer's ideas • employs logical diction, clear syntax, and effective punctuation to create a suitable voice • largely follows standard writing conventions, including accurate citation of sources; minor errors do not interfere with meaning.	The essay • demonstrates a limited style that ineffectively supports the writer's ideas • includes lapses in diction, syntax, or punctuation which may make the writer's voice inconsistent • is affected by errors in standard writing conventions, which interfere with meaning.	The essay • demonstrates a limited style that ineffectively supports the writer's ideas • includes significant lapses in diction, syntax, or punctuation that reflect a confused writer's voice • contains numerous errors in standard writing conventions, which seriously interfere with meaning.

Unpacking Embedded Assessment 2

Learning Strategies

Close Reading
Graphic Organizer
Marking the Text

Learning Targets

- Reflect on concepts, essential questions, and vocabulary relating to the unit.
- Analyze the skills and knowledge needed to complete Embedded Assessment 2 successfully.
- Create a plan for reading independently.

Preview

In this activity, you will revisit this unit's Essential Questions, closely examine the Embedded Assessment 2 assignment, and plan your independent reading.

Making Connections

In the first part of this unit, you examined how various speakers and writers, including reporters, government officials, scientists, and ordinary citizens, contributed to an unfolding narrative about a single event: Hurricane Katrina. You studied the ways that ideological and critical perspectives may surface in the coverage of an event, and you evaluated how a particular critical perspective can help illuminate truths about an event of historical significance. In this part of the unit, you will shift from examining and researching others' texts to creating your own media text. You will collaborate with peers to create an engaging presentation that employs elements of classical speeches to persuade your audience.

Essential Questions

Based on your study of the first part of this unit, how would you answer these questions now?

1. How do media sources influence our understanding of the truth and significance of an issue?

2. How are media texts constructed to cater to media consumers' interests, experiences, assumptions, and biases or to promote a particular agenda?

Unpacking Embedded Assessment 2

Closely read the assignment for Embedded Assessment 2: Presenting an Argument.

Your assignment is to present an argument in a medium of your choice (persuasive speech, short documentary film, video news broadcast, podcast) in which you transform the information you gathered from your research in the first part of the unit into an argument concerning the topic/issue you have chosen. Your presentation should last five to seven minutes. It may be recorded or presented live.

With your classmates, identify the skills and knowledge you will need to complete this assessment successfully. Create a graphic organizer listing all the specific skills and knowledge.

🗔 Planning Independent Reading

For your independent reading during this part of the unit, consider reading additional informational texts related to the topic you will be addressing for the Embedded Assessment. Discuss with your group what information you should seek out in your independent reading in order to support the successful completion of a presentation for the Embedded Assessment.

My Notes

Learning Strategies

Graphic Organizer
Quickwrite
SOAPSTone

My Notes

Learning Targets

- Closely read and analyze a persuasive speech by considering the speaker's purpose, audience, and message.
- Critique and evaluate the characteristics and structural elements of a speech in a written review.

Preview

In this activity, you will read and closely analyze a persuasive speech by President George W. Bush to understand its structure, ideas, and persuasive elements. Then you will work with classmates to write a review of the speech.

About the Speech

President George W. Bush (b. 1946) delivered the following remarks to an audience at Warren Easton Charter High School in New Orleans, Louisiana on August 28, 2015. The former president, along with First Lady Laura Bush, first visited the school in 2006. They returned in 2015 as part of a series of events to mark the tenth anniversary of Hurricane Katrina. The school was the first public high school in the state of Louisiana and became a charter school during the reconstruction period after Hurricane Katrina.

As You Read

- Imagine the audience's reactions to the speech. Jot down notes in the margin to indicate where the audience might laugh or applaud.
- Circle unknown words or phrases. Try to determine the meaning of the words by using context clues, word parts, or a dictionary.

Speech

Remarks by President George W. Bush at Warren Easton Charter High School on the 10th Anniversary of Hurricane Katrina

by **President George W. Bush**

August 28, 2015

1 Thank you all. As has been mentioned, in 2006 Laura and I came here to Warren Easton Charter High School a year after Katrina hit, and we are honored and pleased to be back on the tenth anniversary of that devastating storm. I can't think of a better place to come here in New Orleans, except for

some of the restaurants. The slogan that guided the school when we first visited is true today: "We believe in success." And because of the success that schools like this have achieved, you have given all Americans reason to believe that New Orleans is back and better than ever.

…

2   In a cruel twist, Hurricane Katrina brought despair during what should have been a season of hope—the start of a new school year. Students who had recently gone back to school suddenly had no school to go back to. Many had nowhere to live. The floodwaters, as you all know better than most, claimed schools and homes alike. As Laura mentioned, the ground we're on today was underwater. All of us who are old enough to remember will never forget the images of our fellow Americans amid a sea of misery and ruin. We will always remember the lives lost across the Gulf Coast. Their memories are in our hearts—and I hope you pray for their families.

3   Hurricane Katrina is a story of loss beyond measure; it is also a story of commitment and compassion. I hope you remember what I remember, and that is 30,000 people were saved in the immediate aftermath of the storm by U.S. military personnel, by Louisiana law enforcement, and by citizens who volunteered. I hope you remember what I remember, and that is the thousands who came here on a volunteer basis to provide food for the hungry and to help find shelter for those who had no home to live in. There are people all around our country who prayed for you, many of whom showed up so they could say they helped a fellow citizen who was hurting.

4   One of the groups that stepped forward to serve were the educators of New Orleans. At a time when it would have been easy to walk away from the wreckage, the educators here today thought of the children who would be left behind. You understood that bringing New Orleans back to life required getting students back to school. And even though some of the educators had lost almost everything you owned, you let nothing stand in your way. Today, we celebrate the resurgence of New Orleans schools—and we honor the resilience of a great American city whose levees gave out but whose people never gave up.

5   Out of the devastation of Katrina, you vowed to do more than just open the schools. You vowed to challenge the status quo. Long before the great flood, too many students in this city drifted from grade to grade without ever learning the skills needed for success. Parents lacked choices and the power to intervene. Principals and teachers lacked the authority to chart a more hopeful course. It was a system that stranded more than sixty percent of students failing in schools. It was what I called the "soft bigotry of low expectations."

6   The decisions you made in the dark hours after Katrina sparked a decade of reform. Rather than just reopen the schools, you reorganized many into charter schools[1] that are independently operated but publicly accountable for achieving high standards. More than nine in ten public school students in this city now call a charter school home. Administrators at these schools have the

---

[1] A charter school is an independently operated, publicly funded school.

My Notes

WORD CONNECTIONS

Etymology

The term **status quo** comes from Latin and literally means "the state in which." In English, the term refers to the existing state of something, and it is often used negatively in political discourse to criticize acceptance of current conditions and the slow pace of social or political change. Reread paragraph 5 of the speech and look for Bush's use of the term *status quo*. What does he mean by it in this context?

freedom to slice through red tape and the freedom to innovate. Parents at these schools have choices if dissatisfied. And the results at these schools have been extraordinary. The reason we know is because we measure, and any attempt to undermine accountability in our school system does a huge disservice to the students who go to the schools in New Orleans.

7   According to a new report by the Cowen Institute, the percentage of New Orleans' students graduating on time has soared since Katrina. The percentage of students who attend schools that score better than the state average almost doubled, and so has the percentage of students meeting basic standards. And you've got to ask, "Why?" It just didn't happen. A lot of it was structural, and a lot of it requires strong leadership—people who stared into the eye of a storm and who refused to back down. And so Laura and I are here in New Orleans to remind our country about what strong leadership means, and we're here to salute the leaders.

8   I think of Jenny Rious here at Warren Easton. After Katrina, Jenny left New Orleans, was forced to leave New Orleans. She started a website called Warren Easton in Exile. The site reunited students scattered across the country around a vision for returning to New Orleans, and reopening this school. When Jenny returned to New Orleans, the first place she went was not her house. It was this school. And as she put it, "I would rather see my own house burn down than this school." Jenny would give anything for Easton and today, we give teachers like her our sincere thanks.

9   It's amazing what happened in this city after the storm wiped out the school system. Educational entrepreneurs decided to do something about the devastation, and the failure. I met a lot of them when I was President, and subsequent to my presidency. Neerav Kingsland is one such person. He took a leadership role at an organization called New Schools for New Orleans, where he worked with others to help launch dozens of new schools and to turn ideas into reform into reality. In other words, this isn't just a theoretical exercise. It's important for our country to look at New Orleans and realize this is an exercise of implementing a plan which works.

10   He—Neerav was so encouraged by what he sees here that he—he's talking up the reforms that worked to other cities across the country. Isn't it amazing—the storm that nearly destroys New Orleans, and yet now New Orleans is the beacon for school reform. Neerav represents the virtues that Bill Clinton and I had in mind when we announced the new Presidential Leadership Scholars program—and we're honored that Neerav was among the first class of scholars.

11   Achieving these results took librarians who salvaged their collections from the watery wreckage. Listen, I know something about librarians. I married one. I'm really proud of the Laura Bush Foundation. She talked about the grants; she talked about Pam and Marshall. These are citizens who supported this Foundation who, if they'd been in New Orleans, they didn't stay very long. And yet, like many around the country, they care deeply about the

future of this city. I hope the students here—I'm really thrilled you're here by the way and thank you for staying awake. I hope you realize the compassion of others in helping you realize a good education.

12 It turns out that every good school that's succeeding—a school that's succeeding—a school that's succeeding—and we know it's succeeding, because we measure against other standards—requires strong principals. And there's no doubt that Lexi Medley is a strong leader. I love when she says—when she says, "If you fail, we fail. The student's our product. We don't believe in putting out anything but the best." In order to succeed, in order to lead properly, you've got to set high goals and high expectations. And that's what Lexi and this school have done. As you heard, this school has graduated 100 percent of its seniors for the past five years. Lexi, you've earned our admiration and our gratitude, along with our best wishes for a happy birthday tomorrow.

13 It's the stories of schools like this one and others that we see a determination to rebuild better than before. And it—it's a spirit much stronger than any storm. It's a spirit that's lifted communities laid low by tornadoes or terrorist attacks. It's a spirit that I saw in New Orleans ten years ago, and that is very evident today.

14 We see that spirit in the population that has ticked back up as families settle back down. We see it in the tourists who are drawn here not only by this city's rich heritage but the new hotel rooms and restaurants. We see it in the spirit in Lauren LeDuff. As Laura mentioned—Lauren mentioned—Laura and I first met her in 2006 when she was a senior at Easton. She's happy to be back at the school she loved—she was happy to be back at the school she loved at the time. And you know what she told me? She said, "I want to be a teacher." And here she is as a member of this faculty, teaching English. I probably needed her when I was in high school. When asked how students have overcome adversity, Lauren says, "We teach our kids to be resilient. That's in the culture of this city."

15 Lauren's right. The resilience you teach at Warren Easton is the same resilience that this city showed the world in the wake of Hurricane Katrina. On this anniversary, the work of making a stronger and more hopeful New Orleans goes on. You've achieved a lot over the last ten years. And with belief in success, and a faith in God, New Orleans will achieve even more. The darkness from a decade ago has lifted. The Crescent City has risen again. And its best days lie ahead.

Former President Bush and Laura Bush visit Warren Easton Charter School in New Orleans, 2015.

My Notes

Making Observations
- What emotions does the speech evoke?
- Which statements in the speech are the most thought-provoking?

Working from the Text

1. Choose one or two of the questions you wrote during the first reading of this speech and pose them to your classmates in a small group discussion. Listen and respond as your classmates do the same with their questions. Jot down notes in the space to capture any new understanding or information gained from the questions.

2. With your group, use the **SOAPSTone** strategy to examine the speech "Remarks by President George W. Bush at Warren Easton Charter High School" more closely. Conduct on-the-spot research as needed to find additional details about the speech. Record your analysis and supporting textual evidence in the graphic organizer.

SOAPSTone	Analysis	Textual Support
Speaker What do you know about the speaker?		
Occasion What are the circumstances surrounding the speech?		

SOAPSTone	Analysis	Textual Support
Audience Who is the audience?		
Purpose What is the purpose of this speech?		
Subject What topic(s) is the speech about?		
Tone What is the speaker's tone?		

☑ Focus on the Sentence

Summarize the central thesis of President Bush's speech by expanding the short sentence.

Kernel: They improved schools.

Who? _____

When? _____

Where? _____

How? _____

Expanded Sentence:

_____

_____

Evaluating Characteristics and Structural Elements of a Speech

Now that you have examined the rhetorical context and central message of the speech, you will look more closely at its persuasive elements.

With your group, reread the speech to identify and evaluate the characteristics and structural elements listed in the chart. Use the guiding questions to drive your discussion and to help you assign a score to each characteristic or element. Be prepared to justify the score with evidence from the text and thoughtful analysis.

Characteristic or Element of Argument	Guiding Questions	Score 1 – not effective at all 5 – highly effective
Thesis	What is the thesis of the speech? Is the thesis clearly stated? Is it arguable?	
Evidence	What evidence is presented? Is the evidence credible? Is the evidence convincing?	
Appeals	What appeals to the audience's sense of logic, emotions, or ethics does the president use? How likely is it that each appeal would persuade the audience?	
Treatment of Counterarguments	To what extent does the president acknowledge and respond to counterarguments? How effective is the response to counterarguments?	
Structure of the Argument	How is the argument structured? Is the introduction clear and convincing? Does the argument unfold in a logical manner? Is there a convincing conclusion and call to action?	

3. Based on your group's evaluation of the characteristics and structural elements of the speech, come to consensus about an overall critique. How effective is President Bush's argument? What makes it effective and/or what would make it more effective?

4. Now that your group has evaluated the argumentative characteristics and elements of the speech, share your critique with the rest of the class. To what extent do other groups agree? Do any of the other groups present valid evidence that would convince you to modify your response?

☑ Check Your Understanding

Quickwrite: How can you apply your evaluation and critique of President Bush's speech to the development of your own argumentative speech for Embedded Assessment 2? What elements and characteristics of President Bush's speech might you use as a model? What will you try to do differently?

✍ Writing Prompt: Informational

Write a short review of the speech, "Remarks by President George W. Bush at Warren Easton Charter High School on the 10th Anniversary of Hurricane Katrina." The review should express a thoughtful, critical examination of the speech's argumentative characteristics and structural elements. Be sure to:

- Clearly state your overall critique of the speech.
- Use text evidence and thoughtful commentary to justify your evaluation.
- Write with well-chosen vocabulary and an appropriate level of formality.

My Notes

That Sounds Just Right

© 2021 College Board. All rights reserved.

Learning Strategies

Brainstorming
Discussion Groups
Graphic Organizer

My Notes

Learning Targets

- Participate in a collaborative discussion to plan the creation of an argumentative presentation.
- Analyze and evaluate the ways that presentation elements such as eye contact, speaking rate, enunciation, and gestures contribute to the effective delivery of a speech.

Preview

In this activity, you will work collaboratively to choose a medium through which to present your argument for Embedded Assessment 2. Then you will watch a video of a persuasive speech and evaluate the speaker's delivery.

Planning to Present

Before you actually develop your presentation—whether it takes the form of a documentary, a speech, or another medium—you should begin thinking about some of the basic components of a good plan. Carefully consider the rhetorical context of your presentation: your topic/issue, your audience, why you are writing/creating a work on this particular topic or issue.

1. Discuss the following questions with your group before you go further in planning your presentation.

   Topic/Issue: What is your topic/issue? What event, person, text, or conflict are you focusing on? What critical lens(es) are you using to illuminate that subject for your audience? What messages or interpretation do you wish to convey?

   Purpose: What is your purpose? What do you want your audience to think/feel/know/do as a result of viewing your text?

   Audience: Decide on an audience to whom you will address your argument. Settle on an identifiable audience that you expect will have some interest in your topic. Your target audience should extend beyond your teacher and the other students in your class.

   Speaker: Who are you as the speaker? What is your stake in the topic?

   Occasion: What is the occasion for the presentation of your argument? Are you developing it in response to an incident or event, or to celebrate or acknowledge a situation? Would this be shown in a theater, on television, or online?

   Tone: What tone will best help you achieve your desired purpose? What specific music, visuals, sound effects, language choices, and elements of speech could you use to establish your tone? What tone will evoke the desired response in your audience?

2. Taking into consideration your responses to the questions listed, what presentation format or medium will your group use to present your argument? Help move the group toward the goal of consensus by offering thoughtful and purposeful ideas and judgments as you discuss your options. Make sure you decide on the following:

- Brainstorm a list of media channels that you might use to present your various points of view. Which option would best allow your group to explore your subject?
- Will you present live or use a recorded format for your presentation?
- How will your chosen mode of delivery enable you to communicate your research findings effectively?
- What equipment or materials will your group need to create the presentation?
- How will each group member contribute?

☑ Check Your Understanding

Write down at least five steps you and your group will need to take to create your presentation. Then put a star next to the step you will take first.

Viewing a Speech

In the previous activity, you analyzed and evaluated the text of a speech by President George W. Bush. Now you will view a video of the same speech, or another speech selected by your teacher, paying close attention to the speaker's delivery.

3. When viewing the speech, record your observations and evaluation of the speaker's delivery.

Element of Delivery	Observations	Evaluation
Eye contact		
Speaking rate and pauses		
Volume		
Enunciation		
Gestures		

My Notes

4. With your presentation group, choose one paragraph from the speech and practice delivering it to your group, experimenting with the delivery elements listed in the graphic organizer. What is the effect when you vary the delivery? What makes for the most effective delivery?

5. Write statements summarizing your group's goals for the effective use of each delivery element.

Eye contact:

Speaking rate and pauses:

Volume:

Enunciation:

Gestures:

☑ Check Your Understanding

How will you apply the observations you made of President Bush's delivery to your own presentation?

Turning Research into Persuasion

Learning Targets

- Generate a clear plan for synthesizing information from research to create a coherent presentation that reflects depth of thought.
- Select an organizational structure strategically based on the purpose, audience, topic, and context of a presentation.
- Identify characteristics of your chosen presentation format and plan how to use those genre characteristics in the presentation.

Preview

In this activity, you will work collaboratively to plan elements of your presentation.

Learning Strategies

Brainstorming
Discussion Groups
Graphic Organizer

My Notes

Developing Your Media Text

1. **Revisiting Your Guiding Questions:** Review the guiding questions you previously generated as a group, and write the questions in the following space.

2. **Defining a Common Question:** Work together to define a common guiding question. The goal is to identify a question that is broad enough to be an umbrella under which each of your individual questions falls.

3. **Writing a Thesis Statement:** Once you have your central question, write a strong thesis statement that answers the question.

My Notes

4. **Synthesizing Research:** How will your group thoughtfully synthesize information from your research in order to create an effective argumentative presentation? What information is most useful for each part of the presentation? Are there any gaps in research that you could fill to strengthen your argument or your treatment of counterarguments?

5. **Evaluating Organizational Options:** Revisit the presentation you and other groups delivered for Activity 4.7. What organizational approaches worked best? Why? Which approaches might work best for your current text? What other options might work?

6. **Defining Roles:** Using your collective research on your issue, and considering the medium you have selected, decide what roles each group member will play. If you are creating a documentary, for example, who are your subjects or characters? If your presentation will take the form of a speech, who are the speakers? These may be actual people who were involved in or influenced by the event, or they may be composite characters that represent particular points of view. Decide in your group who will play each role.

INDEPENDENT READING LINK

Read and Connect

Choose one or more of your independent reading texts. Consider what elements from your independent reading text could serve as a model to influence the development of presentation. Select a passage that demonstrates a particularly strong use of structure, language, rhetorical choices, or organization, and share it with your group.

7. Identifying Conventions: Make a list of typical structural and stylistic **conventions** of the medium you have selected for your presentation. You might dissect a professional model to help you identify key features to emulate.

VOCABULARY

ACADEMIC

Conventions are the standard features, practices, and forms associated with the way something is usually done. Different media channels and types of media texts have different genre conventions.

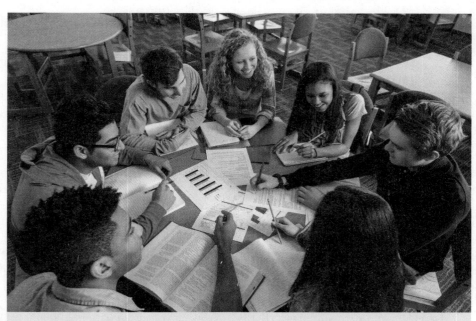

As your group considers the structural and stylistic conventions of your medium, offer ideas or judgments that will move the group toward its goal.

My Notes

Using Digital Media: To evaluate how best to apply digital media to your presentation, discuss the following questions within your group.

- What advantage does the use of digital media have over the use of print media in your presentation?
- How does the use of media impact the audience and their view of your reasoning and evidence?

8. Revising the Presentation: How can the Internet serve as a tool for production, publication, and collaboration? Brainstorm and list ideas and make decisions with your group.

9. Complete the Presentation Plan: Preview the Presentation Plan graphic organizer and then complete it with your group.

Presentation Plan		
Our thesis:		
Our chosen medium/format:		
Conventions of this medium/format:		
What will the audience see? What images will be shown? If filming a video, what angles, framing, and composition will be used?	**What will the audience hear?** What tone are we striving for? How will we use voice, music, or sound effects to achieve our purpose?	**What will the audience think/feel?** What rhetorical devices and appeals will we incorporate to persuade our audience? What will the audience learn? What will they believe/know after the presentation?

Voir Dire: Facing a Jury of Your Peers

Learning Targets

- Use a juror ballot to critically examine and provide feedback about a presentation.
- Reflect on feedback from peers in order to improve the effectiveness of a planned presentation.

Preview

In this activity, you will practice evaluating an argumentative presentation in preparation for serving as a peer jury during your classmates' presentations for Embedded Assessment 2.

Learning Strategies

Discussion Groups
Double-Entry Journal
Paraphrasing

WORD CONNECTIONS

Etymology

Voir dire is a legal term referring to the practice of questioning jurors to evaluate their suitability to serve on a jury. It is derived from an Old French term meaning "to speak the truth."

Juror Ballot

As other groups present their arguments to the class, you will use a juror ballot to take notes and ultimately evaluate their presentations. Becoming familiar with the ballot will not only help you use it effectively during others' presentations but will also help you in your own presentation planning.

1. As you watch a video that presents an argument, complete the following juror ballot. Assess the quality of the argumentative text and the degree to which you think it successfully engages and persuades the intended audience. Read through each section of the ballot before viewing.

Section 1: Make a Double-Entry Journal	
As you view the presentation, record observations you make, evidence you encounter, questions that come to mind, and your interpretations or responses. Be sure to note evidence of the critical perspective(s) that you see expressed through the presentation. Use the same close observation and analysis skills that you would bring to bear on a written text.	
Observations / Evidence / Questions	**Your Interpretation / Response**

Section 2: Identify the Argument

Paraphrase the group's thesis statement, record the main reasons and evidence they provide, and note any treatment of counterarguments.

Paraphrased Thesis:

Reasons and Evidence:

Treatment of Counterargument(s):

Section 3: Respond in a Quickwrite

After viewing the presentation, quickwrite your overall impressions. Be sure to praise the parts of the presentation that are done well.

Section 4: Evaluate the Presentation

For each of the areas listed, discuss the choices made by the group. How effective are these choices at supporting their argument with their target audience?

Structure of the Argument

Chosen Medium

Style and Conventions

Delivery / Production

Section 5: Write a Review

Write a review of the group's final product that shows a thoughtful critique and evaluation of the content and presentation of the argument. Address how effective you think the presentation would be at persuading the audience and illuminating the critical significance of their subject.

2. Partner with a classmate who is not in your presentation group. Compare notes from the juror ballot and briefly share your overall reviews of the video you viewed.

My Notes

3. Next, discuss questions or comments you have about using the ballot. How prepared do you feel to use the ballot while viewing classmates' presentations?

4. Continue working with your partner by exchanging the plans your groups have made so far for your argumentative presentations. Review your partner's plan, evaluating the likely effectiveness of the proposed plan and providing suggestions for how to make it more effective. You might reference the Scoring Guide for Embedded Assessment 2 as you evaluate their proposal.

☑ Check Your Understanding

Based on the feedback you received about your group's presentation plan, decide what changes or additions will make your planned presentation more effective. Write your ideas down and then share them with your presentation group.

⬡ Independent Reading Checkpoint

Review your independent reading selections. What questions can you ask about each text using the critical lenses you have studied? What new understanding or information emerges when you question the texts from these perspectives? Write a short reflection about which critical lenses have been the most revealing over the course of your reading in this unit and beyond. How will you continue using the lenses in your future readings?

Presenting an Argument

ASSIGNMENT

Your assignment is to present an argument in a medium of your choice (persuasive speech, short documentary film, video news broadcast, podcast) in which you transform the information you gathered from your research in the first part of the unit into an argument concerning the topic/issue you have chosen. Your presentation should last five to seven minutes. It may be recorded or presented live.

Planning and Prewriting: Take time to plan for your research and the structure of your presentation.	■ What roles are necessary for the presentation, and who will take on each role? ■ How will you divide up the writing tasks so that everyone has an equal share of work to do? ■ How can you ensure that the group works purposefully to maintain focus and move toward goals?
Drafting: Write a script and a plan for supporting information (visuals, media, etc.).	■ What genre conventions, including elements of classical speeches, will you follow as you create your presentation? ■ What other steps will you need to plan and complete besides writing the script (creating visuals, rehearsing, filming and editing if recording the performance)? ■ How will you appropriately display academic citations and use source materials ethically?
Evaluating and Revising: Create opportunities to review and revise your work.	■ What changes or additions do you need to make in order to ensure that the work of the different group members becomes one coherent presentation? ■ How can you use the feedback of others to improve your work? ■ How can you use the Scoring Guide as a resource to evaluate your draft?
Checking and Editing for Publication: Confirm that your final draft is ready for publication (or delivery).	■ How will you check for adherences to standard English conventions? ■ What sort of outside resources can help you to check your work? ■ How will you ensure that elements of delivery, such as eye contact, volume, and gestures, are used effectively?

Reflection

After completing this Embedded Assessment, think about how you went about accomplishing this assignment, and respond to the following:

- This assessment involved working as a team and combining the ideas of several people. How did the presence of multiple perspectives provide advantages for your group? How did it make the process more difficult?

Juror Ballot

As you view a group's presentation, you will complete this juror ballot. Your task is to assess the quality of the presentation you're viewing and the degree to which you believe it will successfully persuade the intended audience.

Section 1: Make a Double-Entry Journal	

As you view the presentation, record observations you make, evidence you encounter, questions that come to mind, and your interpretations or responses. Be sure to note evidence of the critical perspective(s) that you see expressed through the presentation. Use the same close observation and analysis skills that you would bring to bear on a written text.

Observations / Evidence / Questions	Your Interpretation / Response

Section 2: Identify the Argument	

Paraphrase the group's thesis statement, record the main reasons and evidence they provide, and note any treatment of counterarguments.

Paraphrased Thesis:

Reasons and Evidence:

Treatment of Counterargument(s):

Section 3: Respond in a Quickwrite

After viewing the presentation, quickwrite your overall impressions. Be sure to praise the parts of the presentation that are done well.

Section 4: Evaluate the Presentation

For each of the areas listed, discuss the choices made by the group. How effective are these choices at supporting their argument with their target audience?

Structure of the Argument

Chosen Medium

Style and Conventions

Delivery / Production

Section 5: Write a Review

Write a review of the group's final product that shows a thoughtful critique and evaluation of the content and presentation of the argument. Address how effective you think the presentation would be at persuading the audience and illuminating the critical significance of their subject.

SCORING GUIDE

Scoring Criteria	Exemplary	Proficient	Emerging	Incomplete
Ideas	The presentation • reveals an insightful analysis and mature understanding of the topic through a script and an annotated bibliography • demonstrates thorough investigation, insightful application of the lenses, and thoughtful understanding of the topic • includes a reflective text that demonstrates a thorough and detailed analysis of the entire process.	The presentation • demonstrates careful analysis and clear understanding of the topic • demonstrates adequate investigation, application of the lenses, and clear understanding of the topic • includes a reflective text that demonstrates adequate analysis of the process.	The presentation • reveals a limited analysis and understanding of the topic • demonstrates inadequate investigation and/or misunderstanding of the lenses or how they apply • includes a reflective text that demonstrates inadequate analysis of the complete process.	The presentation • reveals little or no analysis and/or understanding of the topic • demonstrates inadequate investigation and/or misunderstanding of the lenses or how they apply • does not include a reflective text.
Structure	The presentation • is organized in a precisely appropriate way that enhances the intended message for the target audience • features a polished presentation that creates focus and maintains energy • demonstrates equal sharing of responsibility.	The presentation • is organized appropriately for the selected presentation format and makes clear the intended message • features an organized, coherent presentation • demonstrates sharing of responsibility that is mostly balanced.	The presentation • is organized inappropriately for the selected presentation format and may convey an unclear message • includes a disorganized presentation • demonstrates an unequal division of responsibilities.	The presentation • does not use the selected presentation format appropriately • includes a confusing and disorganized presentation • demonstrates an unequal division of responsibilities.
Use of Language	The presentation • demonstrates a mature style that advances the group's ideas • crafts language that is precisely appropriate to the media channel.	The presentation • demonstrates a style that adequately supports the group's ideas • crafts language that is appropriate to the media channel.	The presentation • demonstrates a limited style that ineffectively supports the group's ideas • includes language that is inappropriate to the media channel.	The presentation • demonstrates confusing language that does not support the group's ideas • includes language that is inappropriate for the media channel and presents the topic inaccurately.

Resources

Independent Reading

Learning Strategies

Graphic Organizers

English-Spanish Glossary

Index of Skills

Index of Authors and Titles

Suggestions for Independent Reading

This list, divided into the categories of **Literature** and **Nonfiction/Informational Text**, comprises titles related to the themes and content of the unit. For your independent reading, you can select from this wide array of titles, which have been chosen based on complexity and interest. You can do your own research and select titles that intrigue you.

Unit 1 Independent Reading List: Perception Is Everything

Literature		
Author	Title	Lexile
Bray, Libba	*Going Bovine*	680L
Conrad, Joseph	*Heart of Darkness*	1050L
Cunningham, Michael	*The Hours*	960L
Defoe, Daniel	*Robinson Crusoe*	920L
Far, Sui Sin	*Mrs. Spring Fragrance: A Collection of Chinese-American Short Stories*	N/A
Greene, Graham	*Brighton Rock*	680L
Huxley, Aldous	*Brave New World*	870L
Jordan, Hillary	*Mudbound*	N/A
Kingsolver, Barbara	*The Poisonwood Bible*	960L
Kitamura, Katie	*A Separation*	N/A
Lahiri, Jhumpa	*The Namesake*	1140L
McEwen, Ian	*Atonement*	N/A
Nguyen, Viet Thanh	*The Sympathizer*	N/A
Orwell, George	*Down and Out in Paris and London*	1020L
Orwell, George	*Rebelión en la granja*	1030L
Paton, Alan	*Cry, the Beloved Country*	860L
Plath, Sylvia	*The Bell Jar*	1140L
Salinger, J.D.	*Nine Stories*	N/A
Shihab Nye, Naomi	*19 Varieties of Gazelle: Poems of the Middle East*	N/A
Stevenson, Robert Louis	*The Strange Case of Dr. Jekyll and Mr. Hyde*	1060L

Nonfiction/Informational		
Author	Title	Lexile
Baldwin, James	*The Fire Next Time*	1300L
Bartolettii, Susan Campbell	*Growing Up In Coal Country*	1110L
Cofer, Judith Ortiz	*The Latin Deli: Telling the Lives of Barrio Women*	N/A
Culler, Jonathan	*Literary Theory: A Very Short Introduction*	1370L
Friedan, Betty	*The Feminine Mystique*	N/A
Galbraith, John	*The Affluent Society*	N/A
Goleman, Daniel	*Emotional Intelligence: Why It Can Matter More Than IQ*	N/A
Hershey, John	*Hiroshima*	1190L
James, Henry	*Varieties of Religious Experience*	1360L

Lewis, Michael	*Moneyball*	N/A
McCourt, Frank	*Angela's Ashes: A Memoir*	1110L
Mukherjee, Siddhartha	*The Emperor of All Maladies: A Biography of Cancer*	N/A
Paravisini-Gebert, Lizabeth	*Jamaica Kincaid: A Critical Companion*	1530L
Riis, Jacob	*How the Other Half Lives*	N/A
Vonnegut, Kurt	*A Man Without a Country*	N/A
Wallace, David Foster	*A Supposedly Fun Thing I'll Never Do Again*	N/A
Watson, James	*The Double Helix: A Personal Account of the Discovery of the Structure of DNA*	1201L
Wright, Richard	*Black Boy*	950L

Unit 2 Independent Reading List: The Power of Persuasion

Literature		
Author	Title	Lexile
Albee, Edward	*Who's Afraid of Virginia Woolf?*	N/A
Amis, Kingsley	*Lucky Jim*	930L
Austen, Jane	*Sense and Sensibility*	1180L
Bolt, Robert	*A Man for All Seasons: A Play in Two Acts*	N/A
Brontë, Charlotte	*Jane Eyre*	1040L
Butler, Octavia E.	*Parable of the Sower*	710L
Chopin, Kate	*The Awakening*	960L
Fitzgerald, F. Scott	*The Beautiful and the Damned*	1040L
Gilmore, Charlotte Perkins	*The Yellow Wallpaper*	920L
Greene, Graham	*The Quiet American*	800L
Hansberry, Lorraine	*A Raisin in the Sun*	N/A
Harris, Joanne	*Chocolat*	N/A
Homer	*La Iliada*	930L
Homer	*The Illiad*	1330L
Krisher, Trudy	*Uncommon Faith*	N/A
Leiva, Ángel	*El túnel*	920L
Martin, Richard P.	*Myths of the Ancient Greeks*	N/A
O'Neill, Eugene	*Long Day's Journey Into Night*	N/A
Shelley, Mary	*Frankenstein*	1170L
Steinbeck, John	*Grapes of Wrath*	680L
Uhry, Alfred	*Driving Miss Daisy*	N/A
Walker, Alice	*The Color Purple*	670L
Williams, Tennessee	*Cat on a Hot Tin Roof*	N/A
Woolrich, Cornell	*The Cornell Woolrich Omnibus*	N/A

Nonfiction/Informational		
Author	**Title**	**Lexile**
Bodanis, David	$E = MC^2$: A Biography of the World's Most Famous Equation	1170L
Chesterton, G.K.	George Bernard Shaw	N/A
Gray, Richard	Archetypal Explorations: An Integrative Approach to Human Behavior	1310L
Iaccino, James F.	Jungian Reflections Within the Cinema: A Psychological Analysis of Sci-Fi and Fantasy Archetypes	1510L
Kolbenschlag, Madonna	Kiss Sleeping Beauty Goodbye	N/A
Koloski, Bernard	The Historian's Awakening: Reading Kate Chopin's Classic Novel as Social and Cultural History	N/A
Levine, Lawrence W.	The Unpredictable Past: Explorations in American Cultural History	1460L
Mamet, David	On Directing Film	N/A
Murch, Walter	In the Blink of an Eye: A Perspective on Film Editing	N/A
Pomerance, Murray	An Eye for Hitchcock	1410L
Pratt, Annis	Archetypal Patterns in Women's Fiction	1540L
Roller, Judi M.	The Politics of the Feminist Novel	1290L
Sayers, Sean	Marxism and Human Nature	1250L
Strauss, Rochelle	One Well: The Story of Water on Earth	960L
von Franz, Marie-Louise	Archetypal Patterns in Fairy Tales	N/A

Unit 3 Independent Reading List: Evolving Perspectives

Literature		
Author	**Title**	**Lexile**
Atwood, Margaret	The Handmaid's Tale	750L
Bellow, Saul	Herzog	850L
Brontë, Charlotte	Jane Eyre	1040L
Brontë, Charlotte	Jane Eyre (Spanish)	1040L
Coetzee, J.M.	Waiting for the Barbarians	930L
Dostoevsky, Fyodor	The Eternal Husband and Other Stories	N/A
Hardy, Thomas	Tess of the D'Urbervilles	1110L
Hosseini, Khaled	The Kite Runner	840L
Kafka, Franz	The Metamorphosis	1340L
Lester, Julius	Othello: A Novel	770L
Lloyd, Rosemary	Closer and Closer Apart: Jealousy in Literature	1600L
Morrison, Toni	The Bluest Eye	920L
Naslund, Sena Jeter	Ahab's Wife: Or, The Star-gazer: A Novel	N/A
Robbe-Grillet, Alain	Jealousy	N/A

Roy, Arundhati	The God of Small Things	840L
Shakespeare, William	Otelo: el moro de Venecia	NP
Soyinka, Wole	Death and the King's Horseman: A Play	NP
Stevenson, Robert Louis	El extraño caso del doctor Jekyll y el señor Hyde	1110L
Stevenson, Robert Louis	The Strange Case of Dr. Jekyll and Mr. Hyde	1060L
Stoppard, Tom	Rosencrantz and Guildenstern Are Dead	NP

Nonfiction/Informational

Author	Title	Lexile
Andraka, Jack	Breakthrough: How One Teen Innovator Is Changing the World	940L
Berger, Arthur A.	Cultural Criticism: A Primer of Key Concepts	N/A
Cooper, Alex	Saving Alex: When I Was Fifteen I Told My Mormon Parents I Was Gay, and That's When My Nightmare Began	N/A
Bernard, Jacqueline	Journey Toward Freedom: Sojourner Truth	N/A
de Pizan, Christine	The Treasure of the City of Ladies	N/A
Gladwell, Malcolm	The Tipping Point: How Little Things Can Make a Big Difference	1160L
Grandin, Temple	Animals in Translation	1130L
Harper, Hill	Letters to a Young Brother: Manifest Your Destiny	N/A
Hodgdon, Barbara	The Shakespeare Trade: Performances and Appropriations	N/A
Janik, Vicki (editor)	Fools and Jesters in Literature, Art, and History	1380L
Johnson, David	Shakespeare and South Africa	1640L
Kerrigan, John (editor)	Motives of Woe: Shakespeare and 'Female Complaint'	1330L
Loomba, Ania and Martin Orkina (editors)	Post-Colonial Shakespeares	N/A
Maolem, Sharon	Inheritance: How Our Genes Change Our Lives - and Our Lives Change Our Genes	N/A
O'Hagan, Andrew	The Secret Life: Three True Stories of the Digital Age	N/A
Suzman, Janet	Not Hamlet: Meditations on the Frail Position of Women in Drama	N/A
Winoker, Jon	The Big Book of Irony	N/A
Tannen, Deborah	Gender and Discourse	1270L
Wells, Stanley (editor)	Shakespeare in the Theater: An Anthology of Criticism	1360L
Woolf, Virginia	A Room of One's Own	1220L

Unit 4 Independent Reading List: An American Journey

Literature		
Author	**Title**	**Lexile**
Adichie, Chimamanda Ngozi	*Americanah*	N/A
Brown, Don	*Drowned City*	920L
Calvino, Italo	*Invisible Cities*	1290L
Coelho, Paulo	*The Alchemist*	910L
Egger, Dave	*Zeitoun*	840L
Golding, William	*El señor de las moscas*	760L
Hawkins, Paula	*The Girl on the Train*	760L
Henriques, Diana	*The Wizard of Lies: Bernie Madoff and the Death of Trust*	N/A
Kessler, Lauren	*Clever Girl*	N/A
McCann, Colum	*Let the Great World Spin*	N/A
McLean, Bethany and Peter Elkind	*The Smartest Guys in the Room: The Amazing Rise and Scandalous Fall of Enron*	N/A
Mitchell, David	*Ghostwritten*	N/A
Moore, Alan	*The Watchmen*	N/A
Morrison, Toni	*Song of Solomon*	870L
Pérez, Ashley Hope	*Out of Darkness*	660L
Volponi, Paul	*Hurricane Song*	850L
Ward, Jesmyn	*Salvage the Bones*	890L
Woolf, Virginia	*To the Lighthouse*	1030L

Nonfiction/Informational		
Author	**Title**	**Lexile**
Atkins, Larry	*Skewed: A Critical Thinker's Guide to Media Bias*	N/A
Baum, Dan	*Nine Lives: Mystery, Magic, Death, and Life in New Orleans*	N/A
Bowden, Mark	*The Finish Line*	N/A
Brinkley, Douglas	*The Great Deluge: Hurricane Katrina, New Orleans, and the Mississippi Gulf Coast*	N/A
Dineen, Jacqueline	*Huracanes y tifones (Hurricanes and Typhoons)*	
Diamond, Jared	*Guns, Germs, and Steel: The Fates of Human Societies*	1440L
Donovan, Sandy	*Media: From News Coverage to Political Advertising*	1150L
Fink, Sheri	*Five Days at Memorial*	N/A
Foster, Thomas C.	*How to Read Literature Like a Professor*	820L
Goldberg, Bernard	*A Slobbering Love Affair: The True (And Pathetic) Story of the Torrid Romance Between Barack Obama and the Mainstream Media*	N/A
Greenwald, Glenn	*No Place to Hide: Edward Snowden, the NSA, and the U.S. Surveillance State*	N/A
Konnikova, Maria	*Mastermind: How to Think Like Sherlock Holmes*	N/A
Krakauer, Jon	*Into Thin Air*	

Lule, Jack	*Globalization and Media: Global Village of Babel*	N/A
Momaday, N. Scott	*The Way to Rainy Mountain*	890L
Moore, Wes	*The Other Wes Moore*	990L
Obama, Barack	*Dreams from My Father: A Story of Race and Inheritance*	N/A
Rose, Chris	*1 Dead in Attic*	N/A
Sloan, Wm. David and Jenn Burleson Mackay (editors)	*Media Bias: Finding It, Fixing It*	N/A
Thompson, Neal	*Hurricane Season: A Coach, His Team, and Their Triumph in the Time of Katrina*	1120L

Independent Reading Log

Directions: This log is a place to record your progress and thinking about your independent reading during each unit. Add your log pages to your Reader/Writer Notebook or keep them as a separate place to record your reading insights.

Unit _____

Independent Reading Title _____

Author(s) _____ Text Type _____

Pages read: from _____ to _____

_____
_____
_____
_____
_____
_____

Independent Reading Title _____

Author(s) _____ Text Type _____

Pages read: from _____ to _____

_____
_____
_____
_____
_____
_____

Independent Reading Title _____

Author(s) _____ Text Type _____

Pages read: from _____ to _____

_____
_____
_____
_____
_____
_____
_____

Unit _____

Independent Reading Title _____

Author(s) _____ Text Type _____

Pages read: from _____ to _____

_____

_____

_____

_____

_____

Independent Reading Title _____

Author(s) _____ Text Type _____

Pages read: from _____ to _____

_____

_____

_____

_____

_____

Independent Reading Title _____

Author(s) _____ Text Type _____

Pages read: from _____ to _____

_____

_____

_____

_____

_____

Independent Reading Title _____

Author(s) _____ Text Type _____

Pages read: from _____ to _____

_____

_____

_____

_____

_____

Learning Strategies

Reading Strategies

STRATEGY	DEFINITION	PURPOSE
Activating Prior Knowledge	Providing an opportunity for students to think about what they already know about a concept, place, person, culture, and so on, and share their knowledge with a wider audience	To prepare students to encounter new concepts, places, persons, cultures, and so on, prior to reading a text; an Anticipation Guide and a Quickwrite can be used to activate and assess prior knowledge
Chunking the Text	Breaking the text into smaller, manageable units of sense (e.g., words, sentences, paragraphs) by numbering, separating phrases, drawing boxes	To reduce the intimidation factor when encountering long words, sentences, or whole texts; to increase comprehension of difficult or challenging text
Close Reading	Accessing small chunks of text to read, reread, mark, and annotate key passages, word-for-word, sentence-by-sentence, and line-by-line	To develop comprehensive understanding by engaging in one or more focused readings of a text
Diffusing	Reading a passage, noting unfamiliar words, discovering meaning of unfamiliar words using context clues, dictionaries, and/or thesauruses, using context to distinguish between denotative and connotative meanings, and replacing unfamiliar words with familiar ones	To facilitate a close reading of text, the use of resources, an understanding of synonyms, and increased comprehension of text
Double-Entry Journal	Creating a two-column journal with a student-selected passage in one column and the student's response in the second column (e.g., asking questions of the text, forming personal responses, interpreting the text, reflecting on the process of making meaning of the text)	To assist in note-taking and organizing key textual elements and responses noted during reading in order to generate textual support that can be incorporated into a piece of writing at a later time
Graphic Organizer	Using a visual representation for the organization of information from the text	To facilitate increased comprehension and discussion
Guided Reading	Identifying and modeling a series of strategies to guide students through challenging text (e.g., making predictions, marking the text, skimming the text, diffusing vocabulary)	To model for students the use of multiple strategies to make meaning of challenging texts and help them learn to apply the strategies independently
KWHL Chart	Setting up discussion that allows students to activate prior knowledge by answering, "What do I **know**?"; sets a purpose by answering, "What do I **want** to know?"; helps preview a task by answering, "**How** will I learn it?"; and reflects on new knowledge by answering, "What have I **learned**?"	To organize thinking, access prior knowledge, and reflect on learning to increase comprehension and engagement
Marking the Text	Selecting text by highlighting, underlining, and/or annotating for specific components, such as main idea, imagery, literary devices, and so on	To focus reading for specific purposes, such as author's craft, and to organize information from selections; to facilitate reexamination of a text

STRATEGY	DEFINITION	PURPOSE
Metacognitive Markers	Responding to text with a system of cueing marks where students use a ? for questions about the text; a ! for reactions related to the text; an * for comments about the text; and an underline to signal key ideas	To track responses to texts and use those responses as a point of departure for talking or writing about texts
Note-taking	Making notes about a text to use in a written response	To remember key ideas and information, track connections made to the text, log questions and observations, and gather evidence to use later in writing assignments
OPTIC	Strategy for evaluating visual images. **O** (Overview): Write notes on what the visual appears to be about. **P** (Parts): Zoom in on the parts of the visual and describe any elements or details that seem important. **T** (Title): Highlight the words of the title of the visual (if one is available). **I** (Interrelationships): Use the title as the theory and the parts of the visual as clues to detect and specify how the elements of the graphic are related. **C** (Conclusion): Draw a conclusion about the visual as a whole. What does the visual mean? Summarize the message of the visual in one or two sentences.	To analyze graphic and visual images as forms of text
Predicting	Making guesses about the text by using the title and pictures and/or thinking ahead about events that may occur based on evidence in the text	To help students become actively involved, interested, and mentally prepared to understand ideas
Previewing	Examining a text's structure, features, layout, format, questions, directions, prior to reading	To gain familiarity with the text, make connections to the text, and extend prior knowledge to set a purpose for reading
QHT	Expanding prior knowledge of vocabulary words by marking words with a **Q**, **H**, or **T** (Q signals words students do not know; H signals words students have heard and might be able to identify; T signals words students know well enough to teach to their peers)	To allow students to build on their prior knowledge of words, to provide a forum for peer teaching and learning of new words, and to serve as a prereading exercise to aid in comprehension
Questioning the Text	Developing levels of questions about text; that is, literal, interpretive, and universal questions that prompt deeper thinking about a text before, during, or after reading	To engage more actively and independently with texts, read with greater purpose and focus, and ultimately answer questions to gain greater insight into the text; helps students to comprehend and interpret

STRATEGY	DEFINITION	PURPOSE
Paraphrasing	Restating in one's own words the essential information expressed in a text, whether it be narration, dialogue, or informational text, while maintaining the original text's meaning	To encourage and facilitate comprehension of challenging text
RAFT	Primarily used to generate new text, this strategy can also be used to analyze a text by examining the role of the speaker (R), the intended audience (A), the format of the text (F), and the topic of the text (T)	To initiate reader response; to facilitate an analysis of a text to gain focus prior to creating a new text
Rereading	Encountering the same text with more than one reading	To identify additional details; to clarify meaning and/or reinforce comprehension of texts
SIFT	Analyzing a fictional text by examining stylistic elements, especially symbol, imagery, and figures of speech in order to show how all work together to reveal tone and theme	To focus and facilitate an analysis of a fictional text by examining the title and text for symbolism, identifying images and sensory details, analyzing figurative language, and identifying how all these elements reveal tone and theme
Skimming/Scanning	Skimming by rapid or superficial reading of a text to form an overall impression or to obtain a general understanding of the material; scanning focuses on key words, phrases, or specific details and provides speedy recognition of information	To quickly form an overall impression prior to an in-depth study of a text; to answer specific questions or quickly locate targeted information or detail in a text
SMELL	Analyzing a persuasive speech or essay by asking five essential questions: • **S**ender-receiver relationship—What is the sender-receiver relationship? Who are the images and language meant to attract? Describe the speaker of the text. • **M**essage—What is the message? Summarize the statement made in the text. • **E**motional Strategies—What is the desired effect? • **L**ogical Strategies—What logic is operating? How does it (or its absence) affect the message? Consider the logic of the images as well as the words. • **L**anguage—What does the language of the text describe? How does it affect the meaning and effectiveness of the writing? Consider the language of the images as well as the words.	To analyze a persuasive speech or essay by focusing on five essential characteristics of the genre; analysis is related to rhetorical devices, logical fallacies, and how an author's use of language achieves specific purposes

STRATEGY	DEFINITION	PURPOSE
SOAPSTone	Analyzing text by discussing and identifying **S**peaker, **O**ccasion, **A**udience, **P**urpose, **S**ubject, and **Tone**	To facilitate the analysis of specific elements of nonfiction, literary, and informational texts, and show the relationship among the elements to an understanding of the whole
Summarizing	Giving a brief statement of the main points or essential information expressed in a text, whether it be narration, dialogue, or informational text	To facilitate comprehension and recall of a text
Think Aloud	Talking through a difficult passage or task by using a form of metacognition whereby the reader expresses how he/she has made sense of the text	To reflect on how readers make meaning of challenging texts and to facilitate discussion
TP-CASTT	Analyzing a poetic text by identifying and discussing **T**itle, **P**araphrase, **C**onnotation, **A**ttitude, **S**hift, **T**heme, and **T**itle again	To facilitate the analysis of specific elements of a literary text, especially poetry. To show how the elements work together to create meaning
Visualizing	Forming a picture (mentally and/or literally) while reading a text to deepen understanding	To increase reading comprehension, deepen understanding, and promote active engagement with text
Word Maps	Using a clearly defined graphic organizer such as concept circles or word webs to identify and reinforce word meanings	To provide a visual tool for identifying and remembering multiple aspects of words and word meanings
Word Sort	Organizing and sorting words into categories designated by the teacher or selected by the student and providing a written or oral justification for the classifications	To solidify understanding of word meanings by considering the multiple uses, meanings, and relationships of word parts, words, and groups of words

Writing Strategies

STRATEGY	DEFINITION	PURPOSE
Adding	Enhancing a text by finding areas to add facts, details, examples, and commentary; smoothing out transitions; and clarifying and strengthening ideas and assertions	To improve, refine, and clarify the writer's thoughts during drafting and/or revision
Brainstorming	Using a flexible but deliberate process of listing multiple ideas in a short period of time without excluding any idea from the preliminary list	To generate ideas, concepts, or key words that provide a focus and/or establish organization as part of the prewriting or revision process
Deleting	Enhancing a text by eliminating words, phrases, sentences, or ideas that inhibit clarity and cohesiveness	To improve, refine, and clarify the writer's thoughts during drafting and/or revision
Drafting	Composing a text in its initial form before developing it	To incorporate brainstormed or initial ideas into a written format
Freewriting	Writing freely without constraints in order to generate ideas and capture thinking	To generate ideas when planning a piece of writing, or to refine and clarify thoughts, spark new ideas, and/or generate content during drafting and/or revision
Generating Questions	Clarifying and developing ideas by asking questions of the draft. May be part of self-editing or peer editing	To clarify and develop ideas in a draft; used during drafting and as part of writer response
Graphic Organizer	Organizing ideas and information visually (e.g., Venn diagrams, flowcharts, cluster maps)	To provide a visual system for organizing multiple ideas, details, and/or textual support to be included in a piece of writing
Guided Writing	Modeling the writing that students are expected to produce by guiding students through the planning, generation of ideas, organization, drafting, revision, editing, and publication of texts before students are asked to perform the same process; coconstructing texts with students as part of guided writing	To demonstrate the writing process

Speaking and Listening Strategies

STRATEGY	DEFINITION	PURPOSE
Choral Reading	Reading text lines aloud in student groups and/or individually to present an interpretation	To develop fluency; differentiate between the reading of statements and questions; practice phrasing, pacing, and reading dialogue; show how a character's emotions are captured through vocal stress and intonation
Debate	Engaging in a structured argument to examine both sides of an issue	To provide students with an opportunity to collect and orally present evidence supporting the affirmative and negative arguments of a proposition or issue
Drama Games	Participating in creative dramatics (e.g., pantomime, tableau, role-playing) to reinforce an oral literacy skill or develop a deeper understanding of a concept	To engage students in the reading and presenting of text and to create meaning through a kinesthetic approach
Fishbowl (Inner/outer circles)	Discussing specific topics within groups; some students will form the inner circle and model appropriate discussion techniques while an outer circle of students listens to and evaluates the discussion process of the inner circle in order to respond effectively	To provide students with an opportunity to engage in a formal discussion and to experience roles both as participant and active listener; students also have the responsibility of supporting their opinions and responses using specific textual evidence
Note-taking	Creating a record of information while listening to a speaker or reading a text	To facilitate active listening or close reading; to record and organize ideas that assist in processing information
Oral Reading	Reading aloud one's own text or the texts of others (e.g., echo reading, choral reading, paired readings)	To share one's own work or the work of others; build fluency and increase confidence in presenting to a group
Rehearsal	Encouraging multiple practices of a piece of text prior to a performance	To provide students with an opportunity to clarify the meaning of a text prior to a performance as they refine the use of dramatic conventions (e.g., gestures, vocal interpretations, facial expressions)
Role-Playing	Assuming the role or persona of a character	To develop the voice, emotions, and mannerisms of a character to facilitate improved comprehension of a text
Socratic Seminar	Tying a focused discussion to an essential question, topic, or selected text in which students ask questions of each other; questions initiate a conversation that continues with a series of responses and additional questions	To help students formulate questions that address issues (in lieu of simply stating their opinions) to facilitate their own discussion and arrive at a new understanding; students also have the responsibility of supporting their opinions and responses using specific textual evidence

Collaborative Strategies

STRATEGY	DEFINITION	PURPOSE
Discussion Groups	Engaging in an interactive, small-group discussion, often with an assigned role; to consider a topic, text, or question	To gain new understanding of or insight into a text from multiple perspectives
Jigsaw	In groups, students read different texts or passages from a single text, then share and exchange information from their reading with another group. They then return to their original groups to share their new knowledge.	To summarize and present information to others in a way that facilitates an understanding of a text (or multiple texts) without having each student read the text in its entirety
Literature Circles	Groups of students read the same text to participate in a mutual reading experience; based on the objective(s) of the lesson, students take on a variety of roles throughout the reading experience; texts may be selected based on individual preferences or on the demands of the text.	To provide opportunities for students to interact with one another as they read, respond to, and interpret a common text
Think-Pair-Share	Pairing with a peer to share ideas before sharing ideas and discussion with a larger group	To construct meaning about a topic or question; to test thinking in relation to the ideas of others; to prepare for a discussion with a larger group

Graphic Organizer Directory

Contents

Active Listening Feedback

Presenter's name: _____

Content

What is the presenter's purpose? _____

What is the presenter's main point? _____

Do you agree with the presenter? Why or why not? _____

_____

_____

Form

Did the presenter use a clear, loud voice? ☐ yes ☐ no

Did the presenter make eye contact? ☐ yes ☐ no

One thing I really liked about the presentation:

_____

_____

_____

One question I still have:

_____

_____

_____

Other comments or notes:

Active Listening Notes

Title: _____

Who?

What?

Where?

When?

Why?

How?

Audience Notes and Feedback

Scoring Criteria	Notes/Feedback
Introduction/ Conclusion	
Timing	
Voice	
Eye Contact/ Gestures	
Use of Media, Visuals, Props	
Audience Engagement	

Cause and Effect

Title: _____

Cause: What happened?

Effect: An effect of this is

Cause: What happened?

Effect: An effect of this is

Cause: What happened?

Effect: An effect of this is

Cause: What happened?

Effect: An effect of this is

Character Map

Character name: _____

What does the character look like?

How does the character act and feel?

What do other characters say or think about the character?

Collaborative Dialogue

● Topic: _____

Use the space below to record ideas.

"Wh-" Prompts
Who?   What?   Where?   When?   Why?

Speaker 1

Speaker 2

Conclusion Builder

Evidence

Evidence

Evidence

Based on this evidence, I can conclude

Conflict Map

Title: _____

What is the main conflict in this story?

What causes this conflict?

How is the conflict resolved?

What are some other ways the conflict could have been resolved?

Conversation for Quickwrite

1. Turn to a partner and restate the prompt in your own words.

2. Brainstorm key words to use in your quickwrite response.

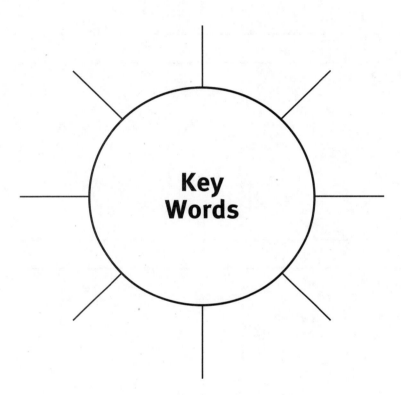

3. Take turns explaining your ideas to your partner. Try using some of the key words you brainstormed.

4. On your own, write a response to the quickwrite.

Definition and Reflection

Academic Vocabulary Word
Definition in own words
Illustration (literal or symbolic)

My experiences with this concept:

- I haven't really thought about this concept.

_____

- I have only thought about this concept in English Language Arts class.

_____

- I have applied this concept in other classes.

_____

- I have applied this concept outside of school.

_____

My level of understanding:

- I am still trying to understand this concept.

_____

- I am familiar with this concept, but I am not comfortable applying it.

_____

- I am very comfortable with this concept and I know how to apply it.

_____

- I could teach this concept to another classmate.

_____

Discourse Starters

Questioning and Discussing a Text

One question I have is _____.

Could this mean _____?

Why do you think the author _____?

I understand _____, but I wonder _____.

I notice that _____.

I think this (word/sentence/paragraph) means _____.

I think _____ because the text says _____.

In paragraph _____, the author says _____.

According to the text, _____.

One way to interpret _____ is _____.

Summarizing

The main events that take place are _____.

The major points of the text are _____.

The main idea of _____ is _____.

One central idea of this text is _____.

Another central idea is _____.

All in all, the message is _____.

The author's main purpose is to _____.

Basically, the author is saying that _____.

Comparing and Contrasting

_____ and _____ are similar because _____.

_____ and _____ are similar in that they both _____.

_____ is _____. Similarly, _____ is _____.

One thing _____ and _____ have in common is _____.

_____ and _____ are different because _____.

_____ and _____ are different in that _____.

_____ is _____. On the other hand, _____ is _____.

One difference between _____ and _____ is _____.

Clarifying

I'm not sure I understand the instructions.

Could you repeat that please?

I have a question about _____.

I am having trouble with _____.

Will you explain that again?

Could you clarify _____?

Would you mind helping me with _____?

Which (page/paragraph/section) are we reading?

How do you spell/pronounce _____?

Discourse Starters

Agreeing and Disagreeing

I agree with the idea that _____ because _____.

I share your point of view because _____.

You made a good point when you said _____.

I agree with (a person) that _____.

Although I agree that _____, I also think _____.

I understand where you're coming from, but _____.

I disagree with the idea that _____ because _____.

I see it a different way because _____.

You have a point, but the evidence suggests _____.

Arguing and Persuading with Evidence

I believe that _____ because _____.

It is clear that _____ because _____.

One reason I think _____ is _____.

Based on evidence in the text, I think _____.

Evidence such as _____ suggests that _____.

An example to support my position is _____.

This is evident because _____.

What evidence supports the idea that _____?

Can you explain why you think _____?

Evaluating

This is effective because _____.

The evidence _____ is strong because _____.

This is convincing because _____.

I see why the author _____, but I think _____.

This is not very effective because _____.

The evidence _____ is weak because _____.

This would have been better if _____.

What do you think about the writer's choice to _____?

Why do you think _____ (is/isn't) effective?

Giving Feedback and Suggesting

The part where you _____ is strong because _____.

What impressed me the most is how you _____.

This is a good start. Maybe you should add _____.

I like how you _____, but I would try _____.

You might consider changing _____.

I would suggest revising _____ so that _____.

One suggestion would be to _____.

Why did you choose _____?

A better choice might be _____.

This would be clearer if _____.

Editor's Checklist

Over the course of the year with SpringBoard, customize this Editor's Checklist as your knowledge of language conventions grows. The three examples below show you how to write a good checklist item.

	Are all the sentences complete?
	Do the subject and verb of each sentence agree?
	Do all the sentences have correct punctuation?

Writer's Checklist

Ideas	
	Does your first paragraph hook the reader?
	Is the purpose of your writing clear (to inform, to make an argument, etc.)?
	Is the genre of writing appropriate for your purpose?
	Is your main idea clear and easy to summarize?
	Does your text contain details and information that support your main idea?
	Are the ideas in the text well organized?
	Do you connect your ideas by using transitions?
	Do you use parallel structure to keep your ideas clear?
	Does each paragraph have a conclusion that transitions to the next paragraph?
	Does your writing end with a strong conclusion that restates the original purpose of the text?

Language	
	Do you keep a consistent point of view throughout?
	Do you use the present tense when writing about a text?
	Are any shifts in verb tense easy to follow and necessary?
	Have you removed unnecessary or confusing words?
	Do you use vivid verbs and descriptive adjectives when appropriate?
	Do you use different styles of language (like figurative or sensory) when appropriate?
	Do you use a variety of sentence types?
	Do you vary the way you begin your sentences?
	Did you split up run-on sentences?
	Are your pronoun references clear?

Evaluating Online Sources

The URL
 • What is its domain?
     • .com = a for-profit organization
     • .gov,.mil,.us (or other country code) = a government site
     • .edu = affiliated with an educational institution
     • .org = a nonprofit organization
 • Is this URL someone's personal page?
 • Do you recognize who is publishing this page?	

Sponsor: • Does the website give information about the organization or group that sponsors it? • Does it have a link (often called "About Us") that leads you to that information? • What do you learn?	
Timeliness: • When was the page last updated (usually this is posted at the top or bottom of the page)? • Is the topic something that changes frequently, like current events or technology?	
Purpose: • What is the purpose of the page? • What is its target audience? • Does it present information, opinion, or both? • Is it primarily objective or subjective? • How do you know?	
Author: • What credentials does the author have? • Is this person or group considered an authority on the topic?	
Links • Does the page provide links? • Do they work? • Are they helpful? • Are they objective or subjective?	

Fallacies 101

Ad Baculum (Scare Tactics)	If you don't support the party's tax plan, you and your family will be reduced to poverty. Chairman of the Board: "All those opposed to my arguments for the opening of a new department, signify by saying, 'I resign.'"
Ad hoc	Person 1: I should have gotten an A on that test. Person 2: You didn't study for that test at all. Person 1: That class is useless!
Ad Hominem (Against the Man)/ Genetic Fallacy	"My opponent, a vicious and evil person, should absolutely never be elected to office." The Volkswagen Beetle is an evil car because it was originally designed by Hitler's army.
Ad Populum	You should turn to channel 6. It's the most watched channel this year. There is always a long line at that restaurant, so the food must be really good.
Appeal To Pity	"Jonathan couldn't have cheated! He's such a nice boy and he tries so hard."
Argument from Outrage	The airline cancelled my flight an hour before takeoff and wouldn't tell me why. This is an outrage! We should all boycott the company.
Circular Reasoning	Emotional support animals should be allowed on airplanes, so the airline should change its policy. The policy should be changed because emotional support animals should be allowed on planes!
Either/Or (False Dilemma)	We can either stop using cars or destroy Earth. We must drill now or we'll remain dependent on foreign oil suppliers.
Faulty Analogies	Buying into the stock market is the same as betting on a horse race.
Hasty Generalization	They hit two home runs in the first inning of the season. This team is going all the way to the World Series!
Non-sequitur	I always see her with a book in her hands. She must hate watching TV.
Post Hoc	I ate a turkey sandwich and now I feel tired, so the turkey must have made me tired.
Red Herring	The new dress code banning t-shirts isn't fair. Students have the right to free speech just like anyone else.
Slippery Slope Fallacy	"If I don't study for the test, then I'm going to get a bad grade. If I get a bad grade on the test, I'll get a bad grade in the class, and I won't get into a good college. Getting into a good college is the most important part of getting a good job; so if I don't study for the test, I won't get a good job!"
Straw Man	People say that Mark Twain was a good author, but I disagree. If he was such a good author, why didn't he write using his own name?

Idea and Argument Evaluator

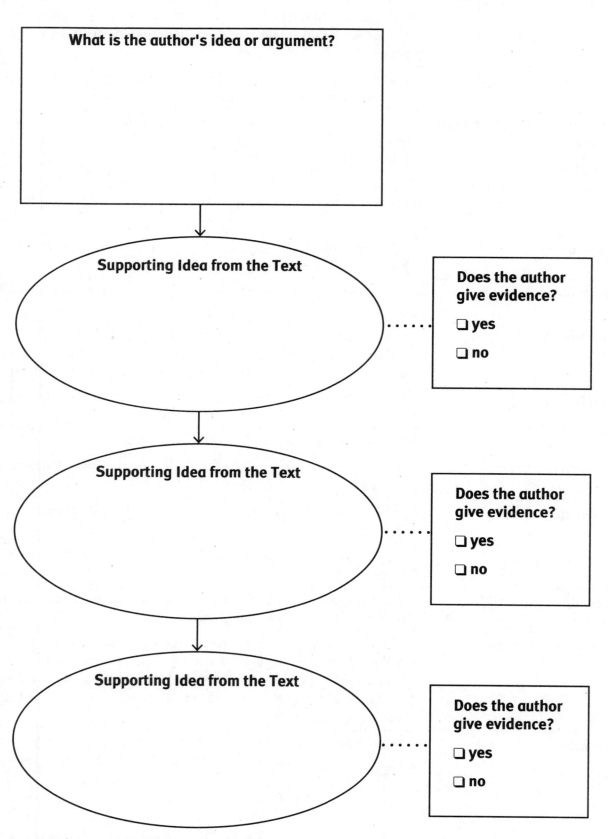

What is the author's idea or argument?

Supporting Idea from the Text

Does the author give evidence?

❑ yes

❑ no

Supporting Idea from the Text

Does the author give evidence?

❑ yes

❑ no

Supporting Idea from the Text

Does the author give evidence?

❑ yes

❑ no

Idea Connector

Directions: Write two simple sentences about the same topic. Next, write transition words around the Idea Connector. Then, choose an appropriate word to connect ideas in the two sentences. Write your combined sentence in the space below.

Sentence One

Sentence Two

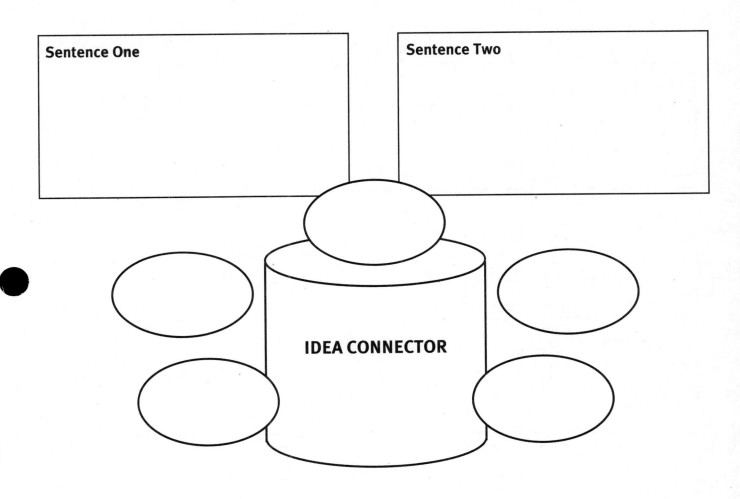

IDEA CONNECTOR

Combined Sentence

Key Idea and Details Chart

Title/Topic _____

Key Idea _____

_____

_____

Supporting detail 1 _____

_____

_____

Supporting detail 2 _____

_____

_____

Supporting detail 3 _____

_____

_____

Supporting detail 4 _____

_____

_____

Restate topic sentence: _____

_____

Concluding sentence: _____

_____

Narrative Analysis and Writing

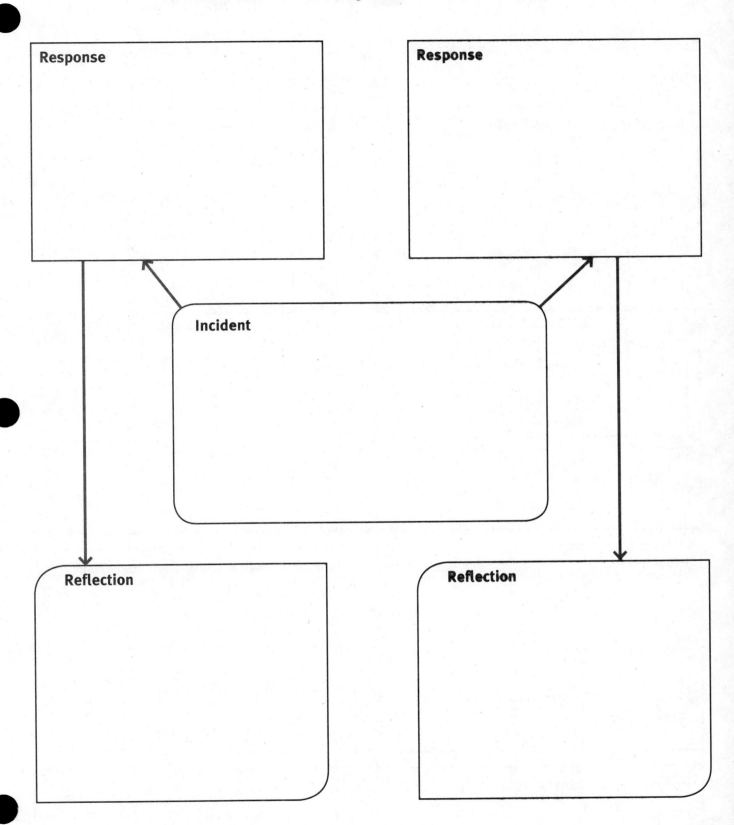

Response

Response

Incident

Reflection

Reflection

Notes for Reading Independently
Fiction

Title: _____

Author: _____

Something interesting I noticed:	**A question I have:**

Summary:

Illustration:	**Connections to my life/other texts I've read:**

How challenging this text was:

Easy	1	2	3	4	5	6	7	8	9	10	Challenging

Notes for Reading Independently
Nonfiction

Title: _____

Author: _____

Main idea:

Facts I learned:

Summary:

Questions I still have:

Connections to my life/other texts I've read:

How challenging this text was:										
Easy	1	2	3	4	5	6	7	8	9	10	Challenging

Opinion Builder

Reason

Reason

Based on these reasons, my opinion is

Reason

Reason

OPTIC

Title of Piece:

Artist: _____ **Type of artwork:** _____

Overview	Look at the artwork for at least 10 seconds. Generate questions; e.g., What is the subject? What strikes you as interesting, odd, etc.? What is happening?
Parts	Look closely at the artwork, making note of important elements and details. Ask additional questions, such as: Who are the figures? What is the setting and time period? What symbols are present? What historical information would aid understanding of this piece?
Title	Consider what the title and any written elements of the text suggest about meaning. How does the title relate to what is portrayed?
Interrelationships	Look for connections between and among the title, caption, and the parts of the art. How are the different elements related?
Conclusion	Form a conclusion about the meaning/theme of the text. Remember the questions you asked when you first examined it. Be prepared to support your conclusions with evidence.

Paragraph Frame for Conclusions

Conclusion Words and Phrases

shows that

based on

suggests that

leads to

indicates that

influences

The _____ (story, poem, play, passage, etc.)
shows that (helps us to conclude that) _____
_____
_____

There are several reasons why. First, _____
_____
_____
_____
_____

A second reason is _____
_____
_____
_____
_____

Finally, _____
_____
_____
_____
_____

In conclusion, _____
_____
_____
_____
_____

Paragraph Frame for Sequencing

Sequence Words and Phrases

at the beginning

in the first place

as a result

later

eventually

in the end

lastly

In the _____ *(story, poem, play, passage, etc.)*

there are three important _____

(events, steps, directions, etc.)

First, _____

_____

_____

_____

_____

Second, _____

_____

_____

_____

_____

Third, _____

_____

_____

_____

_____

Finally, _____

_____

_____

_____

Paraphrasing and Summarizing Map

What does the text say?	How can I say it in my own words?

How can I use my own words to summarize the text?

Peer Editing

Writer's name: _____

Did the writer answer the prompt? ☐ yes ☐ no

Did the writer use appropriate details or evidence to develop their writing? ☐ yes ☐ no

Is the writing organized in a way that makes sense? ☐ yes ☐ no

Did the writer use a variety of sentence types to make the writing more interesting? ☐ yes ☐ no

Are there any spelling or punctuation mistakes? ☐ yes ☐ no

Are there any grammar errors? ☐ yes ☐ no

Two things I really liked about the writer's story:

1. _____
   _____
   _____

2. _____
   _____
   _____

One thing I think the writer could do to improve the writing:

1. _____
   _____
   _____

Other comments or notes:

Persuasive/Argument Writing Map

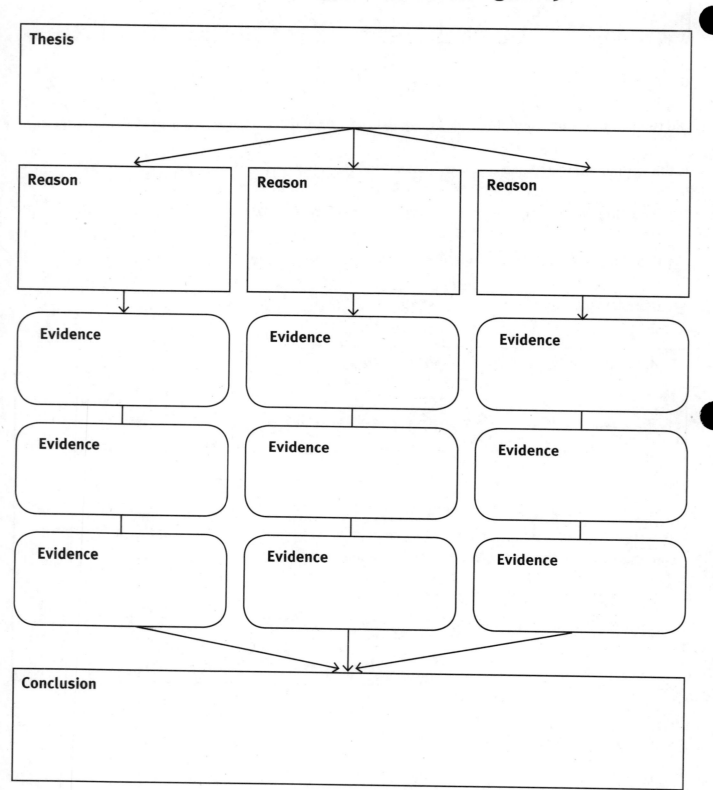

Thesis

Reason

Reason

Reason

Evidence

Evidence

Evidence

Evidence

Evidence

Evidence

Evidence

Evidence

Evidence

Conclusion

Presenting Scoring Guide

Scoring Criteria	Exemplary	Proficient	Emerging	Incomplete
Introduction / Conclusion	The presentation • provides a clear, engaging, and appropriate introduction to the topic or performance • provides a clear, engaging, and appropriate conclusion that closes, summarizes, draws connections to broader themes, or supports the ideas presented.	The presentation • provides a clear and appropriate introduction to the topic or performance • provides a clear and appropriate conclusion that closes, summarizes, draws connections to broader themes, or supports the ideas presented.	The presentation • provides an adequate introduction to the topic or performance • provides an adequate conclusion that closes, summarizes, draws connections to broader themes, or supports the ideas presented.	The presentation • does not provide an introduction to the topic or performance • does not provide a conclusion that closes, summarizes, draws connections to broader themes, or supports the ideas presented.
Timing	The presentation • thoroughly delivers its intended message within the allotted time • is thoughtfully and appropriately paced throughout.	The presentation • mostly delivers its intended message within the allotted time • is appropriately paced most of the time.	The presentation • delivers some of its intended message within the allotted time • is sometimes not paced appropriately.	The presentation • does not deliver its intended message within the allotted time • is not paced appropriately.
Voice (Volume, Enunciation, Rate)	The presentation • is delivered with adequate volume enabling audience members to fully comprehend what is said • is delivered with clear enunciation.	The presentation • is delivered with adequate volume enabling audience members to mostly comprehend what is said • is delivered with mostly clear enunciation.	The presentation • is delivered with somewhat adequate volume enabling audience members to comprehend some of what is said • is delivered with somewhat clear enunciation.	The presentation • is not delivered with adequate volume, so that audience members are unable to comprehend what is said • is delivered with unclear enunciation.
Eye Contact / Gestures	The presentation • is delivered with appropriate eye contact that helps engage audience members • makes use of natural gestures and/or body language to convey meaning.	The presentation • is delivered with some appropriate eye contact that helps engage audience members • makes use of gestures and/or body language to convey meaning.	The presentation • is delivered with occasional eye contact that sometimes engages audience members • makes some use of gestures and/or body language to convey meaning.	The presentation • is not delivered with eye contact to engage audience members • makes little or no use of gestures and/or body language to convey meaning.
Use of Media, Visuals, Props	The presentation • makes use of highly engaging visuals, multimedia, and/or props that enhance delivery.	The presentation • makes use of visuals, multimedia, and/or props that enhance delivery.	The presentation • makes use of some visuals, multimedia, and/or props that somewhat enhance delivery.	The presentation • makes use of few or no visuals, multimedia, and/or props that enhance delivery.
Audience Engagement	The presentation • includes thoughtful and appropriate interactions with and responses to audience members.	The presentation • includes appropriate interactions with and responses to audience members.	The presentation • includes a few interactions with and responses to audience members.	The presentation • does not include interactions with and responses to audience members.

RAFT

Role	Who or what are you as a writer?
Audience	As a writer, to whom are you writing?
Format	As a writer, what format would be appropriate for your audience (essay, letter, speech, poem, etc.)?
Topic	As a writer, what is the subject of your writing? What points do you want to make?

Roots and Affixes Brainstorm

Directions: Write the root or affix in the circle. Brainstorm or use a dictionary to find the meaning of the root or affix and add it to the circle. Then, find words that use that root or affix. Write one word in each box. Write a sentence for each word.

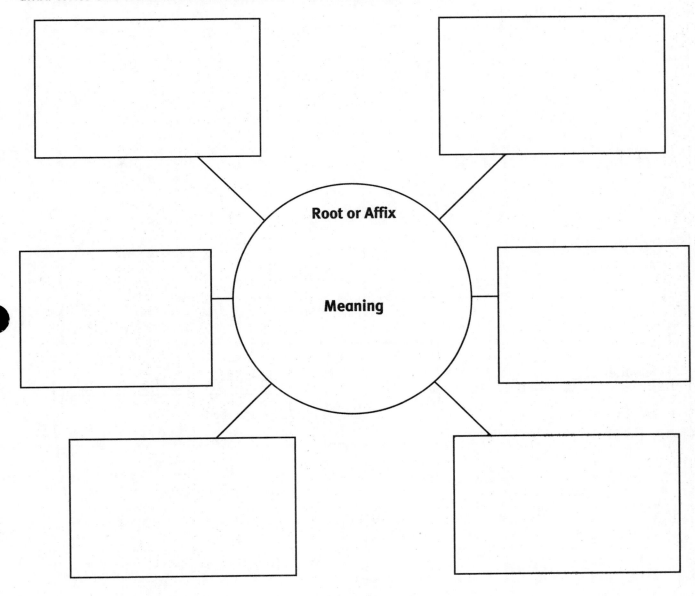

Round Table Discussion

Directions: Write the topic in the center box. One student begins by stating his or her ideas while the student to the left takes notes. Then the next student speaks while the student to his or her left takes notes, and so on.

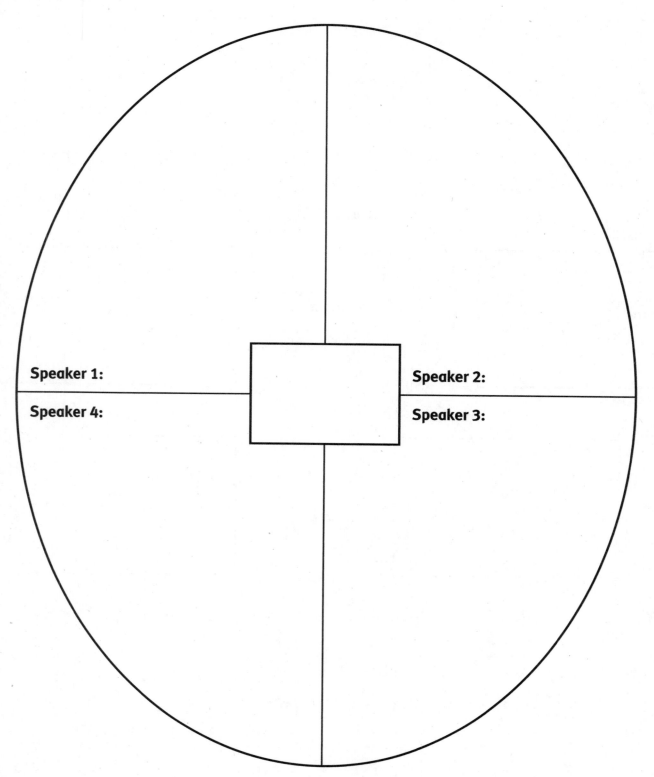

Speaker 1:

Speaker 2:

Speaker 4:

Speaker 3:

Sequence of Events Time Line

Title: _____

What happened first?		Next?

Beginning   Middle   End

Then?		Finally?

SMELL

Sender-Receiver Relationship—Who are the senders and receivers of the message, and what is their relationship (consider what different audiences the text may be addressing)?

Message—What is a literal summary of the content? What is the meaning/significance of this information?

Emotional Strategies—What emotional appeals (*pathos*) are included? What seems to be their desired effect?

Logical Strategies—What logical arguments/appeals (*logos*) are included? What is their effect?

Language—What specific language is used to support the message? How does it affect the text's effectiveness? Consider both images and actual words.

SOAPSTone

SOAPSTone	Analysis	Textual Support
Subject What does the reader know about the writer?		
Occasion What are the circumstances surrounding this text?		
Audience Who is the target audience?		
Purpose Why did the author write this text?		
Subject What is the topic?		
Tone What is the author's tone, or attitude?		

Text Structure Stairs

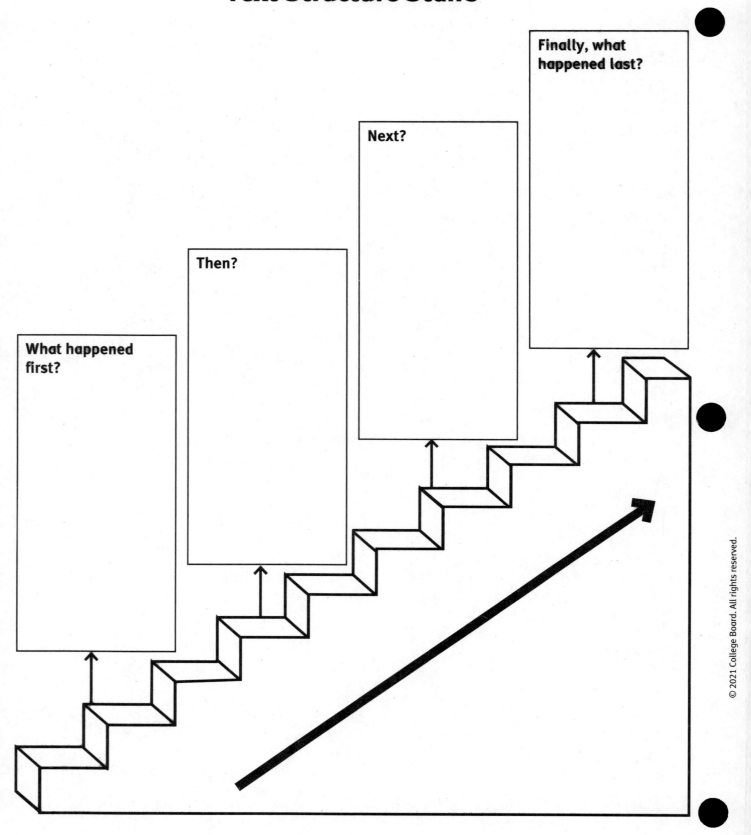

What happened first?

Then?

Next?

Finally, what happened last?

TP-CASTT Analysis

Poem Title:

Author:

Title: Make a Prediction. What do you think the title means before you read the poem?

Paraphrase: Translate the poem in your own words. What is the poem about? Rephrase difficult sections word for word.

Connotation: Look beyond the literal meaning of key words and images to their associations.

Attitude: What is the speaker's attitude? What is the author's attitude? How does the author feel about the speaker, about other characters, about the subject?

Shifts: Where do the shifts in tone, setting, voice, etc., occur? Look for time and place, keywords, punctuation, stanza divisions, changes in length or rhyme, and sentence structure. What is the purpose of each shift? How do they contribute to effect and meaning?

Title: Reexamine the title. What do you think it means now in the context of the poem?

Theme: Think of the literal and metaphorical layers of the poem. Then determine the overall theme. The theme must be written in a complete sentence.

TP-CASTT

Poem Title:

Author:

Title		
Paraphrase		
Connotation		
Attitude		
Shifts		
Title		
Theme		

Unknown Word Solver

Can you find any context clues? List them.

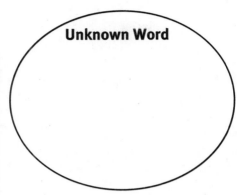

Unknown Word

Do you recognize any word parts?

Prefix:

Root Word:

Suffix:

Do you know another meaning of this word that does not make sense in this context?

Does it look or sound like a word in another language?

What is the dictionary definition?

How can you define the word in your own words?

Venn Diagram for Writing a Comparison

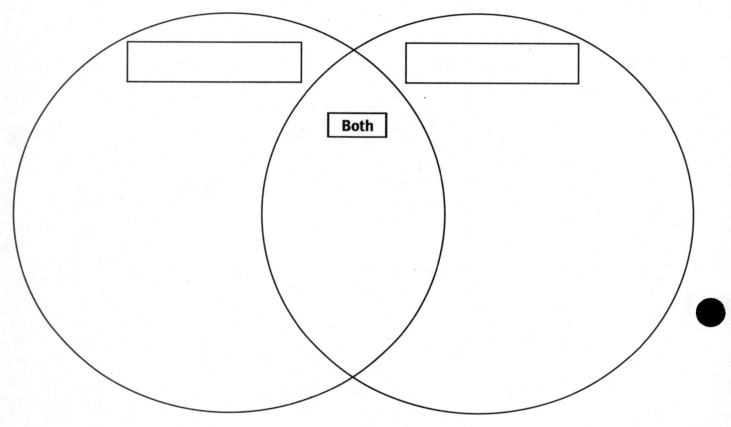

Both

They are similar in that _____
_____
_____
_____
_____
_____
_____

They are different in that _____
_____
_____
_____
_____
_____
_____

Verbal & Visual Word Association

Definition in Your Own Words	Important Elements

Academic Vocabulary Word

Visual Representation	Personal Association

Web Organizer

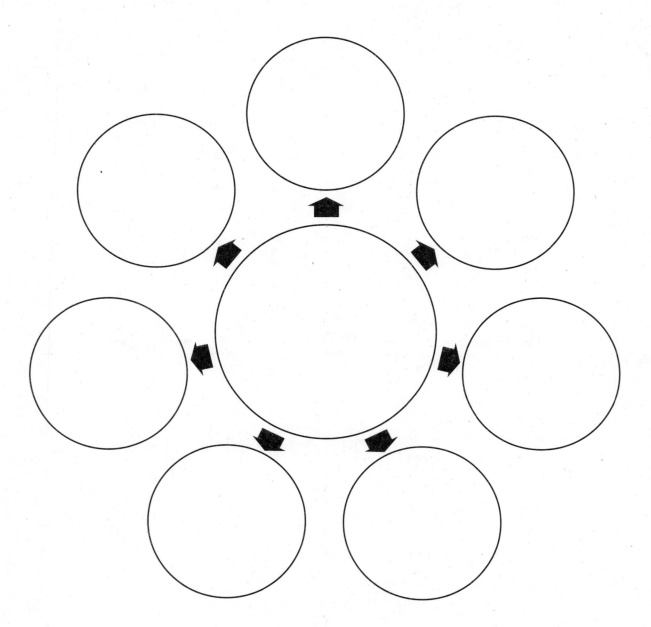

Word Choice Analyzer

Word or phrase from the text	Definition of word or phrase	How can I restate the definition in my own words?	What effect did the author produce by choosing these words?

Explain Your Analysis

The author uses the word or phrase _____, which means

_____

Another way to say this is _____

_____

I think the author chose these words to _____

_____

_____

One way I can modify this sentence to add detail is to _____

_____

Word Map

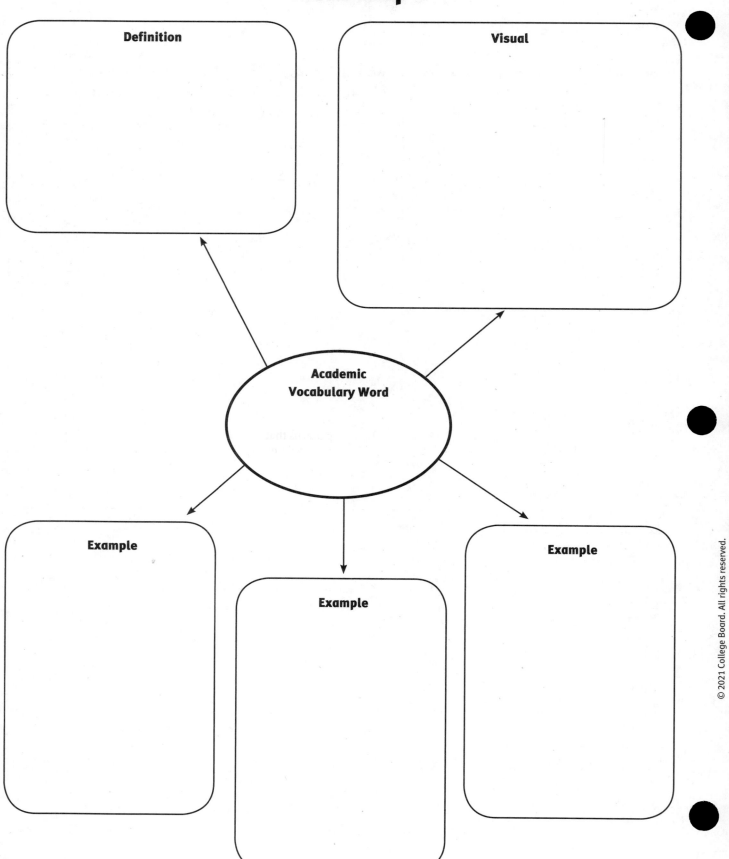

Definition

Visual

Academic Vocabulary Word

Example

Example

Example

Glossary/Glosario

A

active-voice verbs: verbs for which the subject performs the action
verbos en voz activa: forma verbal que indica que el sujeto realiza la acción

advertising techniques: specific methods used in print, graphics, or videos to persuade people to buy a product or use a service
técnicas publicitarias: métodos específicos usados en impresos, gráfica o videos para persuadir a las personas a comprar un producto o usar un servicio

agenda: a secret plan or motivation that causes someone to act in a certain way
agenda: motivación o plan secreto que lleva a alguien a actuar de determinado modo

allegory: a story in which the characters, objects, or actions have a meaning beyond the surface of the story
alegoría: cuento en el que los personajes, objetos o acciones tienen un significado que va más allá de la superficie de la historia

alliteration: the repetition of initial consonant sounds in words that are close together
aliteración: repetición de sonidos consonánticos iniciales en palabras cercanas

allusion: a reference made to a well-known person, event, or place from history, music, art, or another literary work
alusión: referencia a una persona, evento o lugar muy conocidos de la historia, música, arte u otra obra literaria

analogy: a comparison between two things for the purpose of drawing conclusions on one based on its similarities to the other
analogía: comparación entre dos cosas con el propósito de sacar conclusiones sobre las semejanzas que una cosa tiene a otra

anaphora: the repetition of the same word or group of words at the beginnings of two or more clauses or lines
anáfora: repetición de la misma palabra o grupo de palabras al comienzo de una o más cláusulas o versos

anecdotal evidence: evidence based on personal accounts of incidents
evidencia anecdótica: evidencia basada en relatos personales de los hechos

annotated bibliography: a list of sources used in research along with comments or summaries about each source
bibliografía anotada: lista de fuentes utilizadas en la investigación, junto con comentarios o resúmenes acerca de cada fuente

antagonist: the character who opposes or struggles against the main character
antagonista: personaje que se opone o lucha contra el personaje principal

aphorism: a short statement expressing an opinion or general truth
aforismo: afirmación corta que expresa una opinión o verdad general

appeals: the efforts to persuade an audience that a certain concept is true by directing statements toward reasoning or logic, character, or senses and emotions
llamados: serie de esfuerzos que alguien realiza con el fin de convencer a una audiencia de que determinado concepto es verdadero, persuadiéndola de ello mediante el uso del razonamiento o la lógica o bien apelando a su carácter, sentidos o emociones

Archetypal Criticism: criticism that deals with symbols and patterns that recur in the literature of widely diverse cultures
crítica de arquetipos: examinación de la literatura basada en símbolos y diseño

archetypes: universal symbols—images, characters, motifs, or patterns—that recur in the myths, dreams, oral traditions, songs, literature, and other texts of peoples widely separated by time and place
arquetipos: símbolos universales—imágenes, personajes, motivos o patrones—reiterativos en los mitos, el arte y la literatura alrededor del mundo

archival footage: film footage taken from another, previously recorded, source
cortometraje de archivo: fragmento de película tomada de otra fuente grabada previamente

argument: a form of writing that presents a particular claim or idea and supports it with evidence
argumento: forma de redacción que presenta una opinión o idea particular y la apoya con evidencia

argumentation: the act or process of arguing that includes the *hook* (quotation, example, or idea that catches readers' attention), *claim* (the opinion or thesis statement), *support* (evidence in the form of facts, statistics, examples, anecdotes, or expert opinions), *concession* (the writer's admission that the other side of the argument has a valid point), *refutation* (a well-reasoned denial of an opponent's point, based on solid evidence), and *call to action* (a request of readers)

argumentación: la estructura de una argumentación incluye el *gancho* (cita, ejemplo o idea que capta la atención del lector), *afirmación* (declaración de opinión o tesis), *apoyo* (evidencia en forma de hechos, estadísticas, ejemplos, anécdotas u opiniones de expertos), *concesión* (admisión por parte del escritor de que la otra parte del debate tiene un punto válido), *refutación* (negación bien razonada de una opinión del oponente, basada en evidencia sólida) y *llamado a la acción* (petición inspirada de lectores)

argument by analogy: a comparison of two similar situations, implying that the outcome of one will resemble the outcome of the other

argumento por analogía: comparación de dos situaciones semejantes, infiriendo que el resultado de será parecido al resultado de la otra

artistic license: the practice of rewording of dialogue, alteration of language, or reordering of the plot of a text created by another artist

licencia artística: la costumbre de reformular un diálogo, aliteración de palabras, o arreglo de la trama de un texto creado por otro artista

aside: a short speech spoken by an actor directly to the audience and unheard by other actors on stage

aparte: alocución breve dicha por un actor directamente al público y que no escuchan los demás actores que están en el escenario

assonance: the repetition of similar vowel sounds in accented syllables, followed by different consonant sounds, in words that are close together

asonancia: repetición de sonidos vocálicos similares en sílabas acentuadas, seguida de diferentes sonidos consonánticos, en palabras que están cercanas

audience: the intended readers, listeners, or viewers of specific types of written, spoken, or visual texts

público: lectores objetivo, oyentes o espectadores de tipos específicos de textos escritos, hablados o visuales

audience analysis: determination of the characteristics and knowledge of the people who will read a work or hear a speech

análisis del público: determinar las características y conocimiento de las personas que leen una obra o escuchan un discurso

author's purpose: the specific reason or reasons for the writing; what the author hopes to accomplish

propósito del autor: razón específica para escribir; lo que el autor espera lograr

autobiography: an account written by a person about his or her own life

autobiografía: narración de una vida escrita por el propio sujeto del relato

B

balanced sentence: a sentence that presents ideas of equal weight in similar grammatical forms to emphasize the similarity or difference between the ideas

oración balanceada: oración que representa ideas de igual peso en formas gramaticales similares para enfatizar la semejanza o diferencia entre las ideas

bias: an inclination or mental leaning for or against something; prevents impartial judgment

sesgo: inclinación o tendencia mental a favor o en contra de algo, lo que impide una opinión imparcial

bibliography: a list of the sources used for research

bibliografía: lista de fuentes primarias en la preparación de un texto

biography: a description or account of events from a person's life, written by another person

biografía: descripción o narración de la vida de una persona o los sucesos importantes de su vida escritos por otra persona

blank verse: unrhymed verse

verso libre: verso que no tiene rima

block: to create the plan for how actors will position themselves on the stage in relation to one another, the audience, and the objects on the stage

ensayar: establecer un plan para determinar la posición que los actores deberán ocupar en un escenario en relación a sí mismos, a la audiencia, al escenario y a los objetos del mismo

blocking: in drama, the way actors position themselves in relation to one another, the audience, and the objects on the stage

bloqueo: en drama, el modo en que los actores se sitúan entre sí, con el público y los objetos en el escenario

book review: a formal assessment or examination of a book

reseña de libro: evaluación o examinación formal de un libro

C

cacophonous: harsh and unpleasant sounding
cacofónico: sonidos molestos y desagradables

call to action: a restatement of the claim and what the writer wants the reader to do
llamado a la acción: repetición de la afirmación y lo que el escritor quiere que el lector responda

caricature: a visual or verbal representation in which characteristics or traits are exaggerated or distorted for emphasis
caricatura: representación visual o verbal en la que las características o rasgos se exageran o se distorsionan para dar énfasis

catalog poem: a poem that uses repetition and variation in the creation of a list, or catalog, of objects or desires, plans, or memories
lista en poema: poema que usa repetición y variación en la creación de una lista o catálogo, de objetos o deseos o planes o memorias

cause: an action, event, or situation that brings about a particular result
causa: acción, suceso o situación que produce un resultado particular

caveat: a cautionary detail to be thought through carefully when analyzing something
exhortación: advertencia o consejo a tener muy en cuenta a la hora de interpretar o analizar algo

censor: to examine materials for objectionable content
censurar: examinar materiales por contenido desagradable

censorship: the act of suppressing public speech or publication of materials deemed to be offensive by the censor
censura: acto de suprimir un discurso público o publicación de materiales considerados ofensivos por un censor

challenge: to oppose or refute a statement that has been made
poner en duda: oponerse a algo o refutar una declaración que alguien ha hecho

characterization: the methods a writer uses to develop characters
caracterización: métodos que usa un escritor para desarrollar personajes

characters: people, animals, or imaginary creatures that take part in the action of a story. A short story usually centers on a *main character* but may also contain one or more *minor characters*, who are not as complex, but whose thoughts, words, or actions move the plot along. A character who is *dynamic* changes in response to the events of the narrative; a character who is *static* remains the same throughout the narrative. A *round* character is fully developed—he or she shows a variety of traits; a *flat* character is one-dimensional, usually showing only one trait.
personajes: personas, animales o criaturas imaginarias que participan en la acción de un cuento. Un cuento corto normalmente se centra en un *personaje principal*, pero puede también contener uno o más *personajes secundarios*, que no son tan complejos, pero cuyos pensamientos, palabras o acciones hacen avanzar la trama. Un personaje que es *dinámico* cambia según los eventos del relato; un personaje que es *estático* permanece igual a lo largo del relato. Un personaje *complejo* está completamente desarrollado: muestra una diversidad de rasgos; un personaje *simple* es unidimensional, mostrando normalmente sólo un rasgo.

character foil: a character whose actions or thoughts are juxtaposed against those of a major character in order to highlight key attributes of the major character
antagonista: personaje cuyas acciones o pensamientos se yuxtaponen a los de un personaje principal con el fin de destacar atributos clave del personaje principal

character sketch: a brief description of a literary character
reseña del personaje: breve descripción de un personaje literario

chorus: in traditional or classic drama, a group of performers who speak as one and comment on the action of the play
coro: en el drama tradicional o clásico, grupo de actores que hablan al unísono y comentan la acción de la obra teatral

cinematic elements: the features of cinema—movies, film, video—that contribute to its form and structure: *angle* (the view from which the image is shot), *framing* (how a scene is structured), *lighting* (the type of lighting used to light a scene), *mise en scène* (the composition, setting, or staging of an image, or a scene in a film), and *sound* (the sound effects and music accompanying each scene)
elementos cinematográficos: las características del cine—películas, filmaciones, video—que contribuyen a darle forma y estructura: *angulación* (vista desde la cual se toma la imagen), *encuadre* (cómo se estructura una escena), iluminación (tipo de *iluminación* que se usa para una escena), y *montaje* (composición, ambiente o escenificación de una imagen o escena en una película), y *sonido* (efectos sonoros y música que acompañan cada escena)

cinematic techniques: the methods a director uses to communicate meaning and to evoke particular emotional responses from viewers

técnicas cinematográficas: métodos que emplea un director para comunicar un significado y evocar cierta respuesta emocional de los videntes

claim: a thesis statement describing the position the writer is taking on an issue

afirmación: declaración de opinión (o tesis) que asevera una idea o establece un debate hacia una posición específica

cliché: an overused expression or idea

cliché: expresión o idea que se usa en exceso

climax: the point at which the action reaches its peak; the point of greatest interest or suspense in a story; the turning point at which the outcome of a conflict is decided

clímax: punto en el que la acción alcanza su punto culminante; punto de mayor interés en un cuento; punto de inflexión en el que se decide el resultado del conflicto

coherence: the quality of unity or logical connection among ideas; the clear and orderly presentation of ideas in a paragraph or essay

coherencia: calidad de unidad o relación lógica entre las ideas; presentación clara y ordenada de las ideas en un párrafo o ensayo

commentary: the expression of opinions or explanations about an event or situation

comentario: expresión oral o escrita de opiniones o explicaciones sobre una situación, tema o suceso

commentary: explanations about the significance or importance of supporting details or examples in an analysis

comentario: explicaciones acerca de la importancia de los detalles que tienen apoyo o ejemplos en un análisis

complementary: combined in a way that enhances all elements combined

complementario: combinar dos o más elementos de una manera que mejora los dos

complex character: a character that has multiple or conflicting motivations

personaje complejo: personaje que tiene motivaciones multiples o conflictivas

complex sentence: a sentence containing one independent clause and one or more subordinate clauses

oración compleja: oración que contiene una cláusula independiente y una o más cláusulas subordinadas

complications: the events in a plot that develop a conflict; the complications move the plot forward in its rising action

complicaciones: sucesos de una trama que desarrollan el conflicto; las complicaciones hacen avanzar la trama en su acción ascendente

components: the parts or elements of a whole

componentes: partes o elementos que conforman un todo

compound sentence: a sentence containing two independent clauses

oración compuesta: oración que contiene dos cláusulas independientes

concession: an admission in an argument that the opposing side has valid points

concesión: admitir en un debate que el lado opositor tiene opiniones válidas

concluding statement: a statement that follows from and supports the claim made in an argument

declaración concluyente: declaración que sigue de la afirmación, o la apoya, en un argumento

conflict: a struggle or problem in a story. An *internal conflict* occurs when a character struggles between opposing needs or desires or emotions within his or her own mind. An *external conflict* occurs when a character struggles against an outside force. This force may be another character, a societal expectation, or something in the physical world.

conflicto: lucha o problema en un cuento. Un *conflicto interno* ocurre cuando un personaje lucha entre necesidades o deseos o emociones que se contraponen dentro de su mente. Un *conflicto externo* ocurre cuando un personaje lucha contra una fuerza externa. Esta fuerza puede ser otro personaje, una expectativa social o algo del mundo físico.

connotation: the associations and emotional overtones attached to a word beyond its literal definition, or denotation; a connotation may be positive, negative, or neutral

connotación: asociaciones y alusiones emocionales unidas a una palabra más allá de su definición literal o denotación; una connotación puede ser positiva, negativa, o neutra

consonance: the repetition of final consonant sounds in stressed syllables with different vowel sounds

consonancia: repetición de sonidos consonánticos finales en sílabas acentuadas con diferentes sonidos vocálicos

context: the circumstances or conditions in which something exists or takes place

contexto: circunstancias o condiciones en las que algo ocurre

conventions: standard features, practices, and forms associated with the way something is usually done

convenciones: prácticas y formas usuales asociadas con las costumbres de hacer algo

counterarguments: the arguments that can be made to oppose a viewpoint

contraargumentos: argumentos que se presentan para rebatir un punto de vista

counterclaim: a position taken by someone with an opposing viewpoint

contrareclamación: posición que toma una persona con un punto de vista contrario

couplet: two consecutive lines of verse with end rhyme; a couplet usually expresses a complete unit of thought

copla: dos líneas de versos consecutivos con rima final; una copla normalmente expresa una unidad de pensamiento completa

credibility: the quality of being trusted or believed

credibilidad: calidad de ser confiable o creíble

critical lens: a particular identifiable perspective as in Reader Response Criticism, Cultural Criticism, etc., through which a text can be analyzed and interpreted

ojo crítico: punto de vista particular identificable como por ejemplo Teoría de la recepción, Crítica sociocultural, etc., por medio del que se puede analizar e interpretar un texto

cultural conflict: a struggle that occurs when people with different cultural expectations or attitudes interact

conflicto cultural: lucha que ocurre cuando interactúan personas con diferentes expectativas o actitudes culturales

Cultural Criticism: criticism that focuses on the elements of culture and how they affect one's perceptions and understanding of texts

crítica cultural: analizar un texto basándose en elementos culturales y como ellos afectan la percepción y lacomprensión de textos

culture: the shared set of arts, ideals, skills, institutions, customs, attitude, values, and achievements that characterize a group of people, and that are passed on or taught to succeeding generations

cultura: conjunto de artes, ideas, destrezas, instituciones, costumbres, actitud, valores y logros compartidos que caracterizan a un grupo de personas, y que se transfieren o enseñan a las generaciones siguientes

cumulative (or loose) sentence: a sentence in which the main clause comes first, followed by subordinate structures or clauses

oración acumulativa (o frases sueltas): oración cuya cláusula principal viene primero, seguida de estructuras o cláusulas subordinadas

D

deductive reasoning: a process of drawing a specific conclusion from general information

razonamiento deductivo: proceso en que se usa información general para sacar una conclusión específica

defend: to support a statement that has been made

defender: dar apoyo a una declaración que alguien ha hecho

denotation: the precise meaning of a word

denotación: significado literal de una palabra

detail: a specific fact, observation, or incident; any of the small pieces or parts that make up something else

detalle: hecho, observación o incidente específico; cualquiera de las pequeñas piezas o partes que constituyen otra cosa

dialect: the distinctive language—including the sounds, spelling, grammar, and diction—of a specific group or class of people

dialecto: lenguaje distintivo, incluyendo sonidos, ortografía, gramática y dicción, de un grupo o clase específico de personas

dialogue: the words spoken by characters in a narrative or film

diálogo: palabras que dicen los personajes en un relato o película

dialogue tags: the phrases that attribute a quotation to the speaker, for example, *she said* or *he bellowed*

marcas del diálogo: frases que atribuyen la cita de un hablante, por ejemplo, *dijo ella* o *bramó él.*

diction: a writer's word choices, which often convey voice and tone

dicción: selección de palabras por parte del escritor; elemento estilístico que ayuda a transmitir voz y tono

diegetic sound: any sound that can logically be heard by characters on screen

sonido diegético: sonidos lógicos que los personajes pueden oír en una escena en la pantalla

direct characterization: specific information about a character provided by the narrator or author

caracterización directa: información específica sobre un personaje creada por un narrador o autor

discourse: the language or speech used in a particular context or subject

discurso: lenguaje o habla usada en un contexto o tema en particular

documentary or nonfiction film: a genre of filmmaking that provides a visual record of actual events using photographs, video footage, and interviews

documental o película de no-ficción: género cinematográfico que realiza un registro visual de sucesos basados en hechos por medio del uso de fotografías, registro en videos y entrevistas

dominant group: a more powerful group that may perceive another group as marginalized or subordinate

grupo dominante: un grupo más poderoso que puede percibir a otro grupo como maginado o subordinado

drama: a play written for stage, radio, film, or television, usually about a serious topic or situation

drama: obra teatral escrita para representar en un escenario, radio, cine o televisión, normalmente sobre un tema o situación seria

dramatic irony: a form of irony in which the reader or audience knows more about the circumstances or future events than the characters within the scene

ironía dramática: una forma de la ironía en que los lectores o el público sabe más sobre las circunstancias o sucesos futuros que los personajes en la escena

dramaturge: a member of an acting company who helps the director and actors make informed decisions about the performance by researching information relevant to the play and its context

dramaturgo: socio de una compañía teatral que ayuda al director y a los actores tomar decisiones informadas sobre la interpretación investigando información relevante a la obra teatral y su contexto

dynamic (or round) character: a character who evolves and grows in the story and has a complex personality

personaje dinámico: personaje complejo que evoluciona a lo largo de la trama literaria

E

editorial: an article in a newspaper or magazine expressing the opinion of its editor or publisher

editorial: artículo de periódico o revista, que expresa la opinión de su editor

effect: the result or influence of using a specific literary or cinematic device; a result produced by a cause

efecto: resultado o influencia de usar un recurso literario o cinematográfico específico; resultado o producto de una causa

elaborate: to expand on or add information or detail about a point and thus to develop the point more fully

elaborar: extender o agregar información o detalles sobre un asunto, y así desarrollar el asunto de manera más completa

empirical evidence: evidence based on experiences and direct observation through research

evidencia empírica: evidencia basada en experiencias y en la observación directa por medio de la investigación

emulate: to imitate an original work or person

emular: imitar una obra original

enfranchisement: having the rights of citizenship, such as the right to vote

emancipación: tener los derechos de la ciudananía, tales como el derecho al voto

epigram: a short, witty saying

epigrama: dicho corto e ingenioso

epigraph: a phrase, quotation, or poem that is set at the beginning of a document or component

epígrafe: frase, cita, o poema que aparece al comienzo de un documento o componente

epithet: a descriptive word or phrase used in place of or along with a name

epíteto: palabra o frase descriptiva usada en lugar de o junto con un nombre

ethos: (ethical appeal) a rhetorical appeal that focuses on the character or qualifications of the speaker

ethos: (recurso ético) recurso retórico centrado en la ética o en el carácter o capacidades del orador

euphonious: a harmonious or pleasing sound

eufónico: un sonido armonioso y agradable

evaluate: to make a judgment based on an analysis about the value or worth of the information, idea, or object

evaluar: dar una opinión basándose en un análisis sobre el valor o mérito de la información, idea, u objeto

evidence: the information that supports a position in an argument; forms of evidence include facts, statistics (numerical facts), expert opinions, examples, and anecdotes; *see also* anecdotal, empirical, and logical evidence

evidencia: información que apoya o prueba una idea o afirmación; formas de evidencia incluyen hechos, estadística (datos numéricos), opiniones de expertos, ejemplos y anécdotas; *ver también* evidencia anecdótica, empírica y lógica

exaggeration: a statement that represents something as larger, better, or worse than it really is

exageración: representar algo como más grande, mejor o peor que lo que realmente es

exemplification: the act of defining by example by showing specific, relevant examples that fit a writer's definition of a topic or concept

ejemplificación: definir por ejemplo mostrando ejemplos específicos y relevantes que se ajustan a la definición de un tema o concepto del escritor

explanatory writing: a form of writing whose purpose is to explain, describe, or give information about a topic in order to inform a reader

escrito explicativo: forma de la escritura cuyo propósito es explicar, describir o dar información sobre un tema para informar al lector

explicit theme: a theme that is clearly stated by the writer

tema explícito: tema que está claramente establecido por el escritor

exposition: events that give a reader background information needed to understand a story (characters are introduced, the setting is described, and the conflict begins to unfold)

exposición: sucesos que dan al lector los antecedentes necesarios para comprender un cuento. Durante la exposición, se presentan los personajes, se describe el ambiente y se comienza a revelar el conflicto.

extended metaphor: a comparison between two unlike things that continues throughout a series of sentences in a paragraph or lines in a poem

metáfora extendida: metáfora que se extiende por varios versos o a través de un poema completo

external coherence: unity or logical connection between paragraphs with effective transitions and transitional devices

coherencia externa: unidad o conexión lógica entre párrafos con transiciones efectivas y recursos transitionales

eye rhymes: words that appear to rhyme because of identical spelling patterns but do not actually rhyme, for example, *cough* and *through*

falsas rimas: palabras, en inglés, que poseen una terminación idéntica y, por tanto, nos llevan erróneamente a pensar que riman, tales como *cough* y *through*

F

fallacy: a false or misleading argument
falacia: argumento o poema falso o engañoso

falling action: the events in a play, story, or novel that follow the climax, or moment of greatest suspense, and lead to the resolution

acción descendente: sucesos de una obra teatral, cuento o novela posteriores al clímax, o momento de mayor suspenso, y que conllevan a la resolución

faux pas: an embarrassing act or remark in a social situation (borrowed from French)

metedura de pata: comportamiento o comentario embarazoso en el marco de una situación social

Feminist Criticism: criticism that focuses on relationships between genders and examines a text based on the patterns of thought, behavior, values, enfranchisement, and power in relations between and within the sexes

crítica feminista: se enfoca en la relación entre los sexos y examina un texto basándose en el diseño de pensamiento, comportamiento, valores, emancipación, y poder en las relaciones entre los sexos

figurative: symbolic or emblematic; not literal
figurativo: simbólico o emblemático, no literal

figurative language: the use of words to describe one thing in terms of another

lenguaje figurativo: lenguaje imaginativo o figuras retóricas que no pretenden ser tomados literalmente; el lenguaje figurativo usa figuras literarias

film techniques: the methods a director uses to communicate meaning and to evoke particular emotional responses in viewers

técnicas cinematográficas: metodos que usa un director en la comunicación del significado y evocar una respuesta emocional específica en los videntes

fixed form: a form of poetry in which the length and pattern are determined by established usage of tradition, such as a sonnet

forma fija: forma de poesía en la que la longitud y el patrón están determinados por el uso de la tradición, como un soneto

flashback: an interruption or transition to a time before the current events in a narrative

flashback: interrupción en la secuencia de los sucesos para relatar sucesos ocurridos en el pasado

flat (or static) character: a character who is uncomplicated and stays the same without changing or growing during the story

personaje estático: personaje no complicado que permanence del mismo caracter y que no cambia a lo largo de una historia

folktale: a story without a known author that has been preserved through oral retellings

cuento folclórico: cuento sin autor conocido que se ha conservado por medio de relatos orales

footage: literally, a length of film; the expression is still used to refer to digital video clips

metraje: literalmente, la longitud de una película; la expresión aún se usa para referirse a video clips digitales

foreshadowing: the use of hints or clues in a narrative to suggest future action

presagio: uso de claves o pistas en un relato para sugerir una acción futura

form: the particular structure or organization of a work

forma: estructura o organización particular de una obra

found poem: a poem consisting of words, phrases, and/or lines that come directly from another text

poema encontrado: poema compuesto de palabras, frases o pasajes sacados directamente de otros textos

free verse: poetry without a fixed pattern of meter and rhyme

verso libre: poesía que no sigue ningún patrón, ritmo o rima regular

G

genre: a kind or style of literature or art, each with its own specific characteristics. For example, poetry, short story, and novel are literary genres. Painting and sculpture are artistic genres.

género: tipo o estilo de literatura o arte, cada uno con sus propias características específicas. Por ejemplo, la poesía, el cuento corto y la novela son géneros literarios. La pintura y la escultura son géneros artísticos.

genre conventions: the essential features and format that characterize a particular genre, or style of literature or art

convenciones genéricas: características básicas y el formato que caracterizan un género específico

graphic novel: a book-length narrative, or story, in the form of a comic strip rather than words

novela gráfica: narrativa o cuento del largo de un libro, en forma de tira cómica más que palabras

graphics: images or text used to provide information on screen

gráfica: imágenes o texto que se usa para dar información en pantalla

H

hamartia: a tragic hero's fatal flaw; an ingrained character trait that causes a hero to make decisions leading to his or her death or downfall

hamartia: error fatal de un héroe trágico; característica propia de un personaje que causa que un héroe tome decisiones que finalmente llevan a su muerte o caída

hero: the main character or protagonist of a play, with whom audiences become emotionally invested

héroe: personaje principal o protagonista de una obra teatral, con el que el público se involucra emocionalmente

historical context: the circumstances or conditions in which something takes place

contexto historico: circuntancias o condiciones en las cuales algo sucede o pasa

Historical Criticism: criticism used to uncover meaning in a literary text by examining the text in the context of the time period in which it was created

historicismo: método crítico que se usa para revelar el significado de un texto literario mediante el examen de dicho texto en el contexto de la época en que fue escrito

hook: an opening in an argument or a piece of writing that grabs the reader's attention

gancho: cita, anécdota o ejemplo interesante al comienzo de un escrito, que capta la atención del lector

Horatian satire: satire that pokes fun at human foibles and folly with a witty, gentle, even indulgent tone

sátira de Horacio: sátira en que se burla de las debilidades y locuras con un tono suave, ingenioso, hasta indulgente

humor: the quality of being amusing

humor: calidad de ser divertido

hyperbole: exaggeration used to suggest strong emotion or create a comic effect

hipérbole: exageración que se usa para sugerir una emoción fuerte o crear un efecto cómico

I

iamb: a metrical foot that consists of an unstressed syllable followed by a stressed syllable

yambo: pie métrico que consta de una sílaba átona seguida de una sílaba acentuada

iambic pentameter: a rhythmic pattern of five feet (or units), each consisting of one unstressed syllable followed by a stressed syllable

pentámetro yámbico: patrón rítmico de cinco pies (o unidades) de una sílaba átona seguida de una sílaba acentuada

image: a word or phrase that appeals to one of more of the five senses and creates a picture

imagen: palabra o frase que apela a uno o más de los cinco sentido y crea un cuadro

imagery: the verbal expression of sensory experience; descriptive or figurative language used to create word pictures; imagery is created by details that appeal to one or more of the five senses

imaginería: lenguaje descriptivo o figurativo utilizado para crear imágenes verbales; la imaginería es creada por detalles que apelan a uno o más de los cinco sentidos

imperialism: a policy of extending the rule or influence of a country over other countries or colonies; the political, military, or economic domination of one country by another

imperialismo: política de extender el dominio o la influencia de un país sobre otros países o colonias; dominio político; militar o económico de un país sobre otro(s)

implied theme: a theme that is understood through the writer's diction, language construction, and use of literary devices

tema implícito: tema que se entiende a través de la dicción del escritor, construcción lingüística y uso de recursos literarios

indirect characterization: a narrator's or author's development of a character through the character's interactions with others, thoughts about circumstances, or speaking his or her thoughts aloud

caracterización indirecta: el desarrollo de un personaje según un narrador o autor por las interacciones del personaje con otros, pensamientos sobre las circunstancias, o su habilidad de enunciar sus pensamientos en voz alta

inductive reasoning: a process of looking at individual facts to draw a general conclusion

razonamiento inductivo: proceso de observación de hechos individuales para sacar una conclusión general

inference: a conclusion about ideas or information not directly stated

inferencia: conclusion sobre las ideas o información no presentadas directamente

interior monologue: a literary device in which a character's internal emotions and thoughts are presented

monólogo interior: recurso literario en el que se presentan las emociones internas y pensamientos de un personaje

interpretation: the act of making meaning from something, such as a text

interpretación: acto de interpretar un significado de algo, tal como un texto

internal coherence: unity or logical connection within paragraphs

coherencia interna: unidad o conexión lógica entre párrafos

irony: a literary device that exploits readers' expectations; irony occurs when what happens turns out to be quite different from what was expected. *Dramatic irony* is a form of irony in which the reader or audience knows more about the circumstances or future events in a story than the characters within it; *verbal irony* occurs when a speaker or narrator says one thing while meaning the opposite; *situational irony* occurs when an event contradicts the expectations of the characters or the reader.

ironía: recurso literario que explota las expectativas de los lectores; la ironía ocurre cuando lo que se espera resulta ser bastante diferente de lo que realmente ocurre. La *ironía dramática* es una forma de ironía en la que el lector o la audiencia saben más acerca de las circunstancias o sucesos futuros de un cuento que los personajes del mismo; la *ironía verbal* ocurre cuando un orador o narrador dice una cosa queriendo decir lo contrario; la *ironía situacional* ocurre cuando un suceso contradice las expectativas de los personajes o del lector.

J

justice: the quality of being reasonable and fair in the administration of the law; the ideal of rightness or fairness

justicia: calidad de ser razonable e imparcial en la administración de la ley; ideal de rectitud o equidad

Juvenalian satire: satire that denounces, sometimes harshly, human vice and error in dignified and solemn tones

sátira de Juvenal: sátira de denuncia, a veces con aspereza, los vicios y errores humanos con tonos dignos y solemnes

juxtaposition: the arrangement of two or more things for the purpose of comparison

yuxtaposición: ordenamiento de dos o más cosas con el objeto de compararlas

L

lede: an alternative spelling of lead; the opening of a news article or a single sentence that describes the main point of the article

entradilla: comienzo de una información periodística que resume lo más importante de ella

lining out: the process of creating line breaks to add shape and meaning in free verse poetry

llamada y respuesta: proceso de crear rupturas de lineas para dar forma y significado en la poesía del verso libre

literal: explicitly stated in a text; exact

literal: algo expresado de modo explícito y exacto en un texto

literal language: the exact meanings, or denotations, of words

lenguaje literal: los signficados y denotaciones exactos de las palabras

Literary Criticism: the formal practice of interpreting, evaluating, and explaining the meaning and significance of literary works

crítica literaria: práctica formal de interpretar, evaluar y explicar el significado y el valor de obras literarias

literary theory: a systematic study of literature using various methods to analyze texts

teoría literaria: intento de establecer principios para interpretar y evaluar textos literarios

logical evidence: evidence based on facts and a clear rationale

evidencia lógica: evidencia basada en hechos y una clara fundamentación

logical fallacy: a statement that is false because it is based on an error in reasoning

argumento falaz: afirmación de carácter falso por el hecho de estar basada en un error de razonamiento

logos: (logical appeal) a rhetorical appeal to reason or logic

logos: (apelación lógica) apelación retórica que usa la evidencia factual y la lógica para apelar al sentido de la razón

M

main idea: a statement (often one sentence) that summarizes the key details of a text

idea principal: declaración (con frecuencia una oración) que resume los detalles claves de un texto

marginalize: to relegate or confine a person to a lower or outer limit

marginar: relegar o confinar a una persona a un límite bajo o ajeno

Marxist Criticism: criticism that asserts that economics provides the foundation for all social, political, and ideological reality

crítica marxista: ver un text a través de la perspectiva en que la economía proporciona la fundación de toda realidad social, política, e ideológica

media: collectively refers to the organizations that communicate information to the public

medios de comunicación: colectivamente refiere a las organizaciones que comunican información al público

media channel: a method an organization uses to communicate, such as radio, television, website, newspaper, or magazine

canales mediaticos: método que usa una organización en la comunicación como radio, televisión, sitios de web, periódico, o revista

metacognition: the ability to know and be aware of one's own thought processes; self-reflection

metacognición: capacidad de conocer y estar consciente de los propios procesos del pensamiento; introspección

metaphor: a comparison between two unlike things in which one thing is spoken of as if it were another, for example, the moon was a crisp white cracker

metáfora: comparación entre dos cosas diferentes en la que se habla de una cosa como si fuera otra, por ejemplo, la luna era una galletita blanca crujiente

meter: a pattern of stressed and unstressed syllables in poetry

métrica: patrón de sílabas acentuadas y átonas en poesía

mise en scène: the composition, or setting, of a stage

puesta en escena: la composición o el lugar de un escenario

monologue: a dramatic speech delivered by a single character in a play

monólogo: discurso dramático que hace un solo personaje en una obra teatral

montage: a composite picture that is created by bringing together a number of images and arranging them to create a connected whole

montaje: cuadro compuesto que se crea al reunir un número de imágenes y que al organizarlas se crea un todo relacionado

mood: the atmosphere or predominant emotion in a literary work, the effect of the words on the audience

carácter: atmósfera o sentimiento general en una obra literaria

motif: a recurrent image, symbol, theme, character type, subject, or narrative detail that becomes a unifying element in an artistic work or text

motivo: imagen, símbolo, tema, tipo de personaje, tema o detalle narrativo recurrente que se convierte en un elemento unificador en una obra artística

motive: a character's reason for behaving in a certain way
motivación: razón esgrimida por un personaje para obrar de determinado modo

musical (or sound) device: the use of sound to convey and reinforce the meaning or experience of poetry
aparatos musicales: uso del sonido para transmitir y reforzar el significado o experiencia de la poesía

myth: a traditional story that explains the actions of gods or heroes or the origins of the elements of nature
mito: cuento tradicional que explica las acciones de dioses o héroes, o los orígenes de los elementos de la naturaleza

N

narration: the act of telling a story
narración: acto de contar un cuento

narrative: a story about a series of events that includes character development, plot structure, and theme; can be a work of fiction or nonfiction
narrativa: narración sobre una serie de sucesos que incluye el desarrollo de personajes, estructora del argumento, y el tema; puede ser una obra de ficción o no ficción

narrative arc: the story line of a text, including a beginning (*exposition*), a middle (the *rising action*), a high point (*climax*), and an end (the *falling action* and *resolution*)
arco narrativo: línea argumental de un texto, que consta de un comienzo (*exposición*), una parte media (*acción creciente*), un punto culminante (*clímax*) y un final (*acción decreciente y resolución*)

narrative pacing: the speed at which a narrative moves
compás de la narrativa: la rapidez en que una narrativa pasa

narrator: the person telling the story
narrador: persona que cuenta una historia

non-diegetic sound: sound that cannot logically be heard by the characters on screen; examples include mood music and voice-overs
sonido no diegético: voces y comentarios superpuestos; sonidos que no provienen de la acción en pantalla.

nut graf: an abbreviation of the expression *nutshell paragraph*; a statement that tells readers of a news article why they should care about what happened
epítome: texto introductorio que hace entender a los lectores por qué debería importarles la noticia que se relata a continuación

O

objective: based on factual information
objetivo: basado en información de hechos

objective tone: a tone that is more clinical and that is not influenced by emotion
tono objetivo: tono que es mas aséptico y que no se deja influir por la emoción

objectivity: the representation of facts or ideas without injecting personal feelings or biases
objetividad: representación de los hechos o ideas sin agregar sentimientos o prejuicios personales

ode: a lyric poem expressing feelings or thoughts of a speaker, often celebrating a person, event, or thing
oda: poema lírico que expresa sentimientos o pensamientos de un orador, que frecuentemente celebra a una persona, suceso o cosa

omniscient narrator: a narrator who knows all and tells a story from the perspective of multiple characters
narrador omnisciente: narrador que conoce todo lo sucedido sobre un determinado acontecimiento y relata la historia desde la perspectiva de varios personajes

onomatopoeia: the occurrence of a word whose sound suggests its meaning
onomatopeya: palabras cuyo sonido sugiere su significado

oral interpretation: a planned oral reading that expresses the meaning of a written text
interpretación oral: lectura oral planeada que interpreta el signficado de un text escrito

oral tradition: the passing down of stories, tales, proverbs, and other culturally important ideas through oral retellings
tradición oral: traspaso de historias, cuentos, proverbios y otras historias de importancia cultural por medio de relatos orales

oxymoron: words that appear to contradict each other; for example, cold fire
oxímoron: palabras que parecen contradecirse mutuamente; por ejemplo, fuego frío

P

paradox: a statement that contains two seemingly incompatible points
paradoja: declaración que contiene dos asuntos aparentemente incompatibles

parallel structure (parallelism): refers to a grammatical or structural similarity between sentences or parts of a sentence, so that elements of equal importance are equally developed and similarly phrased for emphasis

estructura paralela (paralelismo): se refiere a una similitud gramatical o estructural entre oraciones o partes de una oración, de modo que los elementos de igual importancia se desarrollen por igual y se expresen de manera similar para dar énfasis

paraphrase: to briefly restate ideas from another source in one's own words

parafrasear: volver a presentar las ideas de otra fuente en nuestras propias palabras

parenthetical citations: used for citing sources directly in an essay

citas parentéticas: usadas en citas de fuentes primarias en un ensayo

parody: a literary or artistic work that imitates the characteristic style of an author or a work for comic effect or ridicule

parodia: obra literaria o artística que imita el estilo característico de un autor o una obra para dar un efecto cómico o ridículo

passive-voice verbs: verb form in which the subject receives the action; the passive voice consists of a form of the verb *be* plus a past participle of the verb

verbos en voz pasiva: forma verbal en la que el sujeto recibe la acción; la voz pasiva se forma con el verbo *ser* más el participio pasado de un verbo

pathos: (emotional appeal) a rhetorical appeal to the reader's or listener's senses or emotions

pathos: (apelación emocional) apelación retórica a los sentidos o emociones de los lectores u oyentes

patriarchal: having the male as head of the household and with authority over women and children

patriarcal: sociedad en que el varón es jefe del hogar en el cual mantiene autoridad sobre las mujeres y niños

perception: one person's interpretation of sensory or conceptual information

percepción: interpretación de una persona en cuanto a información sensorial o conceptual

periodic sentence: a sentence that makes sense only when the end of the sentence is reached, that is, when the main clause comes last

oración periódica: oración que tiene sentido sólo cuando se llega al final de la oración, es decir, cuando la cláusula principal viene al final

persona: the voice assumed by a writer to express ideas or beliefs that may not be his or her own

personaje: voz que asume un escritor para expresar ideas o creencias que pueden no ser las propias

personification: a figure of speech that gives human qualities to an animal, object, or idea

personificación: figura literaria que da características humanas a un animal, objeto o idea

perspective: a way of looking at the world or a mental concept about things or events, one that judges relationships within or among things or events

perspectiva: manera de visualizar el mundo o concepto mental de las cosas o sucesos, que juzga las relaciones dentro o entre cosas o sucesos

persuasive argument: an argument that convinces readers to accept or believe a writer's perspective on a topic

argumento persuasivo: argumento que convence a los lectores a aceptar o creer en la perspectiva de un escritor acerca de un tema

photo essay: a collection of photographic images that reveal the author's perspective on a subject

ensayo fotográfico: recolección de imágenes fotográficas que revelan la perspectiva del autor acerca de un tema

plagiarism: the unattributed use of another writer's words or ideas

plagio: usar como propias las palabras o ideas de otro escritor

plot: the sequence of related events that make up a story

trama: secuencia de sucesos relacionados que conforman un cuento o novela

poetic structure: the organization of words, lines, and images as well as ideas

estructura poética: organización de las palabras, versos e imágenes, así como también de las ideas

poetry: language written in lines and stanzas

poesía: género literario que se concreta en un poema y está sujeto a medida o cadencia

point of view: the perspective from which a narrative is told, that is, first person, third-person limited, or third-person omniscient

punto de vista: perspectiva desde la cual se cuenta un relato, es decir, primera persona, tercera persona limitada o tercera persona omnisciente

precept: a rule, instruction, or principle that guides a person's actions and/or moral behavior

precepto: regla, instrucción o principio que guía las acciones de una persona y/o conducta moral de alguien

primary footage: film footage shot by the filmmaker for the text at hand
metraje principal: filmación hecha por el cineasta para el texto que tiene a mano

primary source: an original document or image created by someone who experiences an event first hand
fuente primaria: documento original que contiene información de primera mano acerca de un tema

prologue: the introduction or preface to a literary work
prólogo: introducción o prefacio de una obra literaria

prose: ordinary written or spoken language, using sentences and paragraphs, without deliberate or regular meter or rhyme; not poetry or song
prosa: forma común del lenguaje escrito o hablado, usando oraciones y párrafos, sin métrica o rima deliberada o regular; ni poesía ni canción

prosody: the pattern and rhythm of sounds in poetry, including stress and intonation
prosodia: rasgos fónicos de la métrica de la poesía, incluidos el énfasis y la entonación

protagonist: the central character in a work of literature, the one who is involved in the main conflict in the plot
protagonista: personaje central de una obra literaria, el que participa en el conflicto principal de la trama

proverb: a short saying about a general truth
proverbio: dicho corto sobre una verdad general

Q

qualify: to consider to what extent a statement is true or untrue (to what extent you agree or disagree)
calificar: consider hasta qué punto una declaración es verdadera o falsa

quatrain: a four-line stanza in a poem
cuarteta: en un poema, estrofa de cuatro versos

R

rationale: an explanation for a belief, statement, or behavior
fundamento: cimientos o bases en los que se apoya una creencia, afirmación o comportamiento

Reader Response Criticism: criticism that focuses on a reader's active engagement with a piece of print or nonprint text; shaped by the reader's own experiences, social ethics, moral values, and general views of the world

crítica de reacción del lector: análisis de un texto basado en las experiencias, ética social, valores, y percepciones generales del mundo

reasoning: the thinking or logic used to make a claim in an argument
razonamiento: pensamiento o lógica que se usa para hacer una afirmación en un argumento

rebuttal: a reason why a counterargument is wrong
refutación: razón por la cual un contraargumento es erróneo

refrain: a regularly repeated line or group of lines in a poem or song, usually at the end of a stanza
estribillo: verso o grupo de versos que se repiten con regularidad en un poema o canción, normalmente al final de una estrofa

refutation: the reasoning used to disprove an opposing point
refutación: razonamiento que se usa para rechazar una opinión contraria

reliability: the extent to which a source provides quality and trustworthy information
confiabilidad: grado en el que una fuente da información confiable y de buena calidad

renaissance: a rebirth or revival
renacimiento: un volver a nacer o una reanimación

repetition: the use of any element of language—a sound, a word, a phrase, a line, or a stanza—more than once
repetición: uso de cualquier elemento del lenguaje—un sonido, una palabra, una frase, un verso o una estrofa—más de una vez

resolution (denouement): the end of a text, in which the main conflict is finally resolved
resolución (desenlace): final de una obra teatral, cuento o novela, en el que el conflicto principal finalmente se resuelve

résumé: a document that outlines a person's skills, education, and work history
currículum vitae: documento que resume las destrezas, educación y experiencia laboral de una persona

retrospective: looking back to analyze the events in one's past
retrospectiva: mirar atrás en el tiempo para analizar los acontecimientos del pasado de una persona

revise: to rework or reorganize a piece of writing to improve its logic and flow after completing a first draft
revisar: rehacer o reorganizar un escrito para mejorar su lógica y fluidez tras haber terminado un primer borrador

rhetoric: the art of using words to persuade in writing or speaking

retórica: arte de usar las palabras para persuadir por escrito o de manera hablada

rhetorical appeals: emotional, ethical, and logical arguments used to persuade an audience to agree with the writer or speaker
recursos retóricos: uso de argumentos emocionales, éticos y lógicos para persuadir por escrito o de manera hablada

rhetorical context: the subject, purpose, audience, occasion, or situation in which writing or speaking occurs
contexto retórico: sujeto, propósito, audiencia, ocasión o situación en que ocurre el escrito

rhetorical devices: specific techniques used in writing or speaking to create a literary effect or enhance effectiveness
dispositivos retóricos: técnicas específicas que se usan al escribir o al hablar para crear un efecto literario o mejorar la efectividad

rhetorical question: a question that is asked for effect or one for which the answer is obvious
pregunta retórica: pregunta hecha para producir un efecto o cuya respuesta es obvia

rhetorical slanters: rhetorical devices used to present a subject in a biased way
sesgos retóricos: recursos retóricos que se usan para presentar un determinado asunto de un modo tendencioso

rhyme: the repetition of sounds at the ends of words
rima: repetición de sonidos al final de las palabras

rhyme scheme: a consistent pattern of rhyme throughout a poem
esquema de la rima: patrón consistente de una rima a lo largo de un poema

rhythm: the pattern of stressed and unstressed syllables in spoken or written language, especially in poetry
ritmo: patrón de sílabas acentuadas y no acentuadas en lenguaje hablado o escrito, especialmente en poesía

rising action: the movement of a plot toward a climax or moment of greatest excitement; the rising action is fueled by the characters' responses to the conflict
acción ascendente: movimiento de una trama hacia el clímax o momento de mayor emoción; la acción ascendente es impulsada por las reacciones de los personajes ante el conflicto

dynamic (or round) character: a character who evolves and grows in the story and has a complex personality
personaje dinámico: personaje que evoluciona y crece en la historia y que tiene una personalidad compleja

S

sarcasm: deliberate, often ironic ridicule
sarcasmo: burla deliberada, de carácter generalmente irónico

satire: a manner of writing that mocks social conventions, actions, or attitudes with wit and humor
sátira: manera de escribir en que se burla de convenciones sociales, acciones, o actitudes con ingenio y humor

scenario: an outline, a brief account, a script, or a synopsis of a proposed series of events
escenario: bosquejo, relato breve, libreto o sinopsis de una serie de sucesos propuestos

secondary audience: a group that may receive a message intended for a target audience
audiencia secundaria: grupo que puede recibir un mensaje orientado a una audiencia específica

secondary source: a discussion about or commentary on a primary source; the key feature of a secondary source is that it offers an interpretation of information gathered from primary sources
fuente secundaria: discusión o comentario acerca de una fuente primaria; la característica clave de una fuente secundaria es que ofrece una interpretación de la información recopilada en las fuentes primarias

sensory details: details that appeal to or evoke one or more of the five senses—sight, sound, smell, taste, and touch
detalles sensoriales: detalles que apelan o evocan uno o más de los cinco sentidos—vista, oído, gusto, olfato, y tacto

sensory images: images that appeal to the reader's senses—sight, sound, smell, taste, and touch
imágenes sensoriales: imágenes que apelan a los sentidos del lector—vista, oído, olfato, gusto, y tacto

sequence of events: the order in which things happen in a story
secuencia de eventos: orden en que los sucesos de una historia pasan:

setting: the time and place in which a story happens
ambiente: tiempo y lugar en el que ocurre un relato

simile: a comparison of two different things or ideas using the words *like* or *as*, for example, the moon was as white as milk
símil: comparación entre dos o más cosas o ideas diferentes usando las palabras *como* o *tan*, por ejemplo, la luna estaba tan blanca como la leche

situational irony: a form of irony that occurs when an event contradicts the expectations of the characters or the reader
ironía situacional: ocurre cuando un evento contradice las espectativas de los personajes o el lector

slanters: rhetorical devices used to present the subject in a biased way
soslayo: recursos retóricos para presentar el tema de modo sesgado

slogan: a short, catchy phrase used for advertising by a business, club, or political party
eslogan: frase corta y tendenciosa que usa como publicidad para un negocio, club o partido político

social commentary: an expression of an opinion with the goal of promoting change by appealing to a sense of justice
comentario social: expresión de una opinión con el objeto de promover el cambio al apelar a un sentido de justicia

soliloquy: a long speech delivered by an actor alone on the stage; represents the character's internal thoughts
soliloquio: discurso largo realizado por un actor sobre el escenario que representa sus pensamientos internos

sonnet: a 14-line lyric poem, usually written in iambic pentameter and following a strict pattern of rhyme
soneto: poema lírico de catorce versos, normalmente escrito en un pentámetro yámbico y que sigue un patrón de rima estricto

sound bite: a short excerpt from the recording of a speech or piece of music which captures the essence of the longer recording
cuña: corto fragmento de una grabación o de una pieza musical que capta la esencia de la grabación completa

speaker: the imaginary voice or persona of the writer or author
orador: voz o persona imaginaria del escritor o autor

stage directions: instructions written into the script of a play that indicate stage actions, movements of performers, or production requirements
direcciones escénicas: instrucciones escritas en un guión o drama que indican acción, movimiento de actors, o requisitos de la producción

stakeholder: a person motivated or affected by a course of action
participante: persona motivada o afectada por el curso de una acción

stanza: a group of lines, usually similar in length and pattern, that form a unit within a poem

estrofa: grupo de versos, normalmente similares en longitud y patrón, que forman una unidad dentro de un poema

static (or flat) character: a character who is uncomplicated and remains the same without changing or growing throughout a narrative
personaje estático: personaje que no cambia a lo largo de una narrativa

stereotype: an oversimplified, generalized conception, opinion, and/or image about particular groups of people
estereotipo: concepto generalizado, opinión y/o imagen demasiado simplificada acerca de grupos específicos de personas

stichomythia: in drama, the delivery of dialogue in a rapid, fast-paced manner, with actors speaking emotionally and leaving very little time between speakers
esticomitia: en el drama, es la rendición del diálogo de una manera rápida con actores que hablan con emoción, dejando espacio muy breve entre los hablantes

storyboard: a tool to show images and sequencing for the purpose of visualizing a film or a story
guión gráfico: método de mostrar imágenes y secuencias con el propósito de visualizar una película o historia

strategize: to plan the actions one will take to complete a task
estrategizar: planear las acciones de uno para complir una tarea

structure: the way a literary work is organized; the arrangement of the parts in a literary work
estructura: manera en que la obra literaria está organizada; disposición de las partes en una obra literaria

style: the distinctive way a writer uses language, characterized by elements of diction, syntax, imagery, organization, and so on
estilo: manera distintiva en que un escritor usa el lenguaje, caracterizada por elementos de dicción, sintaxis, lenguaje figurado, etc.

subculture: a smaller subsection of a culture, for example, within the culture of a high school may be many subcultures
subcultura: subsección más pequeña de una cultura, por ejemplo, dentro de la cultura de una escuela secundaria puede haber muchas subculturas

subjective: based on a person's point of view, opinions, values, or emotions
subjetivo: basado en el punto de vista, las opiniones, los valores o las emociones de alguien

subjective tone: a tone that is obviously influenced by the author's feelings or emotions
tono subjetivo: tono obviamente influído por los sentimientos o emociones del autor

subjectivity: judgment based on one's personal point of view, opinion, or values
subjetividad: en base en nuestro punto de vista, opinión o valores personales

subordinate: a person or group that is perceived as having a lower social or economic status
subordinado: persona o grupo percibido de ser de rango social o estado económico bajo

subplot: a secondary or side story that develops from and supports the main plot and usually involves minor characters
argumento secundario: una historia secundaria o periférica que apoya el argumento principal y que suele involucrar a personajes secundarios o menores

subtext: the underlying or implicit meaning in dialogue or the implied relationship between characters in a book, movie, play, or film; the subtext of a work is not explicitly stated
subtexto: significado subyacente o implícito en el diálogo o la relación implícita entre los personajes de un libro, película, u obra teatral. El subtexto de una obra no se establece de manera explícita.

survey: a method of collecting data from a group of people; it can be written, such as a print or online questionnaire, or oral, such as an in-person interview
encuesta: método para recolectar datos de un grupo de personas; puede ser escrita, como un impreso o cuestionario en línea, u oral, como en una entrevista personal

symbol: anything (object, animal, event, person, or place) that represents itself but also stands for something else on a figurative level
símbolo: cualquier cosa (objeto, animal, evento, persona o lugar) que se representa a sí misma, pero también representa otra cosa a nivel figurativo

symbolic: serving as a symbol; involving the use of symbols or symbolism
simbólico: que sirve como símbolo; que implica el uso de símbolos o simbolismo

synecdoche: a figure of speech in which a part is used to represent the whole or vice versa
sinécdoque: figura retórica en que una parte se usa para representar el todo, o vice-versa

syntax: the arrangement of words and the order of grammatical elements in a sentence; the way in which words are put together to make meaningful elements, such as phrases, clauses, and sentences
sintaxis: disposición de las palabras y orden de los elementos gramaticales en una oración; manera en que las palabras se juntan para formar elementos significativos como frases, cláusulas y oraciones

synthesis: the act of combining ideas from different sources to create, express, or support a new idea
síntesis: acto de combinar ideas de diferentes fuentes para crear, expresar o apoyar una nueva idea

synthesize: to combine ideas from different sources to create, express, or support a new idea or claim
sintetizar: combinar ideas procedentes de distintas fuentes para crear, expresar o sustentar una nueva idea o afirmación

T

target audience: the intended group for which a work is designed to appeal or reach
público objetivo: grupo al que se pretende apelar o llegar con una obra

tenor: the intent, tone, or attitude conveyed by the words in a text
tenor: intención, tono o actitud transmitida por las palabras de un texto

textual evidence: the details, quotations, and examples from a text that support the analysis or argument presented
evidencia textual: detalles, citas, y ejemplos de un texto que apoyan el análisis o la argumentación presentada

theatrical elements: elements used by dramatists and directors to tell a story on stage. Elements include *costumes* (the clothing worn by actors to express their characters), *makeup* (cosmetics used to change actors' appearances and express their characters), *props* (objects used to help set the scene, advance a plot, and make a story realistic), *set* (the place where the action takes place, as suggested by objects, such as furniture, placed on a stage), and *acting choices* (gestures, movements, staging, and vocal techniques actors use to convey their characters and tell a story).

elementos teatrales: elementos utilizados por los dramaturgos y directores para contar una historia en el escenario. Los elementos incluyen *vestuario* (ropa que usan los actores para expresar sus personajes), *maquillaje* (cosméticos que se usan para cambiar la apariencia de los actores y expresar sus personajes), *elementos* (objetos que se usan para ayudar a montar la escena, avanzar la trama y crear una historia realista), *plató* (lugar donde tiene lugar la acción, según lo sugieren los objetos, como muebles, colocados sobre un escenario), y *opciones de actuación* (gestos, movimientos, representación y técnicas vocales que se usan para transmitir sus personajes y narrar una historia).

thematic statement: an interpretive statement articulating the central meaning or message of a text
oración temática: afirmación interpretativa que articula el significado o mensaje central de un texto

theme: a writer's central idea or main message; *see also* explicit theme, implied theme
tema: idea central o mensaje principal acerca de la vida de un escritor; *véase también* tema explícito, tema implícito

thesis: the main idea or point of an essay or article; in an argumentative essay the thesis is the writer's position on an issue
tesis: idea o punto principal de un ensayo o artículo; en un ensayo argumentativo, la tesis es la opinión del autor acerca de un tema

thumbnail sketch: a small drawing made to plan the composition of a more detailed or finished image that will be created later
boceto en miniatura: pequeño dibujo realizado para planificar la composición de una imagen más amplia o detallada que será posteriormente creada

tone: a writer's (or speaker's) attitude toward a subject, character, or audience
tono: actitud de un escritor u orador acerca de un tema

topic sentence: a sentence that states the main idea of a paragraph; in an essay, the topic sentence also makes a point that supports the thesis statement
oración principal: oración que establece la idea principal de un párrafo; en un ensayo, la oración principal también establece una proposición que apoya el enunciado de la tesis

tragedy: a dramatic play that tells the story of a character, usually of a noble class, who meets an untimely and unhappy death or downfall, often because of a specific character flaw or twist of fate

tragedia: obra teatral dramática que cuenta la historia de un personaje, normalmente de origen noble, que encuentra una muerte o caída imprevista o infeliz, con frecuencia debido a un defecto específico del personaje o una vuelta del destino

tragic hero: an archetypal hero based on the Greek concept of tragedy; the tragic hero has a flaw that makes him or her vulnerable to downfall or death
héroe trágico: héroe arquetípico basado en el concepto griego de la tragedia; el héroe trágico tiene un defecto que lo hace vulnerable a la caída o a la muerte

transcript: a written copy or record of a conversation that takes place between two or more people
transcripción: copia escrita de una conversación que sucede entre dos o más personas

U

unconventional: eccentric; unusual; original
no convencional: excéntrico; inusual; original

understatement: the representation of something as smaller or less significant than it really is; the opposite of exaggeration or hyperbole
subestimación: representación de algo como más pequeño o menos importante de lo que realmente es; lo opuesto a la exageración o hipérbole

V

valid: believable or truthful
válido: creíble o verídico

validity: the quality of truth or accuracy in a source
validez: calidad de verdad o precisión en una fuente

verbal irony: a form of irony that occurs when a speaker or narrator says one thing while meaning the opposite
ironía verbal: ocurre cuando un hablante o narrador dice una cosa mientras quiere decir lo opuesto

verbatim: in the exact words of a source
textualmente: palabras citadas exactamente como fueron expresadas

verify: to prove or confirm that something is true
verificar: probar o confirmar que algo es verdadero

vignette: a picture or visual or a brief descriptive literary piece
viñeta: ilustración o representación visual o pieza literaria descriptiva breve

visual delivery: the way a performer on stage interprets plot, character, and conflict through movement, gestures, and facial expressions

presentación visual: manera en que un actor en un escenario interpreta trama, carácter, y conflicto a través de movimiento, gestos, y expresiones de la cara

visual rhetoric: an argument or points made by visuals such as photographs or by other visual features of a text

retórica visual: argumentos o asuntos representados en visuales como fotos u otros rasgos visuales de un texto

visualize: to form a mental picture of something

visualizar: formarse una imagen mental de algo

vocal delivery: the way a performer on stage expresses the meaning of a text through volume, pitch, rate or speed of speech, pauses, pronunciation, and articulation

presentación vocal: manera en que se expresan las palabras en el escenario, por medio del volumen, tono, rapidez o velocidad del discurso, pausas, pronunciación y articulación

voice: a writer's (or speaker's) distinctive use of language to express ideas as well as his or her persona

voz: manera en que el escritor u orador usa las palabras y el tono para expresar ideas, así como también su personaje o personalidad

Index of Skills

Literary Skills

Adaptations, 284, 288, 290, 318, 319, 331, 332, 361

Allegory, 36, 37, 43, 140

Alliteration, 21, 338

Allusion, 40, 202, 205, 206

Analogy, 418

Archetypal Criticism, 7, 147–152, 183
  characters, 147, 166, 167, 187
  hero's journey, 147
  images, 147
  motifs, 147
  perspectives, 207, 252, 308, 409, 453
  symbols, 167

Archetype, 7, 147, 148, 152, 153, 161, 162, 163, 166, 167, 168, 173, 187, 189, 192, 194, 197, 222

Argument, 43, 46, 49, 58, 60, 61, 62, 64, 69
  appeals, 43, 54, 60, 61, 62, 64, 71
  characteristics, 54
  counterclaim, 51, 54, 181, 206, 395, 417
  evidence, 54
  graphic organizer, 62, 391
  structure, 54

Argumentative essay, 47–47

Argumentative text, 65–66

Article, 205, 301, 371–374, 381–383, 384–386, 400–402, 419–420, 422–424, 426–428, 436–437

Artistic license, 186

Aside, 304, 305

Assonance, 21

Attitude (*See also* Tone (attitude))
  of author/speaker, 15, 16, 17, 46, 87, 88, 89, 92, 95, 109, 135, 174, 282, 288, 349
  of characters, 136, 137, 180, 182, 191
  of reader, 17, 18, 30, 136, 183
  satire as, 174
  of society, 9, 192, 198, 238, 281, 344, 410

Audience, 4, 28, 30, 40, 43, 45, 46, 47, 51, 52–53, 55, 58, 62, 88, 90, 96, 148, 173, 174, 185, 190, 191, 205, 252, 262, 263, 267, 280, 288, 291, 304, 346, 379, 399, 406, 407, 408, 415, 421, 425, 444, 462, 467, 468, 476, 479

Author background, 12, 14, 22, 24, 26, 36, 40, 47, 55, 71, 77, 82, 84, 92, 101, 112, 124, 153, 155, 166, 190, 201, 211, 225, 243, 245, 259, 274, 292, 332, 371, 380, 384, 400, 404, 426, 436, 462

Author's choices, 4, 21, 23, 25, 26, 30, 31, 35, 39, 40, 43, 45, 46, 52–53, 60, 61, 62, 64, 74, 136, 185, 187, 195, 198, 218, 414

Author's purpose, 40, 45, 46, 47, 49, 52–53, 68, 121, 160, 205, 263, 344, 376, 388, 389, 390, 418, 421

Bias, 4, 147, 199, 368, 379, 395, 425, 444, 455, 456–457

Big ideas, 4, 74, 146, 197, 252, 331, 368

Bulleted lists, 435

Call to action, 55, 58, 62, 392, 468

Characterization, 137, 140, 146, 153, 159, 160, 164, 167, 168, 174, 179, 180, 182, 187, 189, 193, 197, 201, 217, 218, 221, 222, 235, 267, 273, 282, 287, 301, 332
  external factors, 194
  graphic organizer, 321
  internal factors, 194
  motivation, 183

Character(s), 5, 68, 124, 147, 174, 281, 291, 323, 327, 328
  analyzing, 274, 280, 283
  archetypes, 7
  character sketch, 281
  dynamics, 182, 269
  graphic organizer, 182, 270, 271, 307–308
  minor, 307
  motivation, 169, 304, 305, 320, 322, 329
  point of view, 309
  secondary, 353
  social class, 270
  traits, 306

Claims, 58, 60, 61, 62, 64, 71, 291, 348, 376, 416

Climax, 164, 174, 185, 317

Comedy, 172

Comparison, 160, 407, 418

Concept map, 446

Conclusion, 9, 10, 36, 60, 61, 62, 64, 80, 140, 147, 184, 185, 189, 194, 236, 316, 319, 326, 327, 328, 348, 378, 389, 390, 392, 416, 421, 425, 468

Conflict, 9, 68, 110, 113, 135, 137, 164, 167, 174, 175, 182, 183, 186, 218, 238, 270, 273, 280, 298, 309, 317, 320, 411, 470

Connotation, 15, 16, 17, 96

Consonance, 21

Creating meaning, 35, 397

Critical lenses (perspectives), 7, 76, 80, 89, 91, 100, 147, 190, 193, 194, 195, 197, 252, 258, 269, 274, 279, 280, 291, 301, 303, 307, 308, 309, 311, 314, 315, 316, 317, 318, 323, 328, 329, 331, 332, 345, 353, 354, 357, 358, 359, 361, 362, 368, 370, 376, 377, 378, 397, 408, 409, 411, 412, 414, 442, 444, 445, 451, 459, 480
  graphic organizer, 324, 325, 453

Cultural Criticism, 8, 74, 76, 80, 81, 139, 258–249, 279, 280, 281–267, 300, 302, 348, 411, 453
  colonialism, 88
  cultural backgrounds, 80, 136, 258
  cultural context, 96, 263, 281, 346, 451
  cultural perspectives, 89, 281
  dominant culture, 81, 263
  imperialism, 81, 82, 88, 89, 91, 92, 96, 100
  marginalization, 76, 81, 258, 263
  outsider, 298

Defining, 41

Description, 137, 281, 442

Details, 107, 108, 119, 120, 136, 137, 201, 204, 233, 276, 277, 283, 286, 383, 420, 442, 444
  graphic organizer, 34

Dialect, 212

Dialogue, 146, 168, 177, 187, 215, 217, 280

Diction (word choice), 15, 28, 30, 33, 39, 40, 42, 43, 46, 51, 60, 61, 62, 64, 71, 87, 89, 120, 121, 135, 136, 137, 217, 429

Drama, 146, 252
  blocking, 311
  dramatic arc, 164
  dramatic elements, 306, 317, 362
  dramatic structure, 354
  monologue, 284–286
  stereotypes, 297, 298, 299
  structure, 185, 353

Editorial, 415–416

Reading Skills

Writing Skills

Speaking and Listening Skills

Language Skills

Vocabulary Skills

Credits

Unit 1

"In Just-" Copyright 1923, 1951, © 1991 by the Trustees for the E. E. Cummings Trust. Copyright © 1976 by George James Firmage, from *Complete Poems: 1904-1962* by E. E. Cummings, edited by George J. Firmage. Used by permission of Liveright Publishing Corporation.

"Mushrooms" from *The Colossus and Other Poems* by Sylvia Plath, copyright © 1957, 1958, 1959, 1960, 1961, 1962 by Sylvia Plath. Used by permission of Alfred A. Knopf, a division of Random House, Inc.

"Water" by Anne Sexton, from *Poetry*, August 1962.

"I Remember" by Edward Montez, California Poetry Project.

"Prologue," from *Invisible Man* by Ralph Ellison, copyright 1952 by Ralph Ellison. Used by permission of Random House, Inc.

"Clothing Brands Need to Step Up and Keep Women Safe in Their Factories" by Aruna Kashyap, from the Human Rights Watch, July 5, 2018, copyright © 2018 Human Rights Watch.

"Profiting on the Backs of Child Laborers" by Victoria Riskin and Mike Farrell. Copyright © 2000, Human Rights Watch.

"Tipping System Exacerbates Unfair Pay at Restaurants" by Kathleen Kingsbury, from *The Boston Globe,* February 17, 2014, copyright © 2014 The Boston Globe.

"Speaking With Hands" from *The Concrete River*, copyright 1993 by Luis J. Rodriguez. Reprinted with permission of Curbstone Press.

"On Seeing England for the First Time," originally published in Harper's. Copyright © 1991 by Jamaica Kincaid, reprinted with permission of the Wylie Agency, LLC.

"Shooting an Elephant" from *Shooting an Elephant and Other Stories* by George Orwell, copyright © 1950 by Sonia Brownell Orwell and renewed 1978 by Sonia Pitt-Rivers, reprinted by permission of Houghton Mifflin Harcourt Publishing Company.

Once Upon a Time in the East, by Xiaolu Guo. Copyright © Xiaolu Guo 2017. Used with permission of Random House, Inc.

"Stranger in the Village" from *Notes of a Native Son* by James Baldwin. Copyright © 1955, renewed 1983 by James Baldwin. Reprinted by permission of Beacon Press, Boston.

Unit 2

"Orpheus Sings: Pygmalion and the Statue" from *The Metamorphoses of Ovid* translated with an introduction by Mary M. Innes (Penguin Classics, 1955). Copyright © Mary M. Innes, 1955. Used by permission of Penguin Group (UK) Ltd.

"Cinderella, the Legend," from *Kiss Sleeping Beauty Good-Bye* by Madonna Kolbenschlag. Used by permission of Women & Leadership Archives, Loyola University Chicago.

From "Why Women Always Take Advantage of Men," from *Mules and Men* by Zora Neale Hurston. Copyright © 1935 by Zora Neale Hurston; renewed © 1963 by John C. Hurston and Joel Hurston. Reprinted by permission of HarperCollins Publishers.

"The Landlady," from *Kiss Kiss*, by Roald Dahl, text copyright © 2011 by Roald Dahl Nominee Limited. Used by permission of Michael Joseph, a non-fiction imprint of Random House, a division of Random House LLC and David Higham Associates. All rights reserved. Any third party use of this material, outside of this publication, is prohibited. Interested parties must apply directly to Random House LLC for permission.

"The Chaser" by John Henry Noyes Collier from *The New Yorker* by permission of Harold Matson, Agent. Copyright 1940 by John Collier.

Unit 3

The Moor in English Renaissance Drama by Jack D'Amico. Copyright 1991 by University of South Florida Press. Reproduced by permission of the University Press of Florida.

"*Othello* on Stage and Screen" by Sylvan Barnet, copyright © 1963, 1986, 1998 by Sylvan Barnet, from *The Tragedy of Othello* by William Shakespeare, edited by Alvin Kernan. Used by permission of Phyllis Fogelman Books, a division of Penguin Group (USA) Inc.

Unit 4

"How News Has Changed" by Michael Griffin, from *Macalester News*, April 10, 2017, copyright © 2017 Macalester College.

"How Headlines Change the Way We Think" by Maria Konnikova, from *The New Yorker*, December 17, 2014, copyright © 2014 The New Yorker.

"Why Partisans View Mainstream Media as Biased and Ideological Media as Objective" by Matthew C. Nisbet from bigthink.com, copyright © 2011 by Matthew C. Nisbet.

"Daylong Efforts to Repair Levee Fail" by Dan Shea, from the *Times-Picayune*, August 31, 2005.

"An Editorial: It's Time for a Nation to Return the Favor" from the *Times-Picayune*, November 20, 2005.

"Looters Leave Nothing Behind in Storm's Wake" by Mike Perlstein and Brian Thevenot, from *The Times-Picayune*, August 31, 2005.

"Who's a Looter? In Storm's Aftermath, Pictures Kick Up a Different Kind of Tempest" by Tania Ralli, from *The New York Times*, September 5, 2005, copyright © 2005 The New York Times.

"The Press, Race, and Katrina" by Madison Gray, *Time Magazine*, August 30, 2006. Copyright © 2006 Time, Inc.

"'Attitude of Resilience' Helped Create Demo Diva" by Simone Bruni, from *The Chicago Tribune*, September 3, 2015. Copyright © 2015 The Chicago Tribune.

Image Credits